TALK TO ME

TALK TO ME

MONOLOGUE PLAYS

EDITED BY *Eric Lane*

AND *Nina Shengold*

VINTAGE BOOKS

A DIVISION OF RANDOM HOUSE, INC. NEW YORK

A VINTAGE ORIGINAL, NOVEMBER 2004

Library of Congress Cataloging-in-Publication Data
Talk to me : monologue plays / edited by Eric Lane and Nina Shengold.
    p. cm.
    "A Vintage original"—T.p. verso.
    ISBN 1-4000-7615-3 (trade paper)
      1. Monologues, American. 2. American drama—21st century.
    I. Lane, Eric. II. Shengold, Nina.
    PS627.M63T35 2004
    812'.04508—dc22   2004042022

Book design by Mia Risberg

www.vintagebooks.com

Printed in the United States of America
10 9 8 7 6 5 4 3

CONTENTS

EXCERPTS

INTRODUCTION

Like a good character actor, this book wears more than one hat. *Talk to Me* is both a sourcebook for actors in search of exciting new monologues and a fascinating read for anyone interested in the multiplicity of ways in which human beings tell our stories aloud. It includes solo theatre pieces of all lengths, from brief character studies to full-evening one-person shows. It also contains multicharacter plays constructed entirely of monologues for more than one actor—as many as thirty-two, in José Rivera's stunningly diverse *Sonnets for an Old Century*.

In these pages, you'll find an astonishing spectrum of human experience in monologue form. There are dramas, comedies, spoken-word poems, and performance texts for characters of all ages and types. Whether you plan to perform a whole play, or select an audition-length segment, you'll find the complete text for the character that you've chosen right here in this book. What you *won't* find are monologues pulled from the midst of an ongoing scene, and which make little sense out of context or without an acting partner onstage to address. The plays in this book were written to be performed directly to their audience. This makes them a natural choice for auditions and classwork, as well as productions in all sorts of venues, from campus coffeehouses to downtown lofts to Broadway.

As always, the editors of this book received many more scripts than we could possibly publish. We looked for compelling *characters*, rich and vital theatrical creations with interesting stories to tell, and strong, unique voices. As we sifted through hundreds of manuscripts, we gravitated to those plays that (to coin a phrase) talked to us. Some scripts we merely read. Others we *heard*.

Oral historians are fond of the phrase "raw whisky"— uncut, undiluted human speech, as captured verbatim, with all its unique hesitations and phrasing. Anna Deavere Smith's extraordinary theatrical canvas *Twilight: Los Angeles, 1992* was constructed from actual speech, as recorded in interviews shortly following the Rodney King verdict. Danny Hoch doesn't work with a tape recorder, but his ear for the vibrant rhythms of street speech is so finely tuned that the characters in his *Some People* feel absolutely authentic. Other plays in this volume invent a uniquely theatrical language; Mayda Del Valle's exuberant "in the cocina," from Broadway's *Def Poetry Jam,* is a spoken-word poem.

If monologue plays have a wide variety of approaches to oral language, they also take varying forms on the page. Some playwrights write in a breathless gallop, with huge gulps of text tumbling out in continuous paragraphs. Others utilize a free-verse format, separating each phrase with a physical space where the breath would be, as in Betty Shamieh's heartbreaking *Tamam* or Leslie Ayvazian's *Deaf Day,* which is performed in both English and American Sign Language.

Several of the eight full-length plays included here were originally performed by their authors. Performance artist David Cale, a virtuoso chameleon, originated the title role in his lyrical *Lillian,* in which a middle-aged Englishwoman recalls her doomed young lover. The engaging waiter of Aasif Mandvi's *Sakina's Restaurant* deftly conjures an entire subculture of Indian immigrants, all played by one actor. In *The Tricky Part,* Martin Moran spins a tale of seduction, violation, and the attempt to forgive an only-too-human abuser. Lisa Kron's *2.5 Minute Ride* is a breathless experience, twisting and plunging with roller-coaster speed from a midwestern amusement park to a family wedding at a Jewish Center in Canarsie to a far darker visit to Auschwitz.

Jeffrey Hatcher's beautifully written *Three Viewings* is made up of three one-act monologues, each set in the same funeral parlor, with subtle linkages between two very different women and one man who tell us their stories. And how many plays do you find about an obsessed Dutch librarian trying to track down the fine on a book that's 123 years overdue? Glen Berger's *Underneath the Lintel* is, it seems safe to say, in a category of one; it's also both funny and deeply emotional.

The shorter monologue plays in this volume are equally varied. Actresses will find a gold mine of comic material in the struggles of the character actress in Leslie Nipkow's *Guarding Erica* as she desperately attempts to land a job on *All My Children;* and the just-fired, furious tour guide in David Lindsay-Abaire's hilarious "History Lesson." For dramatic monologues, look at Neil LaBute's *medea redux,* in which a latter-day white-trash Medea perpetrates a shocking act of vengeance; Joyce Carol Oates's hypnotic *When I Was a Little Girl and My Mother Didn't Want Me;* and Nina Shengold's haunting *Yahrzeit,* about a grieving child displaced by her mother's remarriage.

Short pieces for men include David Ives' uproarious *Moby-Dude* in which a stoned-out surfer attempts to summarize the plot of an American classic in under two minutes; and Warren Leight's "Jaguar Jesus," a blazing jazz riff from his multi-monologue evening *Stray Cats.* Daniel Gallant's *Josephine Undone* unfurls an outrageous shaggy-dog story; Sam Schwartz's *The Man Who Fell in Love With His Cat* follows an aging widower deep into a feline erotic obsession. In Adam LeFevre's *The Defenestration of Citizen Candidate X,* a politician ignores the advice whispered into his headset by unseen handlers, veering off his scripted farewell into wild free-associative loops.

Two more short plays have multiple casts. Eric Lane's *Glass Stirring* reveals a moving portrait of a World War II family, told by its four members in lyrical monologues; while Lisa D'Amour's multilayered *My California* overlaps monologues by women from three different eras—a Gold Rush pioneer, a flapper, and a runaway '90s teenager—all from the same line of hard-living rebels.

Monologue plays are a modern form of that most ancient of human entertainments, storytelling. Our paleolithic ancestors listened to hunters enacting their sagas in front of a campfire, and members of every human community since have stood up in front of their peers and performed their tales. As Danny Hoch wrote in his introduction to *Some People,* "Solo theatre is actually something very ancient. It predates the Roman and Greek theatrical histories and can be found in the indigenous theatres of Africa, Asia and the Americas (before European colonialism). When the French were colonizing Africa, they used the word *griot* to describe the various solo performers they encountered: people who used drama, comedy, pantomime, storytelling, dance, music, possession and masks to create community performance. The griots reflected, celebrated, reconstructed and questioned the community. In other words—pure unfiltered theatre. They were shamans, teachers, preachers, actors and social critics, all in one."

That's quite a mission statement. The twenty-four playwrights whose works are included in *Talk to Me* are up to the challenge. We leave it to actors, our modern griots, to lift their words off these pages, and talk to us.

NINA SHENGOLD AND ERIC LANE
February 2004

ACKNOWLEDGMENTS

Many people contributed to the creation of this book. We'd like to thank all the literary managers, agents, and publishers who steered us towards hundreds of outstanding plays and helped us secure the rights for our final selections.

Particular thanks go to Michael Bigelow Dixon of the Guthrie Theater, John McCormack at the Zipper Theatre, Pamela Berlin of HB Playwrights Unit, Sarah Bisman, Bill Craver at Writers & Artists, Michael Greaves and Carol Christiansen at Random House, Peter Hagan and Neal Winn at the Gersh Agency, Kenyon Harbison at William Morris Agency, Betsy Kalumer, Michael Kenyon at the Public Theater, Warren Leight, Matt Love and Eleanore Speert at the Drama Book Shop, Maureen Nagy at Overlook Press, Tanya Palmer and Amy Wegener at Actors Theatre of Louisville, Doug Rand of Playscripts Inc., Tom Rowan of Ensemble Studio Theatre, Pier Carlo Talenti at the Mark Taper Forum, Bruce Whitacre at the National Corporate Theatre Fund, Beth Whitaker at Signature Theatre, Gavin Witt at Center Stage, everyone at New Dramatists, the Joyce Ketay Agency, Rosenstone/Wender, and Viking Entertainment. Phyllis Lane and Fritzi Kramer, who are deeply missed. Plus the terrific members of Actors & Writers and Orange Thoughts Productions.

As ever, we thank our own agents, Phyllis Wender and Susie Cohen, and Diana Secker Larson, our wonderful editor at Vintage Books, who made this a pleasure in every way. Also Nayon Cho at Vintage Books Publicity. Our deep appreciation to the Corporation of Yaddo, the Virginia Center for the Creative

Arts, and the St. James Cavalier Centre for Creativity in Malta, for their priceless gift of time and space to work on this collection. Grateful thanks to our fellow travelers Mark Chmiel, Steven Corsano, Shelley Wyant, Shay Youngblood, Nicole Quinn, and Joe Reeder for reminding us how vital theatre for young actors can be, and to Bob Barnett and Maya Shengold for making the journey a whole lot more fun.

Most of all, we'd like to thank the many playwrights who sent us their wonderful work, and we wish to honor the many collaborators—actors, directors, designers, crews, theatres, and audiences—who bring their beautiful words to life.

FULL-LENGTH PLAYS

LILLIAN

David Cale

For Lillian

Lillian premiered at the Goodman Theatre (Robert Falls, Artistic Director; Roche Schulfer, Executive Director) in Chicago, Illinois, on October 27, 1997. It was directed by Joe Mantello; the designer was Robert Brill; the lighting design was by Beverly Emmons. The cast was as follows:

LILLIAN   David Cale

CHARACTER

LILLIAN: An Englishwoman in her early forties.

PART 1

The Present

Chrysanthemums

Stage is bare except for a stool, a microphone, and a small wooden table with a vase of yellow chrysanthemums and a glass of water. Wayne Shorter's "Moto Grosso Feio" plays. LILLIAN *enters holding a single bloom. She stands at the microphone. Music ends.*

LILLIAN

Chrysanthemums are considered to be late bloomers. Originating in China, they date back as far as five hundred years BC. The wild native version of the species has now almost disappeared. Having been completely overshadowed by its more colorful domesticated relative. For optimum results, chrysanthemums require a clay soil, a sunny yet cool location, ideally facing south, and loam. They are what's known as short-day plants, meaning they are light sensitive and produce buds only as the days become shorter and the nights grow longer. To improve the quality of the flowers the first bud that appears should be pinched, that's according to most chrysanthemum experts, in whose ranks I now number myself, thereby increasing the radiance of the subsequent flowers.

(She places the bloom on the stool.)

The other day I overheard a landscape gardener talking to a woman I know who designs plaster gnomes to put on your front lawn: a garden ornament whose appeal has frankly always eluded me. Anyway the landscape gardener says,
"I realized recently that I have been mildly depressed for the last fifteen years."
The gnome lady asked,
"How come you only realize that now?"
He answered,
"Because I don't feel that way anymore."
It's funny what you just happen to overhear.

I wonder if it's true that all the secrets of our lives are whispered into our ears at birth. That the secrets then attach themselves to our unconscious. As years pass occasionally a secret will break free, and make its way up into our daily thoughts. They are then referred to as premonitions. I think we know everything that's going to happen to us.

People come into your life for a reason. There are no accidents. There's nothing haphazard about it. Or coincidental. What may seem random at the time, I think in the end has a kind of correctness.

(*She picks up the flower.*)

I mean, in retrospect, when you look back on your life, if you're able to be honest with yourself, I think you come to realize, it could not have happened any other way.

(*Lights fade. She places the single bloom in the vase.*)

PART 2
Seven Years Earlier

This Jimmy Thing

LILLIAN

(Seated on the stool.)

"The thought of someone else inside you
is something I could never come to terms with,"
Keith had said to me before he went up north
on that job.
"I could get over somebody kissing you, or cuddling,
but if someone else went inside, I don't think I could
ever touch you again."
"Don't be dramatic," I'd said,
"Nobody's going anywhere with me."

Then almost the minute the door shut,
Keith was hardly in his precious Volvo,
when I meet little Jimmy in the store,
fifteen years my junior,
with a look on his face that could drag a shipwreck up
from the bottom of the ocean.

"Wipe that dirty look off your face, Jimmy Foyle," I said.
"And stop trying to put your fingers in my mouth.
I'm a married woman."

I couldn't believe the words were coming out of me.
It was like my husband just flew out the window.

A Jimmy was really what I had in mind for a lover before I
said yes to Keith. He was the kind of person I always wanted
when I was his age, but who never seemed interested in me.
I wasn't generally a Jimmy's type. Jimmys didn't generally
give women like me a second look. We seemed too tame.
Jimmy was a wild one. Rough around the edges. He was a

bit of a devil. Didn't give things a lot of thought the way Keith did. And he was funny. Keith had nothing approaching a sense of humor. Actually Keith was the only person I knew that didn't find me funny in any way.

"I can't believe that Lillian," Jimmy said, "you're a riot."
"How refreshing," I thought, "to be found funny again."

It was really the idea of a Jimmy coming along that kept me from completely giving over to Keith. I'd been holding out for the thought of a Jimmy for a long time. So when he aimed his eyes at me and came on so strong that day, something in me was saying, "It would not be a good idea to turn Jimmy down. It'll be a little fling. You have to work out this Jimmy thing. Lillian, it's between you and yourself."

Jimmy knew Keith was out of town. I think he'd even been watching the precious Volvo to see if it was still in the front. He invitted me over to his house to see his lizards.

"Lizards!" I said.
"Yes lizards," he said.
"How peculiar," I said, "all right Jimmy."

He drove his car like he'd just robbed a bank. We ran a red light.
"Hold on to your seat Lillian," I thought. His car didn't have safety belts.

"I cut them off," he said, "they were uncomfortable."

I thought about Keith. Keith wouldn't start the engine unless everyone was strapped in.

Jimmy's house was lined with tiny aquariums. He got all excited as he told me what the various lizards were, and where they came from. He was quite the authority. Outside of the store he looked much younger.
"God Lillian," I thought, "what are you doing?"

When he made his move on me it was so sudden. Talk about a pounce. Even the lizards scuttled behind their plastic rocks. I immediately felt like I'd been thrown into a wrestling ring. As we were rolling around on his leopard blanket, I must confess my first thought was,

"Am I really enjoying this?"

He was so rough and young. There was no warming up with Jimmy. In fact much to my surprise, it was dreadful. It's funny, I realized I'd gotten used to Keith's mouth. Jimmy had a smaller mouth. I think Keith's tongue was wider too. There was nothing sensual about Jimmy's tongue. It just sort of flickered around in my mouth like the tongues of one of those lizards of his.

Whatever was wrong with Keith, the sexual part was all right. Or maybe I'd overrated it a bit. But he was considerate. Sexually speaking I'd say Keith was like a really good waiter, in a pretty good restaurant. Very good service, but ultimately disappointing food. Jimmy seemed to approach the whole thing like it was some form of kung fu, or that I was something that needed to be overthrown, but really I was just laying there. He was nervous, bless him. I tried to get him to ease up.

"Slow down," I said, in a voice that was supposed to sound seductive, but I have to admit did come out rather motherly.

"If I slow down," he said, "I'll lose the erection."

"God," I thought, "this is dreadful," as he's pulling my sweater over my chin.

Then he breathed into my ears.

"Can I fuck you Lillian?"

And I thought about Keith and what the thought of somebody else being inside me would do to him, and how it really would be the final straw and I said,

"Yes Jimmy, if you want."
He got all excited and ran into another room. Came back
with a Rubber Johnny, and he had trouble opening the
packet. And I'm thinking, "If I let Jimmy inside, then
there's no going back."

He lays back down on top and I put my hand on the erection he was so afraid of losing, which I realized I hadn't even
looked at yet, so I took a peek.
"Oh dear," I thought, "Men's penises are all starting to
look the same," as I helped it find its way inside.

"Is it in?" Jimmy said. He was nervous, bless him.

"Yes, it's in," I said.

Jimmy takes this as his cue to start pounding away at me
with his eyes scrunched shut.

"Christ look at me!" I thought.

I hate it when men shut their eyes and lock off into their
own world.

"You're in my world now," I felt like saying.

And I'm thinking of Keith on that oil rig. Wish Keith had
gotten more excited about doing things. We should have
gone on holidays. Little adventures. It was such a routine.
Wish Keith would get all riled up. Wish he'd get passionate
about something. Oh I don't know, about life, or me, or lose
his temper.
"You know I love you," he'd say, "I don't need to keep
telling you. I wouldn't dream of looking at another
woman."
And he wouldn't.

And I'm looking at Jimmy's lizards. Can they really be happy
in those little tanks, with a lightbulb over their heads morning and night? And I look at Jimmy on top of me, and his
face looks like it's in such pain. His eyes are still squeezed

tight. There's sweat forming on his forehead. And he took so long. God I wish he'd have his orgasm and this could be over. It's starting to feel like a visit to the dentist's, more than a sexual fling. Then Jimmy makes a noise like he's been shot in the leg, and I realize (thank God), he's having his little eruption, bless him.

He rolls over to the other side of the blanket.

"That was sexy," he says.

"Yes," I said, "it was very. Thank you."

Oh Lillian, polite to the end!

But then Jimmy did some really sweet things. He ran a bath. Put something blue in the water. He showed me his muscles.

"Ooooh," I said.

He lit candles. He was quite romantic after all. He was a boy really. I half expected the police to come barging in and arrest me.

"Did I disappoint you?" he said.

"No, of course not," I said.

And for a moment he looked so vulnerable that I thought my heart would break.

We sat in the bath. He was behind me. He did my back. Drew objects on my shoulders in soap and had me guess what they were.

"It's a giraffe," I said.

"No, it's a crane," he said.

"You win," I said.

He was laughing. He looked even younger with his hair wet. He has lovely olive eyes. I didn't realize till we were in the water lit by the birthday candles, bless him. "One day some

young woman's going to really lose her bearings just looking
into those eyes," I thought. And I got a little rush of sadness,
but not anything so big that it would register on my face.

He dried me with a fresh towel. He fixed a snack. We
watched the tele. He had his hand on my thigh. He asked,

"How does your pussy feel?"

I said,

"What did you say?"

He said,

"You heard me."

I said,

"That's for me to know and you to imagine.
Cheeky bugger."
I smiled. He laughed.

"Oh Lillian, you're a riot," he said, for the second time.

What could I say?

"Actually I'm in distinct discomfort."

It would have broken his heart, bless him.

And he was playing with the nape of my neck with his fingers, and it was tickling me in a sort of irritating way, but I
didn't say anything.

And one of Jimmy's lizards is watching us with a large cricket
in its mouth, which it's in the process of crunching on. The
cricket's antennae are waving slowly as its body disappears.

And I'm thinking of Keith in his Volvo, following the tail-
lights of another car, with his radio on. He was probably near
Scotland by then. With that perpetually anxious look on his
face, that he inherited from his father. And Jimmy's giggling
at a commercial on the television. Looking all of sixteen.

And they're both nice men. Sweet men. You know, good people. And as the damn television is chattering away in the background, all I can think is,

"Well my dear, now what?"

(*Wayne Shorter's "Antigua" plays. Lights fade.*)

PART 3
Five Years Later

Brighton

LILLIAN

(*Seated on the stool.*)

When I was young my school reports all said the same thing. "She has potential, but she has a tendency to procrastinate." I didn't know what the word meant. Neither did my mother. She was always saying, "I must buy a dictionary tomorrow and look up that word."

That little memory has always nagged me for some reason. That, and memories of Brighton.

I've always felt a special bond with Brighton. I used to go there as a child. My grandfather had a place. In Hove, to be more precise. Hove is literally next door. They're right side by side. But some people get quite upset if you confuse them. "The working people go to Brighton," my grandfather would say, as if he didn't work. "This family is on its way to Hove." It's so silly really.

On the train down I found myself becoming quite reflective. Keith used to say I spent too much time with my head in the past, and he was probably right.

"Don't dwell," he'd say. "The past is gone."
And he'd bark out the word "gone."

Riding trains always makes me reflective. I'm sure it's all those sights passing you by at such speed does it.
My ex-husband hadn't crossed my mind in a long time but for some reason I found myself thinking about him on the train to Brighton. One thing that's always stayed with me about Keith was the way he'd say, "I know that one day you'll leave." I'd tell him not to think like that, but I knew he was right. Deep down. The moment I met Keith I imagined myself saying good-bye to him.

I'd been working in a bookstore in London for six months, which I did quite enjoy. It was a comfortable position. Civilized kind of customer. There were many days when it didn't seem like work. I've always liked being around books. It's funny, I rarely read them, I just like being in their presence. As if at any point you could pick one up, open it and enhance yourself. I don't know why I won't read. It's as if part of me has always shied away from the idea of any kind of enhancement. It's made all the more peculiar by the fact that I buy books all the time. My house is lined with unread books.

Anyway, I had decided to take a week off work. It was drizzling in London. February. The store was quiet. "Brighton will be empty this time of year," I thought. Time to take some time to recharge. Soon as I get out of the train station there I always feel a sense of both relief and release. Oh the times I've gotten on a train and run back to Brighton.

I'd been there for about a day and a half and it was really doing the trick. There were very few people on the street. Felt like I had the place to myself.

Well I was walking along the front, past the chalets on the beach, when I hear somebody calling my name. I turn around and see this young man with a beard waving at me.

"Who on earth are you?" I thought, and presumed it must be a customer from the shop.

"It's me," said the man with the beard, "it's Jimmy. Don't you remember?"

"Jimmy!" I said, totally taken aback. "You look completely different. I would have walked right past you."

Besides the beard, he was much slimmer, and it's probably my imagination but I think he'd grown.

"What are you doing here?" I asked.

"I live here," he said.

"Since when?"

"Since about four years ago."

I couldn't get over how different he looked.

"I don't lift weights anymore," he said, "I do Tai Chi. Lost a lot of bulk. Don't have the muscles anymore. And I've gone vegetarian."

"And you have the beard now," I chimed in.

"Yeah my wife says it gives me authority."

"Your wife!" I said.

"Can you believe it?" he said. "I got hitched."

The whole episode was quite disorienting. Having Jimmy pop up in the middle of my Brighton, after how many years? Five was it? He asked me if I'd like to grab a bite. Said I would. I have to say though it was immediately comfortable between us. One thing about Jimmy and I, we always got along.

"I don't drink coffee anymore," he said. "Only herb tea. I'm watching my health. But I could have a chamomile tea and a tofu sandwich. I'm very strict."

"Tofu sandwich!" I said. "Oh dear.
I shall be having a glass of wine, a pastry, a cappuccino and
a cigarette. In that order. Health kick!"

He laughed.

"Oh good," I thought, "I'm still amusing to him."

While he wasn't looking I glanced at the side of his face.
He'd become quite beautiful. Delicate almost. In the looks
department, I have to say the little bugger had really come
into his own.

We went to an awful "health" restaurant where they had a
lot of attitude and no pastry, and when I tried to light a cigarette I got a lecture on secondhand smoke. He wanted me
to meet his wife. Thought the two of us would get along.
"Why?" I couldn't help wondering.

"She reminds me of you," he said, "she's a bit older than
me. Very successful in business. Has her own company. I
work for her. She trains executives how to speak in public,
and how to alter their image so they'll become a more effective tool in the marketplace."

The whole enterprise sounded positively creepy. I asked him
what his role in all this was. He said he videotaped the executives speaking and that "Donna"—the wife—would identify their weaknesses, and therefore help to rectify them.

"How old are you now?" I asked, somewhat shifting the
subject.

"Twenty-six," he said. "How old are you?"

"I'm not telling you how old I am," I said.
"Let's put it this way, when I write down my date of birth
now, I put the word 'circa' next to it."

Then he asked if I thought he seemed more mature. Apparently Donna was working on having him project a more
mature version of himself.

"Have you noticed I'm speaking slower?" he said. "Donna got me to do that. She made me watch a video of myself. I had no idea I talked so quickly."

I'd never noticed it.

Poor Jimmy was starting to sound a bit like someone who's had a complete nervous breakdown and who's slowly pasting themselves back together. And I was gaining the impression he'd married Eva Braun.

"She's not pointing any cameras at me," I thought.

Just as some horrendous-looking alfalfa something-or-other arrived, he asked me how what's-his-name was.

"If you mean Keith," I said, "I have no idea. I haven't seen Keith for nearly two years. Last time I tried to talk to Keith he said he still wasn't ready to speak to me yet."

"Was it because of me?" he asked, with a tone of slight self-satisfaction. And I have to say it did irritate me for a moment. I mean there was a reason I stayed with Keith for six years. It wasn't a complete waste of time.

"Let's just say you didn't help."

One thing about Keith he could read me like a book. He knew immediately what had happened with Jimmy. "The way you talked about him in the store. It was obvious," he said.

"It's sad," he'd go on, "you're just like a little girl. You'll fall for anyone who flatters you."

Keith always referred to the thing with Jimmy as "the episode."

"You haven't been the same person since the episode," was how he'd put it.

I really didn't want to meet Donna. I imagined her as exuding sex appeal and confidence and I really wasn't feeling up to comparisons, but I went along with it. For some reason Jimmy was so eager for us to meet. He called her up. Warned her we were on our way, while I excused myself to go to the bathroom, for an emergency one-on-one between myself and my face in the bathroom mirror.

"I hope it's the light in here," I thought. "Either that, my dear, or it's time to lay off the lattes."

Donna was on a business call when we walked in. With her back to us. She was nothing at all like I'd anticipated. Donna was a big girl. Literally. She must have been at least 6'2" and I have to say, and this will sound awfully ungenerous on my part, and it is, but the first thing that drew my attention was her hips. "She's probably given birth to something," I presumed.

When she turned around I thought, "Oh I'm much better looking than you," and I was sort of surprised at myself for how juvenile I was behaving. But I have to say I did suddenly feel in the mood to be a little . . . oh I don't know, yes I do . . . threatening.

Finally she gets off the phone. Waltzes over, extending her hand.

"I'm sorry," she says, "the Americans just think I've got all the time in the world. But they're where the money is, so we can't be complaining too much now can we?"

Then she kissed Jimmy on the mouth in front of me, which seemed a bit unnecessary, and said, "Hello James." "James!" I thought. "James!" Well excuse me! Jimmy may have been many things but one thing he wasn't was a James. Redirecting her attention towards me,

"What line are you in Lillian?" she asks.

"Books," I say, "though I seldom read them."

"Oh publishing?" she says.

"No," says I, "secondhand mostly."

"Oh," she says.
"What a pretty shirt you're wearing."

And I thought,

"You cow!"

I was only there about ten minutes, which was quite long enough. Donna said she had a meeting to go to.

"Oh AA?" I inquired.

"Oh you're hilarious!" she says.

"So are you," I replied.
Which got no response.

She said she was going to Germany for the rest of the week for a conference, and that "James" had the car. Every time she mentioned "James" I had to think for a moment who she was talking about.
"You two can get reacquainted," she said. "You don't need me around now do you?" And for a second it felt like she was throwing him at me.

Jimmy wanted to give me a tour of the south coast, so the following day, after Donna left, he picked me up at the hotel and we went driving in her BMW.

"What happened to your car?" I asked.

"Donna made me get rid of it," he said.

"I liked that car!" I protested. "It suited you."

"She approves of you," he said, "she thought you were down-to-earth."

Which from a pretentious person is not a compliment.

"She said she thinks you're the kind of woman that she could imagine me being with much more than her."

"What does she mean by that?" I asked.

"I don't know," he said, "sometimes I think she's tired of being married to people. I'm her fourth husband."

"Oh," I said and then we just drove for a bit without saying anything. The countryside along the south coast is lovely. And I remembered how much I liked to be in the passenger seat of a car.

While Jimmy was driving I happened to notice his hands on the steering wheel. They looked older. I looked at mine. I'm sure they did too. He slipped in a cassette tape.

(*Jimmy Sommerville's "By Your Side" begins to play, underscoring the following seven lines.*)

I lowered my window. A gust of wind blew through the car. My hair went everywhere. Care and all its relatives seemed to fall out of me. Well I don't know if it was the sea air, the music, too many cappuccinos or Jimmy. But I felt a sudden wave of enthusiasm. He must have thought my mind had just fluttered out the car window.

"Right now," I exclaimed, "I feel like I'm riding the world!"

(*Music crescendos and plays at a louder volume for thirty seconds, then returns to the original level to underscore the next three lines.*)

Driving along the coast we came to a huge funfair. Jimmy wanted to get off the road and investigate. I didn't take much convincing. As we were going in he stopped in his tracks.

(*Music ends.*)

"I always get excited around you," he said.

"I feel the same way," I told him.

And I realized what it was: you see you could be romantic with Jimmy and not feel like a fool. I'd been waiting a long time to be romantic with someone.

Jimmy was immediately drawn to an enormous roller coaster called The Big Plunge. The Big Plunge was a ride that would go up extremely high and then plummet.

Now I have a terrible fear of heights. "There's no way you're going to get me on that thing," I said. "You go if you want to. I'll stay here and have a cigarette."

"Oh Lillian, you're afraid of everything," he said.

"How dare you?" I said. "I am not."

"Come on," he said. "Fear at a certain point just becomes another bad habit."

Which had to have been something he'd picked up from Donna.

The only way I could go on The Big Plunge was by going through a complicated psychological snow job, in which I rationalized that my fear of heights actually represented my terror of life, and that going on The Big Plunge was extremely important for me and could lead to a personal break-through. Besides if ten-year-old children could brave it so could I. Jimmy managed to grab the front seat.

"I'm sure I'm the oldest person to ever take the Plunge," I said, ever the terrified wit, as the ride yanked everyone forward, and the squealing began.

First off I was petrified and then I seemed to push through the fear, and I have to say the whole thing did seem like a personal breakthrough. Donna would have been proud of me. Jimmy held my hand for the duration, which was sweet of him. I've never been able to go on those rides before but I ended up loving it, and went on three more times.

It had become completely easy between us, and midway through the day a strange notion crossed my mind.

"I can imagine myself being with you for a long time," I thought.

By late afternoon I realized I really was getting a little light-headed around Jimmy. I stood at a distance as he was buying tickets for the next ride. Tried to give myself a little talking-to.. "He's 26. He's married. He lives in Brighton," I said to myself.
"Lillian stop it!"

Then out of the blue, on the Ferris wheel, he gave me a peck on the cheek.

"What are you doing?" I asked, trying not to sound delighted, and failing abysmally.

"I wanted to kiss you," he said.

"James," I scolded, "behave!"

The Ferris wheel then abruptly jolted to a halt.
Fortunately with us on the low end.
While we were waiting to move, Jimmy asked what seemed like an out-of-the-blue question:
"If somebody told you your life would end in, say a year, do you think you'd start to really live? Or do you think you'd slip back under the covers and wait for it to be over?"

"I think I'd get a move on," I replied.

Just then the wheel began to turn.

As we were passing the arcade I noticed a photo booth.

"I don't have any pictures of you," I said. "Come on. I need some proof that you exist."

We were clowning around in front of the camera. Pictures took forever to come out. When they finally did emerge from the machine I wasn't quite prepared for what I saw. What took me aback about the photos was that we looked like two people who were completely in love with each other. I'm sure Jimmy picked up on it too. But neither of us said anything.

Driving back to my hotel I started to feel uneasy. I asked him if he wanted to come up to the room for a bit. Dangling the fact that there was a good-sized color TV. I had forgotten how small the room was and it did feel a little awkward. There was nowhere to sit except the bed.

"We have quite a history," I said.

"Yes," he agreed.

"You and me."

Placing his hand on my ankle,
"Your leg feels swollen," he said.
I told him it was the circulation. That my varicose veins were getting worse. Then regretted drawing attention to them. Tried to make a joke.

"I'm not supposed to ever cross my legs again."

"Can't they take them out?" he asked.

"The doctor said it would be for purely cosmetic reasons to remove them," I replied, "and he strongly advised against it."

"Oh," he said, and then went quiet and seemed withdrawn.

"What about wearing a special stocking?"

"Please stop talking about varicose veins.
They don't exactly make me feel like an attractive proposition."

"Are you all right?" I asked.

He didn't say anything. He just nodded. Then I don't know what triggered it exactly but he just started sobbing.

"I fucked up my life," he said.

"What's wrong?" I asked him.

"I wanted to be married to someone. I wanted to make it work. Wanted a family. Didn't want to be like my old man. I hate my life. I want to be a gardener. Want to have a nursery and grow things. I don't want to be videotaping businessmen all day. I hate that world. I want to be outside. Donna says she's not willing to be married to a gardener. She wants to have an open relationship. Wants to be able to see other people. I know she's seeing someone in Germany. She doesn't love me she just likes showing me off to her girlfriends. Cause I'm young. They call me the puppy. You should hear them: "Did you toilet train the puppy yet? Oh Donna, the puppy's so cute.""

"Come on," I said, "stop crying."
"You've got me going now." And I started up.
"Look at the two of us. We're downright unstable."

"Oh Lillian," he cried.

"Come here," I said and put my arms around him. He felt like a different person without the muscles. With that damn beard. He felt like a stranger.

"My Jimmy," I said.

And I don't know what possessed me but I really wanted to kiss him. Even though he was distraught and fragile-seeming, and it was probably most inappropriate. I wanted to push through that to his mouth. So I did. And he didn't pull away. And for a second I thought about Donna, and that I didn't want to go where her lips had been, but then I dismissed that, and I kissed him again. And it was a long kiss. The kind of kiss you could never get bored of. The kind of kiss you could rediscover yourself inside. And it was so tender and unguarded between us, and I knew I was falling and I did nothing to catch myself. It felt like a dam was opening in my chest, and all these feelings that I'd been waiting for years to put into motion, were flooding my entire insides. And I could have had the good sense to get up or ask him to leave, and the dam would have surely blocked, but instead I just let it all come crashing down.

On the train back from Brighton the following day, I stared out of the window for almost the entire ride. Couldn't tell you if the train was crowded or if there was even anyone sitting next to me. I took out the strip of photos we'd taken in the booth. Examined them. As we came into London, the conductor approached and said to me,

"Don't leave anything behind."

I said,

"What did you say?"
Even though I'd heard him the first time.

He said, "Don't leave anything behind."

I put the photos in my bag. I looked at him. He smiled. I smiled.

"I won't," I said, "I won't leave anything behind."

(*Lights dip and then come back up sharply.*)

PART 4
Two Hours Later

Out of Breath

LILLIAN

(*Seated on the stool.*)

When I walked in the door the phone was ringing.
I dropped everything. Ran for the receiver. It was an out-of-breath Jimmy.

"I want to be with you," he says.
"I want you.
I never said that to anyone before.
I'm leaving Donna.
She gets back tomorrow.
I'm telling her tomorrow.
But first I need to check.
Do you want to be with me?"

And he suddenly struck me as so young and a little desperate but I said,

"Yes I do."

I said,

"Yes I do,"

anyway.

(*Wayne Shorter's "Antigua" plays. Lights fade.*)

PART 5
One Year Later

There You Go

LILLIAN

(*Standing. Sipping from the glass of water.*)

I've always felt like somewhat of a mystery to myself. As if there were whole territories inside me that existed beyond the grasp of my comprehension. I love having so much inside remain unknown. That's why I've always distrusted psychoanalysis. To me, at a certain point, it eats away a person's mystery.

"That's not mystery, that's pain," say my friends.

Seemed like everyone I knew was trying to explain themselves. "What about instinct? Gut feeling?" I'd say.

"When I die they'll find intuition at the wheel. (With probably fear still sitting in the backseat trying to bark out directions.) But intuition at the wheel."

"Be warned, Lillian, the way you got him will be the way you lose him," was the general consensus of most of the over-psychoanalyzed people I knew.
"He's a lost and broken boy, and you're not his mother."

(*She places the glass on the stool next to her.*)

When I married Jimmy no one was invited.

"Don't you want anyone to give you away?" he asked.

To which I replied that I would be giving myself away this time, thank you very much.

We were married in a registrar's office by a man whose accent was so thick that to this day I'm not completely clear what I was agreeing to. Not wishing to appear rude by asking him to repeat everything two or three times, I just basically said, yes, yes, yes. There was a plastic cherry blossom tree in each corner of the room, with little fake birds on its branches. Upon closer examination the birds were holding "Love Is Blind" signs between their bills. Looking closer still I noticed the birds had no eyes. "Charming," I thought.

Jimmy showed up wearing a jacket that can best be described as looking like it had been snatched off the back of a small child who'd been on his way to a birthday party, and he came up with the shadiest-looking witness who I had never met before, nor have seen since. I have to say when I first laid eyes on him I did think to myself,

"Keep your eye on your purse." Nonetheless it was quite the little adventure.

First few months we lived together in London. Jimmy got a job pruning trees for the council. One afternoon I finished up work early, thought, "Oh I'll take the scenic route home," when by chance, I happened to run into him. He was perched on the main bough of a sycamore. Lopping branches. Huge sections of tree were falling onto the road. I called out to him. He looked up sharply.

"Don't do that!" he snapped. "You surprised me."

"That poor tree," I said, "the shock'll kill it."

"You have to be brutal about cutting," he said. "The more you cut away, the better they do. It may seem cruel, but it's for the best. Sometimes you have to nearly kill something before it will grow."

And for a good minute we just stared at each other without saying anything.

Later that day, when he came home from work, he laid down and went to sleep. While he was sleeping I pulled back the covers to look at him. He never wore clothes in bed. Always slept the same way; on his side with his hands covering his face.

Well I noticed something on his heel. I thought, "What the hell is that?" He had an ant tattooed on his heel, which I'd never noticed before. It was very tiny and very detailed. A quite perfectly proportioned ant.

I laid down next to him, fell asleep myself, and had this dream that Jimmy's back was covered with faint lines. Faint lines and tattooed roads. Winding through freckles. Crisscrossing his backbone. Occasionally passing through a hair. In the dream I asked him what it was. He answered,

"It's a map of your life."

I laughed, "Oh come on."

He said,

"You started here,"

and he pointed behind himself.

"You're about here now."

And he moved his finger to a place halfway up his back. Over his heart. In the dream I asked him,

"Why does the map end at your shoulder?"

And just as he was about to answer, I woke up.

He had next to nothing in the way of possessions. Everything had belonged to Donna. One of the few things that was actually his was this little tent that he took everywhere. Just in case he ever felt the urge to sleep outside, he'd say.

One Saturday we took a bus ride into the country. Sure enough the little package came along too. No sooner were we off the bus than Jimmy said,
"Let's forget about going home.
I wanna sleep under the sky."
I have to say the idea did appeal. So we bought sandwiches. Supplies. Walked what must have been miles, till we found a spot that met Jimmy's definition of the word remote, by which time the sky was quite black. He set up the little tent and pulled out a sleeping bag that he'd had all along.

By the time we'd eaten it was late and Jimmy was beat so he went pretty much straight to sleep. I, on the other hand, just laid there. The ground was uneven, to put it mildly. I think we were parked on top of a mole community. My spine was wondering what the hell was going on, and it was damp, but I didn't care.

It was so quiet in the open. You could almost hear your moods change. If you laid still enough you could feel your instincts wriggling to the surface.

Hours go by. I'm still wide awake.
Thinking,
"I'm forty-one years old.
It's three o'clock in the morning
and I'm laying in a field."
And the whole thing seemed so absurd, I just started laughing.

"You know what?" I thought.
"Good things are going to happen."
"I'm ready for them now. I wasn't before. I am now."
"Yes," I thought, "I'm ready to roll my sleeves up.
My sleeves are fairly twitching to be rolled.
For the good things."

In the bus on the way back home Jimmy said,
"I can't live without wheels."
But he didn't have two cents to rub together, so I purchased a cheap car. A beaten-up Rover 2000. For a test drive we drove down south to the coast. Just along from Brighton we happened to pass a small cottage for sale with a few acres attached. Four large greenhouses. Quite without thinking I said,
"Pull over Jimmy."

The place had been a nursery. It required work, that was for sure, but there was something about it that I felt immediately drawn to. I took down the name of the estate agent. Gave them a call, just out of curiosity really, to see what it was going for. Well it was surprisingly inexpensive considering it commanded a good view of the sea and came with a little land. The estate agent told me the woman who lived there before had given birth in the house, and had buried her placenta in the garden. And I thought, "Why are

you telling me this?" "Oh good I'll take it. I've been looking for a house with a placenta for the longest time." I mean
really.

But you know, soon as Jimmy and I were inside the place I
knew I wanted to live here.

"We could open a nursery," I said.
"You always wanted to do that. I've always had a houseful
of plants. At school they called me 'Green Fingers.'"

The cottage was empty of furnishings, except on one wall
there was an oil painting of two lizards.
"Look lizards!" I cried.
"It's a sign!"

Jimmy didn't say anything. I could sense hesitation but I bar-
reled on. I felt fired up about the idea in a way I'd never felt
about any potential vocation. I had some savings tucked
away. I did work in a store that had a comprehensive gar-
dening section. On the quiet I made an appointment at my
bank to see about obtaining some kind of small business
loan. Found it to be surprisingly straightforward.

Then, quite impulsively, without discussion of any kind, I
cracked open the nest egg I'd been sitting on, and bought
the place.

Everyone I knew was up in arms.

"It's Jimmy's dream, it isn't yours!
What are you going to do without your financial cushion?
Do you want to end up like some old lady, living on cat
food?"

"Oh for God's sake!" I said.

"This whole episode, and Keith was right, it is an episode,
bears a label with the words 'tragedy in the making' written
all over it."
Said one person.

"No you're wrong," I said. "I've been wearing the tragedy-in-the-making tag around my neck for a long time, and I'm taking it off now."

When it came to packing, I couldn't help thinking about Jimmy cutting that tree and I was ruthless.
"I'll just take my book collection and only what I like.
The past is gone," I said, "I'm not dragging it around anymore."

I just walked away from London and my life there. "I'll get fresh friends," I thought. "I'll start new."

As we were driving down the motorway I felt as though I were on the run from the law, but Jimmy didn't say a word. Didn't play music. Just stared straight ahead.
I asked him,
"What's wrong?"

He said,
"Nothing."

I said,
"Come on, you look like you're on your way to a funeral, or something."

"I don't know anything about you,"
he said.
"You don't know anything about me.
We're as good as strangers."

"You know me," I said.

And had the strongest feeling that I'd been in this situation before.

PART 6
Same Time

Grace

LILLIAN

(Standing.)

We decided the nursery should specialize in chrysanthemums, and Jimmy would do a little landscaping on the side,
for extra money. I soon realized it wasn't Brighton that I had
loved so much as it was being within close proximity to the
sea. From the front of the house, I would find myself transfixed by it.

I loved being outside. Getting my hands dirty. Sometimes I'd
have to force myself to get up out of the flower beds and
call it a day. I'd stand outside in the open sometimes with my
arms in the air. The sun in my face. I swear if you could see
me from the road, you'd think you'd stumbled across some
bizarre cult.

From the moment we moved here though, Jimmy had been
acting strangely. We'd have ridiculous petty arguments. Like
giving the place a name. He thought we should call it "Lillian's." "What about you?" I'd say. "Your name?" And he'd
argue the place was really mine.
"It's your money. You got the loan. I may as well just work
for you."
"It's ours," I'd try to insist. He'd get all sullen, so when customers did start arriving they'd talk to me. They didn't want
to deal with him. One night I tried to confront him. To find
out what was going wrong. And he barked at me,

"We've become ordinary and I haven't got time to be ordinary."

I said,
"I thought this is what you wanted?"

He counteracted,
"Well maybe I've changed my mind."

I put my arms around him once, to try and comfort him and his body was so tense. It was like holding a piece of wood. And he wouldn't look me in the eye.

I said,
"Why won't you look at me?"

He said,
"I can't."

I said,
"Why not?"

He said,
"I just can't."

He'd fall asleep on the couch most every night and I couldn't get him to come to bed. Till it became the norm. He would sleep on the couch. The closer the place came to being finished, the more remote it seemed to become between us. We'd go whole mornings without exchanging a word.

One night it was particularly bad. I thought, "We can't go on like this." So I said, "I think I should leave for a little bit. I'm going to take the car and go for a drive."

"I didn't know you could drive," Jimmy said.

"I only drive if I have to," I said, "and I think I should go for a drive."

"How long will you be?" he asked.

"How long would you like me to be?"

"A few hours would be good," he said.

"Then I'll go for a few hours.
Aren't you going to say good-bye?"

"Why?" he asked. "We'll see each other again.
Won't we?"

and he grinned. And I thought, "That's the first time I've
seen you smile since we got here."

It felt strange to be at the wheel. Winding through lanes at
night. I hadn't driven myself for a long time.
"Where shall we go, Lillian?" I said out loud.
"Don't think," I thought, "just move."
And I put my foot down.
And for a second I wondered,
"Am I dreaming this?"

When I came back to the house it was dark. All the lights
were turned off. I felt considerably apprehensive about
going in. I knew what I'd find. Jimmy was gone. So were his
clothes. I knew that would happen. That's why I left the
house, so he could leave. You see however bad things got,
Jimmy and I understood each other.

But then a strange incident occurred.

(*Wayne Shorter's "Vera Cruz" begins to play, underscoring the next
nineteen lines. Multiple images of single chrysanthemums slowly appear
on a scrim behind* LILLIAN. *They float in and out of focus, in low light.
Moving with the music.*)

I stepped outside the house. Onto the porch. It was pitch
dark. The tall chrysanthemums were in bloom for the first
time. The flowers seemed black at night. They were moving
slightly. As though something were stirring in them. I heard
a noise coming from somewhere in the middle. So I walked
into the chrysanthemums. There was a white dog running
between the rows. The dog kept turning and looking at me.

And every time I'd get close it would start up running again, as though it was leading me somewhere. And I don't know what possessed me but I called out "Jimmy," and the dog stopped in its tracks. Edged towards me. It looked like the kind of dog that no one would want. It licked my hand. For a moment we locked into each other's eyes. "One day some woman's going to really lose her bearings just looking into those eyes," I said out loud. And I got a rush of sadness, but it went away. The dog then turned and started running. I called out "Jimmy," but I didn't call out loud enough. My cry was fainthearted. The dog kept going, deeper into the chrysanthemums.

(*Music and chrysanthemums fade.*)

When Jimmy left, my first impulse was to pack everything and go back to Keith.

When Jimmy left I thought, "I can't do it."

When Jimmy left it felt like placing a child in charge of a child.

When Jimmy left I thought,
"If you don't begin, you're going to go under."

When Jimmy left I took out the strip of photos we'd taken in the booth, and they were completely blank.

Shortly after Jimmy left I ran into Donna in London. Actually she came running after me.

"Don't pretend you didn't see me Lillian," she said.

"Oh Christ," I thought. "What do you want?"

"Look I don't think I made a very good impression on you before," she said, "and I'm sorry. To be honest I was going through a kind of therapy at the time which proved quite disastrous."

"Do you ever hear from our little friend, just out of curiosity?"

I said I hadn't seen "our little friend" for a while, which was true.

"I suppose you know what happened?" she asked. "I came back from Germany, after your visit, and he was gone. No note. No phone call. No good-bye. No nothing. We were going to move the business back to London, which I did. I live here now. He effectively just disappeared on me. It wasn't working between us. Wouldn't have lasted. He pushed me to marry him you know."

Then she asked if I knew how his health was.

I said, "What do you mean?"

She says, "You know, the heart thing.
The arteries are weak, or swollen, I was never quite clear.
They could burst at any time. He could flood inside.
Frankly," she said, "that's one of the reasons why I was
hesitant to marry him. Don't want to set yourself up do
you? Don't mind being a divorcee, but a widow? Now that
ages you."

And she laughed.

"I didn't know him very well," I said, "let's just say we helped each other out,"
and excused myself to leave.

"How's the publishing business going?" she called out.

"Very well," I said. "Thank you for asking."

I heard from Jimmy once. He sent me a photograph of a woman alone on a beach. Wading in the sea. On the back of the photograph was written:
"LILLIAN. Question mark. Love Jimmy."
There was no return address.

For about a week I was feeling an inexplicable sadness. Couldn't figure out what it was. When the phone rang I almost didn't answer it. I knew something was up. It was a woman calling from a hospital in West London. She asked me if I knew Jimmy Foyle. I said I did. She said they'd found a piece of paper in his pocket with my name and number on it. She explained what had happened medically, and I suppose I was in shock or something because I didn't really take in what she was saying. She said they couldn't locate any other friends, or track down his father, that she appreciated this was a bad time, but arrangements had to be made. I said,

"I think I'm going to have to call you back."

I buried Jimmy in the garden. I just couldn't stand the thought of him being among strangers. I planted a hanging cherry tree over him. It fills up with birds sometimes. The singing coming out of that tree is not to be believed. There's flower beds on either side. A lot of people don't know he's there. There's no reason for them to know.

For a couple of months after I realized I'd lost interest in life. I felt as though I were floating. Nothing seemed to connect, or make an impression. But then I said to myself,

"Lillian, enough."

I can't believe where I am sometimes. Any spare moment I can I sit in the garden reading. Occasionally pausing to take in the sea. Right now I'm hovering somewhere between Jacqueline Susann and Grace Paley. I can feel myself opening here. I am exactly where I want to be.

Since I started serving coffee the nursery has become quite the little social spot.

(*She picks up the glass of water from the stool.*)

In warm weather I give caffeinated tours in which you walk through the greenhouses sipping a superbly prepared, even if I do say so myself, espresso or latte, while I give out background information and growing tips.

"With the right application of light, I've discovered a way of keeping chrysanthemums in bloom all year round. They are a hardy annual, but like all plants require effort."

I wonder if we all end up where we're supposed to be.

If you lay out the incidents of our lives, they form the most exquisite poetry.

PART 7
The Present

Chrysanthemums (Reprise)

LILLIAN

(*Standing.*)

There's a man who comes round here.
He buys chrysanthemums from me for a store up the coast.
His name is James. Has the palest eyes.
I find myself just looking at them sometimes in disbelief.

He plays me rock music and tells bad jokes.
The other day he came over all excited.
"Lillian I've finally got a good one.
A snail goes into a used car dealer. Says to the dealer,
'Show me the spiffiest, fastest car you have.'
The dealer points him to a Ford Mustang.
'Fine I'll take it,' says the snail.
'No wait a minute. Paint an *S* on the back.'
So the car dealer paints an *S* on the back of the car.

Snail looks at it, says, 'That's good. Paint an *S*
on the front too.'
The dealer obliges.
'You know what,' says the snail, 'paint an *S* on both
sides.'
So the car dealer paints an *S* on both sides.
'Perfect,' says the snail.
The car dealer looks at the snail curiously.
'I hope you don't mind me asking,
but why did you have me do that?'
The snail answers,
'Because when I drive down the road,
I want people to say, "Look at that *S* car go." ' "

(*She places the glass back on the stool.*)

The two of us completely lost it.
I know he's interested. He lights up, then gets all shy.
Picking out blooms. Averting his pale eyes.
But I'm taking my time. There's no rush. None at all.

(*Jimmy Somerville's recording of "Safe in These Arms" begins to play.*)

I'm not going anywhere.

(*Lights fade. Music continues.*)

SAKINA'S RESTAURANT

Aasif Mandvi

For my parents

Sakina's Restaurant was originally produced at the American Place Theatre in New York City, June 1998. It was then produced at the Bush Theatre in London, November 2001. The play was directed and developed by Kim Hughes; it was performed by the author.

CHARACTERS

AZGI
FARRIDA
HAKIM
SAKINA
ALI
SAMIR

Lights up. We see AZGI standing with his suitcase center stage.

AZGI

Hello, my name is Azgi. I like hamburger, baseball, and Mr. Bob Dylan. You know, I am practicing my introduction because today is a very important day for me, because today I leave my home here in India and I fly on an airplane! (*Motioning with his hands*) And I fly, and I fly, and I fly, and then, I land! (*Motioning with his hands*) And I land and I land and I land and I land, on the other side of the world in America. Oh, I am very excited. Practically the entire village has turned up in my parents' small house to celebrate my departure, can you believe. (*Turning up*) Ha waru me awuchu.

(*Back to front.*)

Okay, let's see. I have my passport, *check*! My ticket, *check*! You know, I am the first person in my entire family to even fly on an airplane. . . . (*Nervous*) I hope no crashing. Oh, and the most important thing I have, a letter! I read . . . for you. (*He reads.*) "Dear Azgi," (*To audience*) That's me. (*Reading*) "America is a wonderful place, and as I told you in response to your letters, that since it was your dream to come here, I would help you as soon as Farrida and I could manage, well Azgi, the time has come. I need help in my restaurant. I can sponsor you, it is hard work, but you can come work for me, live with us, and get to see America, your dream is coming true."

Mr. Hakim is a very very important man, he owns a restaurant in Manhattan! Here is address, 400 East 6th Street . . . NYC . . . USA . . . the World . . . the Galaxy . . . the Universe! (*Triumphantly throwing his arms in the air. Turning up.*) *Ha waru me awuchu.*

(*Turning back, he sees his mother.*)

Ma, Ma, don't cry. Why you crying, Ma? Listen, listen. You know what, you know what, when I go to America, I will write to you every day. I will write to you so much that my hand will fall off. Ma, come on. Ma, you know what? When I go to America, I will write to you from the . . . from the . . . top of the Empire State Building! I will write to you from the . . . from the bottom of the Grand Canyon! I will write to you from every place I go—McDonald's! I will write to you! Hollywood, Graceland, Miami, FL, every place. I will even write to you from Cleveland! Cleveland, Ma! Home of all the Indians! Ma, come on, you know what, you know what? When I go to America, one day I will be very rich! And then I will invite you and you can come and stay with me in my big house with my swimming pool, and my Cadillac. . . .

(*She hands him something.*)

What is this? A stone? You are giving me a stone! Ma, the poorest people in our village will give me more than a stone to take on my journey. How can I tell them that my own mother gave me a stone? The story of the river stone? The story of the river stone? I don't remember the story of the river stone. I don't remember, I don't remember—okay, okay, *Bawa,* I keep the stone. See? I'm keeping it, I'm keeping it. (*He mimes putting it into his pocket and then suddenly pretends to throw it away.*) Oh my God I threw it away! (*Seeing his mother's panic*) I'm joking, I'm joking. It's right here, it's right here, Ma. It was a joke. Look, I keep it, I keep the stone. Okay! There it goes in my pocket, okay! (*Turning upstage and then turning back to face his mother)* Ma, I have to go.

(Music cue rises as AZGI *slowly does salaam to his mother; he kisses her hands and then her feet. He then picks up his suitcase and walks off toward America. He looks back at one point and holds up his hand as if to say good-bye. The lights fade and we hear an airplane fly through the air. When the lights come up accompanied by the song "Little Pink Houses" or any other appropriate song,* AZGI *is standing on a busy New York street. He mimes looking at the buildings around him and attempts to speak to people on the street, all of whom give him a very clear cold shoulder, he tries to say hello to people on the subway and the same thing happens until one solitary person speaks to him; this it turns out is a bum.* AZGI, *somewhat disappointed, gives the man a dime and then is subsequently pickpocketed. He despondently hangs up his coat on the coatrack upstage and turns to face the audience and a brand new American day. Noticing audience.)*

Oh, hello, how are you? Here I am! I made it! Oh my God, this New York is a crazy place. But welcome to Sakina's Restaurant. This is my new job. I am the manager here. . . . Okay, I'm not really the manager . . . I am the *owner!* *(Laughing)* No, no, I fooled you again. No I am not the owner, I am the waiter here but you know it is such a good job— *(He hears someone offstage.)* Oh excuse me. *(Speaking offstage)* Yeah? Oh, okay.

(He begins to set up tables.)

You know Mr. and Mrs. Hakim were waiting for me at the airport when I arrive. I think it is very nice of them to let me stay with them until I find a place of my own. Their two children, Sakina and Samir, are also very nice but they are completely American. Samir, he is only ten years old. He is always playing with his Game Boy. He say to me, he say, "Azgi how are you doing?" I say, "Samir, how am I doing what?" Then everybody start to laugh. Sakina, their daughter, she is older, she is going to be getting married soon. She say to me, she say, "Azgi, don't you worry you will soon catch on." So I just smile and nod my head and say, "Yes, yes, yes, you are absolutely right," even though I have no idea what any of these people are talking about. But I have found that in America, if you just smile and nod your head, and say, "yes, yes, yes, you are absolutely right," people love you!

I have not made any friends yet, because I am here in the restaurant, working, working, working. Mr. Hakim the owner, he is my very good friend, you know when I told him my dream to one day be an American millionaire, he say to me he say (*Mimicking* HAKIM), "Azgi, let me tell you something very profound. (*To audience*) So I listen you know, he say, "In America Azgi, any ordinary idiot can become *rich,* but not any ordinary idiot can be *respected*. I am not any ordinary idiot." (*Confused*) I think about this, and then I smile and nod my head and I say, "Yes, yes, yes, you are absolutely right." Mr. Hakim says I will go very far.

When I told Mrs. Hakim my dream to be an American millionaire, she looked at me and she said, "Azgi, you are smart. Don't be fooled. America can give you nothing that you don't already have." And then she said, "When I was a young girl, I had a dream, just like yours, my dream was to be a classical Indian dancer." I said, "Oh yeah? Show me how you used to dance." She said, "No, I don't dance anymore, but when I first came to America and Sakina was just a baby I used to dance every day," and suddenly she close her eyes and she start to do like this. (*He moves his hips.*)

I didn't know what to say. I said, "Mrs. Hakim!" (*Embarrassed*) I don't think you should do that. But then she say to me, she say, "Azgi, let me teach you how to dance," I say, "No, no, no, I cannot learn, I can only watch," she say, "No! you can learn, let me teach you how to make a bird," so I try you know, (*He begins to move his hands in the style of an Indian dance that represents a bird.*) I make a bird, make a bird, make a bird, make a bird . . . and bird fly away, gone! Bye-bye bird! Okay, okay, okay, I do it for real, I'm sorry I was just kidding. (*Seriously now with real intent to learn*) I make a bird, make a bird, make a bird, make a bird, hey I'm pretty good, and then I do like this (*He shakes his hips.*) and like this and—"Hey Mrs. Hakim you know what? I'm pretty good at this. I think if I had studied like you, I could have been a dancer myself." (*He gets into the dancing.*) I do a little bit of this and a little bit of that—

(*A light change happens simultaneously with a sound cue that sends* AZGI *into slow motion as he continues to dance; the dance becomes more spiritual as he slowly wraps himself with a pink scarf that he picks up from under the stage, and as soon as he does the lights change and we are in the presence of* FARRIDA.)

FARRIDA

(*She is surprised by her husband who has snuck up on her.*) Oh my God! You frightened death out of me. Why you have to sneak up like that? Okay Hakim, please don't be ridiculous, I don't dance like that, I don't dance like this. (*She wiggles her butt.*) I am a very good dancer, okay Hakim you know what, by making fun of me, you are the one who looks ridiculous.

Embarrassed? Embarrassed! Why should I be embarrassed? I am not in the least embarrassed. I just think that there is a thing like that called manners, where you don't just sneak up on someone when they are doing something, and then to, you don't know what I am doing, what if I am doing something I don't want you to see. Okay, very funny, ha ha ha. You saw me dancing, very funny! It is not called *embarrassment,* it is called *politeness.*

(*She picks up her rolling pin and begins to roll out chapati. Throughout most of this piece she is intermittently rolling out chapatis as she speaks to her husband.*)

Well, there are many things about your *new wife* that you

don't know. I am a very talented and mysterious woman. I can do much more than cook your food.

(*He tries to make a sexual advance.*)

Chul, chul, Hakim, come on stop. *Aray* come on, you are being absolutely crazy. Oh my God, you see how you get, you see how you get. You see what happens to you—you work in that restaurant fifteen hours a day, and then you come home and all you are thinking about is hanky-panky. Before you eat, hanky-panky! Before you wash your hands and face, hanky-panky! Okay, Hakim you know what? I won't cook, I won't clean, I won't do anything, me and you we'll just do hanky-panky, hanky-panky, hanky-panky! (*He pinches her and she turns round and tries to whack him with the rolling pin; he however ducks and she misses him.*) You are a lucky man!

That was before, that was long time back, that was before we came to America. In India, how many friends I had, how much family, anybody to help. Now do you know what I do, do you know? I cook, I clean, I take care of Sakina, and at the end of the day when she finally goes to sleep, I have five minutes for dance break which you interrupt with hanky-panky.

What you brought? What present? Go away, you didn't bring any present for me. . . . Really! You brought present for me? Show no. *Aray* show no. Come on, you can't bring present and then not show. Okay. Okay. Okay. I close my eyes you show me? You promise, you promise, okay? (*She covers her eyes.*) Guess? Guess? I can't guess, come on show no! Okay, okay, I guess, I guess . . . no, no, no I want to guess. Okay, you brought something to eat. No, something to wear? No! Something for Sakina? No! (*Excited*) Oh, Hakim, I knew what you brought, I knew what you brought, you brought . . . Something for apartment? *Yes!* New curtains! You brought new curtains!! (*She has taken her hands away from her eyes.*) Okay, okay, okay, I'm closing my eyes. (*She puts them up again.*) New curtains . . . No! Oh. I can't guess anymore. C'mon, I'm looking—Ready, one, two, three— (*She removes her hands from her eyes on the count of three, and she stands there staring in confusion at the sight before her.*)

What you brought? What is this? A *fern?* You brought a fern? Why? Why you brought a fern? Oh my God, Hakim, flowers. Flowers. Flowers means roses, flowers means tulips, flowers does *not* mean fern! My God, what a romantic Rock Hudson I married! No, no, it's very nice. It's very nice, we'll put it in the window, people will come by and say, "Oh look, this lady's husband, he bought her a bush!" (*He wants her to teach him to dance.*) No, no, I can't teach you—please Hakim, I can't teach you to dance. Besides, Hakim, that is a woman's dance. If a man dances like that, people will think he is you-know-what! You go, you dance with your *fern.* (*He seems to insist.*) Okay, okay, I'm sorry, come here you want to learn, come here, okay do like this, like this, make a bird, make a bird, (*She rushes through the hand gestures.*) Okay? Okay, now you are a dancer.

(FARRIDA *pulls on her scarf, so as to give the illusion that he is trying to pull her to him.*)

No, I don't want to kiss you. I don't want to, because *I don't want to.* Hakim, please don't argue with me, I just don't want to. Because, just because, because (*She pulls away from him.*) you smell like cigarette! Are you happy now? Then how come I am smelling cigarette in your mouth right now, when you told me after last time that that was your last pack and now I can smell that you are smoking again.

No, no, I don't want to dance with you, I want to know why you broke your promise. Relax. Relax. How can I relax Hakim, when you told me, you told me with your own mouth. You said, "Farrida, because I love you, I will stop smoking," and what did I say? You don't remember, I will tell you what I said, I said, "No. No. You *will not,* because I know you, and I know the kind of man you are," and what did you say? What did you say? You don't remember, you don't remember what *you* said, okay I will tell you what you said. You said, (*Pointing to God*) *"Khudda Ni Kassam."* Do you remember? *Khudda Ni Kassam* Hakim. And you are a bloody liar! You lie to me, you lie to God, you lie to anybody.

Mane' tara sathe waat aj nai karwi, tara moma si gundhi waas aweche. How can you say that? If you loved me, I would not smell cigarette in your mouth right now. Teach me to dance. You can't even do *one bloody thing* for me! Dramatic. Dramatic. How can I be dramatic? You see me. You see my life. You see my life since I came to this country. Can you imagine? Me. Me. Hakim, I was the girl in India who was always on the go! Movies, theatre, museum, money to burn. Where have you brought me? Where have we come? To this cold country where nobody talks to anybody, where I sit alone in two rooms all day long waiting for you to come home. No friends, no one to talk to, nowhere to go. If I go anywhere, these Americans don't even understand what I am trying to speak.

Look at me, Hakim! I am not even the girl that you married. This is not me, this was not supposed to be my life. I gave up everything for you. For your dream, America! Land of Opportunity! For you, *yes.* For my baby, *yes.* For me, *no.* No opportunity.

How can you say that, how do you know? Even if we do make it, what happens do we just go on smoking and dancing forever? (*Soft music begins to play, signifying that* SAKINA *has woken up.*) See now, Sakina woke up. (*She looks offstage to talk to the apparently crying child.*) *Na ro bacha Mummy aweche. Na ro.* (*She turns back to* HAKIM, *but he is gone.*) That's all right, Hak—. ... you go, I'll take care of her. You go, smoke your cigarette. (*She turns upstage.*) *Na ro, Mummy aweche. Na ro bacha Mummy aweche, Na ro Na ro.*

(FARRIDA *walks upstage and we see her slowly take the scarf from around her neck and it becomes the baby* SAKINA. *She spins around with the baby almost cradling and almost dancing. The scarf is eventually unraveled and we are back in the company of* AZGI, *as he addresses the audience.*)

AZGI

Once upon a time, an eagle and a lark sat on the branch of a giant tree. The eagle pushed out its giant chest and spread its powerful wings, and told the lark of its many adventures. "I have seen the world," said the eagle, "I have seen it seven times over. I have flown over temples and palaces, oceans and rivers, I have swooped down into valleys and I have flown so high that the sun has risen and set below me." The tiny lark had no such adventures of which to speak and it wracked its brain for a story to tell. Finally, it did the only thing it knew how to do. It began to sing. A tiny song, but as it did the tree, the field, the hillside, the entire valley, lifted up out of the earth and rose to heaven.

She doesn't dance anymore. I suppose that eventually she forgot that she could. Or maybe she simply decided it was not worth trying to remember.

Dear Ma, another day in Sakina's Restaurant. I work, and I work, and I work and I work—but I never dance.

(AZGI *is suddenly in the restaurant. He mimes a conversation with a table, tries to clean their dirty silverware by breathing on it, and then wiping it on his pants, he goes to another table and picks up their plates, he spins around in a circle nodding and smiling as if he is dealing with a hundred different tables, he rushes over to the kitchen and screams at Abdul the cook, who is working behind the line.*)

Abdul! I need two *puris* on table five! I need two *lassis* on table six, and this lamb curry is *cold, cold, cold!* Food, Abdul, is supposed to be *hot, hot!* Not *cold!* How come you don't seem to understand that?

(AZGI *runs to speak to one of his tables. To first table.*)

I am very sorry. In all the time I have worked in this restaurant, food is *never* cold, *never*! He is heating it up right now. I will bring it out in two minutes and you just keep enjoying your . . . water.

(*He moves to the second table.*)

Hello, how are you? My name is Azgi, I will be your waiter. How can I help you? Oh yeah, it is kind of spicy, but we have a scale. You see, you can order how spicy you like 1, 2, 3, 4, 5. You decide, he'll make it. What? You want number 5? (AZGI *is a little concerned.*) Sir, don't take number 5, take number 2. No, no, number 2 is better for you, it's very good, you'll like it very much. Please sir, don't take number 5. Sir I am trying to save your life okay. (*Getting angry*) Look, look in my eyes okay, number 2 is better for you. Okay you think about it, I will come back okay.

(*He runs upstage again.*)

Abdul! Where is my lamb curry???? (*The lamb curry seems to have appeared on the line.*) A-ha! (*He runs over to the first table with the imaginary lamb curry. It is very hot and burns his hands.*) Aaaah! There you go. Okay? Piping hot—what happened? Why you look so sad? Not lamb? *Chicken.* Oh my God! No, no, please sit down. Where you going? Please don't leave, sit down, I am very sorry, this is a terrible mistake, I will bring out chicken in just two minutes, please don't leave, whatever you do don't leave.

(*He runs over to second table.*)

Okay, okay, look I tell you what, number 3, number 3 is plenty hot, plenty hot. You don't need number 5. *Listen man! I am from India!* And even in India nobody asks for number 5! It's not a real thing that you can eat, it's just for show. I am not screaming, you are screaming! Look, look, now your wife is crying! I didn't make her cry, you made her cry! Okay, okay. Fine, fine, you want 5, 15, 105! I give you, okay.

Abdul! Listen on dupe 41, I put number 5, but you don't make it number 5, you make it number 2, okay? And this lamb curry is supposed to be chicken curry—because I am telling you, that's why. Because I am the boss right now, Okay? Listen you give me any trouble now, I will have Mr. Hakim fire you! Oh, yeah? Oh, yeah? Come on, come on Abdul. (*He puts up his fists.*) I will take you right now! I will kick your butt so hard that you will be making lamb curry for the tigers in India! Oh, yeah? Come on, Big Guy, come on, Big Guy, come on, Big Guy, come on— (*Suddenly* AZGI *is faced with Abdul who grabs him by the collar.*) BIG GUY! I am joking, man. I am just kidding around, why you take me so seriously? Please don't kill me.

(*Turning.*)

Every night I have the same dream. I am a giant tandoori chicken wearing an Armani suit. I am sitting behind the wheel of a speeding Cadillac. I have no eyes to see, no mouth to speak, and I don't know where I am going.

Mr. Hakim, he come up to me, he say, "Azgi, Azgi, Azgi, you have to calm down, man." He say to me, he say, "Success, Azgi, is like a mountain. From far away it is inspiring, but when you get close, you realize that it is simply made of earth and dirt and rocks, piled one on top of the other until it touches the sky." Mr. Hakim, he is a smart man, but I wonder to myself when God was building the mountain and piling the rocks, one on top of the other, was he working or playing?

(*He begins to ponder his thought, and then suddenly he smiles and goes over to the first table.*)

Hello, my name is Azgi. . . . I am working . . . and playing. (*He goes over to the second table.*) Hello my name is Azgi, I am working and playing . . . how are you? (*He goes over and looks in the direction of Abdul, and blows him a big kiss.*) ABDUL . . . I love you man! (*Phone rings,* AZGI *turns and looks at the audience.*) Phone! (*He picks up the phone.*) Hello, Sakina's Restaurant, Azgi speaking, how may I—Oh, oh Mr. Hakim? No, no he is right here, I will get him—

(AZGI *heads around behind the coatrack as if on his way to find* HAKIM. *When he comes around the other side—with tie in hand—he is* HAKIM.)

HAKIM

(*Into the phone*) Hello, Sakina's, how may I help you? Oh, hello Bob! I am very fine, business is good, business is good, you know, can't complain, how about you? Huh? Dinner for three? Tonight? Oh you must be going to have a big celebration . . . usual table? (*He writes down the reservation.*) Okay, 8 PM. Very good. Oh congratulations, you must be very proud of him. Actually we are also very proud of our Sakina because—(*He is embarrassingly interrupted on the other end of the line.*) Oh, okay Bob, no, no, that's fine, I understand, time is money, got to go. Okay Bob, we'll see you later, okay we'll see you then, bye-bye . . . bye-bye . . . bye-bye. (*Hangs up, and then resumes putting on his tie and grooming himself in mirror and singing a Hindi song of choice. During this, he taps his foot three times, signifying an imaginary knock on the door.*) Come in. (*He turns to see his daughter.*) Hey, hey, hey, hey! Come inside here, close the door, come here, what is this dress? Oh, I see, I see.

(*He talks to his daughter. His distress with his daughter is translated into his ineptness and frustration with his tie that he is trying to secure.*)

You think you are too smart, huh? You think you are too smart? You think you can go anywhere, do anything, wear anything. You think you have become an American Girl! You think the world should care not how you behave, what

you wear, how you dress, nothing! You have got all these
fancy ideas from all your American friends. You are laughing with all your American friends you are saying, "Oh, my
parents are introducing me to an Indian man, nice professional Indian man, going to be a doctor, how foolish of
them," right? How foolish they are. All your American
friends are laughing. They are saying, "Hey, Sakina, life is
not like that. Life is easy, marry who you want to marry,
black guy, white guy—who cares," right? Who cares? In
America, everything is okay! No right, no wrong, no good,
no bad, everything is *cool*! As long as I feel good about
myself, who cares, right? Who cares how my father feels, or
my mother feels, or my grandfather feels, or my grandmother feels. Who cares! It is my business, my life, this is a
free country! Am I right?

(*Phone rings.*)

Hello, Sakina's, how may I help you? Tonight, dinner for
two, Martin . . . can you spell that? (*Writing*) M . . . A . . . R
(*He notices that Sakina is leaving and he tries to get her to come
back in the room while continuing with the customer on the phone.*)
T . . . I . . . N, no I got it, I got it, yes we do, yes we do, free
popadoms, yes all night long, as many as you want. Okay,
we'll see you then, yes I am excited as well, okay then, bye-
bye . . . bye-bye . . . bye-bye.

(*Hangs up.*)

Sakina! Sakina! Come inside. Close the door. I'm talking to
you. Crazy girl, running away. (*He turns to the mirror, notices
his tie is about two inches long with a giant knot and he is a little
embarrassed. He reties it.*) "Oh Dad!" You are saying, "Dad!
Dad! Dad! What do you know about life in America? You
are from India! In America you have to learn to relax,
because everybody in America is very *relaxed* and very *cool*!"
Well, let me tell you something, I have seen all of your cool
and relaxed friends, and you are not fooling anyone—you

will *never* be an American girl. You can *try.* Oh yeah, you can *try.* You can wear your *big hair,* like American hair, and you can wear makeup like American makeup, you can even wear this cheap dress and show off your breasts and your legs and disgrace your whole family—but you will always be an Indian girl, with Indian blood, and these Americans, oh they are very nice, very polite on the face, have a nice day, have a nice day. Welcome to Kmart, very nice. They will even look at you and say, "Oh, she is so pretty, she looks like Paula Abdul." But let me tell you something, the minute you steal one of their good ole boys from them, suddenly you will see how quickly you become an *Indian* again.

(*Phone rings. He speaks in Gujaratti.*)

Hello Sakina's Restaurant how may I help you? *Ahh, came cho bhai. Aray koi divas miltaj nathi, awtaaj nathi. . . . Aje, chullo, na na badha ne layaowjo, na khai takhlif nei, chullo pachi milsu . . .* Okay, bye-bye . . . bye-bye . . . bye-bye.

(*Hangs up and faces his daughter.*)

We love you, Sakina, you are our daughter. But I will never agree to what you are doing with your life. Why do you think we came to this country? For *you!* Why do you think I have this restaurant? For *you!* Why do you think I am working twelve hours a day? For *you and your brother.* So that you could grow up in the richest country in the world, have all the opportunity, all the advantages. We are saving every penny for your college, why? So you can run around with American boys. *No!* So we will be proud of you. Indian children make their parents proud of them. Can your American friends teach you that? Can they teach you about your culture? Your religion? Your language? Can they tell you who you are? Go ask them. I know, I know, I know, it is all fun and games right now, but what will happen? You will marry one of these American boys, have American children, and then what? Then everything will be forgotten.

Everything will be gone. *Tu kai samje che, me su kawchu tane'*. *Tara mugaj ma kai jaiche'*. Answer me, no? No, no, no, no, not in English. Speak to me in Gujaratti. (*He waits, and she does not respond. She is unable to.*) Can't . . . Won't maybe. Look at you, look at what you have become. You will not go to this dance tonight. I will get rid of this "I want to be American" nonsen— (*Exploding in anger*) I don't care! I don't care, I don't care if this is the biggest dance in the country or the world or the entire fucking America! Dancing is important, (*He dances around mocking her.*) but I am not important!

(*The phone rings. He composes himself and answers the phone.*)

Hello, Sakina's, how may I help you? Yes, Bob, how are you? Oh, I am very sorry. Oh, no problem, that's perfectly all right, we'll see you another time. I hope she feels better, thank you for calling Bob. Bye-bye, bye-bye, bye-bye. (*Hangs up, and looks back at* SAKINA.) Tell Azgi that the Cohens have canceled, and go and help your mother . . . in the kitchen.

(*The phone rings, he watches her leave and then he hits the button on the phone. As soon as he does this, we hear the dance music for the next scene.* HAKIM *slowly turns away from the audience, loosens his tie, and unbuttons his shirt. When he turns around he is* AZGI *on the phone in the middle of a wild party.*)

AZGI

(*On phone*) Hey Ma, it is me, Azgi. Yeah, Azgi, I'm calling from New York. You know what, Ma? Next month Sakina is getting married, and tonight she is having a bachelorette party, and I have been invited. I am very excited to be a bachelorette. Hey, yeah, listen to the music. (*He holds up receiver.*) That's the music Ma. You won't believe this party Ma, so many people. Ma . . . I have to go, Ma. I love you, bye.

(*He hangs up the phone and comes downstage dancing. He then dances downstage, he mimes dancing with various different people, each dance*

wilder than the one before, until he ends up in a Rockette-style kick line.
He steps out of that to talk to the audience.)

Sakina told her parents that if she had to marry who they wanted her to marry, then she was going to have the kind of bachelorette party that she wanted to have. She invited seventy-five people, all of them drunk, including myself, and then she had a rock-and-roll band, and just to make sure that her parents would completely disapprove, she paid two hundred dollars for a *male stripper.* I told her, I said, "For two hundred dollars in India, I would run around naked for *one week!*" She said, "Oh, yeah?"

(*The music that has been underlying the previous speech suddenly becomes very loud and* AZGI *begins to strip. He speaks as his clothes are seemingly ripped off his body. First his tie, then his jacket, finally his shirt. He is incredibly embarrassed.*)

No, *no* I cannot strip, no I do not do that kind of thing, I am very modest, I am from India, please do not do this. Okay, okay I tell you what I do, this much, okay? (*He simply opens his shirt a little.*) La la la la . . . that's all I can do so thank you very much. (*His shirt is ripped off him.*) Noooo! Because I was the only man, they decided to turn me into a bachelorette.

(*At this,* AZGI *suddenly runs over to the hat stand and takes the tube dress that has been hanging there. The dress is slipped over his neck as if it were being done to him by the women at the party.*)

No, no, please. I cannot wear this, this is a dress! I am very embarrassed. Please not a *dress,* anything but a dress!

(*His protests of genuine embarrassment are unheeded by the women, who after the dress, proceed to finish off the transformation by squeezing a hair band onto his head, much to* AZGI's *amazement and distress.*)

No. No. I cannot wear this. I won't wear this, please don't make me wear this! AAAAAAAAAAAAAAAAAAAAAA-AHHHHHHH!

(AZGI *stands center stage wearing a tube dress and a hair band.*)

> Once upon a time a man asked God for a new face
> because he was tired of the one he had, so God granted
> the man his wish. The tragedy of this story is that now
> every time the man looks in the mirror, he doesn't know
> who he is.

(AZGI *moves over to the table stage left and sits down. We are now in the presence of* SAKINA. *She primps and preens in a large hand mirror, until she is suddenly surprised by the presence of Tom, who is sitting across the table.*)

SAKINA

Oh my God! (*Embarrassed*) Hi. I didn't see you come in. . . .
Wow you look great, I got your message. I can't stay
long. . . . 'Cause I gotta get upstairs by seven-thirty. Well
we're having this religious festival at our house and all these
people come over and we make this food called *biriani*
and . . . Never mind, I just gotta get back upstairs by seven-
thirty to help my mom get ready for it. (*Pause.*) So, what's
up? I'm just surprised to see you because last time we talked
you were like, "Sakina we are broke up." And then you hung
up the phone. What? That's not true! Is that why you came
here, to tell me that? (*She turns and takes a deep breath and then
turns back to him.*) No, I'm fine, I'm fine, first of all Tom, first
of all, Stacey and I are the ones who started this band and
Stacey and I are the only ones who can— (*She looks up at the
imaginary waiter.*) Hi! No, I'm not eating. . . . No neither is
he, thanks, okay? Thanks. (*The waiter leaves.*) And Stacey and
I are the only ones who can kick anyone out of this band,
which is not even a band yet, because Stacey still needs to
learn how to play the piano and so you are kicking me out ·
of a band that does not even exist yet! No, no, no, no, the
manager manages the band, Tom. He does not kick people
out of the band, that is not his job. What? She said that? She
said that! Stacey said that, Tom, look at me, look at me.

Okay, Stacey is my best friend since eighth grade, and if she said that, Tom, we are totally not friends anymore, so you better not be lying. Oh, my God! I can't believe she said that, I told her why I had to miss those practices, I totally said I have to miss three practices because I have to hang out with that Indian guy that my parents want me to marry—I had to hang out with him—I can't believe she said that, I don't understand, I explained the whole thing to her. (*Tom gets up to leave.*) Where are you going? That's it, that's all you had to say, now you're just gonna leave? (*She reaches for him.*) Wait! Would you please just sit down? (*She stands.*) Please, Tom. (*She bends over and becomes cute and coy in order to lure him back to the table.*) Please, just for two minutes, please just sit down. (*He sits back down.*) Hi, what is going on here Tom? What do you mean, what do I mean? I mean you come here to tell *me* that my best friend is kicking me out of *my* band, and then last week you're like we have to break up 'cause "I need more *space*," and then this week I find out that you're dating *Julie Montgomery*, and I'm calling you every day this week and your Dad is, like, "Tom? Tom's gone to the library," and I'm, like, Tom at the library—I don't think so. No, I don't think I'd be jealous of her. Because, because, because she's a racist pig, that's why. I can't believe you would even date her. I was hoping you came here to tell me of her untimely death. I don't care if I'm not black, it's still disgusting. I didn't say that, I just said she's a racist pig and I wish she'd die. You can still date her. Everyone knows she is, everyone in school knows, have you ever heard her mouth? "Nigger. Nigger. Nigger." (*She suddenly looks around hoping that no one heard her.*) She even called me that word. What's so funny? You're laughing, yes you are, oh my God, you're sick, Tom. This is retarded, I'm leaving. (*Gets up to leave as the waiter returns. She speaks to the waiter.*) Hi! Yeah I have to leave, I have to go upstairs and (*Directing it at Tom*) throw up! What? I don't care if she's sorry, Tom, my problem is not her, my problem is . . . what? (*Realizing that the waiter has taken her seriously*) No I don't need any *Pepto*. It's just *him*, I'm sorry thanks . . . no, no, I'm fine, thanks. (*The waiter leaves. She turns back to Tom.*) My problem is not her, my problem is *you*. It's like I don't even know you anymore. You explained it to her? You explained it to her. Okay, fine this should be great. (*Sitting back down.*) What, Tom, did you explain to her?

(*She listens and then hears something that makes her suddenly furious.*)

Ah ha, . . . and then? And? Okay shut up! No really Tom shut up! Tom, Tom, shut up! Shuuuuuuuut uuuup! Listen to me. I am *not Iranian!* I am *Indian! Indian! Indian!* What do you mean? How could you not know that? Look around, Tom. We dated for *two months*, Tom, *two months!* In that *two* months, I brought you to *this* Indian restaurant like a million times. Where you ate all the "*Oooh*, it's *so good!*" *Indian food* that my Mom put in front of your face. And remember that party I took you to in Brooklyn with all those *Indian* people, wearing *Indian* clothes celebrating *Indian* Independence Day and then you turn around and tell Julie Montgomery, "Hey, Sakina's not a nigger, she's *Iranian!*" Well, there it is isn't it, everything is a big mistake to you. Our whole relationship was a big mistake, remember that one? Oh, my God! I can't believe you, I already explained the whole thing to you. It doesn't mean anything—I am *not* going to marry him. Because I'm not, that's how I know— no, no, no. My parents can't make me, it's not some kind of medieval thing. It's just part of the culture, that's all. It's just a custom, they are just trying to make sure that I am secure in my life, that's all, they're not American, they're not like your parents—I'm not saying that—your parents are great! I'm just saying that my parents have a different attitude about things and if you can just accept that and not make a big deal about it? Well there it is isn't it! If everyone doesn't think like you, talk like you, believe what you believe, then it's all just dumb, right?

(He takes her arm, sexy music comes on.)

What are you doing? No, I can't kiss you . . . because we are in my dad's restaurant. *(She pulls her arm away from him.)* What? *(She suddenly starts giggling based on what he has said. She slowly sensually moves toward him, and as the music gets louder she and Tom engage in a big, sloppy, wet, teenage kiss, she pulls away embarrassed, mortified and turned on, she then slowly realizes that she is chewing "his" gum, she is horrified, and slowly takes it out of her mouth.)* Do you want your gum back? *(She sticks it under the table.)* What? Why? No, you're gonna make fun of him. Because, because you always make fun of him. Okay, if I show you, you promise not to laugh? Do you promise? Say it. Say I promise not to laugh . . . or make fun of him . . . okay.

(She reaches into her purse, and pulls out a photograph and puts it on the table.)

When I was seven, my dad, yeah he gave me this picture of this guy that they betrothed me to, and I just kept it. Because, because, I didn't know I was gonna meet anybody. When you're young and geeky with a funny name and your mom makes you wear harem pants and braids to school every day it's hard to imagine that you're ever gonna meet anyone. I don't suppose you can even relate, Mr. Freethrow Wins the Junior Championship—so it was a good feeling to have a picture of this guy who was like mine, and even though I was different, so was he, and so we were, like, a team. Jeez, I feel totally stupid. I don't even know why I'm telling you this. *(He gets up to leave.)* Where are you going? Where are you going? No, no I will tell him, I couldn't tell him last time, I'm gonna tell him next time. *(She snaps the picture up as he reaches over to tear it up.)* Hey! I think before I tear up his picture, I should tell him that I am not going to marry him, I think that would be courteous. Would you please come back! Why is this such a big deal to you? I'm gonna tell him. Come back, please come back. I will tell him! Fine! Fine, Tom! Just leave! Just leave the way you always do! (*Pause.*) WAAAAAIT!

What you don't understand Tom is that it doesn't make any difference, it's just the way it is. You can kick me outta the band. You can date a racist pig, Stacey can be a total bitch, my parents can cry, and I can even tear up this picture and it doesn't make any difference. (*Pause.*) Okay okay okay okay okay. (*She picks up the picture.*) Fine. . . . Fine. . . . Fine.

(*As music builds* SAKINA *attempts to tear up the picture, but it becomes obvious that she cannot. She holds the picture to her chest, and Tom walks away. Crying, she turns and undresses into* AZGI *again. As the music plays,* AZGI *picks up the strewn clothes and hangs them up. He then puts his shirt on again as the lights come up.*)

AZGI

(*Noticing audience*) Oh hello! How are ya? Oh you know, Sakina's wedding was wonderful. So many people. She looked beautiful, she looked so beautiful, she looked like a gift. The groom. He also looked very handsome. In fact the two of them together, they looked perfect. (*Pause.*) A little uncomfortable, but perfect. The groom, he is a medical student and he is also a very religious Muslim man. In fact, even at his own wedding he was studying for his final exam the next day and praying that he would not fail, can you believe. By watching him, I also start to pray . . . but the only thing I could think of to pray after watching him was, "Please God, don't let me spend my whole life just praying and studying, praying and studying, praying and studying. . . ." Oh, for their honeymoon, they are going to travel all across America. Oh, it sounds very exciting. I am so jealous. They will see everything, the Hollywood and the Redwood, they will ride on wide open Ventura highways, and they will see the Grand Canyon, and the Mississippi. I told the groom, I said, "If I could, I would follow you. I envy the adventure you are going to have." And he looked at me, and said, "Azgi, if I could, I would follow you, I envy the adventure you are going to have."

(*A sudden light change,* AZGI *suddenly doubles over in anguish, he is* ALI.)

ALI

Shut up! Shut up! I have to walk, I have to clear my head, and I have to come back. I have to walk. (*He begins walking upstage.*) I have to clear my head, I have to come back, I have to walk, I have to clear my head, I have to come back. I have to *walk*! I have to clear my head, I have to come—

(*Suddenly he turns and looks up as if someone has opened a door and he is staring into their face. He is visibly nervous, his mouth is dry, and his hands are sweaty.*)

Hello! I only have fifty dollars, I don't know if that's enough or not. Oh, that's fine, whatever you do for fifty dollars is fine. I don't know if I want the complete package anyway. It's probably safer that way, in regards to diseases and such. (*Realizing his faux pas*) I'm sorry, I'm not saying that you have any diseases. Oh no, I ruined the mood. I'm sorry, it's just that I'm a pre-med student, so I'm always thinking about diseases. I don't do this kind of thing normally— *never*! Never before actually, I don't know if that matters to you, but it matters to me, and so I just thought I would share that with you. (*Pulling money out of his pocket and handing it to her*) Look, I'll just give you the money and you can put it over there on the dresser, or in your— (*Noticing that she put it in her underwear, he becomes very embarrassed.*) there! This is very unlikely for me to be in a place like this, I've actually been trying to deepen my religious faith lately. I'm a Muslim, you know. Do you know what that is? (*Pause.*) Yes, it's a type of cloth. What is your name? Angel? Really? (*He laughs.*) No, no, I'm sorry. I was just thinking that that's an ironic name for someone who does what you do for a living. What? No, no, I'm sorry, I'm not a jerk. I'm sorry, that was rude. Look, I think you're very attractive. In fact, that's even the reason I followed you up here from the street . . . was because of the way you look . . . or at least who you look like. Well, you see, you look amazingly like this girl Karen who sits next to me in my Human Anatomy class, and who I cannot stop thinking about, and earlier this evening I was trying to study for my exam tomorrow, but I can't seem to concentrate because I can't stop thinking about Karen, and then when I think about Karen all the time, I think about my parents beating their chests when they realize I've failed all my exams. So I decided to take a walk and pray for some concentration, and that's when I saw you, and you . . . well, you look exactly like her, and you looked at me, and you smiled, and so when you started walking I followed you, and while I was walking up the stairs just now to this little room, I started thinking to myself that you must be a sign . . . a sign from God! That since I'll never be with Karen, I could be with you, and then I could go home and be able to study, and pass my exam and make my parents proud of me! (*He suddenly breaks down into tears.*) I'm sorry, I'm really sorry, I think I've made a terrible mistake. You see I just realized that God would never, never lead me to a place like this. I must be losing my mind. I have to study, I have to go! I need some sleep! I have to study, I'm really sorry. I have obviously wasted your time, I'm really sorry but I have to go. I cannot stay here, I have to go. I'm sorry. (*He leaves, there is a long pause and then he returns.*) I think I should probably get a refund. I don't know what your policy is as far as refunds go. I'm sure that it doesn't come up very often. What? Really? Uh, thank you, that's very kind of you—well I think you're very attractive your-self—no, I can't do that actually. No, I can't. No I really can't—well, because I'm engaged . . . or at least "betrothed" which is actually more like . . . engaged! She's a very nice

girl, Sakina!! Would you like to see a picture? I have one—
no of course not—what I'm trying to say is that she really is
the perfect girl for me, comes from a very similar family,
same religion, same traditions, same values, these things are
important, you know. Besides, Karen is just a distraction. I
mean, she's American. In the long run she would never
accept Indian culture, she would never understand the
importance of an Islamic way of life, she would probably
want to have premarital sex which is something that as a
Muslim I could never do. I know that that probably sounds
ridiculous under the circumstances, but it's true! It's not just
a religion you know, it's a way of life and I have dedicated
my entire spiritual life identity to the complete submission
to the will of God. That's what Islam means. So you see, I
can't just be running around having sex (*He thrusts his pelvis
forward unconsciously.*) like a rabbit (*He does it again, with more
vigor.*) with every woman I am attracted to. (*He does it again
repeatedly with real vigor.*) It would be *sin*! (*He stops, embarrassed
by his pelvis.*) And that is why I have to leave. What? What is
my name? (*He pauses.*) Al! Really! Okay, okay. It's not Al the
way you are thinking of it, like short for Alan or Alvin or
something. It's actually the short form of a very religious
name, a name I can't even say right now, otherwise it would
be a sin—I think. I probably don't even deserve this name.

(*We begin to hear the song* "No Ordinary Love" *[or any such song].
This plays throughout the rest of the piece.*)

What are you doing? No I really don't think you should . . .
remove that! (*He hides behind his hands so as not to look at her,
but then he slowly looks.*) You want me to call you Karen?
Okay!? Karen, Karen, Karen, Karen . . . (*She unbuttons his
pants and begins to perform oral sex; the rest of the lines are delivered while he is receiving a blow job.*) Oh, my God, this is not
me, this is not my life. Oh, shit! (*Looking down*) I'm sorry,
I'm trying not to swear. It's hard, you know, to do the right
thing, you know. (ALI*'s hands spread out for the next few lines*

creating a crucifixion image.) I'm always asking for forgiveness, because I believe that God understands and he is forgiving, and he knows how hard it is, to do the right thing all the time, even when you want to, more than anything else, and if you fail and you disappoint people, you can just try again, right? And you can have the intention to try again even while you're failing . . . failing! I don't suppose there is really any chance of me passing this exam tomorrow. I mean, if I'm going to be punished for this, and I'm sure I will be, that will probably be the punishment, because when you're try-ing to do the right thing and make people proud of you, Satan wants you to fail. And then you end up being a huge disappointment. Well, if I'm not going to be a doctor, I wonder what I will be? Maybe I will be a bum! And Sakina will say, "I can't marry him, he's a *bum*!"

(*He is getting quite worked up at this point as he gets closer to orgasm.*)

And I will say, "Good! Because this bum wouldn't marry you when hell freezes over!" And her parents will say, "How dare you talk to our daughter like that!" And I will say, "I just did!" And my parents will say, "How dare you talk to her parents like that, you are a great disappointment," and I will say, "Mom, Dad, eat (*He orgasms.*) SHIIIT!"

(*He falls to his knees in shock, and slowly as if almost in slow motion he doubles over on the floor, unconsciously going into the Islamic position of prayer. After a few seconds, he regains his composure and attempts to stand and button up his pants.*) Thank you Angel, I mean Kar—I mean Angel. (*He turns, takes off his glasses, turns again and he is* AZGI.)

AZGI

Once upon a time, a hunter wandered into a forest, armed only with a bow and arrow, in order to find food for his family. After some time he came upon a clearing, and in the middle of the clearing stood a goat. The hunter, excited by this, raised his bow and arrow in order to kill the goat, but just as he did, he noticed that the goat was crying. The hunter intrigued by this, asked the animal why it wept. And the goat answered, "I weep because God spoke to me and he told me all the secrets of the Universe." The hunter asked the goat to share the secrets with him, and so the goat did, and after he was done the hunter realized . . . that now, he could never return home.

(*Music and lights change, as* AZGI *slowly sits center stage and contemplates. Suddenly his meditation is broken by a sudden light change and a computerized sound; he gets up and discovers the sound is coming from Samir's Game Boy.*)

(*Looking off*) Samir!! Samir!! Hey how come you leave your stuff lying around man, I got to clean up!

(*Noticing audience.*)

Oh, hello! How are you? You know Samir he leaves his hat and his Game Boy just lying around you know, I have to clean up. I can't be picking up his junk all the time. (*He looks around to make sure nobody is watching and then he vigorously starts playing.*)

(*To audience*) This is a very exciting little game though, apparently the idea is you see, if you can just get your little man to the top of this mountain without getting hit by the falling rocks, then you get to go in the spaceship and fly away . . . it's very good (*Playing*) come on *jump! Jump!* Come on you crazy man, come on, jump! Jump! (*Looking off*) *Hello!* Oh Samir, yeah there you are, I found your hat and your Game Boy because you leave your junk here in the restaurant and then I have to pick up your stuff. No, no, no, you can't have it, because I'm almost to the spaceship. (*Listening and playing at the same time.*) Sakina? Oh yeah, she sent a postcard? From her honeymoon? Oh yeah? Good for you, good for you. To me! To me! She sent a postcard to me? Oh yeah let me see, let me see! Come on it's my postcard man.

Okay, I give you the Game Boy, you give me the postcard, Okay? I put it down, you put the postcard down, ready . . . one . . . two . . . three . . .

(*He puts the Game Boy on the table,* SAMIR *obviously doesn't comply and* AZGI *chases him around the restaurant.*) Hey! Hey! You see how you are? Give me that postcard, come on Samir, come on, give it to me! Hey!

(*He chases* SAMIR *around the stage trying to get the postcard. At a certain point in the chase* AZGI *puts on the hat and becomes* SAMIR. *He squirms around trying to keep a hold of the postcard and then he throws it offstage and runs over to the Game Boy.*)

SAMIR

(*Playing with his Game Boy*) It's on the floor—(*Picking up the Game Boy*) Hey, cool! You're almost in outer space. You know what, you know what, you know what, you know what, you know what Azgi? My sister, she is gonna go all over the country for her honeymoon, and you know what, she said that she would send me a postcard from each place she went, cool right? But you know what the best part is, Azgi? You know what the best part is? When she goes to Disney World she is gonna send me an autographed picture of the Ninja Turtles. Cool right? 'Cause that's where they live! And we were supposed to go to Disney World last year, but we didn't go, 'cause my grandmother died and then we had to go to India. (*He pretends to puke.*) That sucked! And you know what? You know what? You know what? I got into this huge fight with my cousin Mustafa, 'cause you know what, you know what, you know what . . .

(*Light change.*)

Dad! No I didn't punch him, I didn't punch him, I didn't punch him, no listen, I was showing Mustafa this really cool game, but he didn't wanna play, so then I said well . . . let's play anyway! But he was bein' a spoilsport and messin' up the game, and not playin' right, so then I said, "*Fine!* I'm gonna play Ninja Turtles on my Game Boy," and when I was doing that he wanted to play too! All of a sudden! But I said, "No way, Jose!" So then, so then, so then, Mom called me to come upstairs to look at some pictures of Dadi Ma when she was alive and she was young, and ya know what Dad? You were in the picture! Yeah, and you were sitting in her lap and you were just a little baby. Dad, Dad, Dad, do you remember that? Dad, do you remember when you were a baby? Do ya? (*Realizing he cannot change the subject so easily*) So *then*! I said that he could hold my Game Boy for just five minutes. *Just five minutes!* But then, when I came back, he wouldn't give it back to me so I had to give him a Ninja kick in the head!

(*He demonstrates a Ninja kick to the head.*)

That's all that happened, yeah but I didn't punch him, I didn't punch him, he said I punched him, I didn't punch him. So, I don't have to share with a crybaby and a liar if I don't want to. But Dad it's my Game Boy, that I brought on the plane all the way from America remember? Remember, you said nobody could touch it, not even Sakina 'cause it was the only thing that would keep me shut up, remember you said that? Huh? So that just means he's a crybaby that's all. I don't have to share with a crybaby if I don't want. No, no—but I'm not even sorry.

(*His father slaps* SAMIR *on the behind. This is done by* SAMIR *turning himself with his right hand and slapping his own behind with his left hand. Every time that* SAMIR *is slapped in the remainder of this piece, it is done using this method.*)

Hey! How come you're hitting me, he's the one who *stole* my Game Boy. How come no one is hitting him? What? *Naah! Why?* Dad, no! That's totally not fair! No, no, no, I don't want another stupid Game Boy, I just want the one I have. This was my birthday present from Jim's dad, you can't just give my birthday present to any stupid Indian kid that wants it just 'cause they don't have any cool toys here. No, I don't want another one, why can't you buy *him* another one? I'm sick of this. You know what, Mom already gave him my Ninja Turtle high-tops, she already gave him those, yeah the ones with the lights in 'em that go "Kawabunga!" when you jump in 'em, she already gave him those. You're just gonna give him all my stuff. I hate coming to this stupid country. No, no, no, he's not my brother, he's stupid! He smells! He can't even speak English! (*He is slapped again.*) Didn't hurt. (*Slap.*) Didn't hurt more! (*Slap.*) (*Crying*) All right! All right! It hurt!! How come you always hit me when I tell the truth, huh? Yes, you do, yes you do, yes you do, everyone in this country is stupid! And they just want all my cool stuff, 'cause they don't have any cool stuff of their own, and they're just jealous, 'cause we get to live in America, and they're stuck here in ugly, stinky smelly old India, and I never, ever, ever wanna come back here ever, and I don't ever wanna go anywhere with you and Mom ever again 'cause you're just liars! Liars! Liars! Liars! And you abuse your children too! Yes, you do, yes you do! You said we were gonna go to Disney World this year, and we were gonna see the Ninja Turtles like all my friends did. Yeah, well, I don't care. I hate Dadi Ma too! I hate her for dying and ruining everything!

(*This time* SAMIR *is slapped on the face. After the slap* SAMIR *stands in shocked silence as he is about to burst into tears. In that moment he witnesses his father starting to cry. He has never seen this before and is frightened and confused by what he sees.*)

Dad? Are you all right? Dad, I'm sorry! I'm sorry I said that about Dadi Ma. Listen, you know what, Mustafa can have my Game Boy, all right? (*He takes off the hat also, and hands it to his father.*) He can have all my stuff. (SAMIR *reaches out with his hat and Game Boy but his father does not take them.* SAMIR *begins to cry.*) Dad! I'm sorry that your mom died.

(*Slowly he backs upstage and he places the Game Boy and the hat on the nearest table. He is again* AZGI. *The lights change and the area where* FARRIDA *stood is in a pool of light.* AZGI *enters it as himself.*)

AZGI

"This is not me, this was not supposed to be my life," (*Pause.*) she said. (*Moving to the hat and Game Boy*) "I thought we were gonna go to Disney World!" (*Pause.*) he said. (*Moving to where* SAKINA *had sat*) "It doesn't make any difference, it's just the way it is," (*Pause.*) she said. (*Moving to* HAKIM's *area*) "Everything will be forgotten, everything will be gone," (*Pause.*) he said. (*Moving to where* ALI *had stood*) "Well, maybe I should just get a refund," (*Pause.*) he said.

Everyone speaking my voice. Everyone except me. Where did I go, Ma? What happened to the top of the Empire State Building? What happened to the bottom of the Grand Canyon? How did all my adventures and romances end up on other people's postcards? "I don't remember the story of the river stone," (*Pause.*) I said. . . .

Once upon a time, there was a boy, and this boy was standing by a stream, and by his foot he discovered a tiny stone. He picked up the stone because he believed it was the most perfect stone he had ever seen. He immediately threw the tiny stone into the stream because in his young heart he believed that as soon as the stone entered the water and sparkled beneath the sunlight, it would become a diamond. As soon as the stone entered the stream, it began to flow with the current, faster and faster and faster and faster, the boy ran alongside the stream watching his tiny stone, tossing and turning in the water, always moving, always dancing until . . . it disappeared and he could no longer see it. The boy panicked. He ran to the end of the stream, where he discovered that his tiny stone had been washed ashore amidst hundreds and thousands of rocks and stones and pebbles, all of which had taken the same journey down the same stream. The boy searched frantically for his perfect stone, picking up one stone after the next after the next after the next, but he could not find it. He searched day after day, week after week,

month after month, year after year, until the boy became
a man. And then one day he stopped searching, because
he realized that the reason he could not find it was
because he had never really known . . . what it looked like.

(*He pulls out the tiny pebble from the beginning of the play from his
pocket. He looks at it and closes his fist around it. He turns and walks
upstage as the music crescendos. Blackout.*)

SOME PEOPLE

Danny Hoch

For my mother . . . who taught me how to really listen

Some People premiered at PS 122 and opened at the Joseph Papp Public Theater in New York City on October 18, 1994. Jo Bonney directed the production, which was written and performed by Danny Hoch.

CHARACTERS

CARIBBEAN TIGER
MADMAN
KAZMIERCZACK
FLOE
BILL
BLANCA
AL CAPÓN
DORIS
FLEX
CÉSAR
ROUGHNECK CHICKEN

SETS AND COSTUMES

The only set to this show is a black wooden cube about knee-high, a black stool, and a black chair. These three are moved around in different configurations for each character.

Upstage hangs a clothesline from which the minimal costume pieces hang by clothespins.

An open cardboard box for used costumes sits under the clothesline. The costumes are merely accessories to constant black jeans, T-shirt, and shoes. A hat, a sweater, a blazer, or headphones are grabbed from the clothesline and tossed on quickly for each character change.

CARIBBEAN TIGER

The scene is a dimly lit radio studio at around one in the morning. The callers, Daddy Sluggy, Clyde, and Sheila, are prerecorded.

Mmm! Yes ladies and gentlemen of the Big Apple, this is Vaughn Morris your host. Better known to all my fans out there as the Caribbean Tiger! Some people say, what's a tiger doin' in the Caribbean? People well I tell you, livin' up ya inna New York City is like a jungle sometimes and anything can happen, just like a tiger walkin' by upon your radio waves.

Who is listenin' to me? Who is stayin' up with me this early morning, Friday morning, a few minutes after one o'clock people I'd like to know. Call me call me call me. The phone number is 718-555-2828, that's 718-555-2828. The temperature outside right now the weatherman says! About twenty-seven degrees ice cold, people. I tellin' ya, ya better bundle up and stay warm, it's cold outside but never if you're riding with me here upon the radio waves Caribbean Tiger style! Like the man says, you're riding with the Tiger you know it gotta be hot!

Mmm, yes people I'm comin' mixin' up your reggae, rockers, soca, and calypso, oldies but goodies. This hour strictly soca music! We goin' see if you can wind your waist one time. I am lookin' at my telephone switchboard now, my phone lines is blinkin' with people! Wildfire inna studio! Worries and Trouble! I'm going to the phones right now. . . . Hello good morning you're on the air. . . .

DADDY SLUGGY: Ere dat boss. Wha'appnin', Mister Morris?

Who am I talkin' with this morning?

DADDY SLUGGY: Disya Daddy Sluggy, seen.

Daddy Sluggy! Okay Daddy Sluggy, where you callin' from?

DADDY SLUGGY: Me inna Brooklyn, yeh.

Okay Daddy Sluggy from Brooklyn, you ever call before?

DADDY SLUGGY: Na boss. Aeda check you show fe years, but si is a first time me a pick up de phone an' call you pon radio station, seen.

All right Daddy Sluggy, you want to send some greetings out there?

DADDY SLUGGY: Yeah boss. Ya know first I wan say big up to Pudgy, Mikey, Tinga, and Gary over there in East Flatbush Love Productions. Special request to Big Timer crew, Sleepy, and all Jamaican people dem, beca ya know seh Jamaica people dem ago run tings inna New York City.

Okay, respect to you, brother.

DADDY SLUGGY: Yeah and greetin's comin' from Daddy Sluggy.

Okay Daddy Sluggy, you have a good night now. You're riding with the most dangerous DJ on the radio, I am the Caribbean Tiger. Raaarr! Watch out baby! Hello good morning you're on the air. . . .

CLYDE: Eh . . .

Hello good morning.

CLYDE: Yes.

Yes, hello.

CLYDE: Yes. . . . Hello?

Yes good morning sir.

CLYDE: Am I on de radio?

Yes you on the radio, would you like to send some greetings out there?

CLYDE: Oh. Yeah. I want to say hello to Roberta, who just arrive yesterday from Port of Spain.

And this is comin' from?

CLYDE: Excuse me?

Wha is you name sir?

CLYDE: Oh. Clyde.

Okay Clyde, where are you callin' me from Clyde?

CLYDE: . . . Yeah.

Yeah, where are you callin' me from?

CLYDE: Huh?

Where are you? Where are you Clyde?

CLYDE: Brooklyn.

Okay Clyde from Brooklyn, thanks for callin' in all right?

CLYDE: Okay, bye-bye.

Okay yes people, the Caribbean Tiger is in the house tonight! Good mornin' you're on the air.

SHEILA: Good morning, Caribbean Tiger.

Whoa ho ho! The Caribbean Tiger is most definitely in the place tonight! Who is this?

SHEILA: This is Sheila. How are you, Mister Morris?

Fine sweetheart, how are you?

SHEILA: Is this a tape? Or am I really on the radio?

Fine sweetheart, how are you?

SHEILA: No, seriously, is this real?

Hello, good morning?

SHEILA: Is this you, Mister Morris?

Fine sweetheart, how are you?

SHEILA: Stop it, that's no fair.

Ha! Ha! Ha! I'm just playin' with you Sheila. You really tink I'm a tape? Lemme tell you somethin' Sheila, I am live, no jive, never contrive, and I play all you disco forty-five. Raaarr! Where are you callin' me from Sheila?

SHEILA: Brooklyn.

Sheila from Brooklyn, are you married?

SHEILA: No.

Do you have a boyfriend?

SHEILA: Yes.

Do you think your boyfriend would mind if I ask you on a date? Because you sound like the prettiest, most beautifulest lady that has called the station tonight.

SHEILA: Maybe not, you have to ask him.

Wha is you boyfriend's name?

SHEILA: Sorrel.

Sorry? Your boyfriend's name is Sorry?

SHEILA: No, Sorrel, like the drink, Sorrel. It's a nickname.

De man name Sorry? What a pretty lady like you doing with a man call Sorry?

SHEILA: No Sorrel, Sorrel.

I tell you Sheila dear, I am so sorry about that.

SHEILA: Sorrel!

Do you mind if I ask you on a date?

SHEILA: You tryin' to get me in trouble, Mister Morris?

I don't wanna get you in trouble I just wanna get you telephone number. Ha! Ha! Ha! Tiger-Style baby, Worries and Trouble! Send some greetin's out there for me, Sheila.

SHEILA: Can you play that Johnny King song for me?

Johnny King! Soca business! Sheila dear, are you Bajian?

SHEILA: No sir, Guyana.

Guyanese Massive! I'll see if I can't find some Johnny King for you. Thanks for callin' in, Sheila from Brooklyn!

SHEILA: Okay, bye. Love you, Sorrel!

Yes people, the man says lookout, lookout, lookout! Calling all Trinidadian Massive! All Tobagonian! All Bajian, all St. Vincent, all St. Lucian, all Grenadian, all Antiguan, all Guyanese, all Caribbean Massive! The man says this night! Tonight! Friday night! Soca meets calypso over there at the Golden Pavilion over there on Empire Boulevard in Brooklyn, the man says it gonna be HOT! Admission is only ten smackers in this budget deficit time. Security Fort Knox style. The man says is gonna be better than cook food!

And speakin' of cook food people. The records played for you in this fifteen-minute segment is brought to you by Angie's West Indian Restaurant and Bakery over there at 2815 Church Avenue between Nostrand and Rogers avenues and that's in Fun City Brooklyn. Servin up the freshest and most superb in West Indian delicacies. We're talkin about escoviched fish, cow-foot soup, all roti done up just like your grandmother cook it fresh! Tell them you heard it from me the Caribbean Tiger and you get free beef patty. Mmm! Vaughn Morris comes rough every time. Vaughn Morris Is a First-Class Tiger.

MADMAN

It's three in the morning at a Jamaican dance hall spot in the Bronx. One of the live acts for the night, MADMAN, *sporting a leather calabash and sunglasses, pops out of the dark into a spotlight and charms the stage with his romantic ragamuffin style.*

Yes! A . . . A . . . Ahh! Love you. I want to welcome all de people to de number one night spot inna Bronx. Act Three In The Tropics place. Yes. Fresh and Hot. I want to introduce myself to de people dem. Me a de Madman. Dem a call me Madman beca me mad inna me head, but seh me na crazy. Fresh and Hot! Me a de number one dance hall entertainer fe de people dem. I want to big up all de people who come all the way to check me out tonight. Big up to the Bronx people dem. People from de Brooklyn, de Queens, de Manhattan. New Jersey, go home! Staten Island, stay away! Yes! How many people dem out dere make alotta money? Wole up yu han you make money! Com wid it selector. . . . Me bal—me make de money, ya know me make de money. . . . Cease selector! Fresh and Hot! Me a de Madman. Me na ramp, me na joke, me na skin teeth! Me always come 100 percent Gold Ring, Gold Chain, Gold Tooth, Bally Shoe! And whe eva me go, you know seh me haffe mek a ton a cash. Donald Trump celebrity cyaant touch me bwoy! I love you! I blow a kiss to you! Hug an kiss to each and every person. Special big big super hug an kiss to de gyal wid de fat an healthy body. Me say me love de fat-body gyal. Me na wan no skinny gyal, ca de toothpick gyal mussee garbage pan way. Wole up yu han you don hav a Slim-Fast Diet now! Huh! Me a de numba one! I want all my fans to reach out and touch me tonight, because I goin be Fresh and Hot, like magic inna dance-hall place. Touch me, you can touch me, touch me. . . . You cyaant touch me. I am too hot. Me a de hot potato. Yes selector, beca you know seh from me born outta me moda belly, me know me is Fresh and Hot every time. How many people dem out dere you can keep a riddim? How many white people dem can keep a riddim? Not a one, not a one. . . . You can keep a riddim? Follow me. . . .

(*Audience participation.*) All first-row people. All second-row people. All third-row people. Fresh. This is a participatory performance process. We ago do this fe about three hours now. Follow me. . . .

Me a de Madman, me deh from New York City
Me na ramp, me na joke, me na skin teeth, people don tes me
Me hav de style an de class an de personality
Me seh me walk pon street, people admire me
Alla de pretty gyal dem rush me inna hurry
Dem wan fe me cash an fe me jewelry
Eve-ry gyal wan to have my baby
Beca me terrible good-lookin an me neva ugly
When me pickiny, me usee entertainer
Me usee chat lyric pon de corner
Beg likkle money from rich foreigna
Now me big bad, make a million dolla
Me hav one Toyota an one Maxima
One home New York, one home Jamaica
Champagne, Bubble Bath, Leather Sofa
With Gold Chain Pon Me Neck An Ring Pon Me Finga!

Cease! Bally Shoe! Round of applause fe de people dem. I love you. Hug an kiss to each an every person. Me a de Madman! Always come 100 percent Gold Ring, Gold Chain, Gold Tooth. Bally Shoe! Hug an kiss! Love you!

KAZMIERCZACK

KAZMIERCZACK, *handyman for this tenement building, comes to fix the stove in a tenant's apartment in the afternoon. He knocks on the door. No one answers. He sees a familiar face down the hall and waves.*

Anya! Yakshemash! Viglondash bardzo wadnye gishe. . . . Dopshe, dopshe.

(*She leaves. He tries the door again.*)

Halo! Is Kazmierczack! . . . Halo. Kazmierczack. . . . Halo eh, you something broke? Something you break? Something you always never very good? Ah! Kazmierczack, Rama-me, coming you fix. Ah, I fix. Thank you. (*He enters the apartment.*) What you break? Sink good, no good? Ah, good. I no fix. . . . Ah? Cook? Never coming hahh? Only bad? Never this ahh? I look. (*He goes to the stove.*) Maybe you many cook. . . . Ah, is no good. I fix. . . . You many cook? . . . Many cook you? . . . You chodak cook? . . . Chodak. . . . Eh, chodak . . . dook dook dook. . . . Ah, chicken. Never chicken cook? . . . Ah. Is good. You bread cook? . . . Bread? . . . Ah, is good. America, bread, good. Never bad dollar money bread. . . . Ah, America— dollar, my Poland—zwodzhe. Dollar, zwodzhe is all mmm, eh. You wish pay money bread this one Key Food. You maybe, "Halo—can I please one bread?" This, "Thank you very Key Food bread you." My Poland you wish pay money bread, never good dollar. My Poland you wish pay money this automobile, good dollar, you wish pay money bread, bad dollar, is no good. . . . You look? (*He motions to the steel putty in his hand.*) After take ten, eleven minute put ahh, after make aghh! I go aghh, metal, pa! Is good. . . . You work? What you work? . . . Teacher? Oh, I know teacher . . . this . . . small people. You teacher good money? . . . Bad. My wife teacher, this small people. My Poland, teacher good money. America, teacher no money. Is no good. Never money teacher, all small people is go . . . ahhh! Is bad. . . . You cat? . . . Cat. Eh, cat . . . meow . . . Ah, cat. Kazmierczack never look at you cat. Only look you cat . . . box. Cat go . . . ahhh. Ah. . . . Two cat? Oh, bad. My wife . . . cat. One, small. Maybe, one week, after Kazmierczack finish this work, me go this home, for small ten eleven minute sleep me. This shoe go . . . ahh for . . . ah. Cat, one, small, my wife, coming this . . . ehha. Only maybe this one week, cat only always never smell very good. This one week, cat every . . . (*Mimes throwing up.*) Ahhhh. Only ahh. . . . Ah, throw! Throw! This cat is throw, my shoe. After Kazmierczack finish this sleep. Me, go this . . . ah. Look shoe. "Ey, cat! Why you throw this my shoe?" Cat look me, "Ahh never this shoe throw nothing me you this." Is no good. . . . Okay, I fix. Ah, maybe you stop fifteen sixteen minute for . . . hwooh. After come metal. Okay, I fix. You this bread cook, you this chodak cook—ah, chicken cook. Okay, thank you. Dozobachenia. (*He exits.*)

FLOE

FLOE, *a cool sixteenish, sits with two friends and beats hip-hop into the wooden box to supply the music for his rhyme.*

It's the mack motherfuckin', daddy
Never catch me drivin' a caddy

I prefer like a 190E
Imported all the way from Germany

It's the *F* to the *L* to the *O* to the *E*
I tantalize to tickle your throat like Tetley tea

I terrorize, stuff tough trash talkers and bluff tykes
Twist the wrist to grab the microphone and I wear Nikes

Color green, style hi-top, to flex the hip-hop
Born to rip the shop and rock the spot like nonstop, yo . . .

My rhymes are fat, fresh, dumb, dope, down, and groovy
I'm terminatin' suckas like Schwarzenegger in that movie

Sucker emcees I consume, my rhymes boom
I knew I was dope walkin' out my mother's womb

I'll kick you in the head with my Tims, so I could
    squoosh ya
See ya on the street, punk, word up, I'll mush ya

I'm not a pusher, flowin' like a gusher
A fucked-up motherfucker and I live inside Flatbush-uh

I'm makin' dynamite explode, I'm launchin' rockets
I robbed George Jetson, stuck up Spacely Sprockets

My pockets stay fat, with pictures of the presidents
I'm ricochet-bing-bing rockin' rhymes for all ya residents

Of Brooklyn, Queens, Manhattan, and the Bronx
You paid your fifteen dollars, yo I coulda got y'all comps

Every time I rhyme I leave mikes twisted and bent
Never been to Riker's Island, but I almost went

I'm out there murfin', not Papa Smurf and
Foamin' like a Nerf and yeah—I fucked your girlfriend

I smoke suckas mad fast just like the crack
I drop more fuckin' bombs than Bush did on Iraq

I'm stacked and stacked, drink a forty of Similac
Never call me wack because yo, kid, I pack

A pistol, so it's no use holdin' your crystal
I'll shoot ya point-blank in the head, then fuck your sister

I'll throw ya down and step on your head just like a Ring
    Ding
Beat ya ass worse than they did in the Rodney King thing

The rhymes I hit ya with, boy, they ain't no duds
The microphone's the trigger and boom, I'm droppin'
    Scuds

Yeah, and ya don't stop, keep on till the break of dawn
    and . . . (*Freestyle.*)

(*To his boys.*) Ah yeah, you like that, you like that. I fucked it up though. I made up the part about the Scuds yesterday. I was like tryin' to, you know, end on some boom shit but at the same time relate it to like current events. . . . What? You can't have the sample after my verse, man. You already got it after his verse. . . . 'Cause, that shit is mad redundant. You don't know what the fuck you talkin' about.

. . . *A'ight fine, then have the sample after my verse, but then you can't have it after his. . . . Oh my god, shut the fuck up. We ain't even make the demo yet. Wait till we drop the demo, get a record deal, then when you got cash in your pocket you'll shut the fuck up then. . . . 'Cause people are gonna listen to it and be like, "That shit is mad redundant." You *do* get money, 'cause you know you get a advance, right? Like I heard Wu-Tang Clan got like two hundred fifty thousand dollars *each* before the record even came out! Each yo, each, each! But watch, this be just the motherfucker to like, take that money and go buy like a five-hundred bag of Buddha and ten hookers and shit. . . . 'Cause you're stupid. Hey yo, I get that money, I'm goin' to college in two seconds, yup. 'Cause otherwise they just look at you like another dumb rapper and shit. You got a degree in your pocket, niggas give you respect. For real, I'm gonna roll up like Harvard or Yale or some shit. Yo, there's mad honeys at them schools too yo. . . . Nah, bee, you don't need SATs to get into that shit. . . . Nah yo. I roll up in Harvard, a hundred thousand dollars in my pocket, they be like, "A'ight, you in, you in." Trust me. They be like, "Oh hello, welcome" and shit.

. . . What? You don't know what the fuck you're talkin' about. You can't even rhyme for shit anyway. Aha! . . . My mother can't rhyme? Yo, your mother's so stupid, she climbed up a tree 'cause she tryin' to be branch manager. . . . Yo, your mother's so dumb, she got stabbed in a shoot-out. . . .

----

* A'ight: All right

Hah? . . . Oh, why you wanna go there, man? . . . I'm sayin', you dis my moms all you want, but you don't talk about my girl, that's different. . . . I know she ain't my girl no more, that's not the point though. . . . Yo, we broke up, you don't even know the whole story. . . . Nah, I'm sayin', she wanna go roll with some other kid 'cause he got money in his pocket. That's a'ight though. 'Cause wait till we get this record deal and I got money in my pocket, you know she gonna be callin' me up like, ring, ring, "Hi, I'm sorry." I'll be like, "Word?" Click. . . . Nah, actually I can't say that. 'Cause she ain't really the type to do that shit. See, that's why I can't dis her even though we broke up. I mean out of all the girls I been with, I be like, "See ya!" But it's like that's the first girl that like, I don't know. I think honestly I could say like . . . I don't know . . . some shit.

. . . Nah! I'm serious! It's like, even just being with her, we don't even have to be doing nothing, we just be sitting there. Plus she be schooling me, 'cause you know she's in college, right? She's gonna be a sophomore at Hunter next semester. . . . Black and Puerto Rican studies. So I'm sayin', it's like we just be chilling or whatever. And all of the sudden she'll drop the bomb of knowledge on me. Like check this out, there was this whole civilization, livin' on the islands in the Caribbean, mad hundred thousand years before the Europeans came over and fucked that whole shit up. They was called Tainos.

They had a whole civilization, architecture, medicine, culture. . . . Tainos. . . . You ain't never heard of no fuckin' Tainos. This nigga ain't never heard of Fritos talkin' 'bout you heard of that shit. I'm sayin' though, shit was just different with her. . . . That too though. It's like, even when I was fuckin' her. Ah, see I can't even say that 'cause it wasn't like fuckin'. It was like we was making love or some shit. . . . Shut up. Stop laughing. Your mother's so fat she jumped in the air and got stuck, shut the fuck up. . . . Nah, shut the fuck up, stop laughing though. I'm saying, I'm gonna tell you this 'cause it still be buggin' me out to this day. This happened like once, right? . . . I'm not saying I fucked her once, but listen. You know when you be gettin' busy, and like you get all into the moment and shit? Like you get all hot and sweaty and you get into the smells, like you be smelling her neck and shit. You know, you be like, "Ah, lemme smell your neck"? So, I'm saying like one time, we was all in it. And I had closed my eyes and this shit had come over me like I can't even explain it. Like in here, and I had like almost started like, cryin' and shit. I mean I'm not saying I was crying. I'm saying like, a'ight. The only thing I could compare it to is, remember last summer we went to Action Park? . . . Nah, a'ight, bad example, bad example.

I'm sayin', you ever been on a airplane? . . . So you know you be on a airplane and you hit turbulence and the plane drops? And your stomach goes like this, but the rest of your body goes like this? . . . It's like you're separating and you feel like . . . I'm saying, so they got that water slide at Action Park, and when you go down the slide you be like . . . wahh. I'm not sayin' down there, I'm saying like in here. . . . Never mind, man. . . . Nah, forget it, shut up, you're stupid. Watch in like five years, she'll be some college professor, and we'll be on tour at her school. And we'll run into each other and be like, ching! . . . Nah yo, let me shut up, man. I be sounding all sentimental like Sally Jeffrey Rafael and shit. Yo, kick your verse, man, kick your verse! Ya big, can't rhyme for your life. . . . What? Yo, your mother got no arms on *Wheel of Fortune,* talkin 'bout—"Big Money! Big Money!" (FLOE *pounds the box to his homeboy's imaginary verse.*)

BILL

A straight-outta-Jersey pseudo-yuppie with a Jeep runs up to his friend's apartment with him for a would-be two minutes. BILL *talks while his friend struggles with the many locks on the door.*

All right, but just for two minutes because my Jeep is double-parked downstairs and I don't want to get tickets. Can I tell you what your problem is? And this is your problem because I know because I'm very good at telling things about people. You, you don't pay attention to things that are going on around you. It's like you're in this shell. You're like this turtle, you know, crawling along the grass in your shell and bombs are dropping like five centimeters away from you. And you, you're in la-la land. You're like, la-la. Can I give you an example? Let me give you a perfect example. Did you watch Ted Koppel last week? . . . Okay, well, if you would've watched, you would've known that there's little nine-year-olds running around the street with guns, selling crack to babies for sex. . . . You think I'm exaggerating? If you would've watched, you would've known. You also would've known, get this: There's some guy, he killed all these hookers, right? You know, prostitutes? Killed them. But this is the thing, there are all these people and they're in this rage that he shouldn't have killed them. Lemme tell you something, if he didn't kill them they would've wound up spreading AIDS to half the people in this country. . . . Because this is a very serious issue of our time and it affects us all indirectly.

. . . Okay, I'll give you a perfect example. Let's say, some guy he makes a mistake. Not me, but some guy. He goes and uses a prostitute, right? She gives him AIDS, 'cause she's got AIDS, she gives it to him, he goes home to his wife, he gives it to her, she has no idea. Are you following the progression of the story? Then they get a divorce, because of course they're gonna get a divorce because why is the guy with the . . . Anyway, she's out there, you know, on the single scene, whatever you wanna call it. I'm thirty-five years old, I'm a single man. I meet her, she gives me AIDS, I'm dead. You're asking how it affects me? . . . Use a condom? I'm thirty-five years old, I think I'm a little old to use a condom, anyway you're missing the whole point of the story. Listen,

I thought we're coming up here for two minutes so you could shave, this is turning into a whole ordeal here with getting into your apartment. What's with the five locks on your door, what are we in Harlem? Heh . . . It's a joke, you got five locks on your door, you know, Harlem, it's all these people up there? . . . All right, so it's not funny, so now you're a Black Panther all of the sudden? Jesus, it's a joke. Mr. Medeco here. You make me very uncomfortable sometimes.

(BILL *enters apartment*.) Oh, this is nice. . . . I said this is nice, your place. How much do you pay for this? . . . Not bad. Who's the guy that owns the building? The same guy that owns the building on the corner? What's his name? . . . Mohammed? Is he Moroccan? . . . But is he Moroccan? . . . Yeah, but is he Moroccan though? . . . No, I bet he's Moroccan. Because all the Moroccans, they bought up all the real estate, from the Jews . . . No, yes, trust me. They did a whole in-depth report on *MacNeil/Lehrer*, I saw the whole thing. You didn't know the Jews are going poor? Not just that they had to sell . . . Trust me—my friend who's Jewish, he wanted to get for his daughter—what do you call it when they get their own . . . her own phone line—he couldn't get it for her, that's all I'm saying. Anyway that's not the point of the story. The point of the story is that all the Moroccans bought up all the real estate, and all the Baskin-Robbins. And I don't know this just because I watch TV and I'm socially aware, paying attention unlike you—you're in la-la land—but I know this from empirical observation. I was in Baskin-Robbins last month and I'm standing there paying for the cone, and I ask the guy his name. You know I'm always taking advantage of these little small-talk opportunities, you get to know people really well. So the guy says Mohammed. . . . The guy's Moroccan, so he's Moroccan, Libyan, Hindu, Iraqi. They're all connected. They're all in the same little boat there.

Let me ask you something, do you watch Dan Rather? From now on, you have to watch Dan Rather just for educational purposes. Because on Dan Rather, you get the whole complete story. Let me explain something to you. They got this whole Shiite cult, the Buddhists, right? And the thing is they name them all Mohammed so they can't tell the difference between each other. It's like brainwashing. They're brainwashing them into thinking that they're all this one common organism floating around the earth, and they're gonna take over other organisms, and the other ones are innocent law-abiding countries, like ours. I mean they didn't say that exactly on Dan Rather, but you could figure it all out. The Shiites are sort of like the Moonies, it's all inter-woven. Anyway that's not the point, the point is just be careful there's not a bomb in your building. You think these guys got real estate on their minds? I'm thinking not. . . . Where'd you get this, Ikea? . . . This table thing here, I thought it was Ikea. Heh.

Listen, hurry up, because if I got tickets on my Jeep you're paying for them. Hey, you know I'm thirty-five, right? Yeah, I turned thirty-five last week. . . . Thank you, thank you. Anyway, you know I'm old enough to be president, right? You know what I'd do if I was president? You know, to solve all the problems, hatred, racism, killing, stuff? Now keep in mind I'm not prejudice or anything. I'd teach everybody how to speak English. Because that's the problem. I mean, if you don't speak English, how are we supposed to communicate for, you know, peace? Let me give you a perfect example. The other day I finish work, I'm hungry, I feel like having Chinese food. So I go to the Chinese takeout in my neighborhood, I order what I always order—four fried chicken wings, it comes with a small roast pork fried rice. So this day, me, I'm feeling hungrier than normal, so I order a large roast pork fried rice instead of a small, you know? I'll pay for it. So I say to the guy, "Can I have a large instead of a small?" So the guy goes yeah, like he understands what I'm saying. Mistake Number One, the guy doesn't know what the hell I'm saying. You wanna hear

Mistake Number Two? Me, I'm looking out the window making sure my Jeep isn't getting ripped off by, you know, crackhead murderers in the street. Meanwhile, I should be watching, who knows what the hell they're putting in my food? Poison, whatever. . . . You don't know what they put in, they have their little jars of stuff next to the woks. So that's not even the thing. This is the thing. The guy goes to put it in the bag with the duck sauce and everything. Get this, he puts it in the bag behind the counter. So you can't really see what he's putting in the bag, it could be a bomb. . . . You're laughing? You're very unaware.

Can I just tell you, 20/20 did a whole four-part series on bombings, and Barbara was explaining that these bombs went off and nobody would have ever guessed that there was a bomb. . . . Then why do they put it in the bag behind the counter then? They got a whole top of the counter, the top of the counter's clean. Everything is behind the counter, behind the counter. . . . They're very sneaky. So the moral of the story is, I take the bag, I drive all the way home, four blocks. Meanwhile, I could blow up on the way home. I sit down, I take off my shoes, I turn on the TV. I wanna relax, you know. I worked hard all day, I don't know about *these* people. I open the bag, they gave me a small— . . . A small roast pork fried rice . . . are you listening to the story? All right. So me, I'm angry. I'm flustered. I'm looking into the bag and it's like looking into this tunnel of frustration and anger. So I put it back in the bag, I drive all the way back, four blocks, so now it's eight blocks I've driven for this thing already.

I walk in to the guy, see now the guy's not there anymore. Now it's his sister, or his mother, or his wife, his aunt . . . they're all in the family there. : . . Because I know, because I know. So I say to her, "Look, I ordered a large, you gave me a small." So she says, "What?" Already we're having miscommunication. So I tell her, "I. Want. A. Large." She says, "Two-fifty." I say, "No, no, hello, before, earlier . . ." I'm trying to think of all the possible adjectives, I'm like a thesaurus. You know—"Prior to the time when I'm standing before you here now, I already—*then*—ordered a large. You made a mistake." You know, I mean I'm a man, I'm thirty-five years old, I'm not a kid. I want service, you know? So she's going, "Dut dut dut dut dut dut dut dut." Like I'm supposed to understand what she's saying? She's supposed to understand *me*, thank you! So then she turns to her brother or her husband or her uncle— . . . Because just trust me, they are, I know the people in my neighborhood. And she's saying something to him very fast. So I'm trying to listen to what she's saying, she's telling him to blow me up for all I know. So then, 'cause I'm listening, 'cause I'm a listener, I hear her say this thing and I recorded it in my brain and I want to do it for you so shut off the water. She says, "Something something," and then she says, "beaow." What does that mean? That's not a normal sound. . . . Because I went to college, I have a master's degree in business, thank you, I think I know a little something about languages if you give me the benefit of the doubt.

Look, the point of the story is this, these people have got to go through some sort of assimilation program before they come to this country so they can, (a) learn how to speak English, and (b) learn how to function like normal human beings, like us. . . . Because how are you gonna run a business and not speak English? Look at the guy who owns the 7-Elevens, he's from India, he learned how to speak it. Look at the American Indians, they learned to speak it when they came over here. But see these people, they come from out of nowhere, and in twenty-four hours they get a license to open a restaurant. That's like giving a woman a license . . . to fix trucks. I mean not that I'm saying women can't fix trucks, it's just . . . I don't really know what I'm saying actually. The bottom line is this, if you took all these people, from the cleaning people, the nannies, and the maintenance people, the housekeepers, and the kitchens, the guys that work at the place where I get my Jeep washed. If you took

all of them and you sent them back to all of their little terrorist countries, we wouldn't have all this suffering here and
just, things wouldn't be as hard.

. . . Trust me, I'll get somebody to wash it, there'll be
somebody. Oh, you have a cat. I didn't see before. It must
have just come out from wherever it was. That's funny how
all of the sudden they just decide to run out of nowhere.
You don't seem like the cat type. You know it's my favorite
animal? Is it a Persian? . . . I bet its name is Mohammed. Hi,
kitty cat. Hiya, ya big cutie. Ooh too too. What are you
looking at? What are you doing? Where are you going?
Ooh too too. Moo moo mama. Come here, cutie. I'm
gonna get you. I'm gonna get you. (*He picks up the cat.*) . . .
Oh, I got you. Oh. I. Got. You. Oh, you're so heavy, you little small kitty cat. Let's go look in the mirror. Oh, look in
that mirror. Look. In. That. Mirror. Who's that guy behind
you? "I don't know. Some guy." Gimme that paw. Gimme
that paw. Lemme see that paw. How you doing? "I'm okay."
Hah. Oh ribbit ribbit. Moo. Gobble gobble. Meow . . . (*He
abruptly drops the cat.*) Look at all this shit I got all over me
now. Listen, I'm going downstairs. I got a hundred and fifty
tickets on my Jeep already, or they towed it. . . . Trust me,
they're giving out tickets. I just read they hired all these
whatever meter maids, all they do is hand out tickets all
day. . . . Because I read it. What do you think, they write it
for nothing? These guys they got this whole thing connected to those hate groups that were on *60 Minutes*. What
they do these guys, they see my Jeep, they see the Jersey
plate, automatically they assume that I'm white. I mean I
am, but that's not the point. The point is that they think that
Jersey's all white people. Let me tell you, it's not. You come
to my neighborhood, I gotta get five locks on my door. Listen, I'll see ya downstairs. (BILL *exits.*)

BLANCA

BLANCA, *a young twenty-something office worker, stops by her friend's house to borrow shoes.*

Listen, Lisette, lemme borrow your shoes? The short black ones. . . . No, because Manny gets off Foot Locker in twenty minutes and I have to take the bus. . . . But I can't be looking ugly in the bus. . . . So find them! Don't stress me more, all right? My life is already stressed enough, can I tell you? The other day, right? I was at Manny's house, and we was fooling around, and like you know how guys be getting all shy like when they wanna say something really important but they don't say it? Or like they say it, but like their voices be getting all low so you can't hear what they saying? So he was doing that, right, and like I don't be playing that. I was like, "Hello-excuse-me-I-can't-hear-you-what-you-saying," right?

So I figure he's doing that because he wants to ask me to marry him 'cause already we been together one year nine months seventeen days and he ain't asked me nothing. So I look, and he got this thing behind his back, and I figure it's a Hallmark card or something saying like, "Hello Blanca how you doing I love you will you marry me?" Instead, he got a condom, right? . . . Right? So I was like, "Excuse me, who's that for?" He was like, "That's for us." I was like, "Excuse me, I do not think that's for us." But he goes, "No, we have to use it," because he said that he had seen something in like Channel 13 or something, like some thing. He goes, "No, you have to be careful, you don't know what's out there." I was like, "Excuse me, I know what's out there, I'm talking about what's in here," right? I was like, "You ain't sticking no fucking rubber shit up inside me I don't know who touched it. You might as well put a rubber glove and do some Spic and Span in that shit, 'cause I ain't having that." . . . No, 'cause one year nine months seventeen days we been together, now he comes to me with it? *Now* he thinks I'm dirty? I ain't fucking dirty.

And he thinks like I don't know nothing. Like he thought that I thought that you could get it from mosquitoes. Plus it ain't like I just met him. I know his whole family, his parents, his sisters. They're nice people. If I would have got something, I would have got it one year nine months seventeen days ago, right? . . . No, we talked about it, but you think we used it? . . . We started fooling around, I was like, "You seen *this* in Channel 13?" He was like, "No." I was like, "Mmm-hmm."

. . Not those, the black ones you wore last Friday! The short ones with the bows on it. I'm telling you though, Manny be driving me crazy sometimes for the dumb reasons. Like, you know Manny's father's Puerto Rican and his mother's Spanish. So he's Puerto Rican, right? And he's dark and his last name is Sorullo. So when people ask him, he always says Sorulo. 'Cause he says he wants to work in business in Wall Street, and that nobody wants to hire a Sorullo. So I be telling him, "Manny, that's your last name, you can't do that." And he be getting angry at me like, "That's my last name, that's how it's pronounced!" And like, "You got it easier than me, Blanca, 'cause you're lighter than me, 'cause you're a woman." And I'm like, "Excuse me, I'm Puerto Rican too," right? So it was the Puerto Rican Day Parade, and I had gotten us these T-shirts with the Puerto Rican flag in the front, and in the back there's a little coquí and it says "Boricua and Proud." So you would think that he would be like, "Oh, thank you, Blanca, that's so sweet, I love you," right? Instead he starts screaming, "I'm not wearing this shit! I can't believe you got me this! It's ugly!" I was like, "Excuse me, it's not ugly." So he puts on a Ralph Lauren shirt. I was like, "Manny, you think somebody's hiring you for Wall Street at the Puerto Rican Day Parade?" So he goes to me, "Look Blanca, I might be Puerto Rican, but I don't have to walk around looking like one." . . . I was like, "Excuse me. You think that people think that you Swedish? You Puerto Rican." I couldn't believe it. It's like, he wants to wear a condom, but not a T-shirt.

. . . Not those ugly heels, the short ones with the bows. . . . So find them, don't stress me more! It's like I be nice to people and they be having temper tantrums. You're like Lemington. You know my roommate Lemington, right? . . . I know, his name is Lemington, that's weird, right? So you know he's gay, right? And you know if you see Lemington, you be like, "Oh my god this guy is gay." But if you see his boyfriend, you be like, "Oh my god this guy is not gay." 'Cause he's like six foot and all muscular. Like when I first had seen him I was like, "Mmm." Like that, right? But he's gay. And they're not only gay, they're black and gay. Can you believe that? I couldn't believe that. . . . No, 'cause they don't look like those guys from *In Living Color.* At all. But you know I don't care 'cause I'm very liberal. But I think that his boyfriend be beating him 'cause one day Lemington had a cut right here, and I seen those signs in the subway that like if you're gay and your lover beats you. call that number. . . . Right . . . whatever.

So we be getting along, except this one morning I'm getting ready to go to work. It's like seven thirty in the morning and I'm sitting there eating breakfast, I look up and he's wearing my skirt. So I was like, "Lemington, what you doing with my skirt?" He was like, "That's your skirt?" I was like, "Yes, that's my skirt, Lemington, where you got it?" He goes, "In the closet." I was like, "Well that would happen to be my closet, which would happen to be in my room, so that would happen to be—ding!—my skirt," right? I was like, "Lemington, you can't be wearing my skirt." So he starts crying, right? And he's like, "Fine, I won't wear it!" And I can't have him crying in my house at seven thirty in the morning 'cause then the neighbors be thinking like *I'm* beating him or something, right? So we had gotten over it, right? Except that he be leaving me these pamphlets all over the house. Like in the dishes he puts them, in the freezer. So, should I go to get a ice cube, I'll read a pamphlet. Meanwhile I got frozen pamphlets in the freezer. It's this one pamphlet, it's called "Getting to Know Your Body." It's these drawings of these women, looking at themselves, in you know, there, with instructions. Excuse me, but I don't need to be looking there. For what? It's money in there? Plus, what if somebody comes over and they go to get a ice cube, they'll be thinking that I'm looking in there with instructions like, what's this? He thinks that I'm like one of these women that doesn't know nothing about her body and goes and does whatever. (*She puts on some lipstick.*)

But he's sweet though, he got me this cute shirt with all these pictures of famous womens on it. Clara Barton, Nefertiti, Mother Teresa is on the shirt. And he gives it to me and he goes to me, "Rejoice in your womanhood, Blanca, be good to yourself 'cause you're a warrior." I was like, this is some black gay thing or something? He called me a warrior. I picture myself like running through the jungle with a machine gun like, "Look out, it's Blanca coming!"

But the thing is, now he got this little dog, right? And (a) he don't be feeding it, so the dog be eating my curtains, now I don't have no curtains people could just be looking at me naked through the window. And (b) he don't walk it. So the dog be shitting all in my house. And let me tell you, I don't know what the dog be shitting because it got nothing to eat but curtains. It's like little curtain shits is in the floor. The other day I'm getting ready to go to work and I get out the shower in my towel, I step in this little macadamia nut shit. So he goes, "Wipe it." So I wipe it, I took a Bounty but I don't have time to go back in the shower and scrubbing shit out of my foot twenty-four hours. So I go to work. People at work are like, "Ooh you smell like shit." And when I explain to them that, "Excuse me, I do not smell like shit naturally, but I happened to *step* in shit," they're like, "Oh, you stepped in shit? You must be stupid then." And I'll tell you right now, I can't have people calling me stupid, 'cause I ain't stupid.

. . . No, I wanna kick him out, but then he'll think it's 'cause he's gay. I mean it's not that he's gay that his dog shits

in the floor, it's that he's irresponsible. Things are so complicated. Plus I think he got AIDS too, 'cause he's all skinny. . . .
Yeah, Manny's skinny too, but Manny's just skinny. Lemington's gay and skinny, all right? . . . But them people be getting
that shit anyway, right? . . . They do though, right? . . . Right.
You got them? Finally, gimme. I hope they fit. I'm telling you,
you know what is it? (BLANCA *puts on the shoes and checks herself
in the mirror.*) I think my life is stressed because I have to learn
to be nice to myself. 'Cause if you think about it, nobody's
being nice to me. You included. But listen, I have to go
because you making me late. And these shoes are too tight but
I'm wearing them. And let me tell you something. If Manny
comes to me with that whole condom thing again, I'm gonna
tell him like this, "You think I'm dirty? Who do you think I
am? Do you even know who *you* are?"

AL CAPÓN

AL CAPÓN *is a fast-paced disc jockey and radio personality. He is the
Latin American/Spanish-speaking counterpart of Caribbean Tiger. The
stage is dimly lit and he races from time and weather to live advertise-
ments with quick merengue interludes.*

Andando! Holy Moly Guacamole mis amigos. Tenemos las
doce y treinta minutos y estámos con el super éxito de Toño
Rosario! Wow! Yo soy Adalberto Capón, mejor conocido a
ustedes, Al Capón. Aquí estoy en tu SuperPoderosa FM 99.
Holy Moly Guacamole, la temperatura afuera está de vein-
ticinco grados entonces, cuídanse mucho que no cojan gripe
porque hay muchas mongas afuera que coger! Okay okay
okay Cambio! (*Music.*)

   Esta Sábado el 2000 Club presenta directamente de Santo
Domingo la capital del merengue, Jossie Esteban y La
Patrulla 15. Las mujeres entran gratis! Gratis! Gratis! Antes

de las once. Otra vez, Jossie Esteban y La Patrulla 15 Este
Sábado en el 2000 Club en la calle 177 y Broadway en el alto
Manhattan! El 2000 Club!

Okay okay okay. Este segmento de música de quince
minutos está presentado por Kool-Aid. Kool-Aid Kool-Aid
Kool-Aid. Disponible en todos los sabores que te encan-
tarán. Como SuperCherry, SuperGrape, SuperStrawberry y
FunkyFruit! Okay okay okay. Kool-Aid Kool-Aid Kool-
Aid. Andando! (*Music.*)

Este fin de semana en el Gigantic Tomato Supermarket
en Brentwood, Long Island! La SuperVenta del siglo—Holy
Moly! Muslos de pollo Shady Brook Farms—noventa y
nueve centavos por libra! Plátanos SuperVerdes—nueve por
un dólar. Sweetpotato sweetpotato marca Gran Batata—
setenta y nueve centavos por libra! Holy Moly I can't believe
it! Este fin de semana en el Gigantic Tomato Supermarket
en Brentwood, Long Island!

Okay okay okay mis amigos aquí estamos en la capital del
mundo, Nueva York. Y estamos con (*He sings "Happy Birthday," inserting the name "Isabel Santiago del Bronx."*) Okay
okay okay. Muchas felicidades a usted Isabel Santiago del
Bronx de su esposo Manny Santiago, allá en el Bronx tam-
bién por supuesto.

Okay okay okay. Si tú eres good-looking, o si tú eres
looking good, call me baby. Porque yo no soy alcapurria, yo
soy Al Capón, aquí en tu SuperPoderosa Hot FM 99. Holy
Moly Guacamole mis amigos! Andando! (*Music.*)

DORIS

DORIS, *a mother of one in her fifties, is in her kitchen, using her power
tool, the phone, to communicate with some people, while her husband
fixes something in another room.*

Will you shush?! . . . So Shah! Martin, the guy is coming in five minutes. So leave the thing alone! In five minutes he'll be here and he'll fix the whole thing. . . . I know the phone is ringing, I'm letting it ring. . . . So let me let it ring!

Hello? Who is this? . . . Who? . . . Oh, hi! How are you? . . . No, what are you interrupting? You're interrupting nothing. . . . Uy, no, no. I'm sitting here, I'm— . . . What wire, Martin? What wire? I'm supposed to know what wire you're talking about? Oh, that wire, sure. Keep futzing with the wire and blow yourself up. You're not blowing me up!

. . . No, I'm fine. Martin's fine. David's fine. Yeah, in fact, I'm supposed to call my sonny boy in five minutes, so I'll talk quick. . . . No, no he's fine. How's your daughter? . . . Gonna marry to who? Not the same Nigerian guy? . . . Does she love him? . . . So, she loves him and she'll be happy and they'll be happy. Listen, did she make sure he's all tested with all whatever he needs with shots and everything? . . . No, I'm just saying, because especially with he's from Africa, she should make sure, 'cause I saw in the *Times*. . . . How terrible. Isn't it? . . . He's a doctor, the guy? And he's from Nigeria? . . . Eh, well still. . . . No, he doesn't see her anymore. Eh, Roz, to tell you the truth, I had a bad feeling about her when I first met her. She's a sweet girl, and she's attractive, but there was something creepy about her. She had a creepy aura. Anyway. Did I tell you what he's doing now, my son? . . . Oh Roz, he goes with this group of people and they go into all the bad neighborhoods, and I gotta tell ya, I am so— . . . Yeah, I think it's like the Peace Corps, but in New York. . . . Who? David? Hold on, let me ask. . . .

Martin! Does David get insurance with the job? . . . David your son. Does he get insurance with the job, the thing with the— . . . Never mind, you're not understanding me. . . . You're not understanding me, never mind! (*To Roz*) Listen, I'll ask him when I call him. Listen, mameleh, I gotta go, darling, okay? I'll call you back after. Okay, bye.

(*She clicks the phone only to make another call.*) Martin! How do I do the memory with the phone, I forgot? . . . The memory, for David, I know I put for number one, but after I do the star button or before? . . . The pound button? There's no pound button, Martin. . . . There's no pound button, I'm looking at the phone! Uch, I'm doing the star! . . . All right, shush, it's ringing! It's ringing and I can't hear! Will you keep with the wires, keep breaking the thing more, more break it!

. . . Hello, David, sweetheart, it's your mommyface, listen—Hello? Hi, you're there? . . . So what are you screening your phone calls, someone's after you? . . . So pick up the phone, it's your mother calling, it's a secret that you're there? . . . Uch, you make me nervous with this machine, one day I'll call it'll say, "Hi, this is David, I'm not here from they killed me on the train" or wherever. . . . All right, I'm relaxed, I just worry with you in all these . . . uch. . . . Yes, David, but not everyone takes the trains by theirself to the South Bronx or wherever. Sure the people that live there, but they're different . . . I mean not that they're different, they're the same as us, everyone is the same, but, all right, never mind, it's just different, you don't get it, forget it. You can't take a cab sometimes? . . . So let everybody else take the train, you're not them, you have to do what they do? All right, I'm relaxed.

Anyway, bubbeleh, what I wanna ask ya . . . Does your job, do they give you health insurance? . . . So you'll pay the ten dollars and you'll have it. How much more? . . . That's ridiculous, are you sure? . . . All right, so I'll pay it. David, I'm not an extravagant person that I'm saving for a yacht, I'll be happy to pay for it. Or if you want you could go on the plan your father and I have, hold on. . . .

Martin! What's the deductible on the insurance? What's that noise? Now you're drilling? What are you drilling? The guy is coming, Martin! . . . The deductible! On the Blue Cross, the Blue Cross! . . . That's what I'm asking you, how much?! . . . Uh, forget it. Forget! It! . . . Listen, David honey, we'll call the 1-800— . . . Wait, I'm on the phone with David! (*To David*) Hello? (*To Martin*) "*Which* David?!" (*To David*) Uch, wait one second.

Martin! When the guy comes for the thing, you're staying with him, right? . . . What do you mean you're going for a walk? Martin, I'm not letting these people into my house I don't know who they are, the minorities or whoever . . . (*To David*) Uy, you hear this from your father? Where is he walking? In front of a truck he'll walk. . . . You're right, David, they could be anybody. They could be Jewish, whoever, I'm just saying I'm not staying here alone. While he'll be going for a walk they'll be drilling me in the head for the television. . . . All right. David. I said they didn't have to be minorities. Uy, you're such a mensch, you're a sweetheart, you're very caring, I'm very proud of you, mmwa! So listen, tateleh, do you wanna do with the Blue Cross? . . . What no? Everyone has to have health insurance, David. . . . So fine, 36 percent of the country doesn't have it, you're not 36 percent, you're my son. . . . So David, let the 36 percent sit for ten hours waiting in some dirty emergency room somewhere bleeding to death with flies and urine and five hundred sick people with tuberculosis.

. . . My son . . . my son is not gonna sit waiting in some clinic full of people's phlegm all over the floor and everyone's coughing with no air. . . . No, David. God forbid . . . David, God forbid I should be concerned already enough that my son doesn't get shot by some black kid, *or white kid,* in one of these places, but that he should go to a professional Jewish hospital? . . . I know white people shoot people with guns, David, but . . . in other countries. . . . David look, I know I raised you to believe that everyone's equal, and not to be into materials, and to accept people no matter who they are, but David, I am your mother and I know you're an adult, but there are some things about reality that you're not understanding. . . . I can't be concerned about my son? . . . I'm not the one yelling, you're yelling! I just want you to be happy and not dead.

David, don't hang up, I want to talk to you. I am proud of you. I brag to all my friends and they all can't believe it. They all say, "I can't believe it." Is it too much to ask for you to have health insurance? . . . How do you know nothing'll happen? You have a crystal ball? . . . David, they'll have one of their riots these people and you'll be the first one they'll shoot. . . . They shoot people, David, I read *The New York Times.* Not the *Post,* the *Times,* and I see them. They shoot each other. And let me tell you something, David, I feel very bad. I wish these kids didn't have to grow up with all violence and uch, a mess, and my heart goes out to them, it does, but let them shoot each other and not you, that's the way I feel.

. . . I am not racist, David! Don't you dare call me racist! Because if you remember, I let you have all your black and Puerto Rican and Iranian friends at your bar mitzvah, and I treated them just like I treated your Jewish friends. You wanna see racist? Go read with this guy in the paper, "Bloodsuckers," he said. . . . I am not a "Scared-Liberal-Complaining-Reactionary." What does that mean? When they'll wanna stick you in an oven, you'll still defend this guy? You wanna be another martyr, David? You wanna be one of the Jewish kids in Mississippi with the voter registration and they killed them, them and some black guy? . . . How is it possible for Jews to be prejudice when everyone is prejudice all the time against the Jews? David, we had lots of black neighbors before we moved, and we got along fine. My friend Roz's daughter Cynthia is marrying a Nigerian guy and he's a doctor! . . . No, David, the difference is, did I call them bloodsuckers? I said they shoot people, I didn't call names.

. . . How am I guilty? I'm guilty of reading *The New York Times?* David, how come you'll never defend the Jews? You're Jewish but you'll never empathize with your own people. . . . "What is there to empathize?" David, six million—did you see *Schindler's List?* The Jews are still victims. . . . How am I a victim in the suburbs in 1994? . . . Not because I have a juicer and an espresso machine makes me a vict—Black people have juicers and espresso makers too! What are you screaming? What bad thing did I do? I did something bad to them? David, I'm not crazy. You ask people if they'll be in these neighborhoods on the train. . . . Whatever people. You ask them if they'll defend this guy. . . . The black kid who's in jail for murder I should defend? For what? Where do you get this from? Why are you so angry? You're not even black! Why are you angry at your own people? Why are you so angry at me? I'm your mother!

Uy, all right, calm down. Stop yelling! Listen to me. Are you still coming to the seder on Thursday? Your Aunt Barbara's coming and so is your cousin Mark. Mark, the high school principal, gay Mark. And I promise I won't start an argument with you, or Mark. . . . Okay, stop yelling. Are you coming? . . . Well if you don't I'll be very upset. Fine, listen, I'm not angry at you. Are you angry at me? All right, well, it's all right, I'm your mother. Okay, I love you. Bye. . . . Okay, stop screaming. . . . Okay, bye, mmwa! (DORIS *hangs up the phone.*) Martin . . . I'm going for a walk.

FLEX

FLEX, *nineteen, pants sagging, Timbos dragging, five beepers, and a chewstick. He approaches a Chinese takeout restaurant rapping to a song on his Walkman. He enters and stands next to another customer.*

Hey yo, you on line? A'ight then. (FLEX *looks up at the picture menus on the wall above his head. To the restaurant guy*) Hey yo, I'm still lookin', man. Damn, man, niggas try to rush me, man. (*He takes a moment to ponder his order.*) . . . Hey yo, Chinaman! Chinaman! Yo Chinese yo! Lemme get Number Seven yo. . . . Number Seven! Hey yo, I ain't look on there yo, I'm lookin' right there! Niggas got signs up, don't know what the fuck they got up. . . . Hah? Oh, vegetable lo mein? Oh,

I ain't see that right there, good-lookin'. Yo, vegetable lo mein, son, small. Small, you know what I'm sayin' small? Small! . . . Hey yo my man, no mushrooms, no onions in that yo. . . . Mushrooms, you know mushrooms? No mushrooms. And no onion. . . . Onions! You know what a onion is? I don't eat that shit. I'ma tell you what, I find mushrooms and onions in that shit, you could take that shit back, word up. Hey yo son, how long yo? How long? How long? . . . Right, I'ma be back then.

(FLEX *exits to street and sees an old friend.*) Oh shit! Wasup, kid? Oh my god! It's the god! It's the god right now. It's that nigga Al! Oh snap. Wasup with you, man? Goddamn. I ain't seen you in the longest time. What you been up to? . . . Word? I hear dat, I hear dat. . . . Nuttin' man, I'm about to get some food in here right quick, go pick up my little brother from school. Hey yo, it's good to see you, man. Hey yo, check this, I got five beepers, kid, you think I'm lyin'? Check them shits, boy. One, two, three, four, boom! What you wanna do 'bout that? These four are like regular, they go like, beep, beep. But this joint right here, this shit go like this, ooh-ooh! Shit's all disco-style. You should hang out with me for a while and you could hear that shit go off. Hey yo, so what you up to lately, kid? What you gonna do next year though? . . . Get the fuck outta here! Scholarship? See that's 'cause you all on the brainiac trip.

You thought I forgot. I don't forget shit, boy. Remember we used to be in school, and we used to be in the library throwin' shit and the teacher used to come by and we'd be like . . . But you was really readin' that shit though, right? So what you gonna study? You gonna study business, right? My man gonna make mad loot in this piece! . . . Black history? My man said black history yo. Tah-ha. This nigga buggin' yo! Oh shit—(*He mimes staring at a book.*) "Harriet Tubman, Free-dom Fighter." Your ass gonna be broke as hell beggin' in the street and whatnot. . . . Nah, I don't mean to break, man, you get mad props for that shit, you get respect. Somebody gotta do that shit, right? I'm sayin' though, I gotta get that loot, son, word is bond. I'm workin' this job too, I'm makin' bills, boy. You want me to make a phone call, you need some extra cash before you take off to school, I could make that phone call for you. These niggas got me workin' mad hard. Eight to eight every day, liftin' mad concrete-type shit. 'Cause they buildin' this new jail, right, so they need construction heads, seventeen a hour, kid. I'm makin' bank. . . . I don't know what I'ma do next year. I think I'ma start a blunt factory. Nah, I'm playin'. I don't smoke that shit god. . . . I don't smoke nothin'. My lungs is pure yo. This the god right here. I'm sayin' how niggas goin' buy into that? Let them white kids smoke them drugs, man. They make that shit. Yeah right, crack also yo. How black people gonna smoke somethin' that's white? You know mad white people be smokin' it too, but you ain't seen them on CNN gettin' lifted though.

. . . Right, but see, you know what bother me? How one second niggas is like, "Oh yeah, the white man this, white man that." Next second they smokin' Phillies tryin' to watch David Letterman. Explain that. I'm sayin', one second they like, yeah yeah yeah. Next second they like, yeah yeah yeah. You know what I'm sayin'? I'ma tell you like this, Al, it's already 'nuf white kids out here that's tryin' to be black. Peep this, I had to go to Manhattan for this job interview in the Upper West Side. Dead-up word to my moms, I seen this white kid with Filas, Nautica, Philly Blunt shirt, this kid listenin' to X-Clan, walkin' like this. . . . (*He imitates a white kid imitating a black kid.*) What the fuck is this? Nigga look like a Weeble-Wobble and shit. . . . Yeah, yeah! But what you call them white people that don't wash theyself, but they be causin' riots and shit? Yeah, them punk-rock anarchy niggas, right? I seen a bunch of them walkin', all raggedy clothes, rings stickin' out they necks and lips. I seen this one black son in there. I said not the god yo. How a brother gonna be in that shit? Know what I'm sayin'?

I be seein' wild shit! I see them on TV, kid! How a sister gonna sing opera? How a black man gonna sing backup for some Kenny G? Kenny Rogers? Any one of them Kenny motherfuckers. They all from Alabama and shit, Kentucky. . . . Oh, that's where your school at? For real? . . . I'ma see you at that school yo. I got a scholarship too, son. Government-type shit. They gave me five million dollars, right? They gonna teach me how to make AIDS yo. I'ma make AIDS Two, AIDS Three, AIDS Four, up to Ten. I'ma see how many niggas I could kill yo. Boom! And then 'cause I'ma be rich, right, I'ma buy a penthouse, BMWs, check this yo—I'ma own McDonald's, Nike, Levi's, Sony, all that shit. I'ma own Red Lobster. I'ma own that company that make that bomb that we dropped on that nigga Saddam Hussein family. *Bpow!* I'ma make bank! Then, I'ma see your ass in the street beggin'. You know what I'm sayin', you gonna be beggin'! Talkin' 'bout Frederick Douglass was a great man, lemme get ten cent. And I'ma be like, "Oh whatup, Al, remember me? Remember them college days, this and that?" And I'ma hit you off with a twenty spot 'cause you my boy. I'ma get you a job sweepin' up one of my Red Lobsters. Aha . . .

. . . What? . . . I'ma do what I want, son, it's a free country, right? . . . Oh, oh, you gonna tell a black woman she can't sing opera? . . . A'ight then, a'ight then! He wanna talk garbage right now. This the land of opportunity, son, I ain't tryin' to miss mine yo. This nigga tryin' to keep me down now. You sound like this girl yo. I was tryin' to talk to this girl, she wanna go see this art exhibit, right? So you know me, I got a open mind, right? We step up in this museum. Motherfuckers in suits. And it's this art piece on the wall. Motherfuckers is like, "Mmm, yeah, I like that shit." I said straight up, "That's some bullshit right there." She go like this in my face, son, "Maybe if you was more educated you might understand that." I said, "What? Hold up now. I'ma go to school so I could understand that shit?" I'ma tell you what, son . . . Nah, I'ma go to school, I'ma be president and

I'ma blow niggas' whole countries up all over the earth and I'ma make bank! Understand *that* shit!

. . . You see that Lexus right there? That Lexus fat boy. I'ma own Lexus, Jeep . . . Oh shit! I told you I'm gettin' a Jeep? Word to God, kid, red, Cherokee, '91. I'ma have the bomb system in that shit too. Bensi, equalizer . . . 'Cause I had saved up bills from that jail job. Hey yo, seven hundred cells we gonna build in that shit. We gonna lock niggas' heads up all day in that motherfucker, right? So I'm sayin', already I got the Bensi, I got the equalizer. All I got to get is, um, the Jeep, and the insurance. Yo, you should give me your beeper number, we should hang out. . . . You don't got a beeper? How somebody supposed to get in touch with you then? . . . The phone? Daha. This nigga livin' like Fred Flintstone yo.

On the reals though, I gotta pick up my little brother and get my food. I'ma call you then. . . . It's good to see you though, right? Right. Hey yo, Al, they still givin' out applications for that shit that you doin'? I'm sayin' though. Oh, next year? Yeah, I might peep that shit out, definitely though. A'ight then. I'ma call you then. Right. One love god.

(FLEX *takes a moment and reenters the takeout.*) Hey yo, son. Yo, son! Oh, you don't see me now? I said you don't see me right now. You ain't tryin' to serve me now? Never mind, my shit's ready? . . . How you know that's mine though? It's in a bag, I can't see that shit. That could be my man's right there. A'ight then, I'ma tell you what, lemme get extra duck sauce, hot sauce, napkins, all that shit, kid. You know extra? Lemme get extra— . . . Three twenty-five? . . . Three twenty-five. Don't be tryin' to jerk me neither, man. This nigga tryin' to be slick, fuckin' immigrant-ass motherfucker. . . . I said you a immigrant. You know what I'm sayin'? You ain't from here, I'm *from* here. Know that shit.

. . . How I know what? How I know I'm *from* here? Nigga can't even talk English talkin' 'bout how I know. What you know? You don't know shit! I'm American, son. You ain't shit! Gimme my shit yo. (FLEX *takes his food and motions to leave but then turns back.*) Hey yo, boy, you don't say thank you? Yeah, you're welcome. Know your place yo. I know mine.

CÉSAR

CÉSAR *is fiftyish and is at his first visit to a psychotherapist. He wears a traditional guayabera and hat and carries a cowbell and stick. He sings the first verse of Eddie Palmieri's "Te Palo Pa Rumba" and tries to accompany it with the cowbell.*

. . . I don't play, I just hit it. Because is very difficult if you want to play that. Is not just that you hit it. You have to know what's the rhythm, the music, you have to be musician. Lotta people thinking is just that you hit it. No no. I don't sing also but that song my favorite song. "Te Palo Pa Rumba." The guy who make that song is very famous guy. His name is Eddie Palmieri. That guy, hooh, famous. You ever listen to salsa music? He play piano, and also he tell all the musician what to play. So, if is the trombone, or the trumpet, or the drum or whatever. He gonna explain to them, he's a composer, he compose all the music there. He very famous that guy. . . . So you tell me to bring something that I gonna remember what happen, so I bring that (*Cowbell and stick*). That, I buy to my son when he have only one year old. He never really play because he never listen to salsa music. He only wanna listen to the fast music, I don't know how you call it.

. . . Also I bring that (*Hat.*) That I buy to my son when he have ten, eleven years old. He put in the head and he go in the street and he pretend that he Cary Grant. You know Cary Grant? The famous guy? He put in the head for one week and then he throw in the shelf and he never wear. But I keep it because that's my son. So, I supposed to talk to you forty-five minutes, I don't know what you want me to say. . . . No, because my wife, she make me come here. Because in my place if you have a problem, you never talking to a therapist. Forget it. In my place if you go to a therapist, they say you crazy in the head. If my friends know I coming here, forget it. They gonna say, "César go crazy." But I trust her. She's very modern, moderna, you know, modern. Very up-to-date. She reading all the magazine. She gonna look the magazine, then she gonna tell me what I has to do.

Because in my place, if you have a problem, you has to go and talking with un santero o una santera, is like, una consejera. Is a woman, or man, is depend. And she have power, and she take you hand, and she looking you hand, and she tell you what's you problem. Then she tell you you has to take some plant, some herbs, some spices. and you put in the pot. And then you put fire, or some flame there, and you make all the bad thing go out the whole place. Or maybe you put some water, is depend what's you problem.

. . . So my son, he always have a good heart. He never say bad words to nobody, he never punching to nobody. I remember when he have maybe five, six years old. I'm walking to him, with him en the Prospect Park, allá en Brooklyn. And it's the bird. Some bird, the pigeon, is laying in the floor because it's some truck or something gonna come and hit the bird. So the bird laying there in the floor. So my son, he running the bird. He wanna fix it. He say to the bird, "Hey bird, what's the matter with you? You has to get up from there. Is no good that you laying there. You has to go fly . . . up in there." But the bird is only looking in the sky, because the bird know in five minutes, no more. He wanna take the bird home. I say, "You can't take it, the bird is dirty, is from the street." Quería poner como . . . un Band-Aid. But he have a good heart. . . . Maybe when he get a little older, he put some fancy clothes. Not fancy, pero whatever. He put some cologne . . . lotta cologne my son putting there. He go with the girlfriend in the high school.

Because he very handsome. He like me, very handsome. I told to my son, "Be careful." Also I told him, "César, I love you." His name is César like my name is César. I make sure I gonna tell him to that.

Because I see in the TV en *Oprah Winfrey,* is some people. They have five kid, three kid, seven kid. Never say I love you. Only they put the hand, throwing out, and what's the kid? Drug, in the street, problems, whatever. Me and my wife, we only having one kid, César. I always making sure I gonna tell to him, "César, I love you." He say to me all the time, "Papi, I know." Because he don't wanna hear. He wanna be man. But I telling that to him anyway.

. . . When he have one year old, I have a big party for him. I invite all the relative from my family, my wife family. They coming all the way from Puerto Rico. Also we have some people from Dominican Republic, New Jersey, Long Island, Connecticut. All coming to my house in New York City for my son gonna have one year old. Almost one hundred people in my house coming. My wife and her sister is cooking. If you ever taste what they cooking that day, you gonna be like, "Oh my God, forget it." It's a lotta dancing in there. It's one place in the party I say to all the people, "Shut up you mouth. Because my son César gonna play 'Te Palo Pa Rumba.'" That song that I told you before. Because that song is come in the Spanish radio station, en esa época when he have one year old. Maybe fifteen, sixteen years ago. Fifteen years.

So I putting him the lap. I put the bell in the hand. Because is very heavy, he can't lift it, he only have one year. I put the hand the stick. And everybody is looking. And we play "Te Palo Pa Rumba." The whole song. And it's a long song. And everybody is, "Wow!" I never forget that moment there. Because it's very special to me, that time. That whole time, I taking that time, I put it in here. (*He points to his chest.*) . . . Four months ago, he come to me, he say, "Papi, I'm going out." I say, "Where you going?" He say, "To the movie." I say, "Okay, be careful." I told him, "César, I love you." He say, "Papi, I know." . . . That's when I lose him. . . . Is very difficult because the police told is some accident that he's running, the police shooting to him but . . . whatever. No because, my wife she working and then she coming home always cry. And I working, and in the night, I never sleep. How I gonna work if I never sleep? She told me, "You better go to sleep." I told her, "Well, you better stop cry entonces." She told me, "César, if you feeling bad, you has to take all the people in the whole world that love you, and you putting those people here (*He points to his chest again.*), and it's gonna making that you feeling warm in here."

So I thinking, "Who love me? My wife love me, put it here. My sister love me, put it here. My two brother love me. . . . My César love me, put it here." And I know that he love me because that day when he go to the movie he say, "Papi, I love you too." It's the only time he say that, but I hear that. Pero very cold in here. . . . I told my wife, "You has to get some better magazine because that's no working." All the time I thinking that he's sitting there and play that, but whatever. I miss him. Maybe I should never coming here, maybe I go talking to some people because maybe you don't listening to me. . . . (CÉSAR *sings the first verse of "Te Palo Pa Rumba" as lights fade out.*)

ROUGHNECK CHICKEN

Epilogue

ROUGHNECK CHICKEN *is a mythical character somewhere between Jamaican dub poet, Yiddish sage, and chicken. He wears red, gold, and green and sunglasses. He beats on the wooden cube to provide the music for this poem, which is done in song.*

I hope you don't mind if I keep you, just a few likkle minutes after

And if you don't feel like stayin', den get the hell outta de
theatre

But you clap at the end of my show, so I take it you were
listenin'

I hope you have enjoy youself, but listen to this one more
thing

Ey . . .

I know that some of you people have never seen Brooklyn
or Bronx

That's very funny to me hahahahahahaha

But that's not really the subject of this last and final part

So let me collect my thoughts together correctly so that I
can start . . .

And remember you came to see theatre, this ain't no performance art

I want to give you two words, so dat you can take dem
with you

Now don't say dem loud goin' home pon de train, because
somebody might hit you

The first word is Dem. That means Dem, those people
over there

The second word is We. That means Us, these people over
here

Now I hear alotta people talkin', about DemDem, those
people and ting,

Dem Terrorist Muslim Crack Addict AIDS Baby Bad Guy
Doin' De Tiefin'

Now when I hear people say We, they always feelin' happy

Like We make Three-Billion-Dolla Spaceship, put inna
sky, ain't dat nifty?

We make Three Thousand Talk Shows, and the people
love it

We kill Three Billion Chickens this year, and make dem
     inna Chicken Nugget
We made Three Billion Dollars, but We gave money to
     the poor
We dropped big bombs on those evil fucked-up people
     and We won the war
Ey . . .

Last month I talk to a Chicken, by the name of Bingi
So pay attention good now, I goin' tell you what the
     Chicken tole me
Long long time ago . . . Chickens ran de earth
About a Hundred Fifty Thousand Years, before People was
     birth

The Chickens used to live in big mansions, and the other
     birds live in the street
The Chickens used to drive BMW, and the other birds
     walk with dem feet
The Chickens used to say, Look at dem birds, dem filthy
     lazy bum
How can they live like that really, We are so smart and
     Dem so dumb

Well today all de Chickens die, and the other birds fly in
     the sky
That was the end of his story, hahahahahahaha
Ey . . .

Last verse, then you go home . . .

If you don't know my name, me a de Roughneck
     Chicken, me run de area
And any dibby dibby DJ wan to come try tes me dem ago
     get murda
I want you to know I am the number one dance-hall
     chicken inna New York City
And to all de young sexy lady, I want you to know I'm
     young single and free

So if you want my phone number, well you must come
    get it from me
Or take yourself a visit to Brooklyn, and just ask fe de
    Dance-hall Daddy
Ey . . .

SONNETS FOR AN OLD CENTURY

José Rivera

For my father Herminio Rivera

Sonnets for an Old Century was presented in workshop by the Relentless Theatre Company, New York Theatre Workshop, The Mark Taper Forum, The Philadelphia Theatre Company, The La Jolla Playhouse, Ensemble Studio Theatre West, and the California Institute for the Arts.

Sonnets for an Old Century received its world premiere production at the Greenway Arts Alliance, (Pierson Blaetz and Whitney Weston, Artistic Directors) Los Angeles, California, on January 14, 2000. Maricela Ochoa, Oscar Arguello, and Laura Frank were coproducers. The set design was by James Eric; the lighting design was by Cheryl Waters; the costume design was by Naomi Yoshida-Rodriguez; the stage manager was Irma Escamilla; the technical director was Chris "Fin" Finnestead; the director was James Eric.

The original cast was:

Javi Mulero, Whitney Weston, Andrew Carrillo, René Rivera, Masashi Odate, Gary Carter, Diana Larios, James DiStefano, Lynn Dandridge, Michael Teisan, Kevin Kelly, Kiersten Van Horne, Antoinette Abbamonte, Newton Kaneshiro, Steven Ruge, Gretchen German, Mark Ferreira, Billy Kane, Juan Carlos Cisneros, Lesa Carlson, Reiko, Rosana Potter, Wendy Johnson

CHARACTERS

WENDY JOHNSON, JAVI MULERO, CAMILIA SANES, ANNE O'SULLIVAN, DAWNN LEWIS, RICK COCA, MARICELA OCHOA, MICHI BARALL, JOHN ORTIZ, ESTHER SCOTT, SAM WELLINGTON, ROBERT MONTANO, VANESSA MARQUEZ, ANA ORTIZ, CARLO ALBAN, JOHN VARGAS, SVETLANA EFREMOVA, JESSICA HECHT, GENO SILVA, ANTOINETTE ABBAMONTE, KARENJUNE SANCHEZ, YUSEF BULOS, FELICITY JONES, DORIS DIFARNECIO, KEVIN JACKSON, X, MARK FERREIRA, CORDELIA GONZALEZ, KRISTINE NIELSEN, ALENE DAWSON, RENÉ RIVERA, KIERSTEN VAN HORNE

NOTE

Though all the monologues have character names this in no way is meant to limit the type of actor best able to perform that monologue. Consider the names to be a flexible marker as to that character's identity. In many cases the gender, age, and race of the characters is undetermined—in production situations, please aim for the maximum level of diversity possible.

It could be a tunnel, a cave, a warehouse, an airplane hangar, catacombs, or a seedy office building with ugly fluorescent lighting—but it's a large space.

The many people who appear in the space are from various parts of the United States. There are Latinos, blacks, Asians, whites. There are gays and straights, children and old people. All are strangers to each other.

WENDY JOHNSON *speaks to the others.*

WENDY JOHNSON

You stand here and make your statement.

That's it.
You want to fight with existence?
Go for it. You want to scream?
Knock yourself out.

Just remember:
your words go out to the universe, all your
words, to be, I don't know, recycled among
the living—like rain, like part of—
some ecology of the spirit.

It's the last and only time you have
to give your side of the story, as far as I
know.

JAVI MULERO

We would eat liverwurst on black bread
with mustard and onions and have sex.

We would have sex on tattered, sticky pages
of the Sunday *New York Times*.

We would have sex after walking across the
Brooklyn Bridge, cold October afternoons,
staying home from work, angry at our office
jobs among the walking dead and art
wannabes.

We would have sex instead of air.

We would have sex while burning garbage
fell on our fire escape because the maniac
on the floor above us decided devils were
living in his trash.

We would have sex while water dripped
through our ceiling because the maniac on
the floor above us kept the water in his
bathtub running while he went off to visit a
brother on Staten Island who had
communicated with devils and had salient
advice on how to use them for your own
benefit.

We would have sex while the maniac on the
floor above us returned from Staten Island,
fell in the hallway, and pounded the floor
with his fists.

We would have sex after visiting the maniac
on the floor above us, his eyes black and
blue, his shirt saturated with blood, who
told us he was beaten by a gang in Red
Hook who he tried to buy drugs from on his
way to visit his brother in Staten Island.

We had sex after explaining to the maniac
on the floor above us that Red Hook isn't
on the way to Staten Island and we had to
get the super to turn off the water in his tub
and the super is going to recommend that
the maniac on the floor above us, who sees
devils living in many corners of his life, be
evicted immediately for nonpayment of
rent and for constantly coming home from
Red Hook bleeding from the face.

We had sex after an attempted
assassination of the President of the United
States.

We would have sex after returning from
Westchester where her parents lived and
inspired tears and had the power to reduce
her to the status of an undisciplined punk
with no respect for their values and
customs, who had sex out of wedlock with a
Puerto Rican, in many locations and quite
frequently.

We would have sex without protection.

We would have sex while children starved,
racists ran for office, war was waged on the
poor, exotic and never-to-be-duplicated
forms of life were deleted, fundamentalists
dictated the terms of our living, the
hoarding classes perfected devious and
more efficient ways to hoard and the
country drowned in capital, optimism,
envy, and bullshit.

We would have sex when we didn't feel
like it.

We would have sex after bad dreams.

We would have sex after burying our
parents and grandparents, while work
became more and more meaningless, and
friends questioned their marriages.

We would have sex while our children
asked about sex.

We would have sex in spasms, in waves, in
circles, in small violences, in secret
ecstasies, in patient waiting, in doubts, in
forgotten languages, in extreme loneliness,
in promises kept, in wishes left
unacknowledged, in ritual fantasy—in peril
and in peace.

CAMILIA SANES

I was known as quiet and studious.

My glasses embarrassed me
and I hid them often
and suffered the anger of my mother
who also wore glasses,
but she was proud of hers.

She was studious too.
She covered the house in books.
She read in the bathtub
and read to me every night of my life.
Long great hard books full of characters
and interweaving chapters
and sentences with so many commas and
colors. Friendly books with heroes.

I listened so hard.
I settled into my bed
trying to melt into the sheets,
trying to surround my body

with the warm mattress.
I don't think I really heard the words.
I didn't need to.

The words were like waves on the beach,
lifting me softly,
tumbling me in crazy rapids,
pushing me under for moments
of brief, airless, gasping terror,
then delivering me up again—
up to air,
up to sunlight,
up to the light in my small bedroom
and my mother's shape on the bed,
her out-of-style glasses
glistening with mischief and hard work.

The words washed away
the stress of nasty girls
who excluded me on the playground.
The words washed away
the tests that I hated and failed,
despite my glasses and my studying.

The words were invisible fingers
my mother employed
to hold me close and warm,
to squeeze my brain a little tighter,
to hold in firm embrace
my throbbing lungs,
my mighty muscled heart.

She was a dreamer.
She dreamed worlds and they appeared
next to the bathtub in hardcover.

Sometimes I didn't know
if I was really there.

Sometimes I wondered
if maybe she dreamed me too.
She needed a little daughter
who looked and acted like she did
and she forced me by incredible willpower
through the fallopian tubes of her mind
and squeezed me out of her imagination,
blue and bawling,
complete with glasses and gratitude,
asleep at her side in our cozy bed,
dreamer and dream together.

ANNE O'SULLIVAN

Um.
Let's see.
I learned a few things while I was there . . .
over there . . .
wherever there is.
Was.
Is that what I should talk about?
I don't know if I can talk about no sex.

Okay.
What I learned.
Um.
Children?
Children contain all the necessary wisdom
to create a civilization.

Um.
Evil is unexplainable.
So don't even try.
If you suddenly don't understand the words
and actions of your family members or best
friends, think drugs.
Money fucks relationships.
That one's obvious.

All straight men are attracted to all straight
women all the time.
Rice and beans are better than potatoes.

You will never be able to fully forgive your
parents.
Dreams are the Earth's telepathy.
Eat as much as you can, a famine is coming.
Baby boomers have completely run out of
Great Ideas.
Strong moonlight is healing.
Let people know when you're in love with
them. Lies make your lips smaller.
Pay bills a day late.
Strangers are opportunities for mischief—

take advantage.
Paint a classroom.
Wash all your dishes by hand and
contemplate the value of water.
Sins are man-made.
Never trivialize the Supreme Being.
Good prayer is biofeedback.
You can't love a child too much.
Don't fuck with people who believe in you.
Anger is contagious,
so be careful who you sleep with.
Rice and beans are better than pasta.
Grow one edible fruit or vegetable to
supplement your income.
Baseball is a game not a metaphor.
Life is neither a dream nor a cabaret.
You don't have to choose between passion
and security.
There are many parallel Americas and the
rich have the better one.
Listen to your jealousy.

I was shot in the head and I think, to satisfy
the Second Amendment, all Americans should
own one eighteenth-century musket and
that's it.
Religion and spirituality are two completely
different things in America.

DAWNN LEWIS

Night of the unrest,
I was at a screening in Santa Monica.
The week before,
the radio was stolen out of my car.
At the screening, there's no TV,
nobody really knows what's up.
I leave the screening around eleven,
with no idea what's happening,
except I knew the verdict came down
and I'm feeling real sick to my stomach at this point.
And I'm driving back to Pasadena on the 10 . . .
and I see this black towering mass
on the freeway right in front of me,
a huge, black funnel, like, I'm not shittin' you,
someone just let some evil genie out of a bottle,
and I'm all, "Fuck me, it's a tornado!
There's a fucking tornado in L.A.!"
And I'm freaking out!
Then I see *another* one, next to it, *another* one.
Then I realize: no; that's smoke; the city's on fire;
and then I see it's only burning on my *right, south* of the 10
in the black part of town.
And when I understand this . . .
I feel those tornadoes lifting up my car
and spinning me in space and
I'm part of this terrifying wind blowing all our hopes
    away:

the firestorm in the neighborhood
full of old hatreds,
leftover anxiety from the Watts riots,
years of blame and disappointment,
swirling all together in a huge funnel of air,
black and thick, taking me to some anti-Oz
where the yellow brick road's red with blood
and tornadoes don't stop spinning,
and they spin continuously,
to this day, to this minute,
and all I want to do is spin around,
throwing curses and venom in every direction,
at everyone who's forgotten. . . .

RICK COCA

I was waiting outside the house
for almost an hour.
My *novia* was working in this house.
Anglo family.
Watching their children.
They were supposed to get back by eleven
thirty.

It was past midnight.
We didn't think they'd want me in their
house
so I waited in the car on the street in front.

I drove a small and dented Toyota.
The neighborhood was rich.
Big houses, not too much happening at
night. Dead and dark.
Sometimes you see coyotes looking for
food.
Or an opossum crawling across the road.
They are very slow animals.

No wonder so many of them die.
You see their guts spattering all over the
road. They are not pretending then.

Animals fascinate me.
Where I grew up you lived with animals.
You understood their habits.
You paid attention to what they needed
or they would die.
If they die, you die.
I watched them being born!
I got used to blood and birth.
I understood the great variety of shit
in the animal kingdom.

My mother taught me to kill chickens
with my hands.
You grab them around the neck and then
you spin them around.
They struggle and some of them can really
cut you bad if you're not careful.
When I was a child I loved to kill them like
that.

Later I butchered pigs.
I pretended the pig was a condemned man,
a murderer, rapist, with no soul,
who never repented,
and spit at the priest giving him Last Rites
and mocked the sacraments
and the family of the victim,
boasted he raped little girls.
I held the knife tight.
Looked at the struggling, confused pig.
Imagined the rapist or the unrepentant
murderer and I was chosen by the court to
execute this scum. I never smiled.

I never let the pig's—
I mean the prisoner's—
screams distract me.
I plunged the knife into its soft throat—
far as it could go—
and I cut and cut and the animal screamed
like a man and I imagined
the bleeding prisoner
finally understanding the meaning of his
crimes, repenting, fearing God,
believing in God's wisdom,
God's punishment, which I carried out.
I was the messenger of God,
the word of God, I said,
"Don't kill," "Don't rape," "Don't sin," . . .
I was the terrible messenger
and this knife was my message.
I took myself very seriously
when I was ten years old.

I feared nothing except goats.
I wouldn't kill goats.
I wouldn't come near them.
They have haunted eyes, God protect me!
They seem like the reincarnated souls
of madmen.
When they cry out, it sounds like your
name,
I would practically shit myself in fear.
I begged my father to get rid of the goats.

One day—I cried in front of my father
and he was so offended
he hit me over the head
with the handle of a machete
and told me to stop acting like a girl.
He locked me in the goats' pen

for a day to punish me
and those madmen brayed
and shouted at me,
told me their stories,
their past lives.
It was hard to make out their words.
But I understood enough.

One had set his hair on fire.
One had eaten rats.
One believed he was Pope John XXIII.
One had sat in a room twelve years,
sitting in his own shit,
dreaming of space travel.

I screamed at them to stop talking to me.
Worried, my father let me out at dinner-
time—
he was going to make me spend the night
there, but changed his mind,
afraid a night with those madmen
would drive me so insane everyone would
pity him for having an insane child in his
family—
and my father hated people's pity
more than he hated having a sissy son.
I wiped my eyes and walked out the pen.
I never cried in front of him again.

To this day, animals fail to move me
with their dying, their breeding—so what?
The coyotes hurrying through these bigshot
Anglo neighborhoods at night,
ignoring me in my Toyota as I wait for my
girlfriend—so what?

I waited out there nearly an hour.
I was low in my seat,

thinking of my youth in Nicaragua
among animals.
It was dark and quiet.
I was about to fall asleep.
Far away I heard a car.
It wasn't going fast.
I thought "No."
I didn't move.
I could feel the sweat in my hands.
My asshole tightening.
The car had very bright headlights
and it stopped right behind me,
engine running,
lights shining into my car,
I thought "No."

I waited and decided to sit up.
The police lights shot on,
red and blue swirls colliding in my face,
my stomach turning into boiling water,
my mouth dry.
Two men got out.
One of them shined a flashlight in my face.
I waited.
The other cop stood behind the first
and he waited.
Man's eyes were cold.
Man's eyes stared right into me.
I turned my head
and wouldn't look in his eyes
as the other one told me to get out of the
car very, very slow,
hand on his gun,
the night very still,
coyotes long gone,
scared away by the action, instinctual.

I stood there
and explained what my business was
on this street
and one of the cops looked at me
the way I used to look at the pigs
I was about to slaughter,
cold, convinced of my higher duty,
the spokesman of God,
the messenger,
the punisher,
the death-bringer.

MARICELA OCHOA

I wanted to be a ballerina or an astronaut.

In my imagination, day after day,
I practiced dancing on the moon.
If there was life on Mars, I would waltz with
it.

Before the accident, I kept a journal.
I drew pictures of other Life-Forms.
Creatures with sticky tentacles and multiple
eyes—I drew rock monsters, worms with
intelligence, plasma jellies with attitude—
and all of them had rhythm.
They could salsa!
They could tango!
They could do splits!

I learned that dancing on Jupiter is a
challenge. Heavy gas, lots of gravity—
good for slow dancing.
But you can't jitterbug there.

Before I was paralyzed,
my body could do almost anything.

I learned movements instantly.
My body was a library of dance styles.
On long interplanetary voyages
I imagined leading the crew in the
Charleston,
the minuet, the merengue, the hula, and
the mashed potato.

Wars between rival civilizations
in the dark corners of space
would be averted
because my body
would translate between species—
and one-eyed creatures of one world
would read the words
of ten-armed creatures of another world
by following the movements of my hips.

My legs would speak of peace.
My torso would convince
skeptical generals of warlike peoples
that love is a greater conqueror than
conquest.
My body would be a peace treaty.
My limbs would be paragraphs on
disarmament. My eyes would be the
signatures
of diverse universal leaders.

And my toes would be the footnotes.

MICHI BARALL

I have so many questions, I don't know
where to begin. Let's start with the
research I was doing. So is it true? About
the river of galaxies? I have to know this!

The expanding universe—okay?—expands
uniformly in all directions according to the
Big Bang theory. But then we discovered
that the expanding universe wasn't so
uniform after all. That, in fact, there is a
river of galaxies heading off in the direction
of Virgo—a massive flow of galaxies being
sucked into *one direction*, completely at
odds with the Big Bang theory. All over the
scientific community people were freaking
out.

Then a few years ago, my colleagues and I—
we called ourselves the Seven Samurai—we
discovered that a *Massive Great Attractor* is
pulling a quarter of the known universe—a 200 million
light-year region of space—at
the speed of 1.2 million miles per hour.
Pulling it.

Why? What's out there? Are they giving
away immortality? Is it something really
bright and shiny? Is it something musical?
An astronomical Pied Piper hauling a
quarter of the universe's known mass in
one direction? I mean, how good can it be?
Or is it something sinister? Is something
out there eating matter? Is the universe
flat? Should we fear, like the sailors of
antiquity, the horizon—because there's a
point beyond which we can't go? A falling-
off point? I gotta know this!

I had a thing happen to me; I was eight. I
was in my backyard. Alone. My mother
was upstairs taking a nap because the baby
was finally asleep. I was playing with a
sword stabbing invisible enemies.

Then the light around me changed. I
dropped the sword, looked around. And
something on the other side of the yard was
. . . calling me—*pulling* me—to it. I don't
remember well! It was a light, it was a
sound like music, it was warm, it was
friendly, but very stern, it was large, it was
very strong, and I could feel my body
leaning that way. I looked down, and the
grass, too, was leaning that way. The air
seemed to be blowing in that one direction.
I took a step toward this thing, this
Attraction. I noticed my soccer ball rolling
toward it. Getting faster the further it got
from me. I wanted to cry. Each step, it felt
a little stronger, it seemed to get a little
brighter. I was starting to fight it,
breathing very hard, I could hear myself
crying, really crying hard. I noticed all the
trees were bending in that direction too as
if they were pointing something out to me.
I called my mother's name! It was like the
sound of my voice was suddenly grabbed by
big hands and thrown to the other side of
the yard. I saw a few of my tears leave my
face and go right into the swirling eye of
this Big Attraction. There was no sound
but the soft music and my hard crying.

Then it stopped. The whole thing just
stopped. The music, the lights, gone.

Whatever it was, had it gotten what it
wanted? Did it just want a couple of my
tears? The sound of my voice as I called my
mother?

All my life, I've been attracted to stars and
night skies, trying to understand what
happened to me when I was eight: hoping,
with the aid of telescopes and satellites, to
hear that eerie music again and feel that
warmth. I still don't know if the thing
wanted to eat me or love me. I was
attracted to the big dome of the
Planetarium—but when the shaking started
and the whole structure, attracted by
gravity, collapsed on me and sent me here.
Attracted to the Big Questions of the
universe, I think of that river of galaxies,
wondering if it's pulled by the same force
that nearly seduced me in my backyard,
desperately needing to know if it will eat us
or love us.

JOHN ORTIZ

Last year we were in Puerto Rico.
And we were on the beach.
Sun going down.
Beautiful, red, bursting sun, dropping . . .
golden coins into the ocean.
And I was eating a mango.
And it was sticky and sweet.
And Therese was rubbing my back,
real gentle, and sometimes her hand
would come down to my ass.
And someone on the beach
was playing a twelve-string mandolin
and a little girl was singing
in a high stratosphere voice,
pure and brown like her skin . . .
these golden flecks around her greenish eyes . . .

like she'd been kissed there
by the sun's miniature lips . . .
little kiss-tattoos
around the solar system of her mulatto eyes:
her voice bathing me in warm, fat notes,
ancient notes full of slavery and passion.
And I asked myself as I stood there on the beach:
why am I not happy here?
Why don't I stay here and live like this
the rest of my life?
Why, God, isn't this enough?
And I realize now—my ambition
was like a disease in my system.
This disease was commanding me
to leave paradise and kill myself
with work twenty-four hours a day.
And even if this disease destroyed me,
I had to obey it.
It would not let me go
no matter how much I drown it
in mangoes and music and sunshowers.

ESTHER SCOTT

I ran for President.
No one knew me.
All my life I wanted to be President.
The apex of my life!

I went door-to-door
trying to get enough signatures
to put me on the ballot in Michigan.
Most people slammed their doors in my
face.
I never got any media coverage.
But I gathered signatures.
I had a few passionate followers.

I had a message: in 1990, 13 percent of all voters
were from families whose incomes were
under $15,000.

In 1992 that percentage had dropped to
11 percent.

In 1994, of all the families making less than
$15,000 a year, only 7.7 percent bothered to vote.

In 1989 the inequality of wealth
distribution in the United States was at a
sixty-year high.

Imagine what it is now!

The top 1 percent of families ranked by financial
wealth had 48 percent of all the wealth in the
country.

The top 20 percent owned 94 percent of the country's
wealth.

In 1989, 35 percent of all families of color
reported zero or negative net worth.

So I got a few hundred signatures.
I shook a few hundred hands.
In brief moments I made real connection
to real people.
I gave them a little hope.
I made their country a little better for them.
For a couple of minutes there were
a few people who could smell change in the
air. Who witnessed the unlikely birth of a
new nation.

I ate a lot of red meat with the people.
Funny.
I couldn't tell if they were humoring me or
not. But I drank a few cold beers.

SAM WELLINGTON

I'm surrounded by strangers.
I'm trying to just deal.
I want answers.
I'd like to see the man in charge.
I'd like to see a schedule!
I'd like to know when I get to set the pace of
events around here!

I operated a forklift.
And I had my problems with substance
abuse. Okay? But that's all past now.
That shit's gone bye-bye as far as I'm
concerned. As far as I know doing hard
drugs isn't technically a sin in the record
books of any organized religion I'm aware
of.
Last time I checked.

I partied.
Sure, I partied.
I liked to kick back, shoot the shit with a few
friends over a barbecue grill, Coors Light in
one hand, spatula in the other.
Entertain the masses.
I'd drink far more than my share.
I'd get pissed—
been known to happen.
Get a little mellow—
girls look exceptionally good, why not?
Last time I perused the holy pages,
I don't believe beer or pussy
were on the list of frowned-upon human
activities.
I can say pussy if I want!

Consenting adults, of course,
I didn't chase no children,

didn't offer beer or pot to minors.
If I ended up in the arms of a married
woman,
I know I wasn't breaching any kind of
earth-shattering moral responsibility.
As long as I wasn't coveting her.
I wasn't *coveting* her, I was *copulating* her.
And I didn't go for sodomy!
So you can't fault me on that line of
reasoning. And it's not like I'm some kind
of Samson of the love-crowd:
my success rate's pretty single digits most
times. Usually it was drink, drink—puke,
puke—crawl on hands and knees over cold
tile—wish to God I owned a handgun so I
could nullify the drumbeat in the
whimpering bloodpools of my brain.
Thoughts of self-slaughter, even if you read
the fine print under this heading, isn't the
actual event and therefore not covered in
this clause!

Never killed no one.
Never worshipped graven images.
Never had no pictures of Baal or Mithra or
Mothra or whatever those Babylonian
deities were called.
Didn't worship no cows either!
Except a couple of human ones!
Never bought Proctor and Gamble Satanic
products.

I've broken the law.
Sure.
Flat broke so bad, one year, had to steal
medicines when I got sick—
especially my asthma and those inhalers

are marked up to extremes, talk about sin.
So I'd lift a few of those.
Yeah, that's theft, that's stealing, that's,
that's pretty certain, you know, no-holds-
barred sinning.
You got me there.

I remember from the Bible classes, they'd
have a drawing of a quart of milk and that's
your pure, white soul.
But the sinners have little black smudges
on their quarts of milk.
And anything other than actual white milk
in that bottle was fucked.
It ruined the perfection.
And it pretty much ruined your chances of
experiencing the bliss of Heavenly reunion
with the Great Creator—
though I gotta say I'm still waiting for the
bliss part to kick in here.
So I guess my thieveries are showing up on
the outer lining of my soul.
But I'll tell you how unfair that is.
I was hungry, I was having asthma attacks.
I was not greedy.
And I wasn't packing anything.

And, you know, these were Man's laws I
was breaking and I really do think
something as small and temporary as
Man's laws have no real long-term effect on
something as total and permanent as the
human soul.
That's just my opinion.
The opinion of a working man.
I know I can look right into the terrible eyes
of our Lord Jesus and be secure in the

knowledge that the smudges on my eternal
soul are slight and unimportant and simply
the wages of living in an imperfect world
run by Man and his laughable laws.
Looks like I covered most of the territories
of the known sins.

Okay, the only thing, maybe, was . . . while
my father was dying in Jersey . . . and I
couldn't go visit him.
No, it wasn't like I couldn't get time off or I
couldn't afford it or the car died or nothing.
I just couldn't go.
Look at him in the bed.
Legless.
His right arm paralyzed from the strokes.
His power of speech eradicated.
Facial muscles uncontrollable.
Watch him staring at the television all day
long, screaming out the only word his
mouth could form: "Ma!"
Calling my mother.
Ma!
Whenever he needed her to turn him over.
Ma!
Or find him a Mets game on TV.
Ma!
Or turn off the harsh light.
Or put the picture of Lord Baby Jesus just a
little closer, Ma, just a little closer, Ma!
Ma! Ma.

Sorry, I couldn't watch this.
I didn't go.
For years.
I'd let my siblings deal with all that shit
while I continued to not know and not

investigate and not do one blessed thing for
the man, outside of having fantasies of
killing him by suffocation and ending the
pretense, the Bible reading, the hand
clapping, the speaking in tongues, the false
hope, ending it, ending it, for God's sakes
let the poor man die, why don't you?
Just let the poor man die.

Thou shall honor thy mother and thy
father. Jesus.

ROBERT MONTANO

My wife . . .

. . . she gave her old clothes to a local church
. . . she knew the mailman's birthday . . .
she gave to UNICEF . . .
she sent passionate faxes to elected officials . . .
she knew the first
twelve Shakespeare sonnets by heart . . .
she said good-bye to tollbooth people . . .
"bye-bye tollbooth person!" . . .
she returned her library books on time . . .
she visited her eternal grandmother
every faithful summer . . .
the old woman's one remaining pleasure . . .
incontinent, toothless, unhappy . . .
connecting her granddaughter,
through endlessly repeated anecdotes,
to the history written in her blood . . .

. . . she swore she'd buy herself a gun
and shoot herself in the head
before she'd put up with an old age like this . . .
we planned to get ancient together
and do the joint-suicide thing . . .

. . . but there was a guy . . .

. . . a guy who washes car windows
in front of the bank in our neighborhood . . .
young guy . . .
filthy . . .
heroin . . .
always had a skateboard . . .
she'd drive up to the bank . . .
give him a dollar to clean the windshields . . .

. . . they'd hang out and talk . . .
they did this every Saturday morning . . .
he's very good-looking . . .
despite the filth . . .

. . . she used to shoot up, so she understood . . .
I thought they were in love . . .
they had "a thing" . . .
I waited in the car as they laughed . . .
she once gave him a twenty,
got in the car, crying . . .
she said, "I just heard the saddest story" . . .

. . . his new tattoo . . .
I swore it was her name
surrounded by a crown of thorns . . .
the woman he couldn't have . . .
I wanted to kill this man . . .
he was pathetic . . .
smelled like a urinal . . .
she got too *close* to him . . .
I didn't want his clothes to brush her
clothes . . . came home one day . . .
there he is *in the kitchen* . . .
merrily drinking coffee . . .
he's talking to her about movies . . .
big fan of Hitchcock . . .

what the fuck is going on here? . . .
I wanted to unwind . . .
I'm stuck with this putrid drug user
in my kitchen
pontificating about *Strangers on a Train!* . . .

. . . we fought about it that night . . .
I told her: "I come home . . .
I can't even talk to you
because this addict is monopolizing you . . .
all I want is equal rights here!" . . .
she said,
"I already know what you're going to tell
me" . . .
I stare at her . . .
"I *bore* you? . . .
is that it?" . . .
"no," she said quickly . . .
I didn't even stay in bed to hear more . . .
she said, "these people need me" . . .
"I don't need you?" . . .
she said, "not in the same way" . . .
"honey, I need you in profound ways" . . .
she said, "yes I know" . . .
"you're not going to save this man" . . .

. . . I couldn't stop imagining them together . . .
I imagined them sharing a cardboard box . . .
they do it on rusted mattresses . . .
passion heightened by rusted mattress
spikes stabbing their naked butts . . .
in fact, pain is the goal . . .

. . . I imagined they rode skateboards
together . . . panhandling in front of our
house . . .
all our friends staring at her . . .

and she'd look and sound happier
with him than she ever looked and sounded
with me . . .
beneath the layers of traffic soot
and sidewalk dirt
her eyes were full of wisdom and fulfillment
and absolute freedom . . .
the freedom only vaguely imagined
by the housebound . . .
freedom to say "fuck you" . . .
to stare at the drivers
waiting for the light to change . . .
she'd challenge them:
"hey you in the Lexus, are you moral?
empathic? . . .
you think you are . . .
you tell your children you are . . .
in your prayers you boast that you are . . .
yet here I am . . .
LOOK AT ME . . .
I'm staring into the deepest tunnels
of your heart
and I'm not seeing shit . . .
you want me gone . . .
you hope I fall off the edge
of the known world . . .
fall painlessly into oblivion
while you drive to your appointments" . . .

. . . she wanted that power . . .
and that power was something
she could only get from him . . .

. . . then he disappeared . . .

. . . after that we would drive together . . .
anywhere . . .

didn't matter . . .
there they were . . .
like an army of vampires,
bloodless, in their rags and filth . . .
they knew about her . . .
they sought her out . . .
she radiated goodness and they wanted it . . .
they wanted to drink from her kindness
like it was an ancient tribal river . . .
to suck her down into their limbs . . .
to own her . . .

. . . my wife . . .
actually began to disappear in front of my
eyes . . . I watched helpless as she gave away
scraps of herself . . .
first the excess . . .
then the vital tissues . . .
until she disappeared completely from my
sight   down into the tortured piranha pit
of the homeless . . .

. . . away from me . . .
happy . . .
alive . . .
and finally at home.

VANESSA MARQUEZ

I caused the Northridge earthquake.
Me! How did I do it? How do I know?
Because the night of the earthquake
I was in Northridge Hospital.
I was paralyzed from the waist down
from a car accident I got into on the 10.
I was in the hospital for months.
I wasn't improving.

I couldn't stop crying!
But the night of the earthquake,
I was lying in bed,
trying with all my heart and soul
to move my useless legs.
And you know what?
I did! I moved my legs—
and just at that very same second,
the earthquake happened!
I made the whole earth shake with my tiny legs!
Houses fell.
Mountains shifted.
Continents kissed and divorced!
Cracks went down deeper than any hell
I could imagine!
And I did that! Me.
All by myself.

And that terrified me.
And I saw what I did
to all those people and houses
and I cried and asked God to forgive me.
I just didn't know, God!
I was humbled and inspired
and now I can walk.
Now I can walk.

ANA ORTIZ

There's somebody . . . I don't know who he is
. . . I want to take this time to apologize to
him. I don't know your name. I don't know
what you look like.

You were in the Bronx about seven years
ago. Let's see, it was outside the 180th
Street shop on the Two, close to one in the

morning. I don't remember the name of
the street anymore.

But right there, under the elevated tracks,
at the intersection, on the left as you go
east, one night seven years ago . . . I saw you.

It was very dark there. All I wanted to do
was to get home. So I'm walking fast 'cause
I hate that street and I almost didn't see
you. But I did see you.

Two men were holding you by the arms and
they were slamming you headfirst into
the front of a parked car. I couldn't see
your face. The two guys were laughing.
You fell to the ground. I only watched for a
second.

I got out of there as fast as I could. I went
home. I didn't call the cops. I didn't call
for help. I didn't jump in to break it up. I
didn't go back later to see if you were okay.
I didn't do nothing but run. Protect my ass.

For a second I actually convinced myself
that you guys were playing some kind of
game, maybe you were just kids.

I'm sorry. If you're out here. If you're
hearing this. I was the one who walked
away that night and left you there and I
haven't been able to stop thinking about
you in seven years and I thought, here,
now, this would be the time to say I was
sorry. This would be the time.

Please forgive me, sir. Please forgive me.

CARLO ALBAN

I see some gods on the moon.
I also see it moving, just a little, let's
pretend my hand is the moon, it's going like
this.

The moon has too much light.
I think it's the gods.
They're having fires there.
The light shoots!
It goes past all the black air in space and
hits my eyes and I feel the hot too, the hot
light from the gods on the moon.

I can't hear them talking, they're too far
away. I think they're mad at us.
I think they want to blow us up.
They talk whispering.
If we went in the clouds with machine guns
and arrows we could kill them.
We hate them.
The gods have no eyes.
They left their eyes at home.
Their hearts are squish and their blood is
really smooth and warm.
It feels like this.

They waited a long time.
They watch us.
They know everything we do.
Someday we're all going to get real sick
and have a disease and be really dead,
everybody.
Like all the dinosaurs and pterodactyls did.
But faster.
In one night we'll all die and lie down in
bed and fall asleep and be dead.

That's when the gods on the moon will find
their eyes and come down to earth, and
take the whole place over.

JOHN VARGAS

I was obsessed with the veins in her neck!
I could see her blue thick veins
running from her chin down to her chest,
along the velvet hills of her skin,
these arteries full of rich, dark blood,
twisting around like the friggin' streets of L.A.
Every time I drove I felt myself traveling the veins
of her neck, getting lost in her hot Cuban
     bloodstream. . . .

But it was so stupid because
it was so fucking doomed because
even if I wasn't married to her sister,
even if I was single,
I was all wrong for her!
She's into bad boys!
Men with prison records!
Chain smokers! Tattoos!
I didn't even have facial hair!
I hated loud noises!
She liked ex-heroin addicts!
There's a certain romance to men like that!
A mystique!
There was absolutely no friggin' chance for me!
It was pathetic!
It was sickening!
I was disgusted with my life!
I went out west to fucking escape
and my fucking life decided to follow me!
I wasn't a man!

God help me,
I was a parody of a man.

SVETLANA EFREMOVA

I would breathe against the window and
watch the thin white cloud my breath made
on the glass and I would take a finger and
write an X in the mist. Then I would move
ever-so-slightly left or right and I would
exhale again and make another small cloud
on the glass and again I would make an X.
I did this until I had covered the entire
window in that room with the white
anxious smoke of my lungs. Then I would
go to the next window and start over and
make small Xs, row upon row, small exact
Xs, engraved in the temporary surface my
breath made on the cold windowpanes.

I wouldn't even look outside. I never took
my eyes off the small X, then the next virgin
spot on which there wasn't an X. And even
if I had wanted to look outside, it would
have been pointless to look, as the other
side of the window was inches thick with
dirt and car exhaust and pigeon shit. The
light that penetrated that window was a
urine-colored little spit of light, a little piss
of light fighting the compacted air and
finally leaking into the room, yellow and
anxious, like a diabetic's piss.

There were nine windows in the room and
nine is the number of redemption.

I don't know why I made so many Xs. I
was amazed by this activity. I couldn't stop.

Not even when they brought the food. Little
trays with neatly wrapped sandwiches,
which I ignored until I was nearly starving,
but ate quickly because I didn't want to
stop making Xs on those silent nine
windows. In fact hunger only heightened
my desire, motivated me, gave me a heroic
reason to continue the punishment, the
shameful, secret ritual that had locked its
iron jaws around my mind.

I began to despise myself for my weakness:
it wasn't a voice, or a pair of hands, but
some force had seized me and all my
cursing and rebellious fantasies were
wasted on it. Superior and inexhaustible it
commanded, yes, commanded me to
continue.

Why did I obey? I loved food. I loved going
to the bathroom. I loved living in my
dreams. I loved exploring sin, but only in
my imagination. Outside of my
imagination I was terrified of sin and would
never commit one and I'd follow every rule,
man-made or dictated by God, no matter
how absurd, I listened, I followed. Fear
motivated me and I never strayed from the
narrow pathway leading from birth to
death. I let pleasures elude me. I let people
walk away from me, free of my fantasies of
them, innocent of my deeply buried desires
and dreams, the twisting, fantastic, highly
plotted, improbable living dreams in which
I satisfied every need and never paid for it,
never lost a lover, never felt guilt, never
apologized. I turned my back on everything

in order to make little miniature Xs on the
surface of great industrial windows, tightly
interconnected X-patterns as elaborate and
lovely as the Book of Kells.

What was I trying to make? What code was
I trying to break?

At times I was vaguely aware of others in
the room with me. I didn't know if they
were real or ghosts. I was aware of distant
voices, detached and clinical, voices that
freeze your blood and incense your mind,
voices I tried to ignore as I covered those
vast windows in Xs. I wanted to stop and
address the voices. To turn around and
viciously insult whoever it was who spoke
to me in such rude and disrespectful ways.
But I found I couldn't turn around. I
couldn't stop making Xs in the windows.
Night after night, sleepless, nearly starved,
I continued my work in light that obscured
my vision and among voices that confused
my hearing.

I imagined my fists breaking through the
window. I imagined throwing my only
chair through the window. I imagined
great pure sunlight storming into the room:
then air: pure air! And, then, space beyond
the window, space to walk and breathe and
really live. I imagined eating food again
and having lovely bowel movements and
rerunning my sexual fantasies and getting
an apartment and a car and maybe a temp
job in a secure office, some old corporation
that would take good care of me.

I would like that. I would develop as a
human being in that scenario. I would
acquire a small selection of elite books. The
great thoughts of mankind. I'd buy CDs
and listen to the latest tunes. I would
flourish within the context of new
friendships. People would bring me news
of distant places. All would find my story of
the room and the Xs appalling and
fascinating. I would develop a reputation
as an appalling and fascinating individual.
No one at the corporation would suspect
the depth of the quiet and loyal little
functionary in the next cubicle. Storage of
so many secrets would only enhance my
mental powers. I have been a wanderer, an
explorer of the twisting pathways of the
mind. My passport is stamped by nations
grotesque and wonderful.

Over and over again I would be aware of my
moral superiority. Over and over again . . .
over and over again . . . over and over again
. . . as I made my Xs. As I made my Xs in
my urine-colored room I realized how
stupid these fantasies were. How abject
and cruel. My fantasies made me sick. And
in that sickness I found a strange
liberation.

A strange liberation is what you gave me.

JESSICA HECHT

The air killed me.
I was sensitive—
but not any more

than the average person, I think.
I liked to breathe.
Breathing was a good thing.

I had an office on Wilshire and La Brea.
The Asahi Building, eleventh floor,
a balcony that went three-quarters the way
around the building,
you had a view east south and west.
Spectacular sometimes when the air was
invisible. But that was rare:
most times it clung to the ground
like mustard gas,
like some kind of white moss,
like a viral infection
along the tissues of your moist lungs—
like the kiss of death,
like a bad chance,
a freak ghost,
a haunting,
polluted Karma,
warmed-over holistic spiritual bullshit.

I would stand on my balcony
trying to see vistas
and downtown structures
and only see the brown death-clouds
of our automotive suicide
and I'd stand there
coughing and cursing like a tubercular mad
freak, face all red,
phlegm the color of unsanitary blood—
I could taste multinational oil giants
in the unhappy folds of my violated
tastebuds;
I could taste Middle East petrodollars
in my hacking dry wheezing breath

and I'd cough and I'd curse
like some twentieth-century version of Captain
Ahab—I swear I could feel one of my legs
turning into wood—
ranting against the visible air,
shaking my fist at the death-clouds,
spitting at the smudged and indifferent
horizon, straining to see the so-called
beauty
in the so-called mountain ranges
and my eyes slamming into that beige
curtain, that soiled atmosphere,
and I'd curse its opacity and its density;
I'd curse its weight
and its love of gravity and streetlevel;
I'd curse its vile and undefeatable smugness,
its certainty that in this minuscule dance of
death we had together it,
not I, would prevail;
it, not I, would be writing
the obituary for the morning paper.

That was a Monday morning
I had those thoughts.

I went home at six o'clock.
I sat in the eye-clogging, spirit-stomping
traffic traveling the four miles from the
Asahi Building to my home in Los Feliz
in about what seemed like
and couldn't have possibly been less than
one solid hour of nerve-crushing,
soul-spattering numbness.

I got home.
I was in my home.
I was contemplating a wide variety

of Trader Joe's frozen delights.
What will it be tonight, I asked myself.
The frozen Trader Joe's Chicken Burrito?
Or the frozen Trader Joe's Veggie Biryani?

I was staring at my freezer
contemplating another exciting night
of microwave, television, and insomnia . . .
when I notice a bright red smudge
out of the corner of my eye.
I turned to look at it.
It was a pane of glass in the kitchen window
reflecting light.

It was the kind of red
you only dream about
when you dream about absolutes.
The red from the inside of your corpuscles
or the center of a volcano's burning
stomach
or the red of infinite anger
or the deepest passion.

I realized it was reflecting the light
coming in from the living room.
I went to the living room
and looked out the big bay windows.
The windows that face west.
The sun was going down.

How do I explain this?
The dirty air created the most—
it was the most fantastic—
no, it, it, it was the most spectacular—
no, it was an explosion of oranges and reds—
no, that doesn't do it:
that doesn't say how
fuckingly fuckingly fuckingly beautiful

that sunset was that evening
hovering like red liquid over the west,
the airdust twisting and bending
the rays of final sunlight
like the shapes in a Calder mobile,
or the ornate lines
of the Shahnama-yi Shahi,
those rays of light
were twisted and bent
beyond imaginable wavelengths
and color patterns:
I saw lava in the sky,
I saw lung tissue,
I saw rose petals,
I saw bloodied mountains,
I saw red rainbows . . .
and I saw it change
and undulate and tease
and I said to myself,
I gotta go outside
and get a better look at this,
I gotta have one really good experience
in this no exit day.

So I walked down the steps to the driveway
to get a better look at the sunset.

At that very exact moment
my next-door neighbor Lourdes,
a woman about my age,
with a waterfall of churning black hair
and eyes like big radar dishes,
she was coming out of her apartment
to look at the pollution-created,
spectacular, massively red display of,
I don't know: pure glory.
And the both of us

just stood there long minutes
watching this sky-thing
changing and rotating
and I didn't even notice she was there
and we didn't notice each other
as the sun disappeared
and the sky darkened
and I swear I'd never seen this woman in
my life and it turns out we've been
neighbors
for three years
and she lives with two roommates
and it's a little crazy
and lately the walls have been closing in
and I explained I lived alone
and my walls are closing in too
and wasn't that the most incredible looking
sunset any person has ever seen?
And isn't it funny we both decided
it was so beautiful
we had to venture outside
to get a really good look at it?
And why don't you come over
and have some
frozen Trader Joe's Calamari in Oyster
Sauce with me?
And sure that would be fun.

And she came over
and we played my old Lightning Hopkins
records I haven't listened to in half a
century
and she told me stories of loss and sadness
and she cried on my shoulder
and I cried on hers
and we exchanged
fleeting tender fingertip touches

and I do believe
that was the very last time
I ever cursed the air pollution in my life.

GENO SILVA

I grew up with a guy who is now
the most famous TV producer of all time.
Same neighborhood.
Same girlfriends, everything,
and that motherfucker stole the Fonz off me.
We came to Hollywood the same time.
I had an idea for a show.
I said to him two words: "the Fifties."
That's all I said!
And, before you know it,
this cocksucker's got *Happy Days* on the air!
He steals the Fonz from me!
My creation!
The voice, the leather jacket, the hair,
the look, I *did* the "look,"
everything, the cool control Fonzie had,
the way he could just slice through a situation
like a red hot razor blade,
the antihero loneliness,
the outsider metaphysic,
the cleft chin,
all of that, all of that was mine,
and the motherfucker stole it from me
and made a fucking fortune
while I found myself sitting in an office
with a Jew with plugs in his head
pitching to Hispanics!

ANTOINETTE ABBAMONTE

There were three boys.
One on each arm.

They pulled my arms back and it hurt.
I couldn't get loose.
I couldn't kick them.
They weren't very strong
but they were determined.

The third boy was in front of me
trying to dodge my kicks,
looking for an opening,
trying to get a good solid punch in
and I kept fighting
and a couple of other boys
were starting to gather
and laugh
and nobody went to get a teacher
or a parent
and when the boy in front of me
finally saw his opening
he punched me right in the chest
and I felt my head exploding
as if all the blood from his punch
was rushing right up into my face.

I could feel my mouth opening
and saliva coming out of it
and the laughter was even stronger
after that
and I looked up at the school
and I could see a couple of girls
looking down at me
from the second floor window
and they weren't moving or anything,
I think one of them was shaking her head
no,
but no one was rushing down
to save me
and that's when I understood

the depth of the conspiracy against me,
and I started to laugh,
and the next time I looked up
at the second floor of the school,
I could see myself
looking down at myself,
not moving,
like I was another coconspirator,
maybe even the worst one,
maybe the leader,
looking down at myself,
passive,
holding hands with the cold girls at my
side,
just slowly, slowly shaking my head no.

KARENJUNE SANCHEZ

I'm sorry.
I'm just a little freaked out at the moment.
I thought I was going somewhere else.
I thought—
because my father was black
and my mother was Hawaiian—
I'd be going somewhere else.

I'm twenty-eight.
I was born and raised in El Paso.
My father was the king of hardware and
lumber.

There was a hole in the floor next to the
bed.
It was very black.
My mother and father were still very poor—
before Pop became king of hardware and
lumber. We moved into this little house on

the West Side. We weren't there long.
In any case, my father filled that hole
the next day.
But my first night in that house,
I slept in a bed next to that hole in the floor
that was black and deep and quiet.

The first one to climb out of that hole
in the floor called himself Ace Man.
He was a card player from San Antonio
who died in a car accident
the day he quit his job for Bekins
and was speeding through Oklahoma
to see a new girlfriend—
a woman whose furniture he moved
himself.
Ace Man had long ears and a tiny mustache
and was half Mexican, half Hopi.
I was eight years old and we played cards
for hours and he always beat me.

He cried out loud for his lost love
and how he never got to live with her
and how unfair it is to get killed
the day your freedom arrives
and you're on the road
and the radio's playing "Free Bird"
and the earth seems endless
and the people in it seem slightly less evil.

His friends eventually came out of the hole
too: they had funny names
like Little Finger and Clay and Smokes and
Chieftain and Lagrimas and Sparky
and all of them were mixed bloods
of some kind or another
and coming from different
and conflicting cultures

they didn't know what afterlife
to go to
so they hung around this narrow hole in El
Paso for the rest of time
and they all had tales of loss and regret
and told jokes
because the loss and regrets didn't get them
down and they knew how to party
and forget their pain,
and they gave me advice
on how to live in the world
and be myself
and fight my fights,
and see the unusual in the usual,
and turn darkness into light and laughter,
and even with tears in their eyes
they knew how to laugh,
and sometimes the saddest ones
laughed the loudest,
and I thanked those imperfect souls
and I kissed each one goodnight
and each one slipped back
into the hole in the floor
and the next day my father
covered it up forever with cement.

And that's where I always thought I'd end
up: in a covered-up hole in a bedroom floor
in El Paso, Texas.

YUSEF BULOS

Three days in the city.

Day One. I'm walking up Hollywood Blvd.
with my son. We're taking pictures of the
stars on the sidewalk. Trying not to stare at
the people. A man with a hat made of

television parts. Homeless women picking
scabs. Teenagers so thin they disappear like
the sideways view of the rings of Saturn.
Scientologists in neat blue uniforms
walking briskly to their nautical salvation.
In Dayton, you just don't see these
variations. A couple of limos whispering
past us. A few times I thought I recognized
someone from something. Day One in the
city.

We stop at a big candy store. My son has
died and gone to heaven. He buys little
packets of false tattoos. Kids wear them all
the time. I'm dreading what forms of
brilliant rebellion he'll be into by the time
he's a teenager. He puts a little *Jurassic
Park* tattoo on his arm and begs me to put
a tattoo on my arm. I didn't want to. Felt
silly, of course.

But this was the first time in six months
that he and I had spent an entire day
together. Every second of the day was just
him and me. Asks me a million "why"
questions, it's that phase. I can see more of
myself in him than ever before. Recognize
my own reactions.

It wasn't always like this. I resented his
birth. It was unexpected, unplanned. I
went into a nosedive. I fretted about
money so obsessively I went into
counseling. I fought with my wife. I hated
waking up each morning. I looked
longingly at younger unattached women
and dreamed of unattachment. I would
hold my newborn son and feel nothing. His

crying grated on me. I had recurring
fantasies in which I ran away and was never
heard from again.

Then one night, it was two or three in the
morning, and his crying woke me up and I
told my wife I would give him a bottle. The
house was silent. Only one light burned
near us. I was barely awake. I held my son
in the living room—it was only a few
seconds before that miracle happened—
and it was suddenly as if I had just
awakened from a deep and troubling sleep—
and I was instantly aware that I had a son.

A son.

I was looking at him as if I had never seen
him before and in that second, I remember
it so vividly even now, in that second I
remember falling deeply in love with him—
it was the first and only time in my entire
life that I actually experienced the "fall" of
falling in love
a swift endless drop, wind blowing in my
face, down a perfectly delicious abyss . . .
and I just . . . I couldn't control myself . . . I
held him . . . and cried with him and I didn't
want to let go. Not ever. Not for another
second of my life.

Anyway. There we were on Hollywood
Blvd. In this labyrinthine candy store and
he wants me to put this scorpion tattoo on
my arm. Finally, I relent. I apply the
temporary tattoo to my forearm. A big
green scorpion, vivid and nasty: it looks
very convincing.

We walk out onto the boulevard, looking
into absurd little lingerie stores, trying to
explain to this little boy what that's for,
trying not to stand out in general.

Suddenly a couple of young men approach
us. Hispanic boys. They're very young and
their heads are shaven and they wear long
baggy white T-shirts, baggy pants:
chocolate complexions, dark eyes, good-
looking boys, but hardened, their mouths
were set in this frown, it looked permanent,
as if they could easily break out in tears any
second—and I rapidly tried to imagine
their fathers—you know how the mind
works—what do their fathers do, what do
they think of these strong-looking young
men with the permanently sad faces—I
know their fathers must have experienced
the fall I experienced with my son—so how
could they possibly let these vulnerable
little boys out of their sight?—how could
we have gotten to this moment of
confrontation and implied violence?—and
they're looking at me very hard and they
point to the child's tattoo of the scorpion on
my arm and say something very quietly to
me in Spanish. I don't understand what it
is. Then one of them points to his forearm
—he has the tattoo of a spider on his arm.
And I don't understand any of this and my
radar is going, "Get the hell out of there: get
out now"—and I try to move on, and they
won't let me go on and my son's crying and
finally the shorter of the two looks at my
son and notices his *Jurassic Park* tattoo
and realizes my scorpion is just a toy and

not a real tattoo and I'm not in some rival
gang, like who could believe that?—the
Dayton white guy gang?—and this young
man laughs so hard and loud—laughs with
relief—I laugh too—and he says, *"Que vida
mas loca"*—"sorry, mister; whatta crazy
life," in lilting, accented English and moves
on.

Day Two—imagine my surprise: I'm
crossing a street in Beverly Hills, don't
watch my step because I'm eyeing an
extraordinary blonde in a top they would
have prosecuted her in Dayton for, and a
limo plows right into me at top speed,
sending me to the intensive care unit at
Cedars-Sinai Hospital. Day Three and here I
am.

Can you tell me how to get word to my son,
please? I want to tell him not to worry
about me.

FELICITY JONES

They think I lied. I didn't lie! I had an
active imagination but I didn't lie about
this. It was a brain tumor! Jesus Christ!

The deadline had come and gone. I had
finished the script, I really had. But it still
didn't work. It needed tweaking. I told
them down at Universal that it was almost
ready. Give me a couple of weeks to tweak
the stupid thing.

It was a genre picture. I had never done a
genre picture before. New rules I had to
learn. Very strict ones. Movie haiku. I

held my breath and went for it. Stretched
myself.

I always take my time. I'm slow. Sue me
but everyone in the business knows that
going into it and if you can't deal with it,
don't fucking hire me!

So I missed the deadline. No one panics.
Not yet. We agree on another deadline.
That one comes and goes. Tempers under
control, okay good. Another deadline. My
manager is now starting to crack at the
seams. Pieces of him are starting to fall off.
The Universal people are getting ugly.

Look, I had a reputation for being excellent
at my craft. Then I finished the thing and
started having a brain tumor.

I called the studio. The script is close I said
but I can't finish it because I have a brain
tumor. They thought I lied. I didn't lie! I
didn't! I could feel it throbbing in my
cranium. It was like I was having a baby in
my head. Like Athena was pounding the
inside of my face with her big Bronze Age
spear and this tumor started assuming
shapes.

The shapes of an ex-husband. Screaming at
me for being lazy and indecisive. Leaving
me for a younger, happier version of
myself. It was taking on the shape of
famous people. Joan of Arc was being
burned at an imaginary stake in my mind
every night. I could hear the fire in my
sleep. I could smell the smoke. The doctor
said phantom smells were the first sign of a

brain tumor. But it was the screaming that
convinced me.

It wasn't my screaming. It was the
screaming of the brain tumor that had
assumed the shape of Sharon Tate in my
brain, this blob of extra-busy brain cells
that multiplied and conquered and
assumed the shape of famous victims.

I had the operation. They took the tumor
out of my head. I finished the script and
the studio made the movie and I was
nominated for my third Academy Award.
Awesome dress.

I kept the tumor. I kept it in my house. It's
in the refrigerator in a Tupperware-like
container. It's now in the shape of, well,
oddly enough, me. It's a little miniature me
that I talked to and got advice from and all
the neighbors and agents in town and
actors who owed their careers to me
thought I was crazy. But I wasn't. I didn't
lie.

My tumor got on the phone and lied for me.

DORIS DIFARNECIO

I heard the truck's engine.
It was loud.
But not as loud as the wind.
A tornado wind!

I was in the back of the truck.
I was wearing Papa's old army jacket,
big and soft, smelled like him,
the sweat from his travel,
the sweat from his work,

picking oranges and artichokes.
His jacket was alive with memories
of his labors and the sweat mixed in
with the sugar and tears of all those places.
The place by the tracks,
by the slaughterhouse,
at the edge of town:
places where nobody else would live.

We crossed a lot of borders in a truck.
Since before I was born.
Following the seasons,
the rhythms of vegetables, our masters;
little plants told us where to live and when,
and Papa listened and obeyed
and kept his mouth shut
and kept out of sight
and kept listening to the orders of the crops
and we traveled to their places
and did the work we had to do
to keep them alive
and keep America fed
and we obeyed the laws,
all the laws, we had to be careful.

And the truck was full of people that night:
a few strangers we didn't know,
also migrants, also going north.
Papa stopped for them:
I don't know why:
he never does that.

They all got into the truck with me
and Mama and Papa
and we drove north
and then the police followed us.
Papa wouldn't stop.

Maybe the strangers in the truck were afraid.
They must have told him not to stop,
to go faster, and maybe he didn't want
to look weak in their eyes
and we went faster, faster,
and the wind was louder and colder
and the truck's engine was faint,
like it had left me behind. . . .

and I was flying through the night air,
flying like a man-eating spirit,
flying with the demons and unlucky ghosts
of the freeway . . .
and the police wouldn't go away;
they pushed Papa faster . . .
and Papa tried a U-turn . . .
and I remember flying into a storm.

When the storm ended,
my Mama and Papa were gone.
The storm had turned my family to rain.
And the rain fell to the earth.
They disappeared in the thirsty earth
so they could feed the plants
who ruled their lives. Gone.

KEVIN JACKSON

I was looking down at the ocean. I was
nervous. The ocean didn't frighten me. It
was the sharpshooters. They patrolled the
beach every half hour. Through the walls of
the prison they could be heard telling
obscene jokes. Sometimes they were so
bored they would take target practice on
the seagulls. They'd spend their entire
complement of arrows on the seabirds.

No, the ocean didn't frighten me. I loved
heights—my love grew stronger as the
years of incarceration went by. Everything
was far, far below us. The enemies who
imprisoned us seemed no larger than ticks.

Our prison was the tallest structure in the
country. You could see it from a hundred
miles away. And everyone knew that my
father and I, the most wanted criminals in
the country, were trapped there, finally
outsmarted, the genius and his only son
contained in stone and steel, a prison even
his great mind couldn't outwit. Or so they
thought. My father, of course, had other
plans.

At first he wouldn't even trust me with his
scheme. Afraid, maybe, I'd break under
torture and spill my guts. In the morning
he'd draw elaborate diagrams. Study them
all day. Then destroy them every night for
fear the guards would find them during
their periodic raids of his cell.

After a year in prison my father started
asking the guards for extra candles. He was
an avid reader and his eyes were going.
The guards, rightfully suspicious, didn't pay
him any attention. Then he went on a
hunger strike—his tenth, I believe—and
threatened to somehow contact the human
rights groups monitoring our
imprisonment—and this always freaked
out the powers-that-be, and after nearly six
months of strikes, near-deaths, stalemates,
and plain old-fashioned hardball, my father

got what he wanted. Two extra candles every night. I knew, instantly, that a plan was in effect.

But he was subtle. He let another six months pass.

Then my father started to complain that his shit was bloody. He requested that his diet be supplemented with grains. A month passed before he got what he wanted. A handful of grain. Then things started to pick up.

My father would put the grain on the high ledge of his one window. Inevitably a seabird would land and eat the grains. The opening was small and my father would frighten the birds so suddenly they would flap their wings while still on the ledge and inevitably the wild beating of wings against the stone window would shake feathers loose and the feathers would fall to the floor in my father's cell. This happened every day.

And it was this way, slowly, that my father collected his treasure of white feathers.

And he would melt his wax from his two extra candles and glue those feathers together and in a year's time he had fashioned identical pairs of giant wings. Then we fasted until we each weighed less than a hundred pounds.

The day came. I was looking down at the ocean. I was nervous. The ocean didn't frighten me. It was the sharpshooters.

They were on the beach that day. And,
again, bored and stupid, they were wasting
their arrows on the hapless seabirds. When
the tall one shot his very last arrow into the
air, my father said, "Come on."

Through a hole in the wall my father had
patiently carved out of solid rock during the
years of our incarceration, we barely
squeezed ourselves and our mighty wings.

As he predicted the wind was northerly.
For years he had watched the patterns of
the clouds, making mental notes, filed away
in the great cavern of that magnificent
brain, and understood the rhythms of the
air, of temperature, of clouds—and
predicted this day would be cloudless, no
rain, no lightning, no turbulence.

We had to move fast. We climbed through
the hole. We were outside for the first time
in years. We strapped on our wings. The
sharpshooters saw us. The fools started to
shout commands! They started throwing
rocks but of course the tower was much
higher than any man can throw and
seconds after attaching the wings to our
bodies, we were lifted by a current of air.

When my feet left the ground, I gasped! I
had never known such a feeling! I started
to involuntarily kick the air, as if that would
help me fly higher and faster, but it only
dragged me down and my father told me to
knock it off. "It's all in the arms," he said
and he demonstrated and was instantly
high above me, flying homeward, as if he
had been born to it.

I was astonished! And the energy of my
astonishment was the power I used to lift
myself above the prison tower, even as an
army of sharpshooters arrived on the beach
with their arsenal of crossbows.

Now at this point in the story I have to stop
to correct a misconception. It is believed by
many people that it was arrogance and
pride that attracted me to the sun that day
and resulted in my downfall.

No. It was not. It was something
altogether different that brought me down.

The reason I faltered is this: I was sick of
my father's perfection.

I knew I carried his genes in me, knew my
tendency to lose my temper, as well as my
weak left eye and my natural
suspiciousness all came from him. But the
greater gifts, the gifts of the mind, those he
hoarded and kept in the dark locked tower
of his superior IQ. And every day I tried to
match him, I showed him my drawings, my
escape plans, my elaborate and fanciful
weapons—and every time he'd laugh at
me, point out the obvious flaw in each of
them, tell me not to bother myself because
the strain would be too much for my
inferior intellect and of course he was
hatching a foolproof scheme. He'd smile at
me, a condescending smile, the smile an
animal trainer gives to his clever and
limited chimpanzee, the smile I had to
endure my entire life long.

I had a right to think myself superior to him! My legs were longer, my eyes clearer, my endurance greater—but I didn't think myself superior.

That tower was cold, always cold. As we flew upward into the blue air above the ocean, I flew straight for the sun. I flew toward what was warm—away from the cold father whose own heart was buried deep within its private labyrinth, inaccessible to all.

Yes, I wanted to show him his invention was flawed and I knew what that flaw was! I could hear him yelling: "You idiot! You fly too high! Don't fly so high!" "Why not?" I shouted back. "The wings! The wax will melt! You'll ruin the wings!"

That's my story.

I tell it to everyone. I'm telling it to you. You don't have to believe me. I suppose, in this space, you have to tell the truth. I'm telling the truth. That's the story of my father and me, before I came to New York.

The wax melted, I fell out of the sky, I crashed into the ocean, I was rescued by fishermen off the coast of Maine, in a coma. I came to, I begged my doctors to go out to sea and find the remains of my beautiful wings. I was pleasantly and firmly rehabilitated.

I pretended to forget my childhood and my brilliant father and my one incredible flight over the sea. But I won't forget.

I cleave to my story, imagining that
somewhere nearby my father has again
escaped death and is again laughing
brilliantly at all of us.

X

Mixed blood is shit.

You're just fuckin' crazy, lady.

Black man with a story about flying! Shit!

Bring it, bitch! Here I am!

I fucked people up.
Blood was like food to me.
Like a God of the night.
Killed a man in the Bronx seven years ago.
Smashed his face clean into the grill of a
Lincoln Continental with whitewalls,
leather interior, nice shine.
You think I'm sorry?
I'd do it again.
You think I'm afraid?
Don't none of you think I'm going to
change.

MARK FERREIRA

This body is a book.
And in my head I can hear
the voices of ancestors:
they've already spoken richly to my genes.
Left their ironies and paradoxes imprinted
there. The voices of my ancestors are
nightmare voices, insistent, untranslatable.

They want me to remember
what part of my body came from the

Caribbean. What part came from Africa.
Spain.
The Canary Islands.

They ask me: when a nation fights a war are
those battles imprinted on the DNA of the
survivors? What screams are encoded
there?
Battle plans, moments of heroism, a young
soldier pissing his pants . . .
which moments become part of the
collective memory to be translated into
proteins,
affecting the shape of organs,
thickness of marrow,
location of heart valves,
brain circuits,
patterns of sleep?
What does peace mean in this context?
Don't we tear holes in the wind itself when
we make war?

These are my talkative ghosts:
manifestations of the past, acting out old
patterns, tugging on living flesh, inept and
weak, but there, very there, very right now.
History acts on us like big magnets,
like time's fingertips.
A slave's impulses, a leader's perspiration, a
buried son, the color of a flag—
nothing is wasted. Everything is recycled.

I ask my ancestors:
Who had my face before?
Who shaped my brain?
They laugh.
They know I carry my nation's tragedies
with me. I sing its anthems.

Its coastline mirrors the shape of my back.
I know the laughter and faces of my people
are encoded forever in my deep spaces.

CORDELIA GONZALEZ

On my back, *carajo,* exhausted, couldn't
even smoke one fucking cigarette, *esse
maricón* doctor and his stupid rules. The
baby in the nursery, *gracias a Dios;* I didn't
wanna see him. *Dejame quieta,* I know he's
my son but, *puñeta, tu sabes,* at that
moment, flat on my back, *carajo,* I was
grateful for a little rest, maybe watch TV,
catch a soap, though it hadda be an
American soap, Days of Our Fucking Lives,
couldn't expect those fucking white boys to
let me watch *una telenovela, cono.*

I didn't feel too bad. My fucking body. I
could give birth in my sleep, *carajo.* I could
have a baby through my nose! I was so
good at having *niños,* fuck me, I really
couldn't hardly feel him being born.
Sixteen friggin' children! *Cono!* And no
twins! You try it! That's gotta be a world's
record! Somebody gotta look that up in a
book of something. Get me a door prize of
some kind! Sixteen little motherfuckers!

No, I love them, I do, I love every fucking
hair on their little fucking heads. Some of
my girls, bless them, they saved my life,
Dios mio. They do a lotta work.

Now another baby! My body! I look like a
hippopotamus! My skin don't even feel like
skin no more.

So where is he? *Donde esta esse maricón?*
Not here, at his wife's side, not next to the
mother of his sixteen little people, holding
her hand, bringing her ice cubes and shit!
Just like him, Fernando always found an
excuse to miss the birth of his babies.
Sixteen kids and he ain't neer seen one of
the little motherfuckers being born, *carajo.*
Que barbaridad!

So the baby was sleeping. I was resting.
My husband was missing in action. And
I'm mellow and the phone rang. I said,
"What?" No answer. I said, "Who the fuck
is this already?" *Cono!*

So then she answers. She only says one
thing, one sentence. "Well," she says, "you
had his baby last night, but I fucked him."
Click!

Man, I slammed that fucking telephone so
hard! I almost broke my fucking hand!
That bitch! That cheap fucking *hija de la
puñeta! Me cago en tu madre!* She called
me to tell me that. "You had his baby last
night but I fucked him." *Mira que cosa mas*
fucked up! *That's* where that *maricón* was
last night. With his girlfriend and she calls
me to tell me about it! What a class act,
huh? *Cono!*

The day passed okay after that. After I
settled down.

Then the phone rang again. It was my
daughter Lizbeth, the oldest, she's all
hysterical, I can't understand her—"*Que te
pasa, muchacha? Que te pasa?*" She can't

settle down and passes the phone to Julian,
my oldest boy, *y Julian esta llorando
tambien. Ahora me pongo nerviosa.* "*Que
paso, carajo,* what's up with you?" Julian
me dice, "Papi's been hit by a car, Mami."

I don't breathe for a minute. I don't even
think.

Julian goes, "He was walking from a friend's
house." A friend! From that bitch's house,
essa demonia! *"Tu Papa se murio?"* I ask.
"No. But they think he's gonna be
paralyzed, Mami." "Paralyzed where?" I
ask. "Paralyzed from the waist down," he
says. Fernando paralyzed from the waist
down . . .

Julian can't talk. He was crying too hard.
Surprise. I thought Julian hated his father.
Fernando was ruthless with his children
and he gave his worst punishments to
Lizbeth and Julian. Maybe they were
crying from happiness.

KRISTINE NIELSEN

I always came out Wednesday night to drop
my garbage on the curb.
I lived in a quiet neighborhood, mixed, you
know? Basic Seattle.

Neighbors were Chinese—a doctor and
his wife, a guidance counselor. Two
children.

The wife—
she was a very polite woman, very civil.
She wasn't very tall.
She had small shoulders.

Her hair was short and she had a quick,
gasping laugh that made her sound startled
and alert.

I didn't know a lot about psychiatry.
Or how the mind works.
I didn't dream much.
But I studied sounds.

Sounds were my source of knowledge of
people. Especially laughs.
I could gauge intelligence levels from a
good laugh.
I could analyze prejudices, weaknesses,
fears, desires,
from any kind of laugh, from any kind of
person.

God, if you laughed, I could tell you a little
about yourself.
Tell you what kind of day you're having.

God's not laughing today.

Anyway, her laugh was a rich tapestry for
me.

I heard her anxieties in her laughter.
I heard the years of stress.
I heard her husband's coldness and the iron
grip he had on her fate.
I heard her disappointments—
the petty racist remarks she'd hear nearly
each day at school where she worked.
I heard her lamentations in her laugh:
the job is too hard.
she's afraid her children will change,
the neighborhood is getting worse—
this and more were in the sixteenth notes
of her laughter,

the fractured melodies I heard
as clear as symphonies
from the open door of my bedroom,
far from hers,
across the street:
whole light-years and a lifetime away.

ALENE DAWSON

My son had his first day of public school Monday.
We had him in a private school in Van Nuys
but it was a little too far away for us,
too expensive, and he'd come home all sad,
saying, "How come there are no
brown faces in my school, Mom?"
So we finally got him into a magnet in Echo Park
—prestigious—
and there was an assembly Monday
and on the stage the principal got up
to talk to the new students and said,
"Okay kids, now don't you be bringing in
no guns to school in your backpacks!
Hear that, children?
I want no guns, no knives,
no chains in your lockers
or in your backpacks
or on your person."
This is the principal!
This is a magnet school in the humanities!
And she says,
"Stay close to the school,
don't wander away from campus.
There have been drive-bys in this area
so don't leave the school grounds!"
I'm thinking, oh my God!
It's getting out of control.
We're at war.

Citizens killing citizens.
We don't need the government to bomb the city.
We do it to ourselves,
taking the knife to cut open the throats
of our own children,
and then when we're out of hand,
when we're too good at that,
the police are brought in,
like an occupying army, you know,
jackboots all polished up,
hardware all glistening,
big robocop shoulders,
nightsticks ripping open the heads
of our little boys, it makes me crazy.
'Cause you know, it's all their fault!
The economy bad?
It's the black kids!
Air pollution?
The black kids did it!
The dollar down against the yen?
You know who to blame! God!
Made me want to take a rock
and hurl it at some politician,
some bozo running for Mayor,
any of those quicktongued hypocrites
assigned to protect the citizens,
'cause, no, I didn't feel protected,
I felt *exposed*, all opened up,
like some criminal was pointing
his Saturday Night Special at me
and every day I sensed those trigger fingers
out there and I was at the end
of their sights and they were just watching me,
waiting for the right split second
to send a little ounce of screaming steel
into the back of my brain!

God! God! It was not to be believed!
Being a woman in this city,
sometimes, oh my God,
I needed some help!
Especially when my boy went
out that door, you know?
And my imagination has created his killer,
some sweating overanxious rookie cop,
too afraid to piss straight,
slamming into my child at the wrong time,
in the wrong place, 'cause he's thinking,
"Of course, boy's in a gang, it's natural,
they run in packs,
those boys up to no good, you bet.
But what'd you expect?
It's a genetic thing with the black kids,
they're innately less intelligent,
but don't talk to me,
it's already *proven*,
there are *statistics*,
it's testable,
they're naturally more comfortable
with a .45 in their hands
than a volume of Faulkner."
So why the hell not cut the school budget?
Why not send them off
to some genocidal death in the penitentiary?
It's a waste of good American tax money
trying to educate these
unteachable black kids!
Jesus Christ! It's time to build
another super-prison,
you know, with a hundred nautilus machines
and hot tubs and libraries,
'cause, let's face it,
it's a whole lot nicer on the inside

than the corner of Florence and Normandie.
Going to jail is a good career move!
Oh God! If I wasn't a peaceful woman
I would've thrown rocks!

Trouble is, I don't think enough people
believe in the multiplicity of God.
Not enough people understand
God's great face has a nose
and eyes of a thousand shapes and sizes
and all of us, down to the last ugliest
and lowest person, we are all the living,
walking *text* of God.
Yes, the life story of God is
written into each one of us:
we are the pages in the book of God's mind.
And if we'd just take the time
we'd be able to read God
in each other's faces,
read the funny lines as well as the lines
of wisdom and healing—
because the Word of God
isn't written in the Bible, no,
the Word of God is written in your mirror
and on your brother's black face
and in your son's blue eyes.

My son. He's the sweetest thing . . .
actually he's a royal pain in the ass
95 percent of the time . . .
but for 5 sweet percents,
he's my angel of laughter and hope.
My mother is from Guyana.
I was trying to teach my son
a little bit about that heritage,
but it was hard, you know,
that culture's so deep

and I didn't know anything about it.
I told him about South Africa
but, you know, what's that mean?
It's not like the Lakers!
The Lakers you can get up for in the morning!
No, my son's not into Guyana or South Africa.
He's into being a boy.

RENÉ RIVERA

Bueno, I never really made it big as an
actor. I'm not ashamed to say that. I
worked.

The damn business. Competition killed
me. My skin color, my accent, my attitude,
my pride.

I could play a great drug addict. Watching
myself in dailies, I fucking scared myself.

I mugged, I stabbed, I cheated on women
who trusted me, I sold drugs to sixth-grade
inner-city youth. All for NBC.

A line here, five lines there, bit parts, a day
player.

Gangsters, hoodlums, angry spicks, pointy
black shoes. Drunks, losers, punks, washed-
up dreamers, casualties, broken, futureless,
fractured men, always dangerous. Men you
couldn't trust.

I played a dozen rapists with names like
Miguel, Angel, Pedro, José, Juan, Miguel—
did I say Miguel? In one picture alone, I
raped my best friend's wife, my daughter
(twice), a little girl who lived in the
building, white women of every kind.

On prime time, I delivered pizza, I delivered
packages in Manhattan, I snaked clogged
toilets, I was a handyman, a mechanic, a
grape picker, every kind of janitor in every
kind of building, a super super, a petty drug
pusher, a drug kingpin—I've been stabbed
in the heart, tortured, poisoned, raped by
convicts, overdosed eleven times, killed in
the electric chair, hit by a subway train,
eaten alive by ghetto rats, shot by the cops
so often I lost count. I hung myself.

In war pictures I was always the coward. In
prison pictures I was always the traitor who
ratted on his buddies. In westerns I was
the illiterate cook the Indians scalped in the
first reel. I've been a buffoon, an asshole, a
scapegoat, a pretender, a liar, a misfit.
Children and women cheered when I died.
Strangers on the street spit at me. And
what great dialogue I had: "Take that
bitch!" And "I don't care if you kill me,
Sarge, 'cause I'm going straight to hell
anyway!" And "Taste my blade, *cabrón!*"
Eat your heart out, Lorca!

In horror pictures, I was the asshole who
walked into the dark room when the whole
audience was going: "Don't go in there,
asshole!"

I had eleven agents. Fourteen managers.
Countless addresses. I was an angry young
actor, then I swallowed anger, tried to
mellow out, work with the system, I turned
down nothing, I kissed so many asses, I
walked the walk, worked out, stopped
smoking, laid off the nose candy, went to

the right places, shook hands, always
looked sharp anytime of the day or night,
worked on my teeth, got my tattoos burned
off, left my attitude, *mira,* at the door, made
follow-up calls, wrote notes thanking racist
morons for treating me like a bag of come. I
turned anger into ambition. I watched
young studs doing roles I would never get.

Then I got sick.

Now understand me. I was a middle-aged
Latino actor. I was married very young. I
had two daughters and their mother
couldn't stand my guts and she took the
two girls away and moved to Mexico. I
said, "The hell with it," and went out west.
Concentrated on the subtleties of playing
junkies. I had a fantastic body and once or
twice, in the beginning, they called me in to
read for Latin stud roles, usually pimps, but
twice a male prostitute, a gigolo.

So you understand—I'm in town—
separated from the mother of my girls—
I'm the Latin stud prospect of the moment—
I'm free to sleep with whoever I want—
but I can't come out. I come out to nobody.
Nobody in the business.

I go where I had to go. I do what I have to
do. I don't live with nobody for a long time.
I get a fake girlfriend for a little while. I
have sex in secret. Nobody knows.

But I get sick anyway. I get it. I fight
knowing it, but I get it. And I don't tell
nobody.

I get safer. I meet a man. I fall in love.
We're "roommates" now. He's decent and
pure and a lot younger than me and I tell
him, "Babe, you're taking some chances"
and he's the home I never had, the island
where I find some peace, the wall that
surrounds and protects me.

But, you know, I used to drink a lot. And
my liver is like melted dogshit. It's a major
casualty now that I'm bad sick.

Then I meet a young Latino writer, up and
coming, he's all skinny so I nickname him
Flaco and this young man casts me in a role
that's like a Latino King Lear, big, the man
is big, big appetite, big balls, big language,
evil but funny! I never had a part like this
and I had told myself, "No plays; I'm only
concentrating on the film and TV, and no
going out of town!" But this role is the real
thing and I say, "Screw it, I'm taking this
sucker by the balls and I'm going to be
great and show those racist morons what I
can really do!"

And I do the play out of town and Flaco and
me, we become friends. He gives me hope.
He never knows the truth about me but I'm
getting sicker and sicker. My liver, my
blood.

I disappear from sight for a year and a half:
Flaco doesn't know a thing. I make sure
nobody knows.

But one day everything falls apart and I'm
in the hospital and suddenly the word is on

the street: "René's got it. René's sick bad."
And I'm in a crappy-ass hospital in
Hollywood 'cause I'm broke. I didn't want
anyone to visit me but they visit and
eventually even Flaco visits me toward the
end, when I'm bad, really bad and people
are getting emergency phone calls saying,
"You better see René now because you may
never see him again."

And one night I'm barely conscious and
Flaco comes to visit me. And I know he's
there even though I can't talk or open my
eyes. My roommate is there and he's trying
to make me laugh. He's stroking my face,
going, "I know you can hear me René. I
know you want to smile. Give me a smile,
René, come on, I know you can do it,
corazoncito." And I smile.

And Flaco's standing there trying to talk to
me and I don't want him to see me like this.
I want him to remember like I was in his
play, big, big appetite, big language, evil but
funny.

Then one of those pathetic excuses for a
doctor comes in and realizes I'm not getting
any nourishment because the tube they got
running from my arm down to my heart is
collapsed and he's got to pull it out again
and reinsert a new tube that's not
collapsed. So he pulls it out and he's sitting
at my bedside and I'm totally unconscious
and Flaco is there watching all this and the
doctor is trying to insert a new tube in my
veins. And the doctor can't get the tube

back in my vein again and I'm bleeding all
over the place and I can hear that Flaco and
my roommate have stopped talking and I
know they're just watching this and the
doctor is making his pathetic excuses to
Flaco and my roommate and finally I'm so
damn mad, I try to use all my strength to
make a fist and I try to punch the doctor in
the face and I'm grimacing and everything
in my body wants to hurt this man and I
can make my arm move and I take a shot at
him and my fist is shaking like the DTs and
he's still making his excuses and I try three
times to hit him and he tells Flaco he can't
get this tube inside me if I keep trying to
punch him like this and asks Flaco to hold
me down, and I'm so damn mad, and Flaco
grabs my left hand and holds it down and
I'm struggling against him and my mind is
going, "Let me go, let me hit him, let me
keep some dignity, what are you doing here
anyway, this isn't for you, I'm not a damn
show, why don't all of you just leave me
alone?" and another voice in my brain is
going, "Don't get no blood on you, that
damn doctor's got twenty layers of plastic
but you don't have nothing, let go of me
before I bleed on you."

I'm so weak Flaco pushes my arm down so
easy.

He's close to my ear and I can hear him
breathing. His hands are strong. It's
incredible to feel strong skin again, alive
blood, a feverless body, strong. I'm nothing
against that strength and I almost have to

laugh the idea of me punching the doctor, I
almost have to laugh.

KIERSTEN VAN HORNE

The first time someone else's tongue enters
your mouth.

The first time a child trusts you to carry
them to the next room.

The first time you drive safely from
Westfield, Massachusetts to San Diego with
someone you're in love with.

The first time you watch birth.

The first lines of *Paradise Lost*.

The first time you make a decisive three-
point shot in a game that really counts.

The first time you get the dog to shit outside.

The first time you can read "I love you" in a
lover's eyes.

The first time you sleep in after fucking all
night long.

The first family reunion without homicidal
fantasies.

The first love letter.

The first serious talk about love with your
child.

The first time you contemplate suicide and
change your mind.

The first hangover.

The first arrest.

The first acquittal.

The first epiphany.

The first time you hear Lorca in Spanish.

The first real friendship with a person of another race.

The first gray hair.

The first time you see Picasso's *Guernica*.

The first time you visit your birthplace.

The first time you hear Lightnin' Hopkins.

The first visible comet.

The first time you feel attractive and someone calls you "angel."

The first experience with something remotely like a God.

The first recovery after a serious illness.

The first beer with your father.

The first time therapy makes sense.

The first birthday of your firstborn.

The first time you can't walk and your lover carries you to the next room.

The first foul ball you catch in Fenway Park.

The first time you stand alone and you're scared to death and you don't change your position.

The first time you're convinced of your mortality and you laugh.

The first sunrise after the first death of a
parent.

The first time you forgive the unforgivable.

The first time you see the earth from space.

The first time it is truly obvious that it was
better that you had lived, at this time, in
this world.

The first time you decide every moment of
your life should be a work of art.

The first time you die and you breathe
again and you speak to the living.

The first time you realize that it all just
might have been okay.

(*The people in the space look up at the silent sky around them.*

They wait.

No revelations come to them. No answers. No giant bolts of lightning.

Just a slow fade to black.)

END OF PLAY

THREE VIEWINGS

Jeffrey Hatcher

For PEH and CVH

Three Viewings was produced by Manhattan Theatre Club (Lynne Meadow, Artistic Director; Barry Grove, Managing Director), in New York City, on March 14, 1995. It was directed by Mary B. Robinson; the set design was by James Noone; the costume design was by Michael Krass; the lighting design was by Pat Dignan; the sound design was by Bruce Ellman; and the production stage manager was Tom Aberger. The cast was as follows:

EMIL	Buck Henry
MAC	Margaret Whitton
VIRGINIA	Penny Fuller

Three Viewings was first developed by Illusion Theater (Michael Robins and Bonnie Morris, Producing Directors), in Minneapolis, Minnesota, in September 1994. It consists of three connected monologues, written for three actors. Author's notes appear at the end of the script.

CHARACTERS

TELL-TALE
EMIL: A middle-aged man in a conservative suit.

THE THIEF OF TEARS
MAC: A woman in her thirties or forties dressed in black and wearing many sparkling rings.

THIRTEEN THINGS ABOUT ED CARPOLOTTI
VIRGINIA: A woman in her fifties or sixties with a cigarette and lighter.

TIME

Now.

PLACE

A funeral parlor in a small midwestern town.

Tell-Tale

A man, EMIL, *stands downstage in the light. Middle-aged. A conservative charcoal suit and dark tie. His jacket is buttoned.*

Behind him are three floral arrangements with flowers in deep reds and purples.

EMIL *stares out front, slightly off to the side.*

EMIL

(*Lightly—a hushed chant*)

> I love you.
> I love you.
> I love you.
> I love you.
> I love you.
> I love you.
> I love you.
> I love you.
> I love yo—

(*He abruptly snaps his face forward.*)

> She-almost-saw-me! (*A moment to steal a glance back at "her."
> Beat. He breathes a sigh of relief.*)
>   Wheww! That was a close one. Real heart-stopper. The
> beat coming out of my shirt like a bomb about to explode.

Bump-bum! *Bump*-bum! *Bump*-bum! (*He looks off to the side again.*)

This is all getting much more difficult. (*Back to front.*)

I started with just one.

"I love you."

Very quiet, very small. But audible.

"*I love you.*"

Said to the back of her head as she moved through the room. Holding hands. Smiling. Brushing back a tear. If she turns around in the middle of "I love you," I thought, she'll catch me. She'll catch me and she'll hear, and she'll see, and she'll know. She'll catch me, and I'll be happy to be caught. But one "I love you" wasn't really enough. One "I love you" was too . . . subtle. So I advanced to two.

"I love you.

I love you."

Still she didn't turn in time. I went to three.

"I love you.

I love you.

I love you."

Nothing. Now I'm up to *nine*. And this is the first time she's almost seen me say it. What would I have done if she had? It's been nine times since the first, at Carl Grunwald's funeral. Tessie in a red jacket—somewhat inappropriate, admittedly, but it stands out and that's the point—in a red jacket moving through the room, looking for her flowers, handing out her card. I was standing next to the casket, doing what we funeral directors do, when it struck me. All the years I'd known her. Same town, same people, how we're always flung together. Then, suddenly, she's in my mind all the time. First thought at morning, last thought at night. I watched her, me standing next to Carl, Tessie giving her real estate card to Ruth Grunwald. Tessie never presses her card; they always ask, she doesn't push; but they do go home with her card every time. I looked at her in her red jacket and her black hair and her blue eyes and white skin and said:

"I love you."

Even Carl could have heard me. But Tessie didn't. Tessie came up to me.

"Carl looks good," she murmured.

"Thanks. He'd lost a lot of weight in the hospital. Six weeks. I think we brought him back to snuff."

Tessie smiles. Margaret-Mary Walsh approaches the casket, and we turn, Tessie and I turn to face Margaret-Mary, together, at the casket, both of us greeting her. Like a couple. The most natural thing in the world. (*He stares off at "her."*)

It's been nine times now. Next time I'll have to go up to ten. (*Blackout. Lights come up.* EMIL *faces out front.*)

Nettie James died yesterday. She was 103. Been on the verge of death for twenty-eight years. Coal money. Very rich. Terrible woman. The *Herald-Star* made up a headline for her obituary that read "Nettie James FINALLY Dies. Civic And Social Leader Succumbs After A Lifetime of Condescension And Bullying." They didn't print it. It's a big affair. Private service. I got Tessie in. Not that the James family is going to sell the house on Norton Place let alone use Tessie's real estate company, but it's good for Tessie to be seen, and I got her on the list. She's in the visitation room. Nettie James looks very small in her casket. She was tissue paper and cobwebs these last few . . . decades. I'm up to twelve.

I love you.

I love you.

I love you.

I love you.

I love you.

I love you.

I love you.

I love you.

She never turns. Admittedly, I tend to start my chant when she's deep in conversation with someone—Margaret-Mary

Walsh, Bob O'Klock, Art Wise—so there's little *chance* of
her suddenly turning to look at *me*. Wouldn't it be wonderful if she suddenly turned to look at me? What if I could
catch her eyes, suddenly turning to look at me? A man can
always feel a woman's irises clicking in her head when she
turns to steal a glance at him. He can feel it in his peripheral
vision. A little blue and white whip—at you and back. Look
back at her, and the blue whips away. If I could feel that . . .
then I'd know. There's nothing more obvious in life than
one person looking longingly at another—unless it's a person desperately trying *not* to look at all.

I love you.

I love you.

I love you.

I love you.

I hate her name. Tessie. Not Teresa, not Tess—Tessie.
She used to be married. Marvin Vankirk. He's at Winters-
ville High, teaches math. "Expectations plus Marvin equals
reality." They're still friendly. Marvin remarried. Estelle
Calabria. Tessie got her real estate license after the divorce.
Got the idea when Johnny Criss and Joe Bethel and Dale
Featheringham and the rest of the 10 percenters all came
to her mother's funeral. Now Tessie's part of the pack. But
she's different. Maybe I just *think* she's different. (*Beat. He
thinks.*)

No, she's different.

I love you.

I love you.

We go into the service. The Reverend Dr. James A. Zimbro III officiating. I won't say Jim Zimbro's an *unimaginative*
minister, but he *is* known in the trade as "The Rev. Dr.
INSERT DECEASED'S NAME HERE." He begins.

"The love that lasts . . ."

My mind withdraws to other places. It's a depressed real
estate market. That's why Criss, Bethel, the whole bunch
swoop down so. It's harder for Tessie, but she's talented and
she has more than promise. I know. The way she can describe

a house . . . I've almost bought four myself. She's on com-
mission, and it's getting tight. A slow season. She tells me
about wanting to travel, to get away. Mexico. The Berkshires. Spain. I tell her how difficult it is for *me* to get away:
"No slow season."

She laughs. *Her laugh.* Her smile. "Her flashing eyes, her
floating hair."

She has not had an easy life. Father was an alcoholic—
mother spent twelve years dying in the state hospital—the
divorce. And she wears a pacemaker, Tessie—something con-
genital—to regulate her heart.

I love you.

I love you.

I love you.

I have to help her. I will find a way to help her. (*Blackout.*
Lights come up.)

I have started to give Tessie advance word of imminent
deaths. Sometimes I get a warning. Hospital. Police. "A
friend in power." Last week Bill Goodpastor tells me his
wife Marge has a brain tumor, Bill thinks she may not last
the week. Marge looked so old last time she came here. And
Bill, Bill still looks like Paul Newman on sheep-gland injec-
tions. Marge is dying, the house is too big, Bill told me, I
told Tessie.

Unethical? Maybe. It's a slippery slope, but passion is a
bracing lubricant.

I love you.

I love you.

I love you.

I'm up to seventeen now. I'm starting to think she *knows*
I'm saying it, and that's why she *doesn't* turn. I have considered driving past her house at night. The light in the window, the nose pressed against the pane. But I have restrained
myself. That way leads to madness, the padded cell, the perch
in the book depository window. I am not like that. Why
don't I just tell her? What's the worst that could happen?

Mockery. Humiliation. A howl of derision followed by twenty years of averted glances. There should be a kind of safety net for these moments. A magic "shroud" you could use. You go up to the woman, you say:

"I've been meaning to tell you: I love you."

If she says,

"I love you, too,"

great, fantastic, everybody goes to the prom. If she gets red in the face, takes your hand, and says:

"That's *so* flattering, you're *such a friend*,"

then you say,

"Excuse me, but I have to lower the magic shroud now."

And she forgets everything said to her in the last thirty seconds.

"You're such a friend."

A knife in the heart. Anyway, Marge Goodpastor died yesterday. Bill called from his Jaguar. Tessie came early to the visitation—I wanted to introduce her to Bill before the rush and the cremation. I am making this vow: If my "I love you" gambit does not prove fruitful, I will take drastic action. I will tell her my true feelings before the year is out. Tomorrow is Thanksgiving. Jim Zimbro is talking about "the love that lasts." I have thirty-five days. (*Lights fade. Lights come up. Smiles.*)

Tessie said "I hate you" today, and I think there's hope! At the Green Mill. We bumped into each other outside the bank, Christmas shopping. I offered lunch. She said she had to meet Bill Goodpastor to show his house.

"BUT,"

she says . . . and I quote her . . .

"OH—WHAT THE HELL—*LET'S*—*HAVE*—*LUNCH.*" (*Big proud grin and giggle.*)

What do you think of *that!* We were talking about these last few "referrals" I've made her. She sold three houses. Good commissions. She's breathing a little easier now, and she wanted to take *me* to lunch. I told her,

"You know, I can't keep slipping you these tips forever,

we're gonna run out, I'll have to start killing them myself."
(*He laughs, mock-sinister.*)

HEH-HEH-HEH. She laughed. She said,
"You're terrible, I hate you!"

And she *slapped* me! Just my lower arm, across the table,
next to the coffee cup. Her fingers brushed my wrist, near
my watch, skin to skin. I almost jumped. Red face. Adrena-
line. Dizziness. Vertigo. Just a touch on my wrist. This has
happened to me before. This *sort* of thing. It goes away. I let
it run its course. Lasts a few weeks. This one is in its eleventh
month. Is it painful? It hurts . . . but not like hell. I'd rather
have this particular pain than . . . its particular absence. "Desire
plus denial equals . . ." Well, I'm not a Catholic—so I don't
know what the hell it equals. It has gone on too long though.
Fury or humiliation, I will tell her by December 31st. New
Year's Eve. But I wish she'd *guess* it first. I wish she'd tell *me*.
Read my mind, read my lips. Maybe I'll start using code.
Writing "I love you" in the floral tributes or underneath the
lids of the caskets. Cryptography in the swirls of a dead person's hair. "Find the Nina." Suddenly—out of nowhere—
she asks me a question.

"Do you know when you're in love?"

My heart has stopped.

"What?"

"I *said*," she says, "do you know when you're in love."

"Oh yes."

"How?"

I'm stalling for time. I'm trying to think, but I'm on fire,
my brain is swimming, the floor tilts, a descent into mael-
strom. Finally, I manage—a cracked voice at the bottom of
my shoes.

"You always know. Knowing isn't the point. The point is
action. The point is speaking. That kind of action, that kind
of courage . . ."

I'm swirling in her eyes, her hair. She is smart, she is
bright, she has depth and breadth and the world is lit by
lightning!

"Why do you ask?" I ask.

She doesn't smile. She looks at me. Three seconds, eye to eye. One. I love you. Two. I love you. Three. I love you. I'm shouting the words in my mind, *but my lips are sealed,* surely she can hear me, PLEASE, GOD, LET HER HEAR ME! She breaks her stare.

"Never mind."

She'll pay the check, I'll leave the tip. Exiting, I place my hand under her elbow. She allows it. She does not comment. Outside, she kisses me good-bye. Cheek. Another detonation to the skin. My heart is racing. She walks away. The last I see of her is a slip on a patch of ice. Then she rights herself, and turns the corner. Today is December 7th. A date that will live in infamy. I have twenty-four more shopping days. (*Blackout. Lights come up. Tense and angry.*)

Ed Carpolotti died, and Tessie didn't come to the funeral. It was a *three-day affair!* I'd left a message on her machine telling her about Ed. Just the usual. But there was no reply. A day passes. I call her again, get her machine, leave another message. No reply. Two days more, the day of the burial, December 21st, the longest day of the year. I tell Jim Zimbro:

"We should go another day, not everyone who would want to see Ed has had the chance."

Jim looks at me like I'm nuts.

"You want to *extend* it?"

"What about Art Wise," I sputter. "And Johnny Criss. And Joe Bethel and Dale Featheringham and Bill Goodpastor . . ."

"Bill's in Florida," says Jim. "He went down Friday. He and Tessie."

Bump-bum . . . bump-bum . . . bump-bum . . . bump-bum . . . I *slam* down the coffin lid!

"Let's get this goddamn show on the road!"

I *propel* Ed Carpolotti into the service room, the coffin cart banging into the door frame as I take the turn on two wheels! My heart is *pounding!* Had she been seeing him

long? Was it *him* she was talking about at the Green Mill?
Did I *miss* something? Was I *confused*? Was there a *code* she
was using? Had she been saying "I LOVE YOU" TO *ME*
AND I JUST WASN'T LISTENING? DOES SHE HAVE
ANY INKLING AT *ALL*? *AM I A FOOL!* Blood is crashing against the rocks in my ears! *BUMP-BUM! BUMP-
BUM! BUMP-BUM! Will someone not stop this ridiculous
heartbeat! Surely, everyone will hear it! Surely everyone in the room
can HEAR IT!!! (He has reached an explosive crescendo. He finally
stops, looks out, fearing he's been caught. His voice is a hushed rasp.)*

But they do not turn, they do not hear, they do not see.
I am not caught. Afterwards, Margaret-Mary Walsh takes
me aside and tells me she has never been so moved by a
service. The woman has always been good and kind, one of
my "regulars." So I do not hit her. (*Blackout. Lights come up.*)

I was on a bus once in a large city and sitting next to
me was a young man. Across from the man was a beautiful
woman. They were making eye contact. Look at him, look
away—look at her, look away. The tension was enormous.
We all got off at the same stop, and as we stepped onto the
sidewalk, the young man approached the woman and said,

"I noticed you on the bus."

What courage that man had! What faith and daring! He
had seen another face on this planet and thought to himself,

"*I* will not slink into the night regretting the lost opportunities, the might-have-beens. *I* will not die a thousand coward's deaths! I will gather every drop of strength I have! This
will change my life!"

"I NOTICED YOU ON THE BUS!"

And the woman said, "So?" and walked away.

He will always be my hero. (*Beat.*)

The hospital called me at 11:22. An accident on the drive
from the airport. Icy roads after Christmas, a slippery slope,
a Jaguar over the hill. Bill Goodpastor is dead. So is his passenger. (*Pause.*)

As Tessie's family is gone . . . Marvin Vankirk will make the funeral arrangements. Marvin calls me after midnight. Will I take care of her personally? Not one of the assistants, or pop who still comes in occasionally. Me.

"You were such a friend of Terri's."

Terri. Huh.

They bring her in the next afternoon. It's the law, when there has been no previous illness or attending physician at the time of death, to conduct an autopsy on a body. Which means . . . that . . . certain surgical procedures have already been completed. I ask pop to help me in the prep room. I don't want to be alone. He hobbles down, his cane, his shake. I notice her hair. Gray at the roots. Was she letting it grow out? Or did she just not have the chance to color it? I attach the machine, I prepare the instruments—needles, tubes. Her partial plate out, I smooth the crow's-feet around her eyes. I do . . . what we do . . . to her eyes, her lips. What we do is . . . we seal them. (*Pause.*) The funeral is crowded. Johnny Criss is there and Joe Bethel and Dale Featheringham. And Reverend Zimbro, Mr. Fill in the Blank. Zimbro asks Marvin if there is anything he should add to the service. I open my mouth:

"Say something about Mexico, the Berkshires, and Spain."

I've spoken too loudly. Heads have turned. Across the room I see my wife—(*He looks out front.*) Oh yes. Marvin tells us it was Terri . . . 's wish to be cremated.

"Her ashes will be scattered over Mexico," says Marvin, solemnly . . . whenever Marvin and Estelle save up the money to have a "real vacation." We do the final viewing. The final service. The casket is closed. And by three o'clock that afternoon, Teresa is gone. Little-known facts: Some things don't burn in a crematorium. Diamonds. Some metals. Heavier bones. Some things you *can't* burn. Like pacemakers. The heat makes them explode. You can damage the inside of the chamber. So it's important to remove them before you . . . set fire to the body. (*He holds up a small transistor-sized object.*)

I found this in the preparation room. I really should have given it back to . . . someone else. (*He holds it up to his ear.*)

It keeps on ticking. Tonight is New Year's Eve. My wife is upstairs in bed early, and there aren't any customers in the viewing rooms. For the first time in memory . . . we are entirely empty. (*He holds the pacemaker and looks off at "her."*)

Turn around. Turn around. Look at me, sweetie. Please look at me this time. I'll say it again. I'll say it a thousand times until you turn around and catch me. I love you—one I love you—two . . . (*Lights fade to black.*)

THE END

The Thief of Tears

Lights up on MAC, *an attractive woman between the ages of thirty-five and forty-five. Mac wears black. Lots of sparkling rings on her fingers. Behind her are three floral arrangements—white poinsettias.*

MAC

I've been stealing jewelry off corpses for years, Grandma'll be a fuckin' cinch. (*Beat.*)

Let me go back. The phone call of the dead always comes between midnight and 1:00 AM. Before midnight, the call could be anyone for any reason. After one, it's a wrong number dialed in Spain. But if the call comes in *between* midnight and one, the news is a Houseboat on the River Styx and no mistake, Charlie. When I get back to my apartment from the Viper Room, the electronic guy on the answering machine says 12:48. It's Donald's voice.

"Heigh-ho, Mac, father this end. We're at the Philadelphia house. Call us collect ASAP. Hope A-OK your end. Ten-four."

My father never says "good-bye." He says "ten-four" or "A-OK." It's a superstition. If he says "good-bye" he knows he'll die soon in a fiery plane crash. I look at the clock near the bed. Four thirty-six AM. If it's four thirty in Los Angeles that means it's seven thirty in America. They'll be up now in Philadelphia—which is unfortunate because it means my call will not wake them. I pour a drink—vodka—as it's morning. And I dial. Donald picks up.

"It's Nettie," he says. "She died last night. At Norton Place. We're driving down. Are you able to get a flight to Pittsburgh? Do you need anything?"

"Yes," I say, "I can get a flight out. And no, I don't need anything." ("Anything," in our family, means money.)

"Roger, then," says Donald. "Over and out."

We hang up. She's dead. My grandmother, Nettie James, is dead. This is my moment. My destiny has called me. I pour another vodka and rifle through a shoebox in the closet to find the cracked black-and-white photograph I know is there. This photo goes back *with* me. I look at the figure passed out on the bed. Someone in black named Raymond or Charlotte or . . . Lassie. That *won't* go back with me. I should call US Air to see if I can get a flight at nine. But first I look in my wallet. A twenty and three ones. The bank account is overdrawn, and all my plastic is strictly Dead Zone. I need money for a plane ticket and a rental car and three days in the worst place on earth. I will have to work! The *L.A. Times* is delivered early, so I go for the door and head straight to Section D—Rosalind Marquardt. Eighty-three. Tarzana. (*Thinks.*)

No—Elizabeth Quilty. Sixty-nine. West Hollywood. Nup—Miriam Cass. Eighty-six. *Beverly Hills.* Miriam Cass. Survived by her husband, Maurice. Viewing at nine. So I'll get a later flight. By nine o'clock I'm at the funeral home on Sunset Boulevard, my bags in the back of the taxi I've asked to wait. I dawdle until a crowd has formed. A field of blue hair and blue stoles. Maurice must be the old blind guy in the 1964 Savile Row suit. I pay my respects to Maurice, my condolences, how I met Miriam—*MeMee, yes*—on the trip to, to—*Ceylon, exactly!* How MeMee spoke of Maurice—yes, *while* he was sick in their stateroom. I'll just say good-bye. And then there I am in the line, two people away from the— (*Snaps fingers.*)

Score—open casket! I inhale. Swallow. Somehow in this business, it's always the first time. I close my eyes, bite my lips, and the tears well up. I bend over to kiss Miriam good-bye, noting that she is absolutely *encrusted.* Two pecks on the corpse—on either side of the face, in the continental manner. When I pull back, I have my mouth firmly shut—a supreme effort not to lose control of my emotions. Once I'm in the cab I open my mouth and take out the earrings. Ladies and gentlemen, Jack Rubies. My fence will give me three thousand for them, which is enough for an open-end return ticket, a good rental car, and plenty of scratch until I get mine from Nettie James! (*Pause.*)

Four hours later, on the plane over the tundra, a glass of champagne stapled to my palm. Thomas Wolfe once wrote: "You can't go home again." (*Beat.*)

Thomas Wolfe was a putz, of *course* you can go home again, they *make* you go home, *all the time—endlessly!* But this time is different. I'm going to *get* something from *this* trip. High over Ohio, I close my eyes and imagine I'm on *The Charlie Rose Show.* The dark background, the Persian carpet, the good wood. Jodie Foster has just left, and Gore Vidal is in the wings. Charlie turns his cleft to me.

"How'd ya' get your *start* in—well, I guess we'd *have* to call it—heck . . . *corpse-robbing,* right?"

"Right you are, Charlie. *Well,* it was like this, you big, dumb handsome guy they make read books: I had just moved from Stockbridge to L.A., I was broke, not acting. A friend of mine died, a bad death. I hadn't been to a funeral in a long time, and they'd put me in charge of accessorizing him for the viewing, but his wrists were so small, his watch wouldn't fit, so I put it in my purse for later. It wasn't until three days after the funeral that I realized I still had the watch. I was gonna give it back . . . but it was a Rolex in a rough week. And anyway give it back to whom? So I rationalized keeping the watch . . . then selling it . . . then finding ways to do it again. It's kept me in high five figures for eight years now. Never caught, knock on cherry wood or knotty pine. I even know some other people in the business now. We recognize each other at funerals. Tricks of the trade stuff: who's using lubricant, pliers, wire cutters. I saw a chick with a magnet once, she was a fuckin' trip, man. Some jobs are dicier than others, of course. I got a gold tooth once. Don't ask."

"But gosh," says Mr. Rose, "is there anything you *won't* steal?"

"Sure. A wedding ring. A friendship ring. A decoder ring. There are limits."

"But why do you do it? What do you want?"

"Want? The touch of something that has touched another. Bring on Gore Vidal, pal. Ask *him* what *he* wants."

At Pittsburgh I rent a BMW, and an hour out of the airport—past steel mills, past strip mines, past the same farm for fifty miles—I arrive over the river and through the woods to grandmother's funeral. Inside the parlor, the first viewing has begun. My parents, Donald and Dorothy, stand at the first position nearest the head of the casket, receiving the dukes and barons of the town. In the far corner sits my mother's sister, Aunt Teeta, pleasant, smiling, sweet, an idiot. At the rear near the exit is her only son Gerald and my brother, St. David, the Perfect. I look out on a jungle of white poinsettias (it's gotten out that Nettie *loved* white poinsettias). It looks like we're burying her on the set of *Dr. Zhivago*. I squint below a snowy plant and there I see one lone figure. It's Josephine, Nettie's housekeeper on Norton Place. She was my grandmother's H. R. Haldeman.

"You know me, Josephine?"

She nods.

"You remember me, Josephine?"

She does.

"You're the bipolar, bisexual drug addict."

Donald and Dorothy give an imperceptible glance in my direction. It's actually a glare. It wouldn't look like a glare to anyone else, but to a James, it's a glare. Kind of like how only dogs can hear certain sounds. My brother David has suddenly sidled up to me. I can smell the Pepto-Bismol on his breath.

"After the viewing, Mother and Father want to have a talk with us."

Then David slips back to his post near the flowers from something called the First Church of the Charismatic Assumption. I can sense tension in the room. They're all acting—well—they're acting as if someone has *died*. Nettie James was 103 years old. This funeral has been in rehearsal so long it's had replacement casts. But somehow the relaxed jocularity one associates with the death of a very old, very demanding, very rich harridan is entirely absent. I mouth to Josephine:

"What's going on?"

She smiles.

"There's a new will."

Minutes later the family is gathered in a spare viewing parlor where my father, Donald, is interrogating a young local attorney named Danny Spahr about how "it" could have happened.

"Five-point-two million dollars left to the First Church of the Charismatic Assumption? The Norton Place house and the Lake Cottage left to Charismatic Alternative Families, Inc.? My wife's mother left the entire family fortune to a bunch of crazed holy-roller devil-worshippers?"

Danny Spahr shrugs.

"I warned you to disconnect her Cable TV."

The will has been read. The money is gone. This they

will have to get used to. But I have not come for money. I have come for something else. Let me go back. In the black-and-white photograph I've brought with me from L.A. a beautifully coiffed woman in her sixties holds the hand of an equally beautifully coiffed five-year-old girl with red eyes from crying, only you can't see the red in black and white, but you can see the tears. It's 1963, and I'm *not* going to go to the beauty parlor. I'm screaming in the back of the big blue Packard, and my grandmother has decided to calm me down by taking me into the big department store, The Hub. She holds my hand, and when we enter, hundreds of shop clerks rush to greet us, bending, groveling, rubbing their hands. Mrs. Bordenkirker from the shoe department, Miss Carver from the dress department, Morton Lincoff from jewelry. They give her presents. Something especially important seems to come from Morton Lincoff. Something wrapped in a box. Nettie turns to me and says,

"You see? If you're nice to people, they'll give you things. Tell you what: you be a good girl today when you get your hair done, and Nettie'll *give* you what's in this box."

And she opens it. Inside is a beautiful tear-shaped ring. It seems to sparkle with every jewel in the planet. I've never seen such color, so many facets, such light. I will do *anything* to get this ring. So I *am* a good girl, and I *do* calm down, and I *get* my hair done. And when it's all over, and we're back at Norton Place, and Josephine is about to take our picture, I ask my grandmother,

"So where's my present?"

And Nettie says—

"Oh, that was just something I *said*. You can't always get what you *want*."

And the ring goes on her finger.

The family returns to the parlor where the second viewing has begun. There's a crowd around the casket so I decide to take a stroll through the competing parlors. I peer around, casing the joint, when a little old woman who seems to *live* at the funeral home—she has her own *chair*—comes up to me through the white forest. Her name is Margaret-Mary Walsh and she remembers me since I was, I dunno, an *embryo,* sperm with eyelashes. We trade inane nonsense for a while. I sound like a cake-mix lobotomy. Finally she remembers the missing piece in my puzzle:

"And how is your husband and family?"

Imperceptibly, I can feel David flinch, Teeta wince, Donald and Dorothy blush. But I am fine. I tell Margaret-Mary Walsh:

"I'm not married anymore. My husband never fixed the kitchen door."

This seems to satisfy her. The crowd around the coffin has gone on a coffee break, so I make a beeline for the casket. I peer in at my grandmother. A voice nearby murmurs:

"She looks good."

I nod. (She looks like Stalin.) Her hands are folded, touching, one over the other. She always wore the dinner ring on her right hand, aaannnd . . . that's the hand I cannot see. It's covered by the other one. My fingers itch to pick it up, turn it over . . . but I keep my cool.

"Just looking."

How am I going to find out if she's wearing that ring? Suddenly, Donald is at my side:

"Mac, we have a problem. Nettie's new will left instructions specifying certain pieces of jewelry she wanted to be buried with. The funeral home won't take responsibility for the pieces overnight. Their policy is to have the family do the *physical removal* from the body and keep the jewels at home until morning. Now, your mother is in no state to do it, nor is Aunt Teeta. Nor me. Nor your brother, he can't touch dead people."

(David is a surgeon, okay?)

"We'd like *you* to do it, Mac." (*Beat.*)

"Oh, I *couldn't.*"

"MAC: Your mother and I didn't stop you from going to

Los Angeles when you *should* have stayed in the hospital in Stockbridge. We didn't even stop you when you changed your first name from Jane to . . . McTeague. This is a family service we are requesting. One we expect to be performed. Unless you feel you are . . . *incapable*."

I look at my parents. "All *right*," I say, "Sure. I've been stealing jewelry off corpses for years, Grandma'll be a fuckin' cinch." (*She looks at the audience as if to say "This is where you came in."*)

I go to my grandmother. I remove the jewelry. I try to make it all look like it takes longer than it does. Then I very deftly *flip* her left hand off her right. There is *no* tear-shaped dinner ring. Her fingers are bare. I pat her down like a cop at the airport. It's not there. Nothing. In a daze, I give the other pieces to Donald. Then I take my rented BMW, drive to a place called the Green Mill and get drunk with a feed salesman named Duane who can't get his wedding ring off fast enough, an action that makes me so sad and depressed I say horrible things about feed salesmen and go back to Norton Place very alone. I'm in the pink room of my grandmother's home, in the pink bed that's been mine since I was a child. In the darkness, I dream of Jack in the night. Jack in our house in Stockbridge, holding hands with Paul and Lainie at his side.

"Why can't you love the littlest things," he says. "The things you can hold in your hand. What do you *want* from this world?" "There are so many things you can't get or hold on to. Like color, and facets, and light."

And then—in the dream—Jack takes my hand, places three rings on my fingers . . . and says:

"Is that why you tried to kill yourself?" (*Pause.*)

"Yes. I left our bed and I went into the garage, and I sat in the car in the cold, cold night and turned on the ignition. I *tried*. Didn't work out the way I'd planned." (*Pause.*)

The next morning . . . I call the airport to get the soonest possible flight back to L.A. My bags are in the BMW outside the funeral home. *Inside* . . . I'm at my post for the

third and *final* viewing . . . when out of the field of poinsettias, I notice a tiny bald man deep in conversation with
Josephine and Margaret-Mary Walsh. They're whispering
together. They look in my direction, and the bent, hobbled
old gnome approaches. It's *Morton Lincoff*! Morton Lincoff
from The Hub! He's ancient now—like Yoda. And much to
my surprise because what are the chances?—he says to me:

"Where is that husband and those two kids?"

My words come out as ever.

"I am not married now. My husband never fixed the
kitchen door."

I try to walk away. But Morton Lincoff is persistent.

"You know, I remember you coming into the store with
your grandmother—must have been thirty years ago—the
day you were going to get your first hair done. Your grandmother had come in to pick up a ring your grandfather had
me design. A dinner ring. Beautiful thing. The one she's
wearing right now."

I am Morton Lincoff's oxygen, my face so close to his.

"You mean the *tear*-shaped ring?"

"Yes!" he beams. "Beautiful work from a talented whole-
sale genius I had in Hackensack, only came to town twice,
three times a year. Your grandmother had sent it in to be
cleaned before she died. I just give it back to Mister Funeral.
Your grandmother, she wanted she should be buried with it,
and who are we to argue with the dead?"

It's there. It's *there*. Why shouldn't I take it? It was, by
rights—it was by rights . . . *mine*. And I need—I *want*—
The service is about to begin. The family is to pay its last
tributes. One by one. As they do, I go to the powder room,
so that when I return, I will be the last. This is an affront
to protocol, of course, but it's the best method. It's worked
for me a billion times, it'll work for me again. Out of the
bathroom, I sustain the glares, but I am resolute. No one
dare stop the emotional granddaughter from her final embrace. I approach the subject. My grandmother. My mother's

mother. The source of my being. Cold and dusted pink and blue. I look down. The ring is there. The Eagle has landed. I grip the side of the casket. I lean my face to hers. I kiss her cheek—and place my hand upon her hand. Her ring is harder to remove than I had hoped, as if the finger's swelled. I pull. Nothing. I twist. Nothing. I do not want to break her finger. It is an occupational hazard, and I don't want my grandmother to be my first "snapper." And then I look down. Because Nettie's eyes—my grandmother's eyes—are wide open and watching me.

"Grandma?"

"Hello, Jane. Going to steal my ring?"

Uh . . . maybe.

"Sweet Janie. Why have you been lying to my old friends about that family of yours?"

Her hand has mine gripped in a lock so strong, so tight, my fingers will break!

"You've been lying, Jane. I won't let go 'til you tell Grandma where that husband of yours is and my two great-grandchildren."

I am pulling away from her now, but her hand has my wrist, now my elbow, now pulling me deep towards her face!

"Tell me the truth, Janie. Why have you been lying? Where is that husband of yours and my great-grandchildren?"

I am running a cold sweat, I look for my family—my *family!*—and there's no one in the room!

"Where is your family. Where is your family! *Where is your family!*" I shout out.

My husband never fixed the kitchen door! And after I fell asleep in the garage, I finally woke up at the hospital in Stockbridge and I asked where is my husband, where is my daughter, where is my son . . . they explained to me . . . that because the kitchen was attached to the garage, and because the kitchen door had never been fixed, the lock had opened, and the door had opened, and the air from the garage had drifted into the house and into the bedrooms and my family—

my husband, my children, my littlest things—it had killed my family . . . while I slept.

Let me go back. Let me go back! *Let me go back!*

And the ring comes off! Someone touches my shoulder. It's time to close the casket. At the graveside, they place the coffin deep in the ground next to my grandfather's old headstone. The earth begins to hit the top of the casing with the sound that is unmistakably it. I am listening to the minister talk about the gift of the homemaker, the ring clasped tight in my hand. (*Beat.*)

I did not die the day I tried to kill myself. They buried my family before I had a chance to touch them, hold their hands one more time. Jack's wedding ring. Lainie's friendship ring. Paul's decoder ring. All deep in the ground before I woke up. But I am alive, and my grandmother's ring is cold to my touch. It is not what I want or need. At long last, the minister is finished. My mother steps forward and throws in a clump of dirt. Then Aunt Teeta. Then Donald and David and Gerald. Finally, there is me. I go to the hole cut out of the planet. I gather the dirt. And I let it fall. The clump of a clod of earth—the sprinkle of grain and rock—the rain of dust. And the silver note as the ring bounces off the lid and disappears deep into the soil. Forever. (*Pause.* MAC *kneels and begins to remove her rings, until by the end of the next speech, she looks like a mourner from the old country, dressed in black.*)

In Stockbridge, Massachusetts, where I lived for years, there is a place where my other family is buried. I have not yet visited them. But I know the way there. In the darkness, I pray for the touch of a hand that has known my touch too. The call of the dead is not strange in the night. No one can steal anything from my family—ever again. Tears freeze in the cold. When they hit the stone they break into a shattering of colors and facets and light. I gather them close to me, and I am warm like a thief in the night. (*Slow fade.*)

THE END

Thirteen Things about Ed Carpolotti

Lights up on a woman, VIRGINIA. *In her late fifties or sixties, a pleasant suburban matron in expensive, tailored black.* VIRGINIA *sits on a small sofa or love seat. A gold-headed cane leans against the love seat. A purse sits to her side. Next to her purse, unobtrusive, is a small manila envelope.* VIRGINIA *holds an unlit cigarette in one hand, a lighter in the other. Behind her are three floral arrangements in yellows and golds.* VIRGINIA *begins speaking immediately as the lights bump up.*

VIRGINIA

(*Upbeat and energetic.*)

Ed always said I couldn't keep my mouth shut. Well, he didn't *always* say it. I think he said it *once*. He was never a talker. Even *before* we were married. He'd clam up at dinners, parties. He knew I hated him being so quiet. I'd say to him:
"Ed, at least *look* like you're talking to me!"
So he tried. Whenever he didn't have anything to say, he'd turn to me and start to mutter:
"Mary had a little lamb," he'd say.
And I'd come back, "His fleece was white as snow."
"And everywhere that Mary went."
You get the idea. People thought we had quite a rapport! *Well.* Ed gave up smoking four months before he died. When he had his first heart attack, he'd been on "the patch" since early September. Even while he was in the hospital, before the second one hit him and all the "funny" business started to happen, Ed joked he was "down to two and a half patches a day." I told him the biggest change it made was in our sex life. It's just not romantic to turn to the person next to you after it's all over and offer her a small package to stick on her ribcage. He still had one on him pumping away the night he died. That was in Pittsburgh. We'd moved Ed to

Allegheny General when things started to go haywire. St.
Joseph's here in town isn't equipped for that kind of thing—
by which I mean decent hospital care when your life depends
on it. We moved Ed on Thanksgiving morning, during the
broadcast of the Macy's parade. Debbie made all the
arrangements. By the time the ambulance got him up there
his watch and one of his rings had been stolen. They even
got his gold MedicAlert necklace. We should have taken
them off. Debbie said she'd even thought about it but felt
creepy wrestling her father's jewelry off before they carted
him away. Something about it being *"too Dickensian for
words."* (*She looks out front.*)
    I never know what Debbie's talking about. Ed gave up
smoking on Labor Day, he had his first heart attack on Halloween, his second on Thanksgiving, and he died just before
Christmas. Well, he loved holidays. When we brought him
back to the funeral home, the undertaker's assistant asked us
if there was anything else he could do to make Ed look
more natural?
    "Give 'im a goddamn cigarette."
    Natural. He's dead wearing bifocals and a hairpiece,
what's going to help the illusion of reality here? Debbie
picked out the suit and tie. The pocket hankie. The cuff
links shaped like bulldozers. The hairpiece. He had a lot of
them in the bathroom. All of his hair on these little white
heads. You could watch Ed age on those heads. After the
funeral, Debbie told me she'd slipped a pack of Camels into
her father's pocket before they closed the casket—
    "—sort of as a symbol, like the Egyptians or the Vikings
taking a talisman into the great beyond." (*She looks out again.*)
    I never know what she's talking about. Debbie's back
home in Wisconsin now—with her second husband, the
assistant provost, and the twins—and her unfinished novel . . .
about a woman in Wisconsin with her second husband, the
assistant provost, and her twins. I thought about calling her
after the funeral when things started to happen, but she's

listening to Prozac and I don't want to interrupt. I can't remember where or when I met Ed. Tootie Vaughn would remember. Tootie's my best galfriend, and she remembers things like this, but I don't. All I remember was living at home with Mother and Daddy and then there was Ed. He'd left his dad's grocery store and was going to build highways and roads and bridges. He had no money and no prospects and Mother and Daddy did not approve. I had to sneak out of the house to see him once. Mother and Daddy thought I'd gone with Tootie to see Martin and Lewis in *My Friend Irma Goes West,* but I'd gone out to Stone Road with Ed. When I got back Tootie was in our living room with a guilty look on her face, and Daddy quizzed me about where I'd gone. I always know when I've done something wrong. I start to sweat on my . . . well, it's not polite to say it, but . . . my *collarbone.* I flush. I get red there. Nobody can *see* it but I can *feel* it. I lied of course. Said I "had *so* gone to the movies." Daddy said,

"Prove it,"

so I made up an entire plot for *My Friend Irma Goes West.* The next night I went to see *My Friend Irma Goes West* and was surprised to learn just how close I'd got!

I wasn't there when he died. Debbie wasn't either. No one was. Three AM, a week before Christmas. The nurses said he didn't make a sound when the aneurysm hit.

"Why didn't he cry out?" I asked. "Isn't it painful?"

"Oh, yes," they said, "but what with the dementia that set in following the second cardiovascular infarction your husband's responses had become neurologically inappropriate."

At the service, Margaret-Mary Walsh tells me he was lucky to go that way. I guess. He recognized Debbie once towards the end, but he thought we were in Las Vegas. He thought I was his mother. One night he saw a cow in the room standing behind me.

"Yeah," I tell her, "I'd like to die in Las Vegas with my mother and a cow too."

The funeral was . . . Lots of people. Bob O'Klock from the bank. Dino DiSperbio from Smith Trucking. Ed's brother Frank. Funerals make me tired. Even other people's. I don't know how the undertakers do it. They *prefer* the title "mortician" but that always sounds like death with air-freshener to me. "Undertaker" is right. They undertake what we can't bear. (*She looks off.*)

When did I meet Ed? Where did I meet my husband? (*A beat. She focuses again.*)

It was three days before I could get down to the office. The way the will's written I'm president of Ed Carpolotti, Inc. now. *President.* Debbie asks me over the phone if my "first official act will be to recognize Cuba." (*She laughs a trill.*)

I laugh . . . like I know what the hell she's talking about. Ed's secretary, Joy, showed me what our attorney said I needed to see. On paper, it looked like the construction business had been slow—well, business had been *bad* the past year or so. But the files showed assets. We'd be fine. I said that to Joy.

"We'll be fine."

And Joy just *looked* at me. I went to see our attorney the next day. I depend on Danny Spahr, but it's hard to invest a lot of authority in the little boy who used to deliver your milk. I go down to his office at the bank building. Bob O'Klock's bank, where Ed's company did business. Bob smiles and waves at me from behind the glass doors in the lobby. (*She imitates his "call me" hand action.*)

Makes a motion with his hand that either means to give him a call . . . or he wants me to stir his coffee with my finger and then put it in his ear. I wave back. Danny—*Daniel,* excuse me—and I talk for a while, about Ed, about the funeral, about what a wheeler-dealer he was. Then Danny takes out a file marked "BANK."

"Virginia, did Ed ever ask you to sign anything over the last year? Any papers? Documents? Agreements?" (*She touches her neck.*)

I can feel it as Danny Spahr asks that question . . . the heat begins to rise on my collarbone.

"I was *always* signing *something* or other. Ed was such a one-man band, wheeling and dealing. . . ."

Danny's staring at me. Ed always said I couldn't keep my mouth shut. I told Tootie about the papers when I visited her and her new husband in Boca Raton last April. I tell Tootie everything, could she have told—?

"Virginia, did you sign anything that looked official?"

He delivered our milk. You can't lie to a blue-eyed boy who used to deliver your milk. I nod. He hands me the papers from the file. Business loans from Bob O'Klock's bank to Ed Carpolotti, Inc. Secured with equipment, machinery, high-boys, low-boys, tractors, bulldozers. Every asset of the company. Business loans—signed *personally.* Which means— since Ed got me to sign the papers—that I am now person- ally responsible for these loans—totaling over a half million dollars. Danny tells me Ed was behind in payments. Six months behind. The bank has frozen my assets. The CDs, the IRAs, the savings and checking accounts. Frozen, explains Danny, is a euphemism. They're going to *take* the money. Unless I can find a way to pay off the loan . . . within the week. On the way out of the building, I see Bob O'Klock through the glass doors again. His gray suit, his pinstripe hair. What I do next I have not done before in my life. I hurry out of his bank so he will not see me. I turn my head. I run away. (*Pause.*)

I go home to the house on Bray Barton. Still lots of flow- ers and food leftover from the funeral. In the refrigerator there's a casserole made up entirely of boiled apples, Spam, and noodles. Nobody knows who brought it. It's pretty scary, but Debbie said we should keep it until it learns to talk. I go into Ed's den where he spent most of his time . . . at night on the phone—talking to his foreman, Joy. Other men. Sometimes he'd shut the door. I go into the sun- room . . . where *I* live. There are three messages waiting for me on the answering machine Debbie bought us to prove she really phones home on Sundays. The first is from Tootie in Boca Raton, telling me George Erskine died at his office at the glass factory. Keeled over in the middle of a meeting with his auditor. He and Nancy were to go to Hilton Head on Saturday. The second is from Debbie, telling me she's been invited to a writers' conference in Saskatchewan. For some reason she has to pay for it herself—she even mentions the exact amount—and would I like to get away from town and babysit the twins for a week? The third is from a voice I don't know well.

"Gin, hey, this is Dino DiSperbio, like ta' talk to ya', like ta' take ya' ta' lunch, gimme a call. (*Beat.*) I hate these fuckin' things." (*She looks out.*)

Well, that's what he *said.* I find his number in Ed's book, call him back.

"Mr. DiSperbio, I'd love to go to lunch, but to tell you the truth, I'm just not basically up to it yet." There's a pause.

"Well, we have some business to discuss, Gin."

"Well, I'm free now, Mr. D—"

"Hey, not over the phone."

I agree to meet him the next day at the Green Mill Luncheonette. Everybody in town likes to do business at the Green Mill Luncheonette instead of in their offices. I don't know what they do in their offices. Eat lunch, I guess. When I go in, Dino DiSperbio is waiting for me at a booth in the back. I won't say Mr. DiSperbio is fat . . . but almost anyone else would.

"Siddown, Gin." (I do.) "Gin ya' look good. Are you wearing any federal wiretapping equipment?"

This is the first time I have ever been asked this question, but I think I handle it well.

"Uhhh . . . *no.* No, I'm not. Not today anyway. Thank you."

"Gin, I'll get to the point. Ya' know, your husband, Ed, he was a real wheeler-dealer. We had a lotta fun together. Lotta laughs. Lotta cups a' coffee."

He cuts into a piece of peach pie.

"Ed ever ask you to sign any papers?"

My collarbone has been on fire since I heard his voice on the phone the night before.

"See, Ed, he wanted to sell me half of this landfill he owned. I think he needed the money, Gin, and I told him, I said, 'Hey, Ed, I don' think I wanna buy into a partnership, but I tell ya' what: I'll *loan* you some money at a good percentage. How much ya' need?' And Ed told me. And I give it to 'im."

"How much did you give him?" I ask.

"Half a million."

"At what percentage?"

"Fifty."

I am not a financier, but even I know this is not a good rate.

"Do you remember signing a piece a' paper, Gin?"

I nod my head.

"Do you *have* the money, Gin?"

I shake my head.

"Well . . . whadda we gonna *do*?" (*Beat.*)

Dino is the owner of Smith Trucking. They own no trucks and there has never been a Mr. Smith. I go home to the house on Bray Barton. I look at the answering machine—the red light that says I have four messages. The first is from Tootie in Boca Raton saying Art Wise was found dead in the drugstore he owned. The store has been closed by the police. His files have been sealed. The second is from Danny. He has to get back to Bob O'Klock. The third is from Bob O'Klock. Would I like to have lunch at the Green Mill? The fourth is from Debbie. She says her Mazda was in an accident. I assume that means *she* was in an accident, but the way she phrases it, it sounds like the Mazda had a night off and got into trouble. The repairs will cost more than the insurance will pay. She even mentions the exact amount. I have to call somebody. Someone in the family who can help. I pick up the phone and dial Ed's brother Frank.

"What's the problem," he says.

"Not over the phone," I say. The next night I meet Frank up

at the club. In the Grill Room, which we all call the Coal
Room. Because of the Coal Wall the James family donated
in 1959. Debbie says it looks like something Frank Lloyd
Wright would have done if he'd spent too much time in
Appalachia. (*She looks out, shrugs, rolls her eyes.*)

Who knows?

Frank grins from a table in the back.

"How ya' doin', Virginia?"

"Fine," I say, "and I'm not wearing a wire." It's strange to
look at Frank. Seeing the parts of Ed in him. Like he's a
dream of Ed that's not quite right. Frank's a "developer." We
talk about the property market. About his son Randy's pend-
ing marriage to one of the Wickham girls—which pleases
Frank and his wife Lorraine no end. Randy is being groomed
to run the business and still lives at home. Debbie calls him
Boo Radley without the charm. Over the shrimp cocktail,
I start my speech. About Danny, about Bob O'Klock, about
Dino. Finally, I stop. And then Frank speaks:

"Virginia, you know, Ed was a real wheeler-dealer."

"How much did he borrow?"

"It's three hundred thousand, Virginia."

"At 50 percent?" I ask.

Frank looks hurt. "I was his brother, Virginia. (*Beat.*) I
gave him 18 percent and truth be told I'm taking a beating."

I explain to Frank I have no cash, no savings, nothing
that's not frozen or encumbered. Frank's still looking at me.

"You have the *house.*"

I blink at my husband's brother.

"Virginia, Randy's getting married next month, he and
Courtney will be back from St. Bart's on the 1st. They
were thinking of building on some property I have behind
McCauslen Manor, but . . . Well, Randy's always loved your
house. He likes old houses, you know. Big old white houses
with lots of character. Character's very important to
Randy."

He should get one, then, I think.

"And those trees. The big oaks lining the street out front. 'Member how he and Deb used to play together in those trees?"

They *never* played together in those trees. Randy took his pants off and threw rocks at cats from the fourth oak on the right while Debbie stayed in her room reading something called *The Bell Jar.*

"Now, I could arrange to have Rand and Court in there by—well—call it the 15th. New paint, new rugs, Lorraine's got some ideas about the master bedroom . . ."

I go home to the house on Bray Barton. I look at the answering machine—the red light that says I have six messages. The first is from Tootie saying that George Erskine died when it turned out he was embezzling from the glass factory and that Art Wise was a suicide because of some phony prescription-drug deal at the store.

"What's *with* these guys?"

she says, and hangs up. The second is from Danny, who says we have to have a meeting, and he's willing to come to the house. The third is from Bob O'Klock's secretary saying Mr. O'Klock wants to see me, and he's willing to come to the house. The fourth is from Dino, who wants to come by the house with a friend named Vinnie. The fifth is Lorraine, who knows of an apartment for rent behind the shopping mall parking lot. The sixth is from Joy at the office. Do I have any ideas on how to make this week's payroll? (*Pause.*)

I start upstairs to bed. As I go through the hall towards the steps, I stop. Under the front door something sticks out. It's a manila envelope, shoved halfway through. I open the door. It's below zero out. Snow on the lawn, ice on the oaks, the street quiet. I take the envelope and close the door. It's blank. I go upstairs to my bedroom, into my bathroom, lock the door. Ed's hairpieces watch me as I open the manila envelope. It's a white piece of paper with letters pasted on it—like a kidnapper's ransom.

"I HAVE A LIST OF THIRTEEN THINGS ABOUT

ED CARPOLOTTI. EMBARRASSING TO HIM AND TO OTHERS. HAVE ONE MILLION DOLLARS READY BY THIS FRIDAY. SMALL BILLS. UN-MARKED. IN A SUITCASE. OR I WILL RELEASE THE LIST. TELL NO ONE."

Not surprisingly, it is unsigned. (*Pause. During this next section* VIRGINIA *becomes increasingly angry, hurt, confused, and desperate.*)

"George Erskine was embezzling from his own glass factory."

"Art Wise was selling prescription drugs under the counter."

"Ed Carpolotti was . . ."

What will they say about my husband? Will they say thirteen things? More? What is it about these men? Who built their businesses and grew their families and constructed fortresses with their hands and died so frightened and alone? Who could never tell their wives their secrets—their fears? Ed was Catholic, and I am not, and that was a bone many years ago. But I am beginning to understand some things. I am beginning to understand sin. Not the mortal sins or the venial sins. But the sin of failure. The secular sin that knows no organized religion. Who do you go to when you have committed that? Your lawyer? Your banker? Your brother? Your godfather? No one absolves failure. No one lights a candle. You go *mad*. You pray for death and madness. A cow with your mother in a room in Las Vegas. He had run out of ideas, plans, wheeling and dealing. The last place he dreamed of was a land of gamblers in the middle of a desert. I live in my husband's desert now. I owe three times as much money as I thought I had in the world. I am a widow. I am supposed to be drinking gin and tonics on the terrace of a "townhome" in Boca Raton with Tootie Vaughn. I am a widow and we are supposed to buy new cars after our husbands die. I have not told Tootie. I want so *badly* to tell my friend Tootie. I lay out my silver, my china, my crystal, my jewelry, *everything* I have on the dining room table. I don't know where I can sell it all quickly, but . . . It won't come close to what I need. Not for Bob O'Klock or Dino or Frank . . . or whoever has sent me this note. *This note.* Friday is two days away. *There are forty-six messages on the answering machine,* I do *not* return the calls! (*She begins to hold herself and rock back and forth.*)

I have not told a soul, I have not told a soul, I am screaming so slowly, so dimly, so no one can hear. *Where did I meet my husband? Why can't I remember when and where I met my husband?* (*She shuts her eyes, stops rocking, and makes a decision.*)

I pick up the phone and dial Tootie Vaughn in Boca Raton! We trade bits and pieces for a while. Who's sick, who's dead, why Tootie in Boca Raton always seems to know more about what's going on back at home than anyone who actually lives here. Then I ask her my question. (*Long pause.*)

She says she hasn't a clue where I met Ed. Then I fall apart and I tell her everything. (*Silence, then she tries to brighten and picks up her cane.*)

Did you notice this cane? It belonged to my Aunt Stella. I took care of Stella her last few years—about the time Ed bought our house and Debbie was teething. Stella was a crazy old drunk who had one eye, smoked cigars and drank gin from a bucket. In pictures she looks like an ancient female pirate in a wheelchair; wild white hair, a toothless grin behind her black eyepatch. Debbie says she looked like the illegitimate daughter of Miss Havisham and the Hathaway shirt man. (*She looks out.*)

I think I actually *get* that one.

Stella gave me her cane in the nursing home, the day they took her in. I said,

"Stella, now you hold on to this, you may need it."

She shook her head and winked her eye at me.

"Keep it in a safe place for later. *You'll* need it." (*She looks at the cane, admires it.*)

I like this. I won't sell this.

It's amazing how the deadlines come on the same day. The bank's deadline. Smith Trucking. Frank. The note. I am sitting in my sunroom at 8:30 AM, waiting for the hordes to descend upon my door. It helped to tell Tootie about everything, about the list. And she promised not to tell a soul. I am frightened. But I am *ready*. I have my cigarettes and my cane and my answering machine. —Let 'em come! The first call comes at nine AM.

"Ginnie, Bob O'Klock here. Hi. Say: I understand there's a, gee-whillikers, a kinda, kinda *list* somebody's got about Ed and some of his, his wheeling and dealing and well, well, Gin, I just want you to know that I'm sure that whatever's in that list is just a darned pack of lies and the bank will certainly do anything it can to make sure it isn't an embarrassment to you. Or to *anyone else*. We'll do anything. *I'll* do anything. *Anything. Don't worry about the loan.* Just, just keep it to yourself."

And then he hung up. The next call came at 10:42.

"Yo, Gin, Dino here. Hey! This list thing. Whaddaya say we call it even, huh? Square one. Zero-zero. Don't call back. I hate these fuckin' things." The last call came before dinner.

"Virginia, Frank here. Long pause. Randy and Courtney will be living at home for the foreseeable future. Call me if you need. Tootie Vaughn says hello."

Tootie! Tootie's blabbed to everybody. And the idea of that list has scared them off! *What's in that list?* What kind of dealings did Ed have with Bob, with Dino, with Frank, with . . . . whomever? For the rest of Friday, I wait for another demand from the author of the note. But it does not come that Friday. Or the next Friday or the Friday after that. (*Long pause, then briskly.*) Within the month, we begin to dissolve the business, sell off the assets. Since the loans have been *forgiven* and the creditors *quieted*, Danny says I will have some money to invest, retire on, buy a new car. I don't *need* a new car. At the office, Joy handles most of the real work. I just sign the papers. The last one I sign I tell Joy:

"I'm recognizing Cuba."

Joy doesn't know what the hell I'm talking about. I'm flying to Wisconsin tonight to babysit the twins, but first I had to come here to the funeral home. Another service. Somebody dies every day. Joy offered to drive me. We're a little early, and she insists on coming inside to wait with me in the smoking lounge. I say I have my cane and a copy of *The Bell Jar,* so I'm fine, but she says she wants to keep me company, and she seems odd, so I don't say no. We've never been close. Joy loved my husband, and that has always made it strange. So we sit in silence. Finally the last viewing begins. I stand up . . . and Joy is holding a manila envelope, just like the one that was slipped under my door.

"It's from Mr. Carpolotti," she says.

Then she walks away—quickly. I wait until Margaret-Mary Walsh and the rest of the mourners have gone into the parlor. Inside is a list. (*She opens the envelope, takes out a white piece of paper.*)

1) I have never loved any other woman but you.

2) I cannot look at your hand without wanting to hold it.

3) I wanted to build you a house but you loved the one on Bray Barton so much the day we drove by, I never had the chance to change your mind.

4) In my wallet, I keep a picture of you when you were ten years old; I fall in love with you again every time I see it.

5) I think about you every night before I go to bed so I can dream of you in my sleep.

6) *My Friend Irma Goes West* was the best movie I never saw.

7) I have always understood our child more than she could ever imagine.

8) We met at the Green Mill Luncheonette on February 22, 1955.

9) I am writing this in St. Joseph's Hospital. I am less scared than tired.

10) I have made mistakes.

11) *But I think this last plan will work.* Joy has my instructions.

12) You could never keep your mouth shut. I *knew* you would tell Tootie Vaughn about the list and she would tell the world.

13) Mary had a little lamb.

(*She lights her cigarette. The lights fade.*)

END OF PLAY

AUTHOR'S NOTES

Three Viewings consists of three connected monologues for three actors. The running time is 85–90 minutes. There is no intermission. "Tell-Tale" runs 25 minutes. "The Thief of Tears" runs 26–27 minutes. "Thirteen Things about Ed Carpolotti" runs 31–32 minutes. The three actors are never onstage together until the curtain call.

DESIGN

It is possible to perform the play on an almost bare stage. There should be no attempt to duplicate a funeral home in minute detail, nor should a grim "death theme" be emphasized. For example, there should *never* be a coffin onstage.

For the New York production at Manhattan Theatre Club, James Noone designed a simple, elegant, carpeted space with one small sofa, an end table, and, upstage, three recessed bays to house floral arrangements. The three bays revolved between pieces, so that a different set of floral arrangements was displayed for each monologue.

"Tell-Tale" had flowers in deep reds and purples; "The Thief of Tears" had white poinsettias; and "Thirteen Things about Ed Carpolotti" had flowers in yellows and golds. It was a very effective use of color.

Lighting effects should be used sparingly. "Tell-Tale" has precise blackouts noted in the script. "The Thief of Tears" allows for some light shifts in time and mood. "Thirteen Things about Ed Carpolotti" should utilize the least number and least obtrusive of light changes: no blackouts, slow-fades, etc., although a gradual and perhaps imperceptible series of changes could emphasize Virginia's growing fear and isolation until her situation changes at the end.

As for sound, there are no "effects," but there should be music in the brief (seconds) blackouts between each monologue, as the actors move off and onstage. Avoid using low-energy, funereal organ music or other "serious" pieces. Pop and swing come to mind. Frank Sinatra. Rosemary Clooney. Dean Martin and Bobby Darrin. The world of the play is closest to the songs and singers of the 1930s–1950s. Gershwin. Porter. Berlin. Kern. Rodgers and Hart.

STAGING AND MOVEMENT

Buck Henry used the sofa twice in "Tell-Tale," but it isn't necessary for Emil to ever sit. Margaret Whitton played Mac and used the sofa a bit more as her character set different scenes. As Virginia, Penny Fuller sat on the sofa and never rose. This is right. Virginia should *never* stand during her monologue.

ONE TEXT NOTE

In "Thirteen Things about Ed Carpolotti," the date "February 22, 1955" is mentioned. If the actress playing the role of Virginia prefers, this date can be changed to 1945.

CHARACTERS

These are dramatic monologues. They are also *theatrical* monologues. In each play, the character speaks *directly* to the audience. There is no unseen, onstage intermediary—like a priest, a psychiatrist, or God. The characters are storytellers, speaking to the paying customers in the dark—in the present tense, with intimacy, humor, and candor.

In "Tell-Tale" Emil should embody both the buoyancy and the fear of a timid man in the thrall of a great love. We should be able to see and hear his passion overflow his buttoned-down persona.

In "The Thief of Tears" it is important that Mac exhibit the wit, edge, and quicksilver nature of a smart, funny woman who is trying to contain a horrible secret.

In "Thirteen Things about Ed Carpolotti" Virginia should not display her pain or sadness too early—not until deep into the piece at about the time she receives the blackmail threat under her door. At the beginning she is cheerful, funny, and chatty—even (especially) when talking about the circumstances of her husband's death. Obviously, this is a protective mechanism, and it is an essential part of her character. Occasionally this mechanism breaks down for a few seconds ("Where did I meet my husband?"), but she always revs back a moment later. Deeper into the play, as the bad news mounts, the mechanism wavers and finally collapses into bewilderment, panic, and despair (the sequence that begins "George Erskine was embezzling from his own glass factory."), but even as her predicament grows more desperate, it is important that she doesn't slow down into her pain. Drive, speed, and energy are vital to the piece. Virginia should never be played for pathos or sentimentality or "beautiful suffering." And, yes, she must smoke at the end.

In general, I'm convinced that productions of *Three Viewings* should avoid any attempt to overplay the themes of death, loss, and despair, which can lead to a lugubrious and humorless evening. True, each of the three pieces contains passages that must be played with raw emotion and without humor, but audiences bring their own experience of death and loss to the theater, and we don't need to hit them over the head with what they already know.

THE TRICKY PART

Martin Moran

For Henry Stram

The Tricky Part was first presented in a workshop at the Barrow Group (Seth Barrish, Lee Brock, Artistic Directors; Eric Paeper, Managing Director) in November 2003. It premiered at the McGinn/Cazale Theater in New York City in April 2004. It was produced by James B. Freydberg, CTM Productions, Wendy vanden Heuvel, and True Love Productions. It was directed by Seth Barrish; the scenic design was by Paul Steinberg; the lighting design was by Heather Carson; the stage manager was Tom Taylor. The cast was as follows:

MARTY   Martin Moran

The Tricky Part was also developed with the generous support of the Sundance Theater Lab (Philip Himberg, Robert Blacker, Kim Euell); the Long Wharf Theatre (Gordon Edelstein, Artistic Director; Michael Stotts, Managing Director; Carrie Ryan, Dramaturg); the 78th Street Theater Lab (Eric and Ruth Nightengale); John Dias, Dramaturg; Saratoga Stages (Bruce Bouchard, Artistic Director); and the McCarter Theatre (Emily Mann, Artistic Director; Mara Isaacs, Producing Director; Jeffrey Woodward, Managing Director; Janice Paran, Dramaturg).

The playwright would like to acknowledge the profound contribution of the director, Seth Barrish, toward realizing the spirit, structure, and language of this work.

AUTHOR'S NOTE

I have set out to tell the truth about real events. Most names and some details and characters have been altered for the sake of clarity and to respect the privacy of individuals.

PRODUCTION NOTE

The photo used in the play is specific: a boy twelve, standing in a kayak wearing a life jacket, a swimsuit, holding an oar overhead. The performer will need to find a photo similar in detail but, obviously, specific to his physical appearance as a child.

A simple space with a wooden stool and a stand on which sits a photograph of a boy.

Marty enters carrying a small, journal-like book.

Hi everyone. Thanks for making your way here tonight (*Ad-lib appropriate to the place and day.*) . . . um, before we plunge in (*Putting the journal down near the photo*) I wanted to make sure you got a chance to look at this photo. (*He picks up photo and shows it around the room.*) This has followed me around forever. Now it hangs near my desk at home. It's of, you might have guessed, me, thirty-two years ago when I was twelve. Nineteen seventy-two. (*Making the pose as in the picture*) See the resemblance? It was taken on a pond up in the Rockies about two hours outside of Denver, the town where I grew up. Our family—two absent parents (bless them), four scattered kids, lived down in this alphabetical neighborhood—Grape-Glencoe-Holly-Hudson-Ivy-Ivanhoe—rows of identical houses, known as Virginia Vale but, you know, somehow, what seemed most important was that we *belonged* to Christ the King, our church and school up the hill. And I felt a great deal of pride—which is a sin—about my school. I remember they asked me to cover the phone once when the office nun got ill. I just happened to be passing by and, *always* anxious to please, I was thrilled to take her seat for a few minutes. Pretty soon the phone rang—*Hello, Christ the King.* I was in heaven. Or, later, when I was on student council and I had to call out into the worldly world for, you know, bank balances or Styrofoam cups: *HI, this is Christ the King calling.* Usually there'd be this *pause* on the line and I'd get (right here in my breast) this little burst of—(*Prideful gesture*). Most all the kids in my neighborhood went to public school. McMean or Fallis Elementary. I kid you not: *F A double-L I S.* Edwina Fallis Elementary. She was a beloved kindergarten instructor . . . still; I just think it's one thing when your school is named after a dead teacher and another when it's named for the Risen Savior.

I don't know about McMean or Fallis, but every classroom at Christ the King had a clock and a crucifix. Did anyone here go to Catholic school? (*If so . . . ask name of school and ad-lib re: odd names like Our Lady of Perpetual Help or Our Lady of Pity, Our Lady of the Likely Story.*) Anyway . . . the clock and the crucifix hung from the front wall and each day during math or spelling I would stare up and watch the hands ticking past the numbers while Jesus's remained nailed at quarter to three. They were stuck there on the yellow brick like this odd couple that seemed, somehow, to be . . . dueling. I'd look back and forth: Time, Eternity, Earth-Heaven . . . It was like watching Now spin toward the hour of death. Death . . . I had this one nun, Sister Agatha, third grade. She was a heavy woman, in every sense of the word. She wasn't much taller than us nine-year-olds. She was shaped like a box. A black box. A moving cube of church . . . a cube with spectacles. She had a very particular method for teaching cursive. She'd put on 45 records of simple songs for each different letter of the alphabet—"Farmer in the Dell" for *W,* say, or "Three Blind Mice" for G. "Okay, children, letter G, remember the tail; every letter has a tail so they can connect, make meaning." She'd plop on the record, we'd clutch our number 2 pencils: "All right, together now, *Three blind mice,* tail, *Three blind mice, connect!*" And this one day, in the middle of letter *G,* she just froze, staring at her chalk. We sat there until, finally, Carol Buell went to the office to get someone. They came and took Sister out into the hall . . . and we never saw her again.

I did have her for most of the year though and Sister

Agatha was, among the many nuns in my life, the most intense. Often, before we'd go off to the restroom she would turn, face the front wall and raise her cloaked arms in the shape of a V as if pleading to be beamed up. With one hand she indicated the hour and with the other our near-naked Lord. "We line up by one but we live by the other," she would proclaim in this crackly voice. Crackly because there was always something like grief or cheese caught in her throat. And sometimes, you know, right in the midst of a lesson—especially when she was annoyed with you—she would gesture up to the cross and look at you and blurt: "He died to set you free!" And I'd sit there thinking: *Free from what? From where?* There was a brief moment one afternoon (I was really little, first grade) when I thought I'd cracked a piece of the Catholic code. It was when the bell rang, as usual, at 2:45 to release us for the day. Alleluia! I grabbed my satchel and as I did I glanced up to realize that the clock and Jesus told the exact same time and I thought . . . Oh! It's, um . . . but, right away, I knew whatever it was He'd done it was supposed to mean more than just getting to *leave* here— being set *free* to go *home*. Nothing could be that simple, could it? At least not at Christ the King.

CK, as we called it, was situated on a little hill at Eighth and Fairfax, sandwiched between Holy Ghost to the west and Most Precious Blood (a rougher neighborhood) to the east. Little Catholic fiefdoms all over town, fiefdoms of the soul concerned, of course, with matters of the *Hereafter.* That's something you get from the time you're tiny: *AFTER* is what you're shooting for, *After's* what counts. *Here* is basically a problem; you know—a mistake. We fell; we're stuck, *HERE,* in this unreliable flesh struggling to earn our way toward a bodiless eternity somewhere in a nice neighborhood with all the saints. Like Mary . . . and Joseph and . . . Oh. . . .

There was a statue outside of the Virgin Mary—blinding white up on her pedestal, her arms lovingly outstretched, her wrists cocked in this odd way that always made me think she was directing traffic. (*He demonstrates this.*) And if you stood there not far from Mary, you could look out and see the whole front range of the Rockies from Pike's Peak in the south to Long's in the north and all the mountains in between standing jagged and mighty over our *Disturbed Region*. That's what Father Kottenstettie—our priest and sometimes science teacher—told us Denver was called in geologic terms. Really and truly, a Disturbed Region, on account of all the tectonic accidents and violent collisions that create . . . such beauty.

(*With a slight German-Irish dialect.*) He told us: "A rock, a mountain may look at rest, but they most certainly are not. Every*ting* is filled with ceaseless subatomic motion." (*Pause.*)

Anyway, if there was time before 8:30 Mass—that's how we started each day, by the way, 8:30 Mass. It was like the first class of the day, we'd march in, take a pew, sing the opening tune: *Sons of God, hear his holy word, gather round the table of the Lord. Eat his body drink his blood and we'll sing a song of love, Allelu, Allelu, Alleluia* . . . just another tribe starting the day. Well, if there was time before Mass, I used to love to stop and chat with Mary or with the Godly view the way you do, you know? with mountains and statues because you sense that somewhere behind the stillness, behind the scenes, they are *alive* somehow and keeping an eye on things. And not just Mary, but all the martyrs and saints . . . lucky you, you learn this! That there's this huge army of the Good and the Dead just waiting to be called upon, prayed to 'cause they've been through the earthly wringer and *released*. They're part of the oxygen. Their stories are stained into chapel windows and pressed into books and calendars, like Catholic celebrities, sacred movie stars. There's a saint for every day and a holy patron for every profession. St. Cecilia for music, Luke for doctors, St. Genesius for prostitutes . . . and actors. It got so you recognized their hairdos or their particular wounds. Sad St. Lucy with her eyes on a plate, the virgin Agatha with her breasts on a platter, or St. Denis carrying his own head down from Montmartre. I mean . . . Halloween is nothing to a kid from Catholic school. Everywhere you look, there's blood and gore and metaphor.

Sister Agatha (Remember? Cursive?) was passionate about her teaching of the saints. I remember how annoyed she was on the feast day of St. Martin when I replied to her question that I didn't know much about him. She made me stand and read aloud from *Miniature Stories of the Saints*. When I opened to the page devoted to Martin there was this dreamy drawing of him: rockstar hair, handsome face with these brown eyes gazing up toward . . . up, and I knew right away that if he lived here-now instead of Rome-then, he would have been captain of the team and picked me right away. There was this *bond*.

Anyway, it told how he was a soldier who met a freezing beggar in the street one day and, having nothing but the cloak on his back to offer the poor man, Martin took his sword and chopped his cape and gave half of it to the beggar who, lucky for Martin, turned out to be God.

That day during recess Ricky Flynn cornered me and said, "Give me half your Mars bar."

I said, "No."

"Come on," he said. "I'm the beggar, you be the saint." I didn't see how, with his mean eyes and snotty nose, Ricky's could be the face of God but . . . that's the tricky part. So I ripped my candy in half and Ricky laughed with his mouth full. "Thanks St. Martin." I felt so stupid and more unsaintly than ever. See, we're supposed to be like them, the saints, but they're all holy and dead and it's hard to know where to begin. . . .

Consider one particular case of one particular boy . . . me. It was an afternoon we third-graders were having a silent study period, waiting for the hands to reach 2:45. I should have been reading but I was thinking, or dreaming I believe . . . about Wesley, the neighbor boy who occasionally babysat my older sister and me. I didn't know why but I longed to sit next to Wesley as . . . well, as next to a fire on a winter's night but he always remained alone and silent at the end of our living room couch studying his geometry while I sat on the floor doodling his name in my workbook. Well, during my daydream it seems I had stuck my hands in my front pockets and suddenly Sister was in front of my desk.

"Stop that!" she whispered, or hissed really, as if she'd transformed into the serpent of Eden she talked of incessantly. I sat up straight; my hands still caught in my corduroys. "Do you need to make a trip to the toilet?"

"Uh, uh."

"Then stop it." She pointed to my pockets. *Mortified*, I pulled my hands out and folded them on top of *Phonics for Fun*. "That's nothing down there to be toying with," she said, trembling. That's how my mind's eye, my body remembers it: this hallowed nun, quaking at my offense. I didn't understand why but I knew well that my body was fit to blame. She walked to the front of the class and clapped three times—her signal that it was time for another lesson about . . . how we're bad.

"Children . . . if the devil has his way, we'll never reach our greatest desire: *union with God in the life everlasting*." She straightened her little round glasses and looked right at me. Oh gees, this is it, I'm gonna be nailed. "There's a *war* inside of us children because the *Kingdom of God* dwells within but so does our sin and there's not a lot of room in there," she placed a hand on her stomach, "and they're both going at it, white knight and black, angel and devil, tangling us up and if," she raised a finger, "if you *allow* . . . " and she stepped toward me and . . . the bell rang. And she never finished. . . . I'm in Las Vegas, two years ago, right? It's the end of March, 2002. Holy Thursday. That's Catholic for three days before Easter and I'm in Vegas to visit my father. We're at Von's, a fluorescent grocery store roughly the size of Manhattan, waiting in line to pay for pork chops. There's a bank of slot machines near the exit and I'm basically in shock that it's here dad's retired, will likely die.

There, in the checkout line, on the cover of *Time* maga-

zine, is a gray and ominous drawing of the backside of a
bishop and these words: "Can the Catholic Church Save
Itself?" I reach for a copy and suddenly Dad says: "Oh,
Jesus, that's been goin' on for a thousand years." He's jutting
a finger at *Time*. "Did I ever tell you what happened to your
aunt when she was little?"

"No Dad."

"Father Murray, the basement of St. Bede's. I don't know
what went on, but thank God the janitor happened by."

I say to Dad, "Wow," but nothing else because, suddenly,
I'm riveted on a photo, page twenty-eight, of Father Kos
and a Dallas boy age twelve, who killed himself at twenty-
one. I know the story of Kos and his altar boys, I'd cut every
clip of it from the papers in '98 and stuck them in the file
I keep under my desk, but I'd never, until now, seen the
face, God the face, of the boy who shot himself dead. His
tiny-toothed smile, the light in his eyes is absolutely haunting. He's in altar boy frocks, all white and the arm of the
man with the Roman collar is slung behind his slim shoulders. ". . . Do you want me to buy that for you?" my dad
asks. And I look into his old face and wonder, again, what
it would mean, what it would be like, to tell him the
story.

"No, thanks Dad," I say. "I'll get it."

This story that will not let me go.

So, a few evenings later, very beginning of April 2002,
I've left my dad in Vegas and now I'm in Los Angeles to visit
my goddaughter and I'm headed south, possibly east? in the
haze of the Hollywood Freeway when my cell phone
bleeps . . . which means message, *maybe a job!* I pick it up
and press voice mail.

Marty, it's Bob Kominsky. (I hit the brake. The SUV behind
me honks.) *I got your letter saying you'd be traveling west. I'd
dearly love to see you. I'm at the Veterans' Hospital in L.A. Here's
my number. . . .*

I take the next exit and come to a stop in the glare of a

7-Eleven parking lot, stunned that he's *alive*, that my letter
actually found him!

See, I'd lost all track of this guy Bob but, just before taking this trip out west, on a day I was gripped again by the
idea of finding him, I finally mailed a letter with a "Please
Forward," to an old address I had for him—some little town
in California. I never imagined I'd hear from him; let alone
that he'd be in the same . . . I mean, that he's actually in L.A.
at the same time as me! It's just so weird—like God or *someone* is stage-managing this thing.

So, sitting there in the parking lot, I half dial his number,
hang up. Half dial, hang up. *Come on, do it. Just do it* . . . he
answers on the second ring.

"Hello."

The pitch, the tenor of him enters my body like a lance.
So strange, after all these years, him, *him* reduced to a little
human hum across a wireless. Very businesslike, we arrange
to meet.

Thursday, April 4, 2002, the morning of the meeting.

My friend, Jodi, prints out directions from her house in
North Hollywood to the Veterans' Complex off Sepulveda
Boulevard. "Good luck Mart," she says. "Wring his friggin'
neck for me." Jodi's quick to fury on this subject which always
sets me to wondering about anger. My own anger (whatever, wherever it is) feels lost or buried somehow in com-
plicity—as if the sense that I wanted, *allowed?* has squelched
any right I have to wrath or innocence. I remember when I
first told Jodi all that happened she looked at me with such
pity that I just blurted: "Hey doll, I'm okay. It's not like the
guy murdered me." "I'm so sorry that happened to you,"
she said and I saw how she glanced across the room at her
child and the worry that flashed over her face told me that
I'd lived her idea of a parent's nightmare. But I think of
another friend who, when I shared the story said, "Oh,
my . . . weren't you a lucky little boy." When he said it, I
don't know . . . I laughed like a lunatic.

It's a gorgeous day.

Bob's instructions take me to this red-roofed, convalescent home. I park the car. *What am I doing here?* I wonder. I get out and walk by the palm trees and well-kept lawns. A pretty place for mending, I think.

I ask for "Kominsky, please?" Crisp and smiling, the nurse points to the elevator. "Second floor dear."

First I step into the men's room for a pee, for a breath. I stand in a stall and take from my pocket two AA batteries. I'd meant to do this in the car. Forgot. So, standing there in front of a toilet, I snap them into my little tape recorder like a lousy spy. . . . I don't really know why I'm doing this. It's like I'm afraid that without a record I'll forget everything or never believe any of it actually happened . . . so I'm snapping them in thinking: *This is rude, maybe illegal, immoral—fuck it.* I stick the recorder in my jacket pocket and catch myself in the mirror above the sink and . . . break into a crazy grin.

I go up, the corridor is long, hospital white. There are two to a room. I check the names, scrawled in black marker, tucked beneath plastic, next to each door. There are these dazed-looking vets everywhere. Some walking silently, wheeling IVs. Some sitting, staring out the window. The age, the long hair, say Vietnam. As I walk I rehearse lines in my head; afraid I'll go blank:

"Bob . . . do you remember the last time I saw you?

Who was it, exactly, that sent you to prison?"

And then . . . (*whoosh*) there's his name.

The door is open but I'm thinking there must be a mistake because—it says *Kominsky*—but I don't recognize either person in the room. In the far bed, a dark-skinned man is coughing up what appears to be part of his lunch. In the nearer bed, sitting up, is a plump person with a mop of white hair who, at first glance, looks to be someone's grandmother. My first thought is, Are there women vets here? There must be, but, wait, it *is* a man and he—like everyone else—is wearing a rose-colored frock, prison-like, with faint numbers stenciled above the breast pocket. He's holding a plastic fork, poking at some broccoli. Slowly, the face revolves toward the door, blinks once and asks,

"Are you Marty?"

I nod. *His voice,* no question.

And he says, "I never would have recognized you," and in that instant, like a shift from blurry to sharp, I get him. Exactly. Under the mop of grandmother hair I apprehend the features of this vigorous, thirty-year-old man I once knew. *This is him,* the guy who taught me about Buckminster Fuller and geodesic domes, we actually built one. *It's him,* the guy who . . . took me glacier sliding. That was summer after seventh grade; he led a group of us campers up into the Indian Peaks and we came across a huge glacier and he said: "Okay, okay, climb up and slide down!" Nobody moved, everyone was terrified and Bob whispered in my ear: "C'mon, I *know* you can do it." And, I don't know, I just turned and climbed and climbed. It was like a quarter mile long this thing. I got to the top and tied my jacket around my butt and all the other guys linked arms at the bottom of the glacier to keep me from slamming into the rocks. It was insane. I sat . . . aaahhh! screaming the whole way down and they caught me! I was King for a day! Brave for once. This is the guy who woke me late one night at the mountain ranch and said: "Hey, come with me, Marty, you gotta see this!" He grabbed a lantern and took me to the barn. The vet had come in the middle of the night to help deliver a calf. Bob and the vet had their arms all up in there cause the cow was in trouble and suddenly this rickety-legged creature covered with blood and goop came out. Lying there on the barn floor. *Alive!* And Bob turned to me and smiled. And I felt so lucky to be there, to see something so *real* and . . .

Anyway, I say to him,

"I don't want to interrupt your lunch."

"No, no. It's okay," he says, blinking at me through these large, gold-framed glasses. I think of moving in to shake his hand but that seems *ridiculous* and we're in a freeze like, what? Victim facing perpetrator? Or like estranged "ex's." Ex–altar boy, ex–"almost seminarian," ex–friends? enemies? lovers? I don't know. Definitions fail, bleed one into the other. I watch him lay his fork on a paper napkin and I ask,

"How are you?"

He says, "You're catching me at a pretty down time." His eyes are green, he's looking right at me but there's not a glimmer in there and I think: Gees, the light's been bludgeoned out of this guy or maybe he's on something—antipain, antidepressant.

"What happened?" I ask, pointing to his right foot which is enormous, wrapped in white gauze up to the knee like the limb of a mummy.

He says, "Oh, bad infection. They had to amputate a little."

"Wow, sorry."

"Ah, well," he says. "Stepped on a stupid screw in the driveway. Life." (*He shrugs, chuckles.*) "I've got diabetes now. You remember how I liked my Coca-Cola."

"Yep. I do." I glance toward the hall, wanting to move outside, somewhere private.

And he says, "You look good. Your dad had quite a belly by your age."

I'm thrown at his mention, his memory, of my father who he met, I think, maybe twice . . . and I just start chattering. . . .

"Well, I'm . . . an actor, can you believe? . . . and the work's very physical, keeps me fit and . . ." I feel the words buzzing in my skull, how they're utterly weightless . . . and how it's our bodies that are grave, somehow, communicating, catching up. It's like . . . for my bones the whole experience isn't thirty years away, but three feet.

And he asks, "You work in the theater then?"

"Yeah, uh-huh, some TV, plays and musicals. I sing and . . ." *Christ Marty,* I think, *why not just give him an uptune and a ballad.* Lord, he's got just the lost, ugly mug you'd expect in a news item on pedophiles—pasty pale, geeky glasses. ". . . and it's always eight shows a week, very rigorous and . . ." This sharp lament moves through me as I think how much the course of my days has been affected by this broken being in front of me. ". . . but Broadway's great, it pays pretty well, when you can get it. . . ."

I watch him push, with index finger, his glasses up the bridge of his nose, then scoop his bangs to the right. The gesture (*exactly* as I remember it) sends a tremble through my chest. It's as if I'm forty-two and twelve at once.

He asks, "You live in New York?"

"Yeah, I've been in Manhattan twenty years now." This sentence, somehow, gives me a sense of center, of pride. "I live there with my . . . my boyfriend, Henry. We've been together seventeen years." I want him to know, I realize, that I'm all right, that I've found something like success, stability and I ask, "Do you remember the last time we saw each other?"

"I do," he whispers, dropping his head, tripling his chin. "You were what? Fifteen? You drove all the way up to my place in Sunshine Canyon . . . without a license. We sat by my empty fireplace and you told me you were ashamed that we'd ever met and that you never wanted to see me again."

I'm stunned and, oddly, flattered that he remembers it— the scene, my words—exactly as I do. It seems to say that *it,* that I meant a lot. Is that what I've come for? I wonder. To see if I'm as vivid for him as he's been for me? That I was *important,* not just another little boy—an easy target—who gave it up to him?

And he says, "That tore my heart out. I curled into a shell that night, after you left, for nearly two months."

He's speaking the truth, it seems, or, is he playing me? The confusion feels familiar. I finger the button of my recorder but don't push, I'm afraid it will click too loudly.

Then I ask, "Did you know Bob that this coming weekend will be thirty years exactly since we first . . . actually met. April 7, 1972."

"Oh, I'm not aware," he shakes his head, his hair falls back into his eyes. "Dates are fuzzy . . . I couldn't say the exact . . ."

"Oh I can," I tell him. The man in the other bed coughs. He is watching a TV fixed high on the wall. I'm concerned he hears me then, I try not to care: "It was three months after my twelfth birthday. Except for my head, I didn't have a hair on my body. I didn't know a thing, barely what a wet dream might be. . . ."

"Let's go outside," he says, already scooching across the bed toward his wheelchair. I reach out a hand to help and he brushes it away. . . .

I had a teacher, spring of sixth grade. Sister Christine. You know how there always seems to be one nun in the bunch who's different, cool? The one who flies, like Sister Betrille? Well, that was her, Sister Christine. I mean, she couldn't fly exactly but she had a twelve-string guitar and a bucktoothed grin that made you want to sing. She was adorable. She had such an impact on me. She was really tall and she had these reddish brows and, I think, red hair, though that was another mystery that remained just beyond the veil. She still wore hers while most of the other nuns had taken them off. I asked her why once and she said: "I wear my veil as a constant statement of a deeper reality. . . ." "Oh. . . okay." She was full of these sayings . . . like, "It's through discipline that the transcendent enters our lives." Or when we had to *sacrifice,* give something up, for the forty days of Lent— chocolate or TV—she'd always say: "Look, *Virtue* grows through deliberate acts." Or, "Pray for Grace . . . you'll get the help you need." So, here's the thing: she stopped me in the hall one day and looked at me (and she was one of those adults who when they looked at you, really *looked*) she stopped and said, "You know Marty, I think you might be . . . *musical*." So, suddenly, there I was, sitting with her twice a week during recess, learning chords on my cruddy little guitar. (*Miming guitar*) *Tie me kangaroo down sport . . . keep me cockatoo cool Curt . . .* and can I just say how happy I was not to be out on the playground worrying about which kind of ball might hit me in the head . . . *keep me cockatoo cool.* . . . I was making progress and one afternoon Sister suggested that I find a way to earn money for a decent guitar. And that suggestion, gave particular motion to the motion of things.

So . . . I got a job! I became a *Denver Post* paperboy. And the most astonishing thing about this, besides ringing people's doorbells and taking their cash, was that, suddenly, I was friends with George Doyle—chubby, mean, paperboy. The neighborhood menace. Though he was Catholic and lived just around the corner, chances of us ever being pals were slim. He was *Public* (McMean) and two years and most of puberty ahead of me. His idea of fun was dropping a lit M-80 firecracker into the corner mailbox. *Bang!* So I was astonished when, at our paperboy marketing powwows, he seemed to take a shine to me. He gave me advice and I gave him extra rubber bands. It was the bond of capitalism.

He used to call me Marsh, by the way, short for Martian.

"Marsh! *That's* your mistake. Don't ever collect from the Weinstocks on Friday night. Jewish people won't touch money after sundown. It's a Sabbath thing. *Tip death.* As for the Catholics, shoot for cocktail hour. Any day."

It was the Monday after Easter. I finished my paper route and zoomed over to George's place. I dropped my bike on their dried-up grass, ducked under their sickly weeping willow and walked up to the porch. I felt queasy every time I came to fetch George but these nerves, I figured, were a small price to pay for the cachet of hanging out with a bona fide bully.

I knocked on the screen door. Immediately there were heavy steps. I prayed it wasn't his dad. Huge, sullen guy, he was chairman of the local NRA. Had guns hanging all over the house like precious paintings. Whenever he'd see me he'd ask: "Wanna go hunting?" Anyway, I was standing there and I heard:

"Who's there?"

It was Minnie, the live-in housekeeper.

"Minnie, it's me, Marty."

"Oh . . . come in hon." She swung open the door, a big smile on her face cause, well, cause it was me: the Boy from Christ the King. She said, "George ain't home, running late on his route. Trouble at school again." She sat me down, gave me some milk and asked: "Who said Mass this morning?"

"Father Kottenstettie."

"Oh now, he's a saint."

I nodded thinking, God if she only knew what a surly saint.

Father Kottenstettie, our parish priest, was German by way of Ireland and all shriveled from long life as some kind of prisoner of some kind of war somewhere. It was all sad and vague but one thing was clear: Whatever happened to him, it was our fault. He was always angry about something.

On Holy Thursday, the week before, he'd stormed into our sixth grade class and sent Sister Christine and all the girls to the multipurpose room. His face was red, the veins in his neck sticking out.

"Vich one of you boys stole wine from the sacristy?"

I had that reflexive moment (*Starting to raise hand*) where I felt sure I'd done it, but we all knew it was Ricky Flynn. He'd tried every trespass on the list. Ricky didn't fess up so we all got twenty *Hail Marys*. Then, instead of storming out, Father walked to the blackboard and picked up a piece of chalk. We watched as he scribbled:

The Sacred Seed of God

Through his thick tongue, he spoke.

"Vhen you grow from a boy to a man, Got gives you the 'Seed of Life.' In each drop there are a thousand hopeful Catholics. After the sacrament of marriage in the sacred act of intercourse they will race to find the egg inside a woman. The fastest one will penetrate the egg, be born and baptized into the one true church. This will happen in Got's own time." His good gray eye (the other was glass) wandered across our stunned faces. "Your genitalia are for procreation. Do not abuse. If you do, you abuse Got. A mortal sin." With that he dropped the chalk and marched out the door . . . we had this sort of unsupervised moment . . . working through the information. . . .

Anyway, Minnie asked, "Want more milk?"

"No thanks. . . ." Suddenly there was the sound of a key in the door. George poked his head in.

"Come on Marsh."

Minnie yelled: "Dinner's at six!"

We jumped on our bikes and flew past the shoebox-shaped houses and out onto the dirt trails by Cherry Creek. Plump as he was, George was poetry on a bike. I nearly killed myself trying to keep up.

Worn out we dropped our bikes near the creek's edge and slid down the path to the water and George said:

"Marsh, you got to lean into it man . . . you're afraid of everything."

I said, "Am not."

He said, "Are too."

He leaned back and I watched the muddy creek.

"Hey George," I asked, "where's all this water go?"

"Joins the Platte," he said, "the Colorado, dumps into the Gulf of Mexico, I think."

"Wow . . . all that way?" I said. "It's like Virginia Vale is connected to the whole planet by Cherry Creek."

"Don't get weird," he said.

I turned and watched the rise and fall of purple lettering—*Led Zeppelin*—written across George's big chest. His black T-shirt was too small, *Zeppelin* stretched to the limit. The fuzz on his lip had gotten thick lately. He told me how he was planning to use his new razor soon. God, I was miles from all of that, I thought. The hair sprouting and body spurts described in the back of the Scout book (page 273) . . . I was waiting for the big dream, the trigger, wondering if maybe then I'd get big. And strong. And sure.

George grabbed a fistful of dirt and hurled it into the creek, then out of the blue he asked: "Hey Marsh, was that counselor, *Bob,* at Camp Saint Malo the summer you were there?"

"Who?" I asked . . . oh, by the way, Saint Malo was the boys' camp run by the Archdiocese of Denver. Most of the counselors there were, or were thinking about becoming, seminarians—guys training for the priesthood. Beautiful place . . . my dad had gone there, my cousins.

"Who?" I asked.

"Remember that guy, Father Mac's assistant, Bob? He was always taking photos of us, yelling about the right way to do push-ups?"

I did remember, this image popped into my head of him standing next to Father Mac at Chapel . . . tall with dark-framed glasses. He had combat boots but always wore penny loafers to dinner . . . with dimes in them. But I remembered him especially because he told these amazing campfire stories about jungle ghosts and war in Vietnam. He'd been a soldier there and brought back these weird gongs and drums which he used at just the right moment in his stories (*bang-clap scream!*) to scare the shit out of us. After lights-out he'd come around the bunks to make sure we weren't too frightened to sleep. "Are you okay?" he'd whisper, pressing a piece of butterscotch into your hand or leaving a Jolly Rancher perched on your tummy.

I asked George, "You mean the guy with the ghost stories, right? Who slept in the dorm?"

"Yeah that's him."

"He was cool."

"Well," George explained, "he knows my dad from down the Veteran's Club. He's starting a boys' camp of his own on a mountain ranch. He's fixing it up, wants help this weekend, payin' ten bucks. Want to go?"

"A ranch. Wow. I'd have to find someone to cover my route. And 8:30 Mass on Sunday—it's my turn to serve."

"Well, try," George said.

"Okay, I'll ask my mom."

So, that following Friday, right after school, there I was in the cab of a six-wheeled International Harvester. Already, I couldn't wait to tell the guys at school about this. Me in a big yellow truck. Me, on my way to do a job. I was in the middle, George at the open window and Bob, counselor Bob in his red flannel and Levis, was at the wheel. God, this is a chance thrill, I was thinking. Or, as Sister Christine would say: *Nil Sine Numine . . .* which is the Colorado state motto: *Nothing Without Providence.* At the very last second everything—chicka-chicka-chick—just fell into place. Jay Jones said he'd cover my route and Father K. got someone else to serve Sunday Mass and mom said "Yes" and it was Friday and I was free, free to go. We passed the Coors plant, its stacks sending up beer-colored smoke, and climbed up into Clear Creek Canyon.

James Taylor was on the radio. . . .

Lord knows when the cold wind blows it'll turn . . .

And Bob asked, "Have you ever driven a tractor? Or milked a cow?"

I said, "Nope," and Bob's teeth flashed white.

"Well, I'll teach you," he said, "I'll bet you're a quick learner."

I shrugged and felt pride or something leak through the heat of my cheeks. God, the luck of being included. . . .

We were up far and high now—near timberline—snow-capped peaks rising up on all sides. The road was barely a road, more like two tracks of mud through a meadow. The sun had disappeared but the light of day still lingered.

He said, "Watch your knee, Tiger," and I closed my legs, watched his forearm, these marbled blue veins, shift the stick rising from the center of the floor. The truck lurched through the ditches, we rounded a clump of blue spruce and suddenly Bob hit the brakes, cut the engine.

George asked, "Hey man, what's wrong?"

Bob put a finger to his lips. "Shshshshsh . . ." He was staring at the clearing ahead. Something was out there. Then
my eye caught a clue—antlers—a ton of them not eighty,
ninety yards away and I whispered,

"Deer."

"Wapiti," said Bob. "Wild elk." He pointed, "See the
buck at the far end? Look at his rack, he's the king. Bet he's
mounted every doe in the crowd." I looked at Bob looking
at the elk. He belongs here, I thought, he knows about the
wilderness. He used to lead the hard hikes at St. Malo. I
didn't really know him then. He was too important and I
just couldn't believe I was sitting next to him now.

George nudged me, "Look, two are fighting."

And Bob said, "Nah, they're just playing," and stretching
his arm up with a sigh, he let his right hand fall to my nape.
His fingers began to brush up and down over the fuzz there,
you know, sort of inadvertently, but his hand was talking
some story direct from my neck down into the middle of
things and I let . . . let my head do a fall-back press into the
curve of his palm. Something was in there, a bottomless mystery, a long way to tumble. Maybe a friend. And, suddenly, his
hand split to start the engine and we roared ahead as a hundred black and terrified eyes snapped around to see us and in
that instant they ran for their lives, this stampede of fur leap-
ing across the meadow until all the elk had disappeared.

When we got to the ranch we did *real* chores, milked the
two cows by hand, fed the horses. Bob made spaghetti for
dinner and then he led the way down a trail, which ran
alongside the brook and ended at the A-framed cabin. That's
where we'd sleep best, he said, in the loft there.

The sky was *amazing,* just packed with stars. I spotted the
upside-down W, my favorite constellation; I'd learned it in
Scouts. "Cassiopeia, I've never seen it so bright."

And Bob said, "Good eye kid. Cassiopeia." And he
explained, "She was the ancient queen of Ethiopia ya know.
She made the mistake of looking at Medusa's head and was

turned to stone. But then the gods forgave her, split her into pieces and hung her in the sky."

And George said, "Fuck. They call *that* forgiveness?"

Bob laughed and said, "Well, you gotta pay for breaking the rules." He put down his pack and stepped to the side of the path to pee. He undid the buttons of his fly, looked up and said, "Yeah, there's a million stories up there. The stars can guide you. Save your life." He turned and I could see his eyes through the dark. Then his teeth as he smiled at me. "Hey, I'll give you a book on celestial navigation."

I nodded and George said, "Look, a shooting star!"

I just caught it and I blinked, wondering if it really happened.

Bob said, "That star died a thousand, maybe a million years ago."

George said, "Ah, that's *bull* Bob."

And he said, "No, no, it's true. It takes years for light to travel. It's all . . . already happened." (*Crossing to pick up book off table.*)

When I was nearly thirty years old I began writing down what happened next as exactly as I could. This is what I wrote. (*Marty sits, opens the book and continues.*)

Campfire time. (*Finger to lips*) SSShhhhh. (*The lights dim.*)

(*Reading*) When we got to the cabin, Bob stayed downstairs to build a fire and George and I grabbed our sleeping bags and crawled up the ladder to the loft to get ready for bed. It was cold and dimly lit up there and George said to me,

"Marsh, you don't need those dumb pj's man. The more naked you are, the warmer. That's how blood and feathers work, like the Indians did it. Didn't they teach you that in pansy Scouts?"

I looked down at his pink moon of a face poking out of his sleeping bag. "How do you know what the Indians did?"

"Everybody knows dummy."

I dropped my pajamas and slithered into my down sack. The nylon smelled like campfire, icy against my skin.

"Burrr." I tightened the drawstring to my neck and asked, "Hey George. What's Bob *do*? Was he a seminarian?"

"I don't know . . . he quit, I guess. Does construction. Carpentry."

"He's cool, isn't he? I never *knew* there were so many constellations. You know what? He's gonna give me a book about it. George? Did you really see Pegasus when he pointed to it? George? . . . George?"

He was conked. But I was wide-awake. A truck, driving a tractor, milking a cow. I mean, what a day and I was thinking, Okay, I'll wear my boots to school on Monday. All muddy. See if Sister Christine or any of the guys notice. I'm a rancher now.

I heard the rungs of the ladder creaking. Bob climbing. He burped as his head popped up over the floor.

"Hey," he said.

"Hey," I whispered. I thought the noise would wake George. It didn't. He was snoring.

Bob set down a can of Coke and a lantern that had been hooked around his wrist and then he pulled himself the rest of the way up into the loft. He stood, or stooped really, because he was too big for the place and picked up the lantern and hooked it to a nail. It swung there, hissing. He hunched over me.

"George is down for the count, eh?"

I nodded, amazed at how warm my bag had become, how fast my blood was doing its work. George was right about the Indians.

I watched as Bob finished off his Coke and started taking things out of his pocket. A ring of keys. Loose change. A leather wallet. He placed everything just so on top of a battered dresser. He tugged his T-shirt up over his belly. I looked out the one small window—a box of sparks.

Bob's belt buckle hit the floor.

His chest was filled with brown hair growing right down to the stripes of his Fruit of the Looms hanging there from his bony hips . . . just like the loincloth carved on the St. Sebastian outside Sister Joan's office. He took off his glasses and placed them on the dresser. There were dark smudges under his eyes. I hadn't noticed them until now. They made him look sad, the same look Sister Christine had when she talked of paradise. A look that made you want to help.

I sat up because suddenly I thought of my teeth and whispered, "I forgot to brush. I better go down. My mom's really strict about it."

"One night off won't ruin you," he said, arranging his sleeping bag so that our zippers touched. "You gotta break the routine now and again." I could smell the sweat of him. His calves were next to me. White and huge, they made me think of a Sunday roast. He reached up and with a sudden flick of his arm the lantern was out and he rummaged through a drawer. I lay back down and watched him move like a ghost in the million-year-old light. His briefs glowed in the dark and the whole floor bounced when he walked. He unsnapped his Breitling—the watch he told me his grandfather had given him, the one he used in Vietnam—it sparkled as he laid it next to his bed.

"Here's an extra pillow," he said. "Lift up."

"Okay."

He slithered into his bag.

We listened for a time to George's snore, to the wind and branches outside.

Bob said, "Tomorrow's supposed to be good weather. We'll get an early start."

His fingers found my neck and started their talking. I held absolutely still but there was the one little muscle that dared to insist, like a current moving through me I didn't own, it rose, willful, curious. And my heart was going crazy like it wanted out. I was still as a mountain but full of motion.

He fumbled around the edge of my bag—looking for the zipper—and when he found it he tugged it quickly downward. I felt a stream of cold air run from my shoulder to my hip, right past a thousand years of what I knew was taboo. He reached over and with large hands, scooped me into his bag. I remained limp. My body *seemed* to know, to want whatever this was—but *I* didn't want to help. Not one bit. I needed to save some part of me for looking Sister Christine in the eye. I couldn't hear for all the blood pounding in my head but I knew that someone, somewhere, was saying: *stop.*

He turned me on my side so that my back was to him, then wrapped his arms around me, tenderly, tightly. My head fit right under his chin; the hair on his chest tickled my shoulder blades and I simply could not believe the *size* of him, all the surface of him—endless skin on skin, like I was being swallowed into another planet.

He reached down to slip off my underwear. I let him. As my shorts slid past my knees, suddenly, into my mind came a picture that hung from the chalkboard in Father Kottenstettie's science class: a color-coded chart of all the layers of the earth from crust to core and it was the liquid core I was thinking of—the orange ball of fire hidden under a million layers because it's too dangerous. The secret urge buried at the center of everything, the *force* that pushes up the trees and the mountains too. How did I slip here so fast? I wondered. To the secret at the center of bodies. The center of *him.*

God, oh God, is this you?

Bob pressed against me as though he'd found all he ever wanted. I was it and I was terrified, amazed to be the one, as if I was a magnet and he stuck on me. My whole body humming with . . . *touch,* a force mightier than church or family or anything I'd ever found in a book. This must be *it,* I thought, the grown-up world, the way it is and with a swift move of his hand, he placed himself, just so, between my legs. A part of my mind, the part asking: *What in the world is he doing?* was looking on now, as if observing us from overhead, as if observing a collision I was in and I knew there'd be damage. Real trouble.

Come on now! I thought. *One word, one scream, one virtuous move and you could change the course of everything. Couldn't you? Choose to wake George, startle Bob. Stop the accident.*

But I didn't. I *allowed* . . . it was as though he was touching me into being and I was dying to find out who I was.

One of his arms circled my chest as with his other hand he reached around and cupped himself between the very top of my thighs. The smell of Johnson's Baby Lotion filled the room as he slid himself along my legs. I heard a tiny cry, a flutter through his throat as he squeezed the air out of my lungs. *This must be what a man does with a woman and what does that make me?* He squished me again, gave another soft cry, and suddenly there was warm liquid on my legs. *My God,* I thought. *What is it?* It smelled like swimming at the JCC. Oh, wait . . . is it? it must be . . . thousands of Catholics, searching for an egg. This guy is a murderer. What a mess, a massacre. What a jerk!

I wanted to yell down to the drowning Catholics. *Sorry, I know this isn't what you expected.*

His hands were fast all over, plucking and playing with me, and there was a wave at the center of me rising. A motion that threatened to burst, to split me open and I panicked thinking I might spill piss everywhere.

"No!" I whispered, trying to move his hand away . . . but he insisted and then, nothing in heaven or on earth could stop it now, up from the core of me coming, my first, my very own seed splitting up and out and swimming away down my belly. What happened? Did it really happen? Over in a second, like the shooting star. I tried to steady my breath, to lie as still as I could.

After a while he moved his hand away and shifted so we were both on our backs. I turned my face away into the scratchy pillow and right there next to my nose, his precious Breitling was glowing. Hands ticking past the numbers: *11:49, 7 April '72,* burned itself into my brain. Every second hereafter I'd be different. I was twelve years, three months and nine days old. This was the end of? . . . the beginning of? . . . over in a second. Nothing like the Scout book—page 273, *Nocturnal Emission*—said it would be. In a dream all of my own. A dream with a girl.

I tucked myself back into my bag. He was silent, George snored. I brushed my fingers across my stomach, over the evidence, wondering at the blame stuck there, at how fast you can fall. I looked toward the window, to the stars and space beyond, and tried to strike a deal.

(*Whispered heavenward.*)

God, please . . . this has to be just ours. Top Secret.

(MARTIN *closes the book. The lights brighten; he continues.*)

At the end of that weekend, Sunday evening, we were in the truck heading back into Denver. George was at the window, Bob at the wheel. We passed the green sign that says: *Welcome, You're One Mile High.* The streetlamps were just coming on.

George was dropped first then Bob drove around the block toward my street. I watched the squares of light go by—the glow from my neighbors' kitchen windows—the McCoys', the Tynans', the Pecks'. . . . I had the strangest feeling that I'd been to the other side of the world and back again and my house might not be there anymore. We stopped at the corner of Exposition. There was no traffic but Bob didn't make the turn. We just sat there, engine idling. I saw Mrs. Lachada kneeling in her front yard, digging . . . crazy gardener. I'd help her sometimes . . . with chores. . . . Led Zeppelin was on the radio: *There's a lady who's sure all that glitters is gold and she's* . . . Bob reached over and clicked it off. The silence pressed me close to the passenger door. And he said, "George smokes dope, you know."

"What?" I asked.

"Dope, do you?"

"No," I said. I grabbed my knapsack off the floor and stuck it on my lap.

"I'm glad," Bob said. "And I hope you never do Marty

cause you've got talent coming out of your ears." He shoved the stick and made the turn. I wrapped my fingers around the door handle . . . the Fosters' house; the Starmans' . . .

I said, "This is it!" I glanced at the kitchen window, relieved no one was looking out.

Bob said, "Thanks again for your help."

I nodded and pushed the door open.

"Marty. I'm glad George invited you. I hope you'll come work again soon."

The cab rocked gently.

"Marty."

I turned but couldn't really see his face. He was staring at the dash and the light from the instruments made his cheeks green, his eyes like . . . empty sockets.

He said, "Our friendship . . . it's different you know. Because it's . . ." I took a quick look at the house. No movement there but this flickering blue light from the den window. *Wonderful World of Disney* or *Mission: Impossible,* that's where they must be. Sunday night television, Dad on the floor, curled around his vodka tonic, smoking his filterless Phillips. Mom on the couch, adding up household receipts. Little brother, sisters. I'll say a quick hi, take out the trash (my Sunday chore) and go straight to my room.

And Bob whispered, "In another time and place, you know, what we shared is *good.* Really. It's all right. Everything's okay . . . you know why?"

I stared ahead toward the sign at the corner: *Children at Play.*

And he said, "Because there's *love,* you know and . . . it's between us."

I looked at his drooping, unshaven cheek and something like . . . hate took hold of me. I hated that he used the word *love* and I had a sudden sense he'd said all this before to someone else, others. And I realized he was scared of what I might do and I felt this mean rush of power and for an instant then, our eyes met as he reached over to take my shoulder. But before he could touch me I was out the truck and moving toward the house, toward the flickering blue light. I could hear the engine stuck there, idling, but I didn't look back, I kept walking. I opened the yellow front door of my house and there came from the den this deep, commanding voice. The one you'd hear every Sunday after the fireworks of Disney were finished, just before the top secret assignment self-destructs: *"Your mission, Mr. Phelps, should you decide to accept it . . ."*

"I'm home."

And I heard the truck pulling away, and then the sizzling sound of fire as I entered the room and found my family gathered, staring at the Magnavox where the secret agent's impossible mission was going up in smoke. . . .

I talked before about *anger.* I said that I often wonder . . . where mine went. Well . . . I think I know where *some* of it went. . . .

Over the next three years, at some point, I began stealing these orange and yellow pills from my mom, one or two at a time. I hid them in a sandwich baggie at the back of my sock drawer waiting for the moment to stuff them down my throat. I was fifteen when I finally did it, a few months after I finally broke away from Bob and shortly after I heard he was going to jail. (*Beat.*)

Lots of throwing up, one visit to a shrink and nothing else said.

That fall, in an effort to save my life, I switched to public school.

A year later I tried with a rifle, a .22 my dad had left behind when he moved out. I tried to put it to my head but, thank God, I ended up shooting the thing through the paneling of my bedroom wall and the bullet went through the banister of the basement steps and ended up somewhere in the storeroom. Years and years later, when I heard my mom had sold the house—I was in a show at the time in New York, a musical, you only have Monday off—and I flew from

New York to Denver and back on the one day off because, suddenly, I wanted to see if the bullet hole was really there. That it all *actually* happened. It was there.

I touched it. . . .

. . . Bob and I are just outside the Veterans' Hospital now. I've finally clicked on the tape recorder, I feel it buzzing, proof in my pocket this whole thing's happening. It's April 4, 2002—two years ago, right? We're sitting under a palm tree, me on a bench, Bob in his wheelchair and I am so aware of the *face-off,* of all my grown-up effort, my thousands in therapy for this: to be frank.

This brown sparrow arrives . . . flutters really close to Bob's head and disappears. Then Bob speaks first:

"I must have read your letter a dozen times to try and see . . ."

"What I wanted?" I ask.

He nods then looks at his hands clasped in his lap. And he says, "To try and see your *state of mind* I guess. I fix up old cars for a living. Can't work anymore . . ." (he nods toward his bandage) ". . . lost my lease." His right hand becomes a fist now which he's squeezing around his left index finger, it makes me think of a little boy who's got to pee bad. So . . . he looks up and says, "I mean if you're thinking of suing me . . . I don't have anything."

His lips lift with this hint of a grin, his eyes saying: *your move.* And I'm . . . *is he joking?* But then I think, no, he's worried. It's all over the papers, isn't it? Younger Catholic men like me, nailing older ones like him—seeking answers, damages.

And I say, "Look, I'm not here for that."

He unclasps his hands and says, "It was my fault, mentally . . . I don't know the words . . . mentally, it's like I was the same age as you . . . but, but I have to take it on my shoulders." (*Short beat.*) This strikes me as a sentence from his psychiatrist and I say,

"Yeah, it was your fault. You were the adult. I was a *child* and I did not have consent to give." I feel this sudden heat beneath my sternum, like the breath of the twelve-year-old I'm here to represent, as if he's in there saying: "Yeah . . . that's good. Say that, get me off the hook, please."

And Bob says, "I, I, wanted to help you. You were such a gentle soul. . . ."

"Soul?" I say. "My soul? You went for me the very first chance you had. Didn't even wait for a second date." He seems, chooses? not to hear this remark and says,

"Mentally, you were way ahead of the other boys. You were special."

And I say, "Now that I *hate*. What does that mean, *special*? How many *specials* can you have Bob?"

He holds up a hand and says, "Look, yes . . . there were others . . . but not like you. You were so curious about things but you were afraid. . . ."

I say, "Afraid? What do you mean?"

"Well," he says, "you were . . . kind of wimpy. . . ."

"Oh, don't say that," and he goes:

"No, no, I mean you were shy and I wanted to teach you about the land and animals and help you gain confidence and you did. . . ." (*Beat.*) *I* want to disown it but it flashes through me that with this guy: I rafted a river, watched a calf being born, cleared a field, conquered a glacier, learned a heifer from a Holstein, a spruce from a cedar. He says, "I watched you grow to be a young man."

And I say, "Yeah, you did, didn't you?"

He says, "There were lots of levels to what we shared." And he drops his head again.

The brown sparrow is back, circling the crown of Bob's head as if tracing a halo. As if it might land . . . and Bob is slumping there, his silver head shimmering in the California sun, completely unaware, it seems, of the bird and I wonder, in some . . . Catholic way, if the creature bears a message from On High: *Be gentle,* the fluttering spirit seems to say. *I've come to bless him to whom you speak.* Then it's like: *Marty, STOP IT. The bird's scoping for food, or nesting material.*

I ask him, "Who was it that sent you to prison? A camper?" (*Beat*.)

He nods, "Yeah, the boy's family , . . and the archdiocese. They hounded me. It got the attention off the priests who'd been fooling around at St. Malo. I was a scapegoat."

I have the sense that he's lying, exaggerating . . . I don't know and I ask, "I heard you got five years, Canyon City. Is that true?"

He shrugs, nods.

I say, "Must have been awful."

"You can't imagine," he says. "It made my eighteen months in Nam look like a walk in the park. . . ."

Suddenly this black guy sits down on the bench next to me, same hospital uniform as Bob, smoking a cigarette. Bob lets out a rude growl, says, "Let's go," and wheels himself down to the shade at the next bench where he launches into a monologue about the good parent he's tried to be for his daughter who's nearly thirty and "doin' great." He speaks of his troubled ex wife, Karen—whom I knew as his nineteen-year-old cocounselor and girlfriend back at summer camp. After a time I try to interrupt, to get back to the "us" of this but, "Just let me finish," he says, raising his hand sharply and somehow this, more than anything, tells me I really don't like the guy and my candy-striper quotient just evaporates and I say,

"Hey, I had sex with both of you . . . several times. Remember? You, me and Karen. One morning there was blood in the bed. I thought something terrible had happened until you explained it was her period."

This shuts him up. Then he says,

"It was an awkward attempt, I guess, at helping you be more, you know . . . a man. I knew you were worried about . . ."

"Being gay?" I ask.

He nods.

I tell him, "You used to say to me that homosexuals were people without love . . . interesting thinking."

"I wasn't thinking," says he and I ask,

"Have you ever figured . . . you might be gay?"

He brings his hands to his face and says, "I've had to climb so many walls in this life, I suppose there's some things I never could . . . really look at."

I say, "Imagine Bob, what our friendship might have been if . . ."

"If what?" he asks.

"If you hadn't crossed the line. Do you *know* what it does? Did? *The utter chaos* when you walk back into Mass, or your sixth grade classroom and you're standing there in your muddy boots, listening to your teacher thinking: this *thing's* happened . . . wow . . . I'm gonna be a man. But it's happened *all wrong,* I'm broken, I broke the rules, I *can't* belong here and God knows where you turn because even the mountains and the statues look at you differently and because—*no one speaks of such things in our Catholic world* with all our secrets and our terror of the body. And crazily enough then Bob, the *only* place to find five minutes of relief, five seconds of what felt like . . . forgiveness . . . was back in your arms, again and again." He looks away and I tell him, "You know, I grew up to be insanely sexually compulsive— I mean back alleys, bathhouses, hurtful *crazy* secrets . . . from my family, my lover . . . you name it . . . and it has a lot to do, I think, with all that happened between us. (*Beat.*) I mean . . . Bob, *I was twelve.* . . ."

He shakes his head, he's looking at his tangled fingers and I wonder if I could ever convey to him how that was too young to get shot up with desire—split into pieces and hung in the sky—and suddenly, you know, I'm thinking of the boy on page twenty-eight of *Time* magazine, the one who didn't make it and I want to ask Bob what he thinks of that! And I'm wondering if he remembers the photograph that *he* took of a fine-boned boy standing in a kayak on a pond where we went, just the two of us, three weekends after it first happened. (*Beat.*) I'm a tiny twelve, holding up the oar, wearing the life jacket he gave me, lest I might drown.

And all at once I want to make clear to this man in the wheelchair how much he's haunted me, of the terror that lives in me still of repeating, in some way, his trespass. I wonder if I could describe for him the kind of overwhelming tenderness I feel toward kids the age I was then; how there isn't a time I don't squeeze with crazy joy and affection my gorgeous eleven-year-old nephew and think to myself: Oh God, careful, careful now. (*Beat.*) I want him to know . . . how I know this child is sacred, and to respect this child, a moral imperative. A certainty. This I know in my body, in this world, now: that *HERE is the Face of God*.

But I can't find the words or the will to say any of this to the wounded vet sitting at my side, and all that finally comes out is: "You know Bob, I almost didn't make it."

He glances at me, then off to the hospital roofs and says, "I guess, on the one hand I wanted to build you up, but on the other, I was tearing you down."

"Okay," I tell him. . . . I'm hearing Sister Agatha's words, you know, about the *tangle inside* . . . and I'm looking at this guy, this wreck of a *guy*. I'm looking at *his* face and I can see that some part of him means, meant to be good; and at a time I was lost—my father drinking, my mom gearing for divorce, in he clomped and, in some way, his love and my love for him, helped me. I've thought it. Stranger things have happened in these Disturbed Regions.

And he says, "I'm sorry you went through all of this." I don't know if *sorry* was the sound I was after, but suddenly it's all *enough* and I stand to go and I ask,

"Will you be here in the hospital long?"

"Another month, at least," he says. "I'd sure like to hear from you."

I say, "Oh . . . well, you've got my info, right?" It comes out cold like a "We'll do lunch," because underneath my thought is: *You've had enough of me for this lifetime.*

He backs up his chair a foot or two. "I hope," he says looking down at the grass, "I hope you don't hate me."

"Bob," and my words just spill, "whatever else there

might have been, there was kindness too. You were kind and I don't *hate* you."

He hunches forward as if hit in the gut and takes the wheels of his chair. "Once," he says, "we were shopping, you were riding in the cart and you grabbed a box of cereal and said: 'Let's get this Dad.'" He looks up at me. "Do you remember that?" I say nothing thinking, God, that can't be true, even as this image floats through my mind—a Friday night, a fluorescent aisle. He says, "You don't remember?"

(*Shaking head*) "No."

And he says, "Maybe it was just a slip that you said *Dad* but . . . I nearly fell through the floor. . . . It was one of the happiest moments of my life."

And . . . my hand moves to his shoulder—whoosh—just like that . . . and I squeeze the loose flesh. I think, God . . . there it is . . . *touch*.

He extends his hand to shake and we do, like two gentlemen and I say to him,

"Sometimes I wonder who I might be if I'd never met you."

"I can understand that," he says, his face going hard.

I pull away and move down the sunny sidewalk toward the stairs to the parking lot. I feel his eyes on me. I think he's waiting for me to turn, to give some sign. When I reach the door of my rent-a-car I spin around and, sure enough, he's positioning his chair at the edge of the steps where he can watch me go. He's silhouetted against the white brick and I am just amazed that he's there, that he gave me this stab at the past and, without permission, my hand flies into the air and waves . . . jauntily . . . ever the boy from Christ the King. And when Bob raises his arm to wave back I'm filled with the strangest, strongest feeling, that this very good-bye was contained in the first moment I ever laid eyes on him. (*Beat.*) Is it possible that what harms us might come to restore us?

I turn away and get in the car and shut the door thinking, *That's it. I came, I met him, I did it, I was frank . . . this'll put an end to all of it. Right? That's why I've come.* But the grip of it, of him, it's still there. . . . *God, what do you have to do?*

Then, I thought of something Sister Christine said all those years ago . . . that with the really rough things it would always come down to *Grace*—a gift from the beyond that *moves us toward* our own salvation. And as I crawled out into the thick Los Angeles traffic, what I kept hearing in my head was this prayer, a plea repeating: Okay, Grace please, to let it go—LET HIM BE, for heaven's sake, LET HIM REST. And I mean Bob, of course, but then . . . I realize I'm really talking about someone else . . . the twelve-year-old, the sweet kid caught in a photo still talking his way out. . . .

(*Turning to the photo which has become brightly lit.*)

Him. And, you know, I'm not sure how in the world to let him rest. Not yet anyway . . .

(*Lights slowly fade on* MARTY, *then slowly, lights fade on the photo of the boy.*)

2.5 MINUTE RIDE

Lisa Kron

For my family who generously let me use their lives and haven't yet disowned me.

For the Five Lesbian Brothers who took me apart and put me back together as a better actor and something closer to a writer.

Most especially for Peg Healey—who has given me the gift of true devotion as well as all of the best ideas.

PRODUCTION HISTORY

The script for 2.5 Minute Ride was developed through collaboration with Lowry Marshall.

2.5 Minute Ride premiered at La Jolla Playhouse on September 24, 1996. It was directed by Lowry Marshall. The set was designed by Richard Ortenblad, Jr., the lights by Trevor Norton, and the sound and original music by Dan Froot. The production stage manager was Beth Robertson.

After changes to the script, a workshop production of 2.5 Minute Ride opened in New York at Soho Rep in association with David Binder on April 2, 1997. Directorial consultants were Dan Hurlin and Peg Healey. The lighting design was by Susan A. White, sound design by Darron L. West, and original music by Dan Froot. The production stage manager was Liza Dunn.

2.5 Minute Ride opened at The Joseph Papp Public Theater/New York Shakespeare Festival in New York on March 17, 1999. It was directed by Mark Brokaw. The set was designed by Allen Moyer, the lights by Kenneth Posner, the costume by Jess Goldstein, the sound by Darron L. West, and original music by Dan Froot. The production stage manager was Bess Marie Glorioso.

PRODUCTION NOTES

2.5 Minute Ride is, on its face, a story about my family, in particular about my father, but it is my intention that the stories serve as a template, a framework into which audiences project their own relationships and experiences. The theatrical dynamic of the piece lies in the intersection between what is presented onstage and the imagination of the viewer. To that end, the design elements are intentionally devoid of specific or easily recognizable denotation, but the elements of light and sound do serve to keep the play moving, to push the performer from one story to the next.

There are four basic playing areas: upstage left there is a stool which serves as a place to set down the laser pointer and slide clicker. On it also rests the cigarette and a glass of water. The opening slides, and most of the subsequent slides as well, are described from this area. On the back wall is a black scrim upon which the slides are projected. There are no actual images but blank squares of colored light which are made with lighting specials rather than a projector. There is an area of light downstage left which is used for most of the stories about the wedding. Mid-stage right is an old-fashioned, school-library-type, wooden straight-backed chair upon, and around which, stories about the trip to Germany and Auschwitz are generally told. The chair eventually comes to feel like a sort of surrogate for the car. Center stage is used for a variety of stories and descriptions. The matching of story location with stage location becomes less rigid as the piece progresses.

The music used for the production was original solo saxophone music composed by Dan Froot. It became clear fairly early in the development of the piece that, because the subject of the Holocaust is so overwhelmingly evocative, we wanted to steer clear of any music that would tap into the audience's well of previous emotional associations: Bach, for instance, or identifiably Jewish-sounding music such as klezmer. Dan's compositions worked extremely well because the nature of the piece moves abruptly between humor and horror and the saxophone is an instrument that naturally communicates at each end of that continuum.

Finally, a note about performance style. The piece juxtaposes stories of three different journeys. There are no written transitions between these stories. The intuitive performance choice is to create internal transitions with a pause, a breath, a drop of focus. But chief among the many great directional contributions of Mark Brokaw was his insistence that I make the counterintuitive, but dynamic, choice to never pause or drop my focus. The thread of each story is kept suspended throughout the piece—not dropped and picked up again later. The sections do not end but are interrupted, overlapped by the next.

2.5 Minute Ride is written to be performed as if spoken for the first time directly to the people who are sitting in the audience. The energy which animates the performer is meant to be the same as that which animates a storyteller in real life—the desire to amuse, interest, and move the listener. The sense should not be that the performer entered the room with every word planned out, but that the energy exchanged by the teller and the listener is building the story in the moment and taking it in unforeseen directions.

The audience hears the sound of a slide projector advancing to the next slide, as the lights come up on a woman holding a slide projector clicker and a laser pointer. She describes the following "slides" (not actually photographs, but squares of colored light), projected on a scrim. As she talks, she indicates what she sees with the pointer.

These are my grandparents. My father's parents. This, as you can see, is their wedding picture. I never knew them, actually. My father left his hometown in Germany in 1937, by himself, when he was fifteen years old, as part of a program to get Jewish children out of Germany. I'm making a videotape about my father—about his experiences—well, actually about this trip we took together to his hometown in Germany and then to Auschwitz.

(Changes the slide with the clicker. The sound of an advancing slide projector is heard as a new square of light replaces the old one.)

Okay. This is my father's hometown. And here you can see we're looking down on the town from the clock tower. It was originally a walled city—I think you can see a little bit of the wall right here. *(Indicates with the laser pointer.)* It's very beautiful, all these red roofs. My dad remembers every cobblestone in this city. He knows its history from its inception in the Middle Ages and I think he considers himself a part of that continuum. It was incredible, actually, when we were driving around. He can't see too well anymore but he'd say things to me like, "Now if you look to your left, you should see two dirt tracks," and there would be two dirt tracks, and he'd say, "That road was built by Napoleon." Then he'd say, "All right now we're going to go over a bump in the road," and we'd go over a bump, and then he'd say, "And if it's still there, you'll see to your right, a hill with a ditch at the bottom," and there would be a hill and a ditch, and he'd say, "I remember when I was a boy I used to ride my bike as fast as I could down that hill and try not to get caught by the group of boys who were chasing me but if I did I developed a method in which I would lie down in that ditch and pull one of the boys on top of me to use as a human shield."

(*Changes the slide.*)

Okay. This is my dad, you can see, and he's standing outside this apartment building where he lived when he was about three or four years old and here you can see that he's pointing up to this second-story window and he was telling me here about how, when he was about three or four years old, he put his head through the glass in that window. He said, "I planned it out very carefully. If I put my head through at the right angle and with the right amount of force it would pop right through the glass and then I could watch the parade going on down in the street." And I said, you know, "Did you hurt yourself?" And he said, "No, no. It worked out about the way I'd planned." We took this trip about seven or eight years ago, now. My dad had been back to Germany several times and I had been there once but we'd never gone together and this was something we always really wanted to do. So . . .

(*Changes the slide.*)

Okay, we're still in Germany. A little earlier in time, you can see here. This is my father and his father and they're here in the synagogue where his father was the cantor and also the teacher in the Jewish school. This was taken, I think, a few days before my dad left Germany to come to the United States. When he came here, he lived with a foster family in New Haven, Connecticut, and he received letters from his parents about once a week until one week, instead, he received a letter from the Red Cross informing him that his parents had been deported to the Litzmannstadt Ghetto which was in Poland. And that was the last time he heard directly from them.

(*Changes the slide.*)

Okay. This is something I might use in the videotape actually. This is a letter that my father received in 1947 from a man who had been with his parents in the Lizmannstadt Ghetto. I had it translated and it says (*As she reads, she traces the lines with the pointer.*), "Unfortunately, I must inform you that your parents were among the first transports sent to Auschwitz from the Ghetto." (*Traces ahead with the pointer.*) And then skipping down here a little . . . "I was a close friend of your parents and I know quite well how attached to you they were and how often you were talked about." So, the other part of this trip was that we went to Auschwitz where neither one of us had ever been before. And the trip was extraordinary. It was so much more than either of us had imagined and when I returned I decided to make this video because my father has so many incredible stories and I wanted to make a record.

(*Changes the slide.*)

Okay. This is my Dutch "sister" Elizabeth—Elizabeth Klip—who was an exchange student who lived with our family when I was in college. She's extremely bright and so good-hearted, you know, and a little high-strung, I think you can see here, a little bit around the eyes. (*Indicates the eyes with the pointer.*) She's completely devoted to my parents and she drove down from Holland to Germany to pick us up and take us to Auschwitz which is in Poland which was so great for us and a very nice vacation for her, too, as you can imagine.

(*Changes the slide.*)

Okay, this is my friend Mary who I asked to shoot this video for me. She's an accomplished videographer. She's done some wonderful pieces about her family and I asked her to accompany me and my girlfriend, my partner Peg, to Lansing, Michigan, where I grew up, where my parents still live, to shoot some interviews with my dad and then also to accompany us along with my entire extended midwestern family on our annual trip to the Cedar Point amusement park in Sandusky, Ohio, where my dad loves to ride the roller coasters, so we wanted to get that on tape as well, but anyway, here you can see Mary is in my mother's study, which is in the back hall of my parents' house, and here you can see she's showing me this little file cabinet of my mother's with all these little tiny drawers each meticulously labeled, and you can see here that she's pointing to this drawer marked "stamps," and she was showing me here how my mother has organized all of her postage stamps with these little handmade dividers by denomination. And she was saying to me here, "You know, your father's story is interesting but *this* would make a great video." My mother knows that everything has a purpose and throwing things away is a sin. She says, "You know, you all make fun of me for hanging on to everything, but when someone needs something they always come to me." My father always says, "I'd like to live in a stainless steel house with a drain in the middle."

(*Changes the slide.*)

Okay. Um. Okay, I don't know how this one got in here. This is Peg's family. This is from a huge family party I went to at Peg's parents' house several years ago. It was incredible. There were hundreds of them: Healeys, Dohertys, Flaher-

tys . . . They were all healthy and Irish and good-looking.
They all played sports all day. And at one point in the afternoon, another one of the in-laws asked me, "Does your
family have parties like this?" And I said, "No, no. My family's all either dead or crippled."

(*Changes the slide.*)

Okay. This is something that I might also use in the video.
This is my dad here in his office, you can see—we were taping some interviews here—and behind him you can see this
watercolor portrait that was done of him when he was an
American GI. I think he paid a German soldier something
like three packs of cigarettes to paint this for him. It's really
so beautiful. My dad was drafted by the American army,
after he managed to get himself declassified as an enemy
alien, and then he was sent back to Germany where he
worked as an army interrogator, questioning German . . .
well, I was going to say POWs but they weren't really
POWs. They were . . . arrestees, I guess you'd call them . . .
or maybe detainees is a better word. If they were "arrestees"
I guess they'd be Greek. (*Chuckles at her own stupid joke.*)

(*Changes the slide.*)

Okay, this is my family—my mother's side of the family—
the ones I actually know. And here you can see we're about
to leave for Cedar Point—we're here in front of my cousins'
house. There are about nine or ten of us who take this trip
every year, and when we do we separate out into three great
big American-made cars. You can see here my parents' Mer-
cury Marquis, and here's my cousins' Buick Skylark, and
here I think you can see just the corner of my brother's full-
sized Ford Econoline van. Cedar Point is, I would say, about
three, maybe three and a half, hours from Lansing, and
when we take this trip every year we set aside three whole
days so that we have a full day at the park and then an entire
day for travel on either side. And during this epic cross-
country trek these three vehicles remain in contact at all

times with the use of—I think you can see a little bit here on my parents' dashboard—walkie-talkies. I brought this picture because my mother says that I exaggerate when I talk about the family but, I mean, look at the pictures.

My mother is horrified at the prospect of people in her house with video cameras and she keeps bringing up that 1970s PBS series on the Loud family. And on our second day in Michigan she takes all of us over to the Pilgrim House so that we can buy all new chairs for the living room. Now, my parents have been in a solidly upper-middle-class tax bracket for at least thirty-five years but they've never owned a piece of furniture that wasn't previously owned by someone else, but I think that it's the threat of immortality by video that brings out in my mother an almost irresistible urge to redecorate. And we buy all this brand-new furniture. And that night, after everyone has gone to sleep, my mother and I stay up and push big, big pieces of furniture back and forth and back and forth around the living room floor. My mom has these incredible, inexplicable swings in physical ability. One second she can barely hobble from her La-Z-Boy to the bathroom and the next second she's like Jack LaLanne pulling a sofa across the living room with a strap in her teeth.

I'm trying to remember how many times we actually went to Cedar Point as a family when I was growing up. It's occurring to me that it's one of those fake "traditions" my mother uses to get me to come home more often. Like how she asks me every year, "Are you going to make it home for Christmas this year?" And I say, "I don't come home for Christmas, Mom. I never have come home for Christmas. We are not Christians. Stop trying to trick me!"

(*Sound of a car passing. She leaves the clicker and pointer on the stool and crosses to chair. Sits.*)

Elizabeth drives like a demon over pitch-dark Polish roads. Dad sits in the back and tells us stories. I ask questions. I keep my voice firm. I keep my crying to myself.

"Were you looking for your parents?"

"No, I had done that the summer before."

"And was it hard to accept it? Was it shocking?"

"No, I don't think it was hard to accept because I don't think I did accept it. I knew but I think somewhere I thought maybe they were still alive. I don't think I accepted it until a few years ago, in Lansing. It was the winter and it was so cold and I was shivering. In my coat. And I realized this would only happen to them once. They were old and they stood outside, lined up in the cold and they were of no use to anyone and they were killed."

(*Crosses to center.*)

At the entrance to the Magnum there are signs all over which say under no circumstances is this ride suitable for people who are elderly, diabetic or have heart conditions. I look at my father. He can't read the signs because, in addition to having all the conditions listed, he is also legally blind. I tell him what it says and I say, "Are you sure this is a good idea?" And he says, "I don't have to do anything. All I have to do is sit there." And then he pops a nitroglycerin in his mouth. "Well, then, why are you doing that?" I say. "Just in case." I try to get him to pretend to take another one so that Mary can tape him doing it. This might make a very nice video moment. But he says no because he's worried that if the girls who run the rides see him taking a pill they won't let him on.

(*The sound of a car passing pulls her back to the chair. She sits.*)

A horrible moment in the parking lot. We think they're going to make us pay to go in. No way, no way, no way. In the car we don't say anything to each other but it's clear to all of us that we can't pay an admission fee for Auschwitz. Oh. They're only charging us for parking. Well. Okay.

(*Slightly dark, but energetic, sax music plays. She crosses to the "wedding area."*)

My brother is getting married. In Peg's family when someone's getting married, her parents say, "Oh, isn't it exciting?
They're so in love." In my family, when someone's getting
married my parents say, "Well, I hope they know what
they're doing. They seem to be crazy about each other." My
brother lived on the third floor of my parents' house until a
few years ago when my mother asked him to go live in the
attic of my dead grandmother's house. Peg and I had spent
a month living in that house the summer after my grandmother died, about seven or eight years ago, to help my
mom organize an estate sale. The house was packed, floor to
ceiling, with things. Like, there was a whole room full of
Avon my grandmother had bought because she felt sorry for
the Avon lady. We tried to sell as much of her stuff as we
could but there was just too much, and there was the added
problem of my mother's attitude. When someone would ask
for a lower price on something, my mother would snatch
the item out of their hands and say, "I know exactly how
much my mother paid for this item twenty-five years ago
and if you don't want it for that price I'll just keep it
myself." So now, eight years later, the house is still full of
this stuff although it has all been organized on the first floor
on steel shelving, along with the large collection of gay
male pornography left by my grandmother's brother, my
great-uncle Robert, who also lived in the house, who was a
horribly twisted and bitter old closet case who never had a
cheerful or generous word to say to anyone. His two most-
often-used phrases, actually, were, "My God in heaven" and
"99.9 percent of the people," which he would combine into
sentences sometimes, such as, "My God in heaven! 99.9
percent of the people who go to that breakfast bar over
at the Big Boy restaurant just shovel the food into their
mouths! *They just shovel it in!*" The month we stayed in
Lansing to help out we lived in the house with him. He
refused to learn Peggy's name and referred to her only as,
"That girl you people call Peggy!" Anyway, now my uncle

is dead and my brother lives in the house so that my mother can keep it insured. Peg says that David better never get in trouble with the law because he lives like a serial killer. "I mean look at the facts," she says, "he lives in the attic of his dead grandmother's house filled with gay male pornography because his mother makes him."

My brother met his fiancée on the computer. He wanted to meet a Jewish girl and he lives in Lansing, Michigan, so he signed onto America Online and went right to the Jewish singles room where he got down to the business of finding a wife. Every girl seemed really great to him. I tried to figure out his standards. They seemed to me to be something like, "Well, she doesn't seem to have a criminal record. I think I'll marry her." Finally, though, finally, he met the right girl. Shoshi Rivkin from Brooklyn. They asked us to be bridesmaids. "Yes, we'd love to!" we said, when they called to tell us they were engaged. It seemed like such a funny joke. A few days later we realized we had agreed to be *bridesmaids*. I, in particular, realized I had agreed to wear a matching outfit with my girlfriend. This seemed to me to be a special kind of nightmare. I called to tell Shoshi how terribly honored we were but we just couldn't be bridesmaids but we would be happy to sing. I don't know why I told her that. I wanted to write a funny song for the reception. Peggy was horrified. "What kind of a funny song?" she said: "David, we thought you were a neuter/until you met a girl on the computer?" Then they wanted us to sing a Hebrew song in the ceremony. Then they told us we couldn't sing because their rabbi is Orthodox and he told them that Orthodox men cannot be in the presence of a singing woman. They said they hoped we weren't offended by that. "Hey," I said, "it's your wedding and we want what you want." I'm trying to take my mother's advice. She says, "I'm just going to go to that wedding and pretend I'm watching a National Geographic special on TV." But I have a horrible vision. I can see myself at their wedding wearing a man's suit and chomping a big cigar and I'm afraid that every time the rabbi walks by I will compulsively sing at him, "There's No Business Like Show Business!"

(*A new slide clicks into place. This brings her back to the stool. She picks up the laser pointer and describes the new "image."*)

Ah. This is poor Mary standing on the exit stairs of the Iron Dragon. Under no circumstances would they let us bring a video camera on a roller coaster but one of the girls told us that Mary could go up the exit stairs and shoot from the platform on the other side. But when she got there they gave her a really hard time and she was getting really pissed off, you know, because these little high school amusement park girls were getting all snippy with her and making her stand in the sun and she already had that kind of aggravated look that lesbians get in amusement parks in Ohio. So she told me that I would have to go first and convince the girls to let her onto the exit platform. And I found a method that worked pretty well, actually. I'd say, "Can my friend shoot here?" And the girls would say, "Well . . . uh-uh." Then I'd say, "We're doing a documentary video about my father. He's a seventy-five-year-old, blind, diabetic Holocaust survivor with a heart condition." And they'd say, (*Full of wide-eyed, schoolgirl sympathy*) "Ooh. Oh. Okay." It's painfully easy to place the weight of the world right on a teenage girl's shoulders.

(*Sound of a plane passing overhead. She crosses to stand next to the chair.*)

We flew from Michigan to France, to save money, and then traveled by train to Germany. The train trip was a nightmare. Dad had brought four bags as if he was traveling with a valet when in fact there was only me. Also I couldn't read any of the signs because I don't speak German, and he speaks German of course, but he can't see to read them and so I had to sound them out. This was an exercise in pure humiliation. I'd say, (*Making a great effort to be clear but quiet enough to avoid attention. She has no idea how to pronounce these words.*) "Waehlen . . . Sie . . . jetzt . . . die Vorwahl . . . und (*Long pause culminating in a deep sigh of impending defeat.*) gewuenschte . . . Ruf . . . Rufnummer . . ." And he'd say, "What? Speak up. I can't hear you." And I'd think to myself, HOW'D YOU LIKE TO BE PUSHED OUT OF THE TRAIN, OLD MAN!?

(*Crosses to center.*)

There's nothing like watching someone else watch your family to really give you some perspective. I keep catching Peggy and Mary staring at various members of my family like this—(*Hands rush to her face and she staggers backward as if witnessing a scene of horror.*) They don't understand why my family likes to come here. Now that they bring it up, I guess I don't really either. Three members of my family are—to use an expression I think you are not supposed to use anymore but it is the expression my family uses to describe itself—"crippled." As in the phrase: "So crippled-up we can hardly walk." In addition to being crippled they are also in great, great pain. They gasp and moan with pain all day. It is in this state that my family, once a year, tackles a fifteen-acre amusement park. This year, along with her wheelchair, my Aunt Francie is also dependent on an oxygen tank which must be wheeled alongside of her. It's so hot that the park is nearly deserted and my mother and my aunt consider anything above fifty degrees a heat wave. The sad truth is that my family comes to Cedar Point for the food. I can't bear it. A few years ago, after a little therapy, I began to be aware that the women in my family often say things like: "Oh, I'm really not hungry. I couldn't eat a thing. I think I'll just have some pudding." Or: "I just need a little something light, maybe some pie." And as soon as we arrive at Cedar Point, Aunt Francie, true to form, says, "I really don't feel good. I think I need a hamburger." The day has just begun and already I'm feeling trapped, trapped, trapped with my family. I involuntarily leave my body and squish my whole self into my brain where a voice in my head is ranting: "A hamburger will not make you feel better! Shut up! Shut up about hamburgers! It's ten o'clock in the morning for God sakes! Eating the hamburgers at Cedar Point is probably what put you in that wheelchair in the first place!" My therapy brain kicks in. I think, Now, Lisa, this reaction seems a little extreme. Is it your aunt you are despising or the part of you that is capable of eating a hamburger at ten o'clock in the morning? These thoughts must be leaking out of my brain onto my face because I see Peggy giving me the "chill-out-it's-only-ten-o'clock" look! I try to reenter my body but when I do I see that Aunt Francie is eating—from out of her purse—several cold sausages left over from breakfast at the Bob Evans. I concentrate on making my face blank and just following Peggy, and I try not to think about how last night at the Friendly's my aunt went on for ten minutes to the waiter about what foods make her choke.

(*Crosses back to the chair and sits.*)

When Elizabeth doesn't eat she gets insane. (*We hear the sound of screeching car tires.*) She drives up on curbs and the wrong way down one-way streets. I try to coax her to eat. "Would you like a cookie?" "No!" she says. "I can't stand those cookies. I can't even look at them anymore. They make me sick." And she hurls them into the backseat where my father looks bewildered, thinking something is blowing in through the windows. I say, "I think you're really hungry." This is so stupid. It's like when you're little and your mother says, "You're acting tired," which, I don't know about you, but inevitably made me furious. And Elizabeth yells at me, "I'M NOT HUNGRY! I'M JUST DRIVING BUT THIS COUNTRY IS STUPID AND POLISH PEOPLE ARE STUPID AND THERE'S NO FOOD HERE AND THAT'S FINE. I DON'T CARE. I'M NOT HUNGRY." As she continues this rant she picks up speed, at one point hitting about sixty-five miles per hour on a dirt road. She's right though. There is no food in Poland. Well, maybe there is, but they keep it a secret. Where are the big neon signs? That's my question. How do you locate food without big neon signs? I'm also sick of the little Dutch anise cookies we've been eating for three days although, unlike Elizabeth, that hasn't stopped me from eating them. "Wait, stop," I say, "there's a restaurant!" "No," Elizabeth says, "I don't care." "Elizabeth, honey, we have to eat something. Come on, Elizabeth, we have to go to the restaurant. Oh my God. Come on Elizabeth you have to stop the car. Elizabeth, stop this car! Elizabeth, stop this car NOW!" (*She reaches over with her foot and stomps on an imaginary brake, as we hear the sound of a car screeching to a halt.*) Thank you.

We've found a Polish pizza parlor. There's only one thing on the menu. Pizza. We each order two pieces of this pizza even though we are fully aware of its nature: a piece of white toast with melted American cheese and ketchup poured on top. We eat the pizza and we like it. This might actually go over big in the Midwest where cheese is a vital component of every dish. No food is considered edible in the Midwest unless it's fried and covered with melted cheese. Health food in the Midwest is anything in a pita. Like a Big Mac in a pita would be considered health food in the Midwest. And so I settle back into my midwestern heritage and I enjoy the greasy, cheesy toast. I order a third.

(*The sound of a new slide clicking into place brings her back up to the stool to describe the new "image."*)

Okay, we're going back a little bit in time here. This is a picture from 1983, and here you can see me and my dad and we're standing in front of the Demon Drop which is a three-story free fall. Cedar Point is known as America's Roller Coast because it has more roller coasters than any other amusement park in America—and every year they add a new one. And in 1983 they added the Demon Drop and Dad asked me if I wanted to ride it. And I laughed. I thought he was joking because at that time my family didn't ride the roller coasters. We mostly stuck to the more handicapped-accessible rides. Like the Riverboat Ride was one of our favorites, which is a scenic tour down the mighty quarter-mile-long Cedar River where you pass a number of mannequins—you know, animated mannequins—engaged in a variety of activities like, oh, you know, playing the banjo, getting caught in the outhouse, engaging in a feud, a scalping, that sort of thing. . . . But this first year of the Demon Drop, Dad asked and asked and asked about it. He brought it up in the morning at Jungle Larry's Safari and then again during lunch at Frontier Village and at the end of the day, when we were heading back to the parking lot via the Swiss Chalet Sky Ride, he asked about it again and all of a sudden it dawned on me: "Do you want to ride the Demon Drop?" I said. And he said, "Oh. Well, if that's what would make you happy."

It's hard . . . it's hard to describe a three-story free fall. It's not bad, really. It's not good. It's just like— (*A sudden, shocked exhalation of all the air in her lungs, as if kicked in the stomach.*) —When it was over, about a second and a half after it began, I was speechless, I was aghast. I looked at my dad. He was grinning. A crazy sort of a grin.

That first ride on the Demon Drop was the summer before he lost most of his vision. Before that time he had just a small blind spot in his left eye. Someone told me that my mother thought that maybe it was that first ride on the Demon Drop that caused the hemorrhage that took the rest of his center vision leaving him with just peripheral sight. All of a sudden the middle was gone. Only the edges remained. Dad doesn't think the Demon Drop caused his vision loss. And even if it did, he says, "The damage is done."

At his office we tape him showing us all the tools he has to help him see. The closed-circuit TV, the overhead projector and, of course, the big bag of eyeglasses worth two thousand dollars, that he carries with him everywhere. He has one pair of thick half-glasses he uses so that he can sign a check or a credit card slip, and one pair of binoculars mounted on glasses frames that enable him to make out a telephone number written in big digits on a notepad and, of course, his ten-power monocular that lets him read a sign far away, word for word. He says to us, "It's interesting how the brain compensates. For instance, Lisa, where your head is, I see a . . . a flower pattern."

(*Sound of church bells draws her attention. She crosses and stands behind the chair.*)

In Poland we see men carrying hay in horse-drawn wagons, old women digging potatoes, empty streets in run-down cities. I thought I'd be so fascinated to see this world where the clock had stopped fifty years before but now, to my horror, I find I'm just like Edna from the World Apart Travel Agency in Lansing, Michigan, who had said to me before I left, "Eastern Europe? Oh, cripes, that's depressing."

Where is the mall? That's what I'd love to see, the Polish mall where I could look at the different items in the Polish card shops and buy funny things to bring home for the cousins and for Peg. I'd feel so much better if I could just buy something. How did I end up in Poland anyway when where I really wanted to be was Polish Land where I could go to the Pierogi Hut and buy a kielbasa hero from a fresh-faced high school student. I don't speak Polish. I don't speak German either but at least when I was there I could tell where the words begin and end. Here I feel like I'm listening to gibberish. One time we stop at a bus stop to ask a man for directions and when he answers me I start to laugh. I laugh right in his face. I'm not laughing at him. I'm laughing at how absurd it is that I'm listening to him as if I had the vaguest idea what he is saying. He gestures that he wants to get into our car. He's going to ride with us so he can point us in the right direction. He directs us to his house.

Then he gets out and says something like, "Blah, blah, blah. Pointy, pointy, point. Polish, Polish, Polish, Polish . . ."

It's a good thing Elizabeth has a sixth sense about where we're going. I'm supposedly the navigator, but in Poland I'm hopeless. The roads are all tiny and curvy and it's hard to identify which is which since they all seem to be spelled: C-Z-Y-C-N-Z-S-Y. But Elizabeth just glances at the map and she's off. Speeding us in the direction of Auschwitz.

(*Sax music moves her to center and fades out as she begins to speak.*)

What is my mother going to do about this wedding? This is exactly the kind of event she's been studiously avoiding for the past thirty years. In a certain way we wonder why my brother would even have a wedding when it means putting my mother in this situation? She hates ceremony. She hates ritual. She has a law that she never goes anywhere where you have to wear panty hose. And then there is the No Picture Rule. This is really the thing. This is the heart of the matter. We do not take pictures of my mother. And this isn't a joke. No sneaking up is allowed. We never, never take pictures of my mother and it's funny really, because she loves pictures of other people. She loves them so much that sometimes I think she would like to have a copy of every picture taken of every person she ever met. She can't bear to think of a moment being lost when it could have been recorded. (*To someone in the audience*) If you were ever recorded on video and you tell my mother about it she'll say, "Oh, I'd like to have a copy of that." So it's funny really, that she won't let us take pictures of her.

(*A series of slides appears on the scrim. One dissolves into the next as she describes them.*)

My mother looks girlish and womanish and very happy and she's beaming out of a tiny color photo in a big, blue picture hat. Behind her, my father, with his hand on her shoulder, purses his lips and rolls his eyes up, mugging away, unbeknownst to her. It is their wedding picture. There are a few pictures after that. Their trip to Europe. I was conceived in Venice, you know. (Well, not actually in Venice, but in the nearby town of Mestra where the hotels are a lot cheaper.) In these pictures she's windblown and beautiful and so happy. My dad is dark and mysterious. Thick dark hair. Huge brown eyes. Mom showed me letters he wrote to her when they were first married. Scores of them. Describing their life together. All written as if to someone else. "My new wife Ann and I are very much in love, etc. . . ." He mailed them to her from the corner. Then there are some pictures of her as a young mother and then there are no more. She was still happy with her husband and she was happy with her two children but she was no longer happy with the way she looked and so that was the end of the pictures. And so there have been no pictures of my mother for a span of about thirty years.

(*The last slide of the series disappears.*)

I can't picture how she's going to cope with this wedding and I'm worried she's going to get sick, you know, really, really sick, and have to miss it. She told me she threw up during a midnight grocery shopping run at Meijer's Thrifty Acres. She seems okay about it . . . I don't know. She always told us when we were growing up that she wanted us to elope and I never had any doubt that she meant it. When I came out as a lesbian I'm sure one of her first thoughts was, Oh, thank God I won't have to go to her wedding.

(*Sax music, beginning with a long plaintive note, interrupts her. She walks to the chair and sits.*)

What month was it? October. It's so cold. Elizabeth's car has separate controls for heating the driver and the passenger. On my side, I've pushed the little lever all the way over to hot. I don't think we listened to much music. Oh no. We did. Bach. Seems appropriate for the night before Auschwitz.

Dinner at the Orbis Hotel. Dad says, "How funny, tonight we're having a beer with dinner and tomorrow we'll be at Auschwitz." (*Music fades out.*) Dad and I, we've been waiting for this our whole lives. We don't know how to feel. Tomorrow we'll be at the place where his parents' bodies lie. No, they were burned. Will we step on their ashes? Will we see a wooden pallet where they slept? Will we kick a stone they also kicked? Will they be hovering above the place, watching us? Are they waiting for their boy? Have they waited all this time for their little boy to come and say good-bye to them?

(*Stands.*)

I almost had a nervous breakdown before this trip. I lost a friend over it. She told me she was sick of hearing about it. She's an asshole, but I did sound like a broken record, I'm sure. But what will I do, I thought, if my father cries? I've never seen him cry. What if he falls to the ground and sobs and curses the heavens? On the one hand I think I have these maternal feelings toward him and on the other hand I couldn't handle it if I really have to hold him like I were his mother.

Oh. The room is full of hair. Is that my grandmother's hair? Is she here? Elizabeth is just pregnant and she feels sick. If you believe a baby can be marked, you shouldn't come to Auschwitz. A room full of eyeglasses. They stumbled off blind to their deaths. A room full of suitcases. The smell, ugh, the smell. A room full of artificial limbs.

The Israelis are here. A big group with a huge Israeli flag. Huge enough for my father to easily see all day the big blue Mogen David. What a blessing they're here today. He doesn't say too much but I know that these Israelis are his little safety valve. A reminder that the world of Auschwitz is no more. I'm glad they're here too, although after my initial feelings of comradeship, I'm just irritated all day with these irritating Israelis. If I get shoved one more time . . .

We've read every word of every exhibit. I have to read them out loud to Dad, of course. "Okay. This is a poem by a woman named Zofia . . . (*Stumbles over the pronunciation*) Groch-o-wal-ska Abromowicz. (*Realizing he can't hear*) I'm sorry. (*She repeats herself significantly louder.*) Abromowicz. It says: (*Continuing loudly*)

1944.

*Wheels speed along the tracks
rushing toward the victory of crime,
transporting, transporting people to gas,
people to a cremator,
people to a petrol sprayed pyre.
Smoke floats, thick, foul smoke . . .*

(*Seeing the next line of the poem, her face crumples. Instead of the words, a sob comes out. She turns and covers her face.*)

I bury my head in my father's shoulder to hide my contorted face. He pats my back. He's okay. He's a good dad. I feel all shaky and helpless. I pull myself together. Really! The day is just beginning. (*Turns back to face the poem.*) I repeat the words that have undone me: "People burn people here."

(*Pivots around to stand behind the chair.*)

We go on the Mean Streak which is a new wooden roller coaster with a 2.5-minute ride. As soon as we take off, I know that it's a mistake. Dad is clinging to the bar and he has a look on his face like a horse in a fire. I feel like my teeth are rattling out of my head. I hold on to my dad's arm, trying to pump some kind of rays into his body that will keep him from having a heart attack. I think, Oh, my dear God, what have I done? This is really going to kill him. Two-point-five minutes is a really long time on a roller coaster if you are having a good time. If you think the experience is killing your father it's a really *really* long time. For a split second I can see Mary selling this videotape to *A Current Affair*. The lead-in will

read: BIZARRE MURDER!!! LESBIAN FORCES BLIND HOLOCAUST VIC-
TIM ON ROLLER COASTER! KILLS OWN FATHER! I'm so relieved
when we get to the end I'm almost weeping. I want to carry
him to the first-aid station. I wonder if he can walk. He stumbles out of the car. (*She stumbles to center.*) Walks right up to
the video camera, as if for a postgame interview, and says,
"That one was the best." And asks me if I want to go again.

The first Auschwitz camp is like a college campus. Red
brick buildings and swaying birch trees. A beautiful wrought
iron fence with a sign that says: "arbeit macht frei" . . . *work
will make you free.* You have to use your imagination here to
comprehend what went on. In the afternoon we drive the
three miles to the second camp—Birkenau. Here, you need
no imagination. This one looks like what it was. It was
sunny three miles away. Here there is no sun. This is malev-
olent ground. On the way in, I ask Dad and Elizabeth if
they want a snack from the car. "No," they say. They can't
eat here. I can. I feel defiant as I shove a cracker into my
mouth and walk through the gates.

They give us a map and we go exploring. The day alternates between a feeling of horror and a feeling we're at Disney. We look at the map and say, "Well, where should we go
next? To the pits where they buried bodies in mass graves or
the fields where they piled them up and burned them." We
have to laugh. We especially laugh at the bookstores which
we refer to as the Auschwitz gift shop. They sell postcards
there. "Greetings from Auschwitz, wish you were here." We
make gruesome jokes about what gifts they might sell . . .
lamp shades and soap. I actually go into one of the shops to
buy a book but it's full of pictures of the pope and I turn
around and walk out.

(*There is a long, very long, still pause—an almost unbearable silence—
as she realizes the thing she's about to say.*)

I'd been so afraid I wouldn't feel anything here.

(*The silence hangs as she realizes.*)

I think that was my biggest fear.

(*Then she gets drawn into the explanation of her memory.*)

But when I enter the crematorium for the first time in my life I feel horror. Physical repulsion. I can feel my face contort, my lips pull back. In the gas chambers my father stops to take his two o'clock pill. This breaks my heart. I stand to the side and cry. Hard. I can feel . . . I can feel the bottom. It's clear to me now that everything in my life before this has been a shadow. This is the only reality: what happened to my father and his parents fifty years ago. Elizabeth sees me crying and says, "Oh, no."

(*The following feels like an actual break from the play. The audience should have the disconcerting feeling that the woman has abandoned her performance persona and is speaking spontaneously and directly to them. As a result, the words change slightly with each audience. If someone answers one of the questions posed, that answer is acknowledged and incorporated.*)

I don't know why I'm telling you this. You all already know what this looks like, right? You've seen these images before. You don't need me to describe this to you. You know, it's occurring to me that there's a fairly good chance there's someone sitting here who's been to Auschwitz before. And you don't need me to tell you what this looks like, do you? It's insulting, really. It's upsetting and it's insulting. Even if you've never been there you've seen these images before, right? In the movies—*Sophie's Choice* . . . *Schindler's List! Schindler's List!* Is there anyone sitting here right now who *didn't* see *Schindler's List?* (*Scans the audience for takers.*) Really. Really. And you know what? That's exactly what it looks like when you go there. That movie was really well done. That's exactly what it looks like. If you missed the movies you've seen it on TV, right? On public television or the History Channel? Sometimes I feel like they show these images every fifteen minutes or something. You know the ones I'm talking about, the films from the liberation of the camps with the bulldozers and the bodies. Right? You all know what this looks like. I don't know what I'm doing. I feel like a cliché. I'm reminding myself, actually, of this crazy woman that I met this one time. She and I were seated together at this dinner and everyone else knew she was crazy but I had just arrived at this place and I did not know this and so, of course, I got into a conversation with her and she said to me, "Well, yes, my mother hated me. And she treated me like shit and she hit me and she's never had the slightest interest in any of my work but *that's not my point.*" That's how I feel right now. I feel like I'm evading the issue here but I don't know what the issue is. Yes! Yes! I wanted to tell you about our trip. No. No! *"That's not my point!"* I wanted to tell you about my father!

(*Pause, stunned at her own revelation. All of a sudden the woman realizes she has totally exposed herself. Not sure how she got here or how to get out of it, she is at a total loss. She really has no idea what to say next. This should be a truly horrible moment.*)

But what? Umm . . . I don't know. I really don't know. Uh . . . He's . . . a . . . guy. You know, he's an ordinary guy. He's a dad. He's my dad. (*Suddenly she comes downstage, almost into the audience, stepping disconcertingly into their space in her need to make this connection—to make them hear and understand what she is about to say.*) Do you know what he told us when we were growing up? When we were growing up he told us many, many times, "If it weren't for the good fortune of being born a Jew I might have become a Nazi." And then he'd tell us this story: he'd gone to school with a boy named Lohmann who was the only other boy in his class at school who didn't wear a Hitler Youth uniform. My father wasn't allowed to wear one, of course, because he was a Jew, and he was beaten by the other boys regularly for that, but Lohmann didn't wear one because he refused. "I often wonder," my father would tell us when we were growing up, "I often wonder. If I had had the opportunity to wear that uniform if I would have had the *courage of Lohmann*? I'm lucky to be a Jew so I didn't have to *make that choice.*"

(*Stops herself, suddenly realizing she has gone too far and her intensity has become overwhelming.*)

Aahh. When I try to tell his stories I begin to hyperventilate or something. Do you hear that? I keep inhaling and I don't exhale, something like that. I can't tell you his stories. I don't have any filter for them. Or maybe the opposite is true. They're full of myth. I can hear the myths and the awe creep into my voice and it makes me feel sick because I don't know what that has to do with him. You should go to Lansing and meet him. He'll cook you dinner. I am so not kidding, he'll cook all of you dinner. You'll have to stay up really late because they eat at around eleven o'clock or midnight, but both of my parents would tell you these stories. Incredible stories! And then after dinner, if you want, my mother will take you to see Meijer's Thrifty Acres. It's incredible. It's like the showplace of Lansing. It's one store, not a mall, but one store where you can buy anything, you could buy anything at Meijer's Thrifty Acres! You could buy a loaf of bread, you could buy a bra, you could buy an aboveground pool there if you wanted to! You could buy a gun. It's incredible! It's open twenty-four hours.

(*The sound of a slide interrupts her and she runs upstage to describe the following onslaught of blank images.*)

This is one of the extra-wide parking spaces at Meijer's. It's one of my mother's favorite things about the store. (*The slide changes.*) This is a picture of my dad on a roller coaster. (*The slide changes.*) This is a picture of my mom and dad having dinner at the Olive Garden at the mall which is directly across Saginaw highway from Meijer's. (*The slide changes.*) This is a picture of my dad getting his insulin shot. (*The slide changes.*) This is a picture of me not being able to hold his world in my head. (*The slide changes.*) This is a picture of my father's funeral—which is odd because my father's still alive. (*The slide changes.*) This is a picture of my hands. And here you can see I'm holding my grandmother and my grandfather and his students from the Jewish school and the chairs that they sat in and the streets they walked on and the way they held a pen and the funniest joke they ever told and their particular Jewish German accent and the things that made them cry, and all these things have slipped through my fingers because *I couldn't remember any of it.*

(*The sound of one final slide click. Then we hear the sound of crickets. The woman picks up a cigarette from the stool and takes a drag, and, in doing so, takes on the persona of her father. She goes to the chair, moves it into a square of light center stage and sits down. It is nighttime.*)

During the Second World War, Lisa, I was working as an army interrogator and one of the prisoners who was assigned to me for interrogation had acknowledged having worked with the Gestapo. He held an SS rank usually reserved for Gestapo agents, but he insisted he had been only a driver. This seemed a little strange but he was very self-possessed and I could make no real dent in his preposterous story. So, I sent him back to camp—not to his regular barracks but to solitary confinement. Every two or three days I had him returned to me. Each of these interrogations took only five or ten minutes, but every time I sent him back to his cell I had his conditions made a little more severe. His food rations were reduced. His window was boarded up. His blankets were taken away. And on the morning of his last interrogation, he was obviously tired and not as sharp as usual. I started with the routine questions and got the routine answers. Then I asked him if he'd ever made any arrests in the Kraków Ghetto and he said no. I asked him if he had ever driven a car inside the Ghetto and he said yes. So I asked him if he thought it was a lot of fun to go joyriding inside the Ghetto and, of course, he said no. So I said, "Then you did participate in arrests?" And, for some reason, this time this crazy Marx Brothers' routine worked, and he said yes. And when it came to him what he had said, he admitted that he had been a Gestapo agent. And then he broke down and he cried. And then the dam burst. And he said:

(*Leaning forward.*)

"I can't stand it. I can't live like this anymore. I never thought I did anything wrong and now everyone is telling me I'm a criminal. I was fourteen when my father joined the Nazi party. I grew up believing this movement was the salvation of the German people. I wanted to be a patriotic German and a good and moral human being and now you and those like you come and tell me that everything I thought was good and moral and patriotic was, in fact, evil. And the things I was told were destructive and treasonous and evil, were really good and proper. So here I am, at the age of thirty-two, and I have an ulcer and I hurt and I'm being told that if only I'd done my job badly there might be some hope for me, and I can't live like that," he said, "and I can't accept that."

(*Leaning back.*)

I looked across my desk at this man, and I knew he could have been me. If I hadn't had the "good fortune" of being born a Jew, I might well have been sitting where he was sitting and saying the things he was saying. I, too, am capable of becoming enamored of ideas or ideologies. I, too, can take refuge, if I need it, in the saying, "You can't make an omelette without breaking eggs." So there he sat, this Gestapo agent, across the table from me, and I knew how very much alike we were and that he, in a very real sense, was my brother. And I felt very close to him.

And then I had to decide what to do with this man whom I thought of as a brother. And I said to myself, Well, it doesn't really much matter what he believed.

We're all responsible for our actions. And I ordered him turned over to the Polish liaison officer. I knew what would probably happen to him because the communist officers had indicated they would take him on the train as far as we would pay the railroad fare, and when they crossed the border, they would take him off the train, make him dig a hole, and shoot him into it. I'm not entirely certain that that's what happened, but I think it likely. I think it likely that I sent this man whom I thought of at that moment as a brother to be killed after digging his own grave.

(*Stands.*)

The park is closing in ten minutes. (*She returns the chair to its place and sits.*) We split up a little at the end so that some of us can ride the Mantis, a new stand-up roller coaster, and some of us can get one last batch of Cedar Point fries and maybe a shake for the ride home and maybe some . . . fudge. The caravan of cars is parked right by the gate, in the handicapped zone, of course, and then we've all made it back except for Dad and Aunt Kitty. I've reached my family-day limit and I am ready to go. "Buckle your seat belts," I say to Peg and Mary, "they'll be here in a minute." And we wait. "Let's go, go, go," I say. And we wait some more. Finally they wander into the headlights of the cars. Peg says, "Oh my God, Lisa. Your dad doesn't look so good." "He's okay," I say. Peg says he looks a little green. Their walk out of the front gates of Cedar Point to the front seat of the car is torturously slow. Peg and Mary watch intently and send Catholic prayers with every step. I slump in the backseat and mutter impatiently: "He's fine."

About six months later Dad has triple bypass surgery. Somebody, he or my mom, casually mentions that he thinks he probably had a little heart attack on the way out of Cedar Point last summer. Peg says she is not going to Cedar Point with my family again. "You people are insane!" she says. My mother always says, "You know the doctors told us that your grandmother was near death at least a hundred times and she turned out to be fine. Well, okay, eventually she did die, but that was the exception, not the rule."

(*Stands.*)

At the end of the day I'm feeling giddy, almost euphoric. We've done it. It's over. Check. Dad says, "Where is my bag of glasses?" And I say, "I'm sure they're in the car. I must have left them in the car, Dad. I know they're in the car." They're not in the car and now it's nearly dark. We can't leave without them. Dad says it's all right but his face is ashen.

(*A breathless, nervous sax solo begins to play, underscoring the rest of this section.*)

Elizabeth talks to the guard in German. He says we can drive in, along the railroad tracks. It's pitch dark. We drive to the end of the tracks. Now there's Auschwitz dirt on Elizabeth's car. We leave Dad in the car and take two little flashlights to look on the monument where I'd changed film in the camera. I have to be careful and look where I'm going so that I don't fall into the ruins of the gas chambers. Elizabeth has lost her mind. She's racing all over the monument and screaming, "I don't see them. Do you see them, Lisa? Oh, God, oh, God, I don't see them. Are they here? Do you see them?" We get back in the car. We drive back to the front gate. The other place I could have left them was in the barracks. I had stopped to take pictures in the barracks where there was writing on the rafters in old German script that said things like: "One louse and you're dead. Honesty endures longest. Cleanliness is healthiness." We can't drive the car over the tracks. So I go with the guard on foot to look. He's taking me into all the barracks. There are a hundred or so. He speaks a little German. I speak none but I manage to put together the sentence, "Barrack mit Schreiben." He takes me right to the barracks with the writing. I have to run to keep up with him. When he gets too far ahead I'm in pitch dark. How does this man work here? All day the air has smelled like smoke and we've heard dogs barking in the distance. My dad says that Jews and dogs don't get along. I've never in my whole life been so frightened.

The glasses are not here. We'll find them the next day at the visitors' center but tonight we don't know that and we're feeling broken. We thought we could walk away from this. I can't bear that there's a piece of us left here somewhere. I know that my dad has lost much more important things than his glasses in this place, but that was a long time ago. I have an image now that he has a bubble around his life that's complete and apart from this place and now I've broken the circle and lost a piece of him here.

(*Music fades out.*)

I thought I could come here for a day and then get on with my life and now we have to come back here in the morning.

(*Sax music moves her to the wedding area and fades out as she begins to speak.*)

My mother has begun to prepare for the wedding. She's had her hair cut and styled. This is something she hasn't done in thirty years. She's never worn makeup but she's asked me to hire a professional makeup person to do her face the day of the wedding. This is an unprecedented amount of money for my mother to spend on herself but she's got it all figured out. She's telling everyone, "Listen, I'm going to make this last. When they're done with me I'm going to have my face shellacked." The other thing is that she's started buying all these dresses. Now my mother has been wearing the same style of Sears catalog housedress since 1963. But now she's buying dresses by the bagload and bringing them home to try on for my father, whose opinion is a little suspect, as you can imagine.

But on the day of the wedding none of us can take our eyes off her. She looks so beautiful. My brother and my aunts are really glad to get pictures. "I hate to say this," David says, "but at least when she's gone we'll have some photos." But you know, I don't think the pictures look like her. She doesn't look like a photograph to me. I think that must be it. I think we must learn over time to make the translation from live person to still photo and I never did that with my mother. I see her in my mind. She looks like a laughing girl.

(*Crosses back to center.*)

So we went to this wedding. I didn't even buy new panty hose. I just put on some old dress from the back of the closet and Peggy dug something up, and off we went to the Seaview Jewish Center in Canarsie. Shoshi had asked us to come early to help her get dressed. Because we're in the theater. And so we know something about costumes.

The Seaview Jewish Center sports a wonderful design out of a 1972 James Bond movie with mirror sculptures on the walls and little fountains in the corners with colored lights that dance and shimmer when you plug the brown cord into the eye-level wall socket just to the left. The floors are peel-and-stick parquet and the rooms are separated with those big motorized accordion partitions which run on tracks in the floor. You know the kind of partitions—the kind that, it was always rumored, had crushed a child to death in gym class. Peg and I went into the "bride's room," as instructed, and there was Shoshi surrounded by women in pastel lace dresses having her makeup done by an Orthodox woman with one of those turbany scarfy hats covering her hair. Shoshi pointed to me and Peg and said, "Everybody, I want you to meet my two new sisters!" And all the women turned to look at us and the makeup lady said, "Really? Wow! You two don't look like sisters at all!" And we said, "No, we're not sisters. We're . . . We're . . . You know . . ." What? Really, what? Girlfriends? Too insubstantial. "Spouse" might have been a good word but I got afraid it was too strong. I had a horrible vision that if I said the word "spouse" these women's heads would explode leaving a tattered charcoaly ball sitting on their necks. And so I said, "We're partners." And the women went, "Oh . . . oh . . ." And I could see them thinking, Partners in what?

For some reason it made me think of the time Peg and I went camping down south. Peg got really frustrated with me during the trip because the whole time we were in the South I kept repeating over and over, "Those two girls were kissin' so I had to kill 'em."

(Crosses to stand behind the chair.)

My parents had a small wedding. My mother didn't let anyone come except her mother and her best friend. She says, "Well, I don't know what else I was supposed to do. I didn't expect your father to show up." The way my father tells the story, on the day of their wedding he put on a suit and he put his laundry in the backseat of the car and thought to himself, Well, either I'll get married or I'll go to Ohio and do my laundry. He told me once that he married her for her walk. He told me another time that he married her because she's a person who acts morally rather than one who thinks about what kind of acts are moral—which is what he thinks he does.

(Crosses back to center.)

My mother had planned for the day after David and Shoshi's wedding what she called a postmortem, which was basically a get-together in which all the members of our family would gather for the purpose of making fun of the wedding. But an unexpected thing happened at my brother's wedding. I became enchanted. We all became enchanted by this wedding. When the lights came on, I had never seen any place as beautiful as the Seaview Jewish Center in

Canarsie. And when the band began to play I danced and my cousins danced and Peg twirled my aunt around in her wheelchair, and during the dinner Peg got everyone at our table whipped up into a frenzy yelling: "Table twelve rules the wedding!" And everyone got so excited! And this guy that I grew up with turned to me and said, "Peg is incredible." And I said, "Well, yes, she's got that Irish Catholic camp counselor thing going." And he said, "Well it really works. I mean for just a second I found myself thinking, I think table twelve is the best."

And during the service, when my parents walked my brother in and stood with him under the Chupah . . . I cried.

You know, a couple of years ago I went to see the movie, *Little Women.* And it was in a big theater and there were only about thirty people there and they were all women and we were all sitting separately, scattered about in this huge theater. And when Beth dies, all the women in the theater seemed to cry, but it wasn't the usual quiet sniffling you hear sometimes in a theater. These women were racked with sobs. All around me I could hear noises like— (*Makes huge, hiccuping, wailing, crying noises.*)

And that's how I was crying at my brother's wedding.

It had never dawned on me in a million years that I would feel anything other than a big, judgey reaction to the whole thing. But, when I saw my father standing there all I could see was the soul in this little old man who'd lost his mother and his father and his country and his culture and it's all gone forever and this was the closest he was ever going to come to it again and it didn't feel like enough and it felt like too much for me, and so I cried and then I made everyone sitting around me take an oath that they hadn't seen me doing it because I can't be going around crying at weddings.

(*A slide clicks onto the scrim. The woman turns around to look at it. Then she turns back to the audience.*)

I have a checklist in my head: things I have to do before my father dies. Number one: look him in the eye and tell him that I love him. Okay. I did that. Check. Number two: go with him to see the place where his parents were killed. Okay. I did that. Check. Number three: make this video about his life. I've been trying to look at the videotape. It's excruciating. Peg and Mary and I are taping him in his study, at his office, in the park. We say, "Can you show us about your glasses? Great, that was really good. Can you tell us the story about saying good-bye to your parents? Great, great. You know what? That was really, really good. Can you tell it to us again but make it a little more concise? Stop, stop. Hold on. A truck is going by. Hold on. Okay, can you say that again?"

There he is in front of the camera all by himself trying so hard.

"Stop," we say, "can you say that again?"

(*Looks back at the slide for a moment, then turns back to the audience.*)

He's lived in Michigan for forty years. He eats in front of the TV. He takes a cardiac fitness class at the community college. His life in Lansing is like a translucent overlay that doesn't quite match up. The edges are blurred.

Then we got to Germany and my father was home. Friends picked us up and it felt as if they cared for us like we were little babies. They fed us and they gave us feather beds to sleep in and they drove us wherever we needed to go, and my father was home. He's in focus here, I thought. He's in context.

(*Turns back to look at the slide and utters a small gasp as if seeing it anew. She quietly describes what she sees.*)

My father is a small man, contained and neat. He smells like lavender. He's wearing a suit.

(*Turns back to the audience.*)

I tried to imagine seeing my grandparents and I had a fantasy I would see them in Meijer's Thrifty Acres. They'd be hovering over the frozen foods section. It's so cold there. They'd be at a thirty-degree angle. Bobbing a little. A small smile on their lips. They'd be arm in arm. In my fantasy I ask my grandparents if they want to see my father. I pluck them out of the air and sit them gently in the car—the big, American Oldsmobile. I take them to his office. I carry them inside. "Wait here," I say. I knock on my father's door. "Dad, there's someone here to see you!" "What?" he says. He's seventy-five years old. He's hard of hearing. "Wait here." I bring them in. They see him. "Valter," they say.

He can't tell who they are. When he looks at their heads, he sees only flowers.

When I was in college I was taught that if you are standing near a piece of furniture onstage you should put your hand on it because that will make you look bigger.

(*Crosses to the chair. Puts her hand on it.*)

See? See how that works?

(*Her hand drops and then she slowly replaces it.*)

I'm putting my hand on my father's life.

(*Lights fade to black.*)

END OF PLAY

UNDERNEATH THE LINTEL

AN IMPRESSIVE PRESENTATION
OF LOVELY EVIDENCES

Glen Berger

Underneath the Lintel was first presented at the Yale Summer Cabaret, in New Haven, for three nights in August 1999, with the author playing THE LIBRARIAN.

Underneath the Lintel was produced by the Actors' Gang (Patti McGuire, producer) in Los Angeles for a limited run in May 2001. The director and designer was Brent Hinkley; the stage manager was Byrne Lethnik. The cast was as follows:

THE LIBRARIAN   Brian T. Finney

Underneath the Lintel premiered off-Broadway at the Soho Playhouse, opening on October 23, 2001. It was produced by Scott Morfee, Tom Wirtshafter, and Dana Matthow. The director was Randy White; the set designer was Lauren Helpern; the projection design consultant was Elaine McCarthy; the lighting designer was Tyler Micoleau; the sound designer was Paul Adams; the costume designer was Miranda Hoffman; the production stage manager was Richard Hodge; the production coordinator was Cris Buchner. The cast was as follows:

THE LIBRARIAN   T. Ryder Smith

In January 2002, David Chandler took over the role of THE LIBRARIAN.

CHARACTER

THE LIBRARIAN

SETTING

Here.

TIME

Now.

SET

The Librarian has rented the space for the night, and from what we know of the Librarian, we can assume he didn't have much to spend for it. Perhaps the auditorium we're in has been dark for some time, or perhaps the theater is "between shows." Props and other detritus from other shows can litter the back of the stage, or be seen in an exposed back room. An air of dilapidation wouldn't be a bad thing. I've always pictured the Librarian as giving this lecture in a not-so-good part of town, on a rainy night, to perhaps only four or five down-and-outs more interested in getting dry from the rain than listening to a lecture by a Dutchman. Over the course of the evening, however, the "lecture" should imperceptibly turn into "theater." The detritus, unnoticed and seemingly unimportant at first, can unexpectedly take on significance, alluding to scenes and history mentioned in the play. The lighting can become warmer, more "theatrical," etc., and what seemed like a random strewing of objects, or a random water stain on the wall, for instance, can turn out to be not so random after all.

CHARACTER NOTE

Why a Dutchman? The Dutch have a wonderfully bureaucratic streak in them (or so I'm told). They also tend to have a facility for other European languages, and I've known more than one person from the Netherlands whose English was truly remarkable, with a nearly imperceptible accent. (I also just have a soft spot for the Dutch.) My point is that the accent should be very light, and the actor should pay more attention to developing the "idiolect," meaning "an individual's unique way of speaking."

Stage contains a chair (which should never be used for sitting), a large chalkboard (to be used at director's discretion). There is also a battered screen for showing slides, the slide projector to be operated by the actor. A rather old and disheveled man in a decrepit suit shuffles onto the stage carrying a battered suitcase full of scraps. The suitcase, once open, may have various homemade contrivances to display the "evidences." (Perhaps he also keeps certain evidences in his pockets, with evidence tags dangling out.) He wears a date stamper tied with string around his neck.

THE LIBRARIAN

So. Right. We'll proceed. I have only one night for this . . . I'd like to have more, oh yes, but due to the extortionary rates demanded by the proprietors of this auditorium . . . I have only one night for this. Still. We'll proceed. (*He points significantly to suitcase he has set down.*) Box of scraps. Significant scraps. Or rather . . . they're all I have . . . to prove a life. . . . To prove one life . . . and justify another . . . and if you're thinking "that's a tall order for a box of scraps," well just you wait. (*With ominous significance*) They're not just scraps. (*Announcing*) An Impressive Presentation of Lovely Evidences. Hold on to your hats, gentlemen. Bonnets, ladies. Hold on . . . (*Scanning seats*) . . . is this all there is? I don't know what more I can do! I put up signs, I did, on the poles, "Impressive Presentation!" but as soon as I turn my back, they're plastered over! With other signs! And mine were nicer. And important. And tomorrow, I'll be gone. . . . (*Pon-*

dering it on a more personal level) . . . in no time at all . . . I'll be
gone. . . . (*But pulls himself out of it*) . . . Still. We'll proceed.

I am . . . a librarian. From Hoofddorp, that's Holland. Or
rather, I was, before I was fired. Or rather, I retired. Against
my will. Without my pension. Or rather, that's no concern
of yours. Or rather, it will be, but not yet. My special duty
for more than many years being to check in the books that
came in overnight through the overnight slot. In the back of
every book, you see, there's a little envelope, and in this little envelope, there's a little card, and on that little card . . .
the little date the book is due.

(*Holds up stamper.*)This is my stamper. Oh yes, I wasn't letting them keep this. It's lovely— It contains every date there
ever was. You don't believe me? (*Closes eyes, fiddles with stamper dials.*) "August 27, 1883" . . . there, that's the date Mount
Perboewaten explodes in Krakatoa, thirty-six thousand people
perish under the ash. It's all in here! All the trials and joys of
history. (*Closes eyes, fiddles with dials.*) "January 25, 1971" . . .
oh, January 25, 1971 . . . Helen . . . Shattock is walking her
dog in Dayton when a frozen block of urine from the lavatory
of a Pan Am jet falls, and hits her on the head, killing her
instantly. Mind you, (*Fiddles with stamper.*) same date, "1836,"
Cetewayo, King of the Zulus is born! Oh yes, this stamper
contains every birth in this room, not just Cetewayo's. And
death. Yes, our deaths too . . . somewhere. . . . My death is in
here . . . somewhere . . . I just don't know . . . where. . . . Still.
Gives you a bit of respect for it, doesn't it. The stamper.

So. Yes. So, each and every day I woke up, took the bus, no,
no wife, no children, I lived alone, got to the bibliotheque,
put my labeled lunch in the employees' icebox, gave a but-
just-perceptible nod to Brody van Brummelen, works in
reference fine fellow I'm sure except that I'm sure that he's
not and always angling for the acquisitions position that by
all rights is mine, that is, I'm next in line! . . . em, arrived at

my desk, yes that's next, quieted the patrons with a well-timed "ssh" and advanced the date on my little stamper . . . one notch.

Now listen, the overnight slot is strictly for those books *not overdue.* But we checked anyway. That was my job. To check. Now and then you'd find a book a day or two overdue. Sometimes a week. Once, it is said, a book was returned, in the *slot* mind you, three months overdue—well we got over it, but we weren't amused. And neither was the violator when he saw the fine ho ho. Still. We'll proceed.

One morning . . . (*He writes "1986" on the chalkboard.*) . . . one fine and miserable and typical morning, nothing to give an inkling of what was to come—(*Significantly*) I found this book in the pile. (*He takes out a battered book from the box with a tag attached to it labeled "Evidence #1."*) We'll label it Evey-dence # 1. It is a Baedeker's travel guide, in deplorable condition. Well, I was just about to give the little card my stamp with the old stamper when my eyes suddenly sprang out of my head and rolled about on the floor and under the table. And why? Because I saw that this book was checked out in *1873* and no . . . no—never returned til it was returned. Do you understand? (*Writes "1873" on the chalkboard.*) That's one hundred and thirteen years . . . overdue! Astounded out of my wits I was. It must have been his great great grandson returning the book, a blot on the family only now being remedied. And in the overnight slot no less! Appalling. If you have a book one hundred and thirteen years over-due . . . you go to the counter, you admit your lapse, you pay the fine. Well, he wasn't getting away with it, not a chance, I checked the files—oh yes, we keep all the files, and I found the page and here it is. (*Takes out a page from a ledger labeled*) Eveydence #2. (*Reads*) "Baedeker's Travel Guide, checked out November 12th, 1873 by capital *A* . . . period." (*Writes "A." on chalkboard.*) That's his name. Capital *A.* Period. About as vague as they come, but never mind, what's his address, so I can send him the fine of his life. (*Reads*) "Post Office Box 121, Dingtao."

Well, Dingtao didn't ring any bells so I got out the old Atlas. (*He procures an Atlas and pages through it.*) I've always liked Atlases. They allow you to travel all over the world—*without the expense.* Yes, it's true, I had never left Holland. I had rarely left Hoofddorp. I went to Gouda once to see how they made the cheese. But the tour wasn't given that day, they were closed, so never mind. Here it is, Dingtao, near Kaifeng. And no, it seems Kaifeng is not near Hoofddorp. No. Nor Rotterdam. No. It's China! Now how a Chinaman managed to check out a book from a Dutch library without a residence in the Netherlands, well—that would be the first of many puzzlers in this twisty mystery of a tale. And was he even a Chinaman? After all, the notes scrawled in the margins of the book were written in every language under the sun. Including Welsh. Well, it was none of my business. I filled out the standard form notifying our man of the pretty fine awaiting him, and bunged it off to China, and that was that.

But was that really that? No. That was not in any way . . . that. I couldn't get the miscreant out of my mind. I didn't reshelve the book, no, I thumbed through it. I took it home with me. I carried it about. And one day as I was flipping through it, I came upon this. (*Pulls from book*) Eveydence # 3. Bookmark. But not just any bookmark. No. A bookmark *by proxy.* An unredeemed claim ticket for one pair of trousers left in a Chinese Laundering establishment. Oh, in China? No. In London. In (*Writes on chalkboard.*) *1913,* seventy-three years previous.

Well. My life went on, the bus, the books, the "how are you today, Brody," and "no, I don't think my lunch is taking up too much room in the icebox, Brody, no, well, I'm sorry you feel that way," and the organizing of the cart and a "have a good night yourself" and then off with the lights·

and home again, but I'll say this . . . I got to thinking about those trousers. In fact, I couldn't *stop* thinking about those trousers. In fact I had more than one *dream* about those trousers, Trousers, Trousers, Trousers, Trousers until I couldn't take it anymore. Never claimed! Oh sure, the shop probably went defunct years ago, but perhaps . . . not! Anyway I was loath to fritter away my vacation days just to go to London for some nonexistent trousers . . . so I *applied* to travel to London on *library business*—to claim the trousers you see on behalf of the library to recoup some of the losses the library would no doubt accrue from the unpaid fine. It was the most daring gambit I had ever devised, but I felt I was on solid ground, and what do you know, the application was . . . rejected. Flat out. With a reprimand attached about "frivolous requests." Oh I was beside myself and I did a bit of inconspicuous sulking, and also some very discreet running up and down the stack up and down in a frenzy until I was calm again. . . . But damn it to hell, I still couldn't get the pants out of my head, so I went to London all the same. . . .

(*We hear the thirties tune, "Life Begins at Oxford Circus," or similarly jaunty thirties-vintage tune from an English "sweet" band.*)

. . . expending . . . precious . . . vacation . . . time.

(*And we see slides of London.*)

London. Dear God the chaos! The bustle! Oh this was a terrible mistake, why wasn't I home in Hoofddorp in front of the goggle box, cup of tea, nothing ever on but I didn't mind, tall red buses and sweet shops run by Pakistanis—and not very good sweets at that—and I watched the changing of the guard til I had to be changed myself, and the Bloody Tower and the Roman Wall and to think this all used to be swamps and mastodons. "What's this? Something for the French tourist—*Les Misérables*? That looks interesting—'the miserable'—It's all about me in London," I thought, and I had never seen a play before, so I paid, and it's true, after two hours, I was more "miserables" than I had ever been before. Still, we'll proceed.

To the Holloway Road and the Chinese Laundry and . . . well what do you know, it was still there. The shop. So I strode in, waved around my claim ticket, and I came out with a pair of trousers. (*From the box he extrudes*—) Eveydence #4. Trousers. And never cleaned in all that time because they were in such a state of disrepair to begin with. A common laundry policy it seems, to protect the shop from accusations of negligence, and I was all the gladder for it, because it meant that any clues would be left *in situ* as they say.

And I was rewarded. I checked the pockets and I found . . . this. (*Extrudes from pocket with evidence tag attached*—) A used tram ticket. Eveydence #5. From *1912*. A tram that ran in Bonn. Ger-ma-ny.

(*And we hear the tune "Ungarwein" by von Geezy and his Orchestra, or similarly vaguely Germanic thirties-vintage upbeat and librarian-inspiring tune [e.g., a song by the Comedian Harmonists] and see a slide of Bonn and the Municipal Transportation Headquarters.*)

Well I don't know what got into me, feverish, I took a bus to Bonn, to the Municipal Transportation Headquarters to read up on Incident reports for the month of March 1912. Oh yes, I was a regular detective now. It was a shot in the dark, I know, but I figured any scofflaw making loose with library rules might have made some trouble on a tram in Bonn as well. Well you never know. And hey ho, this is what I found. (*Takes out from his box.*) A photeystat I'll label #6, and reads, in the German, as written by the tram conductor, as follows— "*Ein Mann mit einem Bart und einem neu*"— (*Stops short, to audience*) *Sprechen sie*—oh, no, yes of course . . . em, let's see . . . (*And he translates*) "A man with beard and curious hat and smelling truly foul, boarded the tram at Potsdamer Platz with a mangy dog. Although there were plenty of seats, he *refused to sit,* and instead paced up and down the aisle with his dog distracting the other passengers and myself. A dirty Jew, I threw him off at Wittlesbach."

Well, surely this wasn't the same man as the man who owned these trousers, but there was a chance, slim, and I was hooked. And I hated it! What was I doing in Bonn, sauerkraut gives me . . . (*He's said too much and now it's too late.*) . . . well . . . flatus. Wind. Yes, it's a . . . problem. . . . (*Quickly turning to* Baedeker's.) Bonn, devastated by the Normans, rebuilt, devastated by Frederick III, rebuilt, devastated yet again in World War II . . . rebuilt! In a chocolate shop I knocked over an enormous display of marzipan and by the end of the day, it was . . . rebuilt. Moved to tears by the humanity of it all. The persistence, the forbearance. Or I would have been, if "A Period" hadn't kept doing the backstroke across my brain, who is he! No no, I needed a distraction. Quick—I ducked into a playhouse, showing a play called (*Perplexed and dismayed*) . . . *Les Misérables.* It was exactly the same. Only worse. And it was no distraction!— The tram, the trousers, the travel guide, I had to find out more about this man. But how? A dead end it seemed. "Curious hat" "smelling foul" "threw him off at Wittlesbach." Hang on. What's that about a dog. (*Draws a dog on the chalkboard.*) He had a dog, it said, in Germany, in 1912. And he was in England in *1913* long enough to drop off his trousers. But! For the past hundred years, there's been a law in England—all dogs from foreign countries must be put in quarantine (*Draws prison cell around dog.*) for six months on the grounds of Rabies Prevention, there being no rabies in England. Could it be then that our man was forced to leave his dog in English quarantine? Because, if so, there would be records! I called in to Hoofddorp extending my vacation, ignored the grumblings on the other end, worried a little about giving Brody the one-up but I'd attend to that, and like a shot, I was back on British soil, rifling through files for dogs deposited between March 1912 and November 1913, and here was something very curious—only one dog, stay with me here, one dog alone, was put in quarantine during that period, who, after six months, was not reclaimed. That dog's name was . . . (*Writes on chalkboard*.) . . . Sabrina. . . .

(*We hear a scratchy recording of "It's a Long Way to Tipperary" [preferably by John McCormack] or similar WWI-vintage war song, and see a slide of soldiers in trenches*.)

Sabrina. October 1914 and Sabrina still not claimed. World War I had started by then, ten million men would be slaughtered by the end, and the German dog, Sabrina, she too was put down, at last. . . . Gassed . . . And as I stood there in that office, I began to wonder . . . (*Looks about.*) What was I doing here?! But! And yet! What was that dog doing here. And what was anybody doing in those trenches in 1914— (*To slide of soldier*) —oh but you doughboys had a song for that, didn't you, how did it go— (*Sings waveringly the old soldier song [to the tune of "Auld Lang Syne"]*) "We're here because we're here because we're here because we're here. . . . " Yes, well enough of that.

The veterinarian's report on Sabrina is a tearjerker and reads in part— (*Reading scrap of paper with Evidence label dangling on it*) "This dog was brought to us with its footpads torn to shreds. And yet, when we told the dog to sit, it whined and whimpered, and refused to sit, and cowered in terror, as if sitting would bring with it a terrible beating." Poor Sabrina! And remember now, our man in the tram was reported as pacing up and down, *refusing to sit*. Well. This was getting interesting. Not riveting. But interesting. And nothing else of note except this, Except this!— (*Reveals, attached to the report, with its own evidence tag*) —a release statement, handwritten by our Mister Mystery, oh yes, matching to a tee all the loops of the ells and ees that we have here in the margins of the bloody *Baedeker's!* And he signed it—*"A" period*. And he wrote, "I give full authorization to these fellows to keep for the prescribed allotment of time, my dog, *Zebrina.*" Not Sabrina. But "Ze." With a *Z, E* Zebrina. Well. "What sort of a name is that?" I wondered. So I looked it up in the dictionary, and encyclopédia, and one of those "name-the-baby" books and do you know what I found? Nothing. Still. I tucked it away in the back of the thinking thing that I cleverly carry around with me, sometimes, and there was this too—our man was required on this form to leave the name and address of a man in the Country who could vouch for him, and he wrote "The estate of the Lord of Derby, Attention: Thomas Wright."

And here's where things take a turn. And I'm talking about my stomach, for one. And here's why. I did a bit of research. Thomas Wright did live on the estate of the Lord of Derby but it was almost two hundred years previous to the date of the Release Statement, Thomas Wright lived on the estate of the Lord of Derby from 1720 to 1754. *Seventeen* fifty-four. Two hundred and thirty-two years before the *Baedeker's* book was returned. Well this didn't make any sense. I was a bit scared now . . . no one lives that long . . . surely he wrote down the first name that came to his head, having no one truly who could vouch for him in England. . . . Surely! But if you think I wasn't up in Derby the next day, to the archives now overseen by the National Trust, sifting through the account books of Thomas Wright, well, you'd be wrong. This was getting funny, and I didn't like it.

Eveydence #9. A page from Wright's Account Book. Whose now? Thomas Wright's. He kept the accounts of the estate of the Lord of Derby. How many chamber pots ordered and whatnot. And a diligent man was he. And good for us. And here's why. Year, 1748. Page 112, line 8—"Earth-stopper—hired for week. Four pence." So what? So this—in the margins next to the line, and on the back of the page, Wright scribbled the following— (*And he acts out the following in a clearly rehearsed, but rather stiltedly rendered performance [though still managing to impart an air of mystery to the "man in the funnel-shaped hat."])*

Whilst riding in coach, early evening, encountered a most curious man wearing faded yellow funnel-shaped hat roaming grounds of estate.

"Sir," I said, "you are trespassing on private ground belonging to the Lord of Derby, you don't belong here."

"I don't belong here, I don't belong anywhere at all, but I'm everywhere nonetheless and you can thank your Lord for that."

"Do you have a grievance with my Lord?"

"You don't know the half of it," he replied, in an accent impossible to place, but if I had to venture, I would say half-French, half . . . monkey.

"May I ask how my Lord has grieved you, sir?"

"You may ask, but I mayn't answer—I'm not allowed to tell you how he has wronged me."

"Then how do you expect my Lord of Derby to make amends," I said, rather exasperated. And here, the curious man doubled over, and said that was the funniest joke he had ever heard. He said evidently we have been talking about two different Lords. Well, obviously an escapee from Bedlam, but suddenly remembering that I was in desperate need of an earthstopper for tomorrow's hunt, I took the liberty of asking this crooked man if he would like a night's employment. At the word "earthstopper," his eyes lit up.

Hold on. Stop the narrative. What's earthstopping. Well, let's look it up. (*We see a slide of Joseph Wright's nineteenth-century painting* The Earthstopper.) Oh yes, here's a picture of it and a faded miserable picture it is. Apparently it's a little tactic developed by the foxhunting gentry. Foxes, apparently, live in dens, snug little places. . . . At night, the foxes leave their dens, and skulk about, looking for supper. Otherwise, it's the dens for them. Well, if you live on a big estate, and you're throwing a foxhunting party in the morning, you don't want all the foxes in their dens, no. Your guests will say, one and all, "Well that was a lousy party." So what do you do. You employ an *earthstopper,* who goes out with his lantern and spade the night before, and while the fox is out, he stops up his den right up to the top with earth. When the fox returns, he can't find his home. "What miserable earth-stopper's done this," says the fox, "burying my wife and all my lovelies, and now I must roam the hills til morn and find a fix to this conundrum." And, of course, in the morn—while the fox is aroaming—the dogs, the horns, the horses, the slaughter. Lovely. Now back to the narrative.

> . . . At the word "earthstopper," his eyes lit up.
> "Oh, are you one who appreciates a good hunt?"
> "Well no, I like the idea of the little fox roaming about with no place to return to—it's . . . funny." As he appeared exhausted I bade him ride in the coach, which he did, but he would not sit. When I insisted he sit, he insisted with equal force he would not. Unable to abide by a man who insists on standing stooped in front of me in a coach, I bade him walk on behind until . . .

And here the little anecdote suddenly and forever stops, the next page missing, you see . . . Thomas Wright, you see, grew liquidy in the mind, over time, and the little children would steal in, and steal his official papers to use for kites, and the life of Wright got snagged in trees and down drain-pipes. (*With unexpected bitterness*) And whose doesn't.

But! We have this. A man who wouldn't sit on a coach, a man who wouldn't sit on a tram, a man's dog who wouldn't sit in a kennel, a man with a grievance against some lord, and a man with a funny hat. Well. I'm no mathematician, but even I could see that it was beginning to add up. (*Beat.*) Not that I was bad in mathematics, mind you. Next to Rosa van der Werff, I was top in my class, for a year. And that's where I met her actually. Rosa. In math. Oh she had a won-

derful brain for . . . what are those things . . . variables. We'd
do our homework after school, that's how it started. Fine
old time though—giggling, of all things . . . I wasn't even
supposed to be in her class but I was transferred over, heaven
knows why . . . (*Now intensely introspective*) . . . there's a
thought for you. . . . (*And comes out of it when he notices the
audience*) Oh, yes, well enough of that, em, look at this.

(*We see a slide projected.*)

This is a page from a fourteenth-century German manu-
script, depicting a man with a yellow funnel shaped hat.
He's of the Hebraic faith. How do I know? Because all men
of the Hebraic faith had to wear a funny hat just like this
one. *In the fourteenth century,* that is. All of this weighed heavily on the mind as I returned to the day-to-day in Hoofddorp. I stamped, oh yes, I filed, I fined, but *inside* the brains
were churning like the machinery in a cheese factory. When
it *isn't* closed. I had clues, eveydence, but what did it mean?
The patrons were noisy, I didn't care, overdue books came
in, I didn't care, someone stole my lunch from the icebox,
I . . . cared, but not as much as I would have.

And then, one day, *it happened*. I was manning the information
desk, when I received an urgent call, ring, ring, from a patron
inquiring about the amount of direct sunlight one should
allow a Zebra Plant. Well I got out the handy reference guide
to houseplants, turned to the index, looked up Zebra Plant,
and what do you think I saw right below it? "Zebrina!"
With a *Z, E,* as in the dog! "Zebrina Pendula. Page 130."
Surely it meant absolutely nothing, but I flipped violently to
the page all the same and there at the top (*And he reads in his
houseplant book*), "Zebrina Pendula, Latin for the common
houseplant Tradescantia" . . . and then . . . a shiver . . . for in
parentheses . . . "also known as . . . the Wandering Jew . . . ."

I swallowed hard. For in a little-used musty little corner of
my head, I remembered hearing something once about a
myth of a Wandering Jew. Oh Great Guns! In a flash I

dashed to the card catalog, "move out of my way, Brody," and "damn it, Brody, this is *more* important," and "oh wouldn't *you* like to know," and "scramoosh, scramoosh, good-bye, scramoosh" . . . made sure the coast was clear . . . looked up *W* for "Wandering" . . . (*Taps head.*) . . . and found it! (*And he demonstrates a tattered library catalog card.*) *Tales of the Wandering Jew.*

As the story goes, and it's been going for centuries, there once was a cobbler, a Jew, kept to himself, never married, stayed out of trouble, living in Judea, around 36 anno Domini, although no one in the world knew it was 36 anno Domini . . . not knowing there was a *dominus* in their midst to make it anno Domini. And can you blame them. Would *you* recognize a miracle if you saw one? What if you think, "Oh, I'll never see a miracle." Or what if you think, "Well at least I'm sure I haven't seen one yet." What if . . . you're wrong?

It was April, hot day it was in Judea, the smells of the Pesach meal the night before still lingering, and he, our Jewish cobbler, at work with awl and lace, in his little shop, on a shoe—when there was a terrific shouting and haroo outside his window. He went out on his front step and there on the street, a procession of soldiers and convicted men toting their crosses, no doubt to Golgotha. The cobbler had seen it all before, and had little to say about it—like I said, he minded his own affairs. When suddenly, one of the frailest and sorriest of the convicted lot collapsed, right there, right on the steps, right by the door of the cobbler. The name of the collapsed man was Yeshua, and he was a mess. Well. "What do I do," thought the cobbler. Underneath the lintel, he stood. The lintel. The top of the doorframe. He stood under it. Yes? Good. Underneath the lintel he stood. Not lentil . . . *lintel.* You have to understand this or all is lost. Underneath the lintel he stood, and tussled with his quaking brain. "Let him lie on your step a minute, let him catch his breath, it can do no harm." But already Roman soldiers were pressing this

Yeshua to get up, and telling the cobbler to cease in this aiding and abetting or he'd have to answer for it himself *with a cross of his own!,* and the cobbler was shot through and through with fear, he had a great fear of the law, you see, and a greater fear of death, and his hand was forced besides, and he thought, "I don't know this Yeshua, he's probably a thief, a murderer even, although he doesn't look like a murderer, but a troublemaker no doubt," and this was trouble the cobbler could do without, so the cobbler says to this Yeshua, he says to this man with the cross . . . "get off my step . . . go on . . . move on . . . enough tarrying . . . do your resting somewhere else!" . . . And this Yeshua did get up, calmly, and turned to the cobbler and said— "I will go . . . but you, you will tarry til I come again."

And off he went, and there we go, and the cobbler didn't think twice about that little episode, and he lived to be an old man and knew his end was near, which was fine by him, by now he was sick of living. He got ill . . . wrote out his will . . . and then . . . he got well. Lived a few more years, got sick again, called everyone to his bedside . . . and then . . . fie upon it, he got well again. And then he began to notice an even curiouser phenomenon. He noticed, upon reaching the age of eighty, that instead of appearing older, he was looking, well, younger. And he suddenly got the urge to go for a walk, and he left his house and was never seen by his family again.

For fifty years he lived in this vagabond state, incognito, getting younger all the while, and then, he started to get older again, which went on for fifty years, and then, younger again, and fifty years of that, and on and on, older, younger, older, younger. And by this time there was more than a little groundswell claiming that this man Yeshua with the cross was more than he seemed to be, indeed . . . indeed, that he was the son of God . . . of all things . . . and that He would come again at the end of days as the long-awaited meshiach, and the cobbler hearing these rumors began to put two and two together, what was it that that Yeshua said? "I will go, but you, you will tarry til I come again." Holy Scamander, it all made sense to him now. He was going to be stuck on this lousy old earth until the Second Coming. "So there was a God after all," he thought. Well that's good. And God had it in for him specifically. Not good. Bad. Really awful. For over time, this Jew discovered two stipulations of this unique curse which made the thing more than unbearable. One—that he may never rest. Physically impossible for him. That means never sleep. Never lie down. Never sit down. Never kneel. Could he lean? A little. But just a little. So that's one stipulation, and not very nice—I mean . . . sitting down . . . it's a wonderful thing, a little rest, when you're exhausted, it isn't asking much, and if you're not allowed to sit, you become *beyond* exhausted, you just want to stop, for a moment, and if you can't stop, then at least crawl, on your knees, but if you're not allowed to crawl, then you just want to die, and if you're not allowed to die. . . . It's grisly. But Number Two Stipulation is just as worse, in a way, and it's this—the Jew *can never identify himself.* He is never allowed to confirm his own existence to his fellow man. He can be nothing more than a myth, whether he's a myth or not.

Now then. Let's get one thing absolutely clear. The Wandering Jew *is* a myth. Not the houseplant, mind you. No—

(*We see a slide of a houseplant.*)

—this is a picture of the houseplant, and as you can see, the tendrils are, shall we say, wandering, from the pot, yes, and so it became known as the Wandering Jew. And this is a picture of it. And it's mine. A documented photeygraph of the Wandering Jew Zebrina Pendula houseplant. I do not have a documented photeygraph of the Wandering Jew *Jew.* Everyone knows after all that it's just a myth. A myth. As in God is a myth. As in that old myth that life has any meaning or significance. A myth. But more and more I was becoming convinced that although the Wandering Jew was just a myth, I was in possession . . . of that myth's . . . *pants*.

The woman on hold . . . waiting to hear about her Zebra Plant . . . was, regrettably, forgotten, completely. That is, until the next day when she sent a letter of complaint to my superiors—I, who had never received a complaint in my life! Oh it made dear Brody's month, I don't know how he found out about it. He even gave me a chocolate for consolation. (*Steeped in bitterness*) I didn't need his chocolate. (*Clarifying*) I ate it, but I didn't need it. So yes . . . yes . . . it was becoming clear that this overdue book was beginning to interfere . . . with my work. . . . And yet I couldn't stop thinking about it!

Because . . . what if he *did* exist . . . I mean, a man (*Perhaps draws a man on the chalkboard.*) living immortally, incognito, somewhere on this earth, well that's odd enough, but if he existed, it meant something even odder existed too . . . God . . . *God*. . . . And all the irate Zebra Plant owners and reference department rivals in the world suddenly seemed . . . a little less important than they did before. . . . I used to lose sleep over them. . . . Now I lost sleep over something else. . . . Mister A period. Oh yes, I forgot to mention another confounding coincidence—that in more than one source, the name of the Wandering Jew is *Ahasuerus,* do you see? Ahasuerus. As in "please initial the rental contract here, here and here Mister Ahasuerus." "Righteeo—A period, A period . . . *A Period!*"

Well. I got to thinking. If I were in such a predicament, in which a superior had foisted an unreasonable condition upon me, well there's two ways you can go, either (A) accept your new condition grovelingly, or (B) find a way around it. I've always been more of the option (A) sort of man. If you can call that a man. But what if you've been practicing option (A) for over a thousand years, and now you're getting a little weary of it? A superior makes an unreasonable demand—in this case—your life, your history, your trials and suffering, can never be authenticated, or even communicated, no, no, after a thousand years, option (B) begins to look better and better—find a way around it. Trousers, claim tickets, incident reports—what if these things weren't as incidental, as accidental, or casual and trivial as they *seemed.* Just hypothetically speaking, if *you* were the hypothetical Wandering Jew, wouldn't *you* drop little clues, from time to time, nothing overt mind you, nothing to catch His notice, but just little things . . . like . . . oh, I don't know . . . conveniently leaving your *pants,* for instance. . . . Or taking out a discreet post office box in China.

(*Slaps hand to forehead.*)

China! Of course! The man has a post office box in China! If I really wanted to settle this once and for all, be done with this nonsense, all I had to do was go to China. But! I mean . . . China . . . that seemed just a little bit further away than, say . . . Neptune. (*Drawing a brain on the chalkboard*) I put my brain under some good hard scrutiny—it had been playing fast and loose for too long and it needed an audit. (*Speaks to drawing*) "Brain! What in heaven's name are you doing to me? Do you truly believe that this mysterious man is—" "No!" says the brain, "certainly not . . . or . . . oh . . . I don't know anymore. . . . "

. . . Thus spoke the brain . . . thus began the beginning of the end . . . because I felt myself more and more believing . . . I who had never believed anything in my life! *Accepted,* oh yes, I accepted plenty. But the act of *accepting* and the act of *believing* are two very different things. What was happening to me now, was a very different thing indeed. . . . A book drops into my lap one morning. Was it just an overdue book . . . or a *challenge.* . . . Would *I* recognize a miracle if I saw one . . . ? And yet No, this was mad mad mad mad mad. Back to my desk, stamp stamp away, turn the notch one each day and forget about it. What was I going to do, spend all my money to go to China! I, who had Hunan Chicken, once, Once! . . . and got the runs for a week! . . . And there was this too . . . my superiors wouldn't look kindly at any more gallivanting anytime soon. The overnight slot was still clogged with piled-up books, and even though I had plenty of vacation time left, I was forced to sit if I had any desire to keep my job.

And so . . . I got ill. Oh yes, a cough, a sneeze, a swoon, and I was sent home. But . . . (*Confiding*) . . . it was all a ruse! I wasn't sick at all, no!, but I had a week of sick leave to show for it! Oh clever librarian—had anybody ever thought of that before—*pretend* you're sick to get out of work—no, I don't think so, that's a new one in the books I bet. . . . Well I took the plunge . . . (*Now realizing the weight of what he's done*) . . . now take the leap . . . absurd, but no choice, it was off with you . . . to the land of rice, the Great Wall, and . . . rice.

(*We hear some chinoiserie number of a 1920s/30s vintage, e.g., "Limehouse Blues" [preferably by Ambrose and his Orchestra], and see a slide of an overcrowded Chinese city.*)

China! A billion people. In Beijing less than a day and I believed it. At least a billion. And yet, it's funny, I think the death of even a cricket is noticed because as far as I could tell, they keep them all in cages for pets. Back in Hoofddorp, a million insects are caught in a million balls of lint behind a million couches every day and dying and nobody knows. Mind you, (*Fiddles with dials of stamper.*) in 1887 in Honan, China, a flood—like that!—Drownded three million people, three million! And no one in Hoofddorp batted an eye at that either, so the insects behind the couches shouldn't take it personally, that's just the way it is. It may have been three million and one people who drownded, by the way, but what's that one to anyone but that one. If it isn't someone you know, then it's all just—behind the couch. Which begs the question, if I snuffed it tomorrow, would anyone notice? Oh yes, plenty. Or rather, a few. Or rather, Brody. But in two hundred years, five hundred, ten thousand, will anyone care that *he* perished? No. Or any of us here? . . . No. Lord Harry, we're all behind the couch, mutely struggling with our lint . . . not a cheery thought. Standing in Jaiseng Road in Beijing surrounded by a billion other souls can do that to your thoughts, a diversion was needed, I tried to get tickets for a show in town called . . . *Les Misérables*—yes, I like it, I admit it—but I was mistakenly given tickets to the Peking Opera instead, and I went, and . . . I liked that too . . . I didn't know what was happening to me . . . I had heard that travel broadened the mind but at this rate I would need a sombrero soon. But on to Dingtao, where I greased a palm, a very easy thing to do in Dingtao, as if our man had foreseen it all, and I obtained access to the Post Office Box of Mister A period.

Inside . . . was one letter . . . (*He takes letter from box with great anticipation, then opens it, to great disappointment.*) . . . from me, informing him of his pretty fine. (*Then spots another letter.*) And one letter, and one letter! dated January 6, 1906, and here it is, Eveydence #11, written to our man by one Esther Gelfer. In Yiddish. And of all things . . . a love letter. An excerpt of which reads as follows— "If you must know . . . I am in love with you. Hopelessly. You probably don't remember me, but I remember you. In our town of misery, you suddenly appeared, and whistling that *funny little song.*" Make a note of that. (*Draws a musical note on the blackboard.*) . . . "I had never seen you in Zabludow before that day two years ago, the day the man with the phoneygraph came to get our voices on that machine, but I was smitten—you were shy, and knew every language under the sun, and I invited you back to my embarrassing little room. I was young, I was confused and you gallantly refused to lie with me. You refused to even sit down, in fact, and you left in a hurry, in a sweat, nervously, endearingly, and left your jacket behind. At any rate, I know you are well-traveled, and I have emigrated to Amerikay and this is my address and if ever you wish to reclaim your jacket, it is here . . . and I am here . . . both of us . . . waiting. . . ." . . . Lovely . . . (*Strangely affected by the letter*) . . . lovely . . .

(*He snaps out of it and we see slide with map of Zabludow and a slide of Polish protesters.*)

She must have left Zabludow after the Revolution of 1905, Radical Jews in Russia and Congress Poland joining Anti Czarists demanding democratic elections, and Czarist authorities instigating pogroms to divert the masses . . . heads chopped off to divert the masses . . . from their heads, I suppose. . . . Well I couldn't stop now. No time for fried rice, it was a slow boat to Amerikay for me, to seek Esther Gelfer . . . out!

(*And we hear "Yiddisher Charleston" by the old Gilt-Edged Four, or an appropriate klezmer tune of 1920s/30s vintage.*)

Well I got to New York. A slog and a half, but I did it, I did it. Heart pounding, I looked up addresses, made call after call, and at last do you know what I found? That after being in New York for a year and a month, Esther Gelfer moved. To Australia. Shoot me through the eyes.

Well, feeling down, I thought about seeing a play that night to cheer me up, a certain French play, but I took in a concert instead, outside, it was free and what the heck, and then I went swing dancing, of all things—there's a revival apparently—(*We hear romantic swing music, and he gradually, haltingly, rediscovers his feet.*) —and I hadn't danced like that since . . . well since . . . Rosa van der Werff was in my arms in Hoofddorp too many years ago . . . oh I was high as a kite that New York night, and I bored a Japanese couple senseless explaining the Dewey Decimal System while we shared

a horse and buggy through Central Park at midnight, oh it
was capital *T* Wonderful. I mean Thrilling. Both. And. In
the morning I jamfled over to the YIVO Institute for Jewish Research and its Archives of Sound Recordings and
Photo Archives, oh yes, we librarians know just where to go
for the references, and I unearthed this little item.

(*We see a slide of a shtetl in 1904 with ethnographic surveyor with
recording equipment.*)

Eveydence #13A—an ethnographic surveyor with recording equipment in *Zabludow* in April 1904. And do you know
who that is, that gentleman to the left with his head just out
of view? (*Significantly*) Neither do I.

But! Eveydence #13B happens to be this— (*Holds up a battered tape recorder [preferably quite out of date].*) —a recording from
an Edison cylinder— (*Also holds up an Edison cylinder.*) —one
of the very ones made on that Zabludow day. Now listen.

(*He plays tape, and we hear scratchy recording of person speaking Yiddish, with whistling very faintly in background.*)

That's Yiddish you're hearing, but listen harder. Do you
hear that? In the background? That . . . whistling? What is
that? Do you recognize it? It isn't a Polish folk song, no, nor
a Jewish one neither, no. No, it's a little number entitled
"When It's Nighttime in Italy"— (*Sings*) "When it's Nighttime in Italy, It's Wednesday over here. When it's Fish Day
in Germany, You can't get shaved in Massachusetts" et cetera.
First recorded and released by Billy Jones and his Orchestra,
in *New York* in *April 1904*! (*Significantly*) And now here it is
being whistled by— (*Perhaps circling drawing of man and the
musical note*) —some unidentified personage in a tiny remote
shtetl in Poland *the very same month*!? Well wouldn't it be just
like our well-traveled man, as Esther writes, and I quote—to
"whistle that funny little song" in the background thus ensur-
ing that he would be recorded—incognito, but *in perpetuity*—
that he would *leave his mark*!

Well it was on to Australia!, find Gelfer, I had to. And it was on the way, and only then, that I remembered something. . . . I only had a week of sick leave . . . and I had been gone . . . (*Figures in head*) a month and a half . . . I . . . was screwed. (*Disturbed*) Still. We'll . . . proceed. We'll proceed.

(*We see a slide of Australia.*)

Australia, and what did I find. Dear Esther Gelfer. Dead. For thirty-five years. And what did I expect? A one-hundred-and-twenty-one-year-old woman to answer all my questions? Yes. I did find a chest of Esther's effects (*Indicating suitcase of scraps*), there in the attic of her niece, now living outside Brisbane. Dear . . . dead . . . Esther Gelfer, there I stood . . . amongst the ephemera of your life. (*More introspective*) There's a word. Ephemera. From "ephemeral"—short-lived—like those insects, the ephemerids (*Draws a mayfly on the chalkboard.*), mayflies living a day and all to find their perfect mate, and then . . . die. . . . (*He erases the mayfly.*) . . . Esther Gelfer . . . never married . . . Did you live with regrets? "Settle down," you said to him. "Settle down" you said to a man who might have been the *Wandering Jew,* oh poor Esther . . . Cupid *is* cruel . . . or just blind and ignorant. If we're all cruel, it's just out of blind ignorance. Underneath the lintel . . . a cobbler told a man with a cross to shove on . . . and that made all the difference. (*Suddenly, he seems overcome, voice cracking.*) . . . Underneath the lintel . . . underneath the lintel . . . it's supposed to be an innocent place . . . where boys kiss their sweethearts good night . . . in the first bloom of love . . . Rosa Van der Werff . . . wearing those eyes of hers . . . (*Weeps.*) . . . she *did* love me . . . she said so . . . and what did I do? . . . And what did I do? . . . I must have been standing in an ice bucket— blazing heart . . . cold feet . . . (*Pause.*) . . . and she married another . . . (*Pause.*) . . . well you can't live with regrets . . . how was I to know she was the one . . . and only . . . (*Fighting tears and losing*) . . . no, move on . . . move on. . . . A . . . a . . . magician tells you to choose any card in the deck (*Increas-*

ingly bitter), and so with free will you do choose . . . but you don't realize the magician has already subtly forced you to pick the exact card he wanted you to pick. Magicians call that a "Hobson's Choice." And in life we think we make choices . . . but they're Hobson's Choices. So who is this Hobson . . . who is this magician? That's the question. Something named Chance? Or Fate? (_Looking up_) Or Something Else . . .

(_Still fragile from breakdown_) There in Esther's hope chest— (_Pulls from box_) a raggedy old jacket, and on the jacket, a faded yellow star, yes, like the type Jews were forced to wear in Augsburg _in the fifteenth century,_ yes, and in the jacket— a coin. An old coin. A Roman coin, from the time of Tiberius. Issued? 37 AD. Eveydence? #16, underlined, circled, with exclamation points and arrows pointing to it!

(_Emotionally_) That night, outside Brisbane, I stared up at the stars until the old orbs watered—"how very . . . high they are. . . ." . . . Unreachable, that's the word . . . and a line from Job out of the blue blazed across the brain like a comet— "Hitherto shalt thou come . . . but no further. . . ." But no, I'd have none of that talk. I was in for it now, Hobson knows I hadn't a choice, it was a world tour to track down this rapscallion, with the _Baedeker's_ as my guide and clue-filled companion, for curse it all, if it's really him, then he lives, he lives!

(_We hear the jaunty "Freilach Yidelach" by Dave Tarras [or a similarly spirited klezmer tune of 20s/30s vintage by Tarras or Naftule Brandwein]._)

(_Paging through_ Baedeker's, _looking at margins_) Let's see, he knows German, and Italian . . . so I went to Germany, then Italy, then all over the world, where I found graffiti written in every language, including Welsh, and saying only this— (_Writes on board or wall._) "I Was Here."

(_We see slides of Acropolis and bathroom stall._)

To Greece, then France, and I found the words on the side of the Acropolis, and in a bathroom stall in the Paris Metro, "I was here," "I was here—"

(*We see slides of Norwegian coast, totem pole, Mayan temple, etc.*)

—on a rock in Norway, on a totem pole near Juneau, on the thirty-first step of a Mayan temple in Uxmal . . . on a park bench in Stamford, Connecticut, on a statue on Easter Island . . . "I was here," "I was here," "I was here," (*Perhaps writes on wall.*) "I was here . . . !"

(*Music out. Pause. And calmly.*)

But you might say . . . "Yes, but look here . . . those words could have been written by anyone. Perhaps you're not looking for the Wandering Jew at all, but Kilroy." And I would say to that . . . (*Searches for an answer and finally flipping the bird with both hands at the audience, in exasperation*) . . . Fuck you! (*Then sincerely shocked at his behavior*) And then I would apologize *profusely*, and dig about in my box of scraps for some more tangible proof. . . . (*Thinks, eyes light up, and pulls from box, now a little uncomfortably frantic*) . . . Ah! Oh hoh! Look at this! Now look at this, look at this. . . . Ripped from the *Baedeker's* . . . I took it from the *Baedeker's* . . . (*He holds up scrap with label dangling from it.*) . . . an illustration of the ruins in Rome. But by now I was learning to shift my focus, follow the blur in the periphery, look in the margins, the fringes, for that's where our man and The Truth have set up shop. So I peered very closely at the illustration of the ruins, and there in the corner, very small, a drawing of moths, for flavor . . .

(*We see series of slides of the illustration, zooming in until we see the moths, with words on the wing, backwards—as if an impression from the page opposite.*)

. . . But look at the wings—there's words on them, a ghostly vestige—they must have come from the page oppo-

site, from years of the two pages being pressed together—
you see? Yes? Yes? Yes? —But no! The words don't corre-
spond, so we can only assume that at one point a piece of
paper had been inserted *between* the pages, and there was!,
and I tracked it down!, and it's this!—a theatrical pro-
gramme! Eveydence #77, from the year 1777!, in *Holland,*
for a performance entitled "The Wandering . . . (*Reads surprised and profoundly deflated*) . . . Minstrel"? (*Beat.*) "Minstrel"? No. This said "Jew." This said "Jew." (*Stares at paper in
disbelief.*) I swear to you, it was Jew. It said *Wandering Jew,*
I *saw* it. . . . (*Now quite lost on the stage, he reads, softly to self,
working hard to help himself make sense of this setback.*) . . .
"Wandering Minstrel" . . . (*Then*) . . . Mind you . . . there's
a smoked herring . . . called a red herring . . . that was used
at one time to lay trails to train hunting dogs, so the dogs
could learn to track the *aforementioned earthstopped fox.* Well.
For *advanced* training, the red herring was used to *divert* the
dog from the trail. All very confusing for the dog but there's
solace in this—a herring may have been a false herring, but
every false herring still *had its purpose.* (*Perhaps looking at scrap
then heavenward*) *There's never an accidental herring,* oh no,
every red herring, every digression, is a step, perhaps a step
sideways or backwards, but it keeps you moving nonethe-
less . . . (*Softly, perhaps realizing for first time*) . . . and there's
joy . . . too . . . in that. . . .

Yes . . . yes, I was back in *Holland* to dig this one up. Strode
into the Hoofddorp library, as if I hadn't been gone a day,
Brody was head of acquisitions now, I almost felt sorry for
him, chained to a desk all the day as he was. And after a few
gawping stares from the library patrons, and some rather
unkind remarks about the hum wafting off my unwashed self,
I was called into the offices of my superiors and told . . . to
shove on. (*Humbled*) It was quite a blow. ". . . oh . . .
well . . . oh . . . all right then . . . but what about my pension," I said. "Nothing doing," they said. "But . . . but then

how will I manage? How will I enjoy a well-earned rest in my waning days?" "You won't. We're striking your name from the files, it will be as if . . . you were never here at all. . . . " And I was shown out. And there on the steps, eating my chocolate from Brody, I stared in a daze from the other side of the door. At my old haunt, my second home. Underneath the lintel I stood, grappling with a thought. Yes? Should I? No? . . . Yes! And I marched back in, strode straight to my desk, stole my stamper, got out the sharpest letter opener I could find, and carved deep and irrevocably into my former desk so no one could ever be mistaken, "I WAS HERE. . . . I WAS HERE." And then, oh boy did I run away, but fast.

Fine . . . (*Significance of losing job sinking in a bit*) . . . fine, I lost my job. . . . (*Now more desperate*) I lost my job . . . (*And full enormity hitting him*) I lost my job . . . (*Clutches stamper, spluttering*) . . . but I had the history of man in my hand, and, and (*Desperately*) I have this. . . . (*And pulls from box an old horse brush [or some other antique worthless object].*) This . . . is . . . a brush. (*Stares at thing with ever-growing incomprehension.*) Still. We'll proceed. (*More desperately, he pulls from box an item in small pouch with label attached.*) Ah! Look at this . . . look at this . . . this . . . now look at this . . . this this may *look* small and insignificant, but it is actually . . . the fossilized excrement of an ancient turtle. Oh yes. And you may ask, "What does this have to do . . . with the Wandering . . . Jew. . . . " (*Long pause, as he stares at fossilized excrement. Looks all about the stage as if quite lost. All confidence in his scraps has now left him, and he says, softly*) I don't know . . . I don't know . . . I don't know . . . gone . . . gone the turtle goes . . . but leaves a testament more enduring than any of us can hope for. . . . (*To excrement/audience*) . . . Do you know how Aeschylus died, that towering playwright of ancient Greece? It has to do with turtles. Apparently eagles pick up turtles and carry them aloft until they find a suitable rock to drop them on, to crack them open. One day, an eagle thought

Aeschylus' bald head . . . was a rock. Exit Aeschylus. And if you think, "Oh dear that's an awfully trivial death for such a grand person," not to worry—fourteen people in America die every year by vending machines falling on top of them. Vending machines—after shaking them for the fifty cents they just devoured. . . . Life . . . fifty cents . . . (*Bitterly despairing*) And it's not just the trivial deaths, no—all death has a way of making one's life, no matter how grand, seem silly and small—it's as if, as if Life were Beethoven's *Ninth,* but instead of culminating with a choir, a hundred-strong, it culminates with . . . the squeak of a dog toy. (*Becoming increasingly agitated, bewildered, intensely bitter and tearful*) No, no "Ode to Joy," nothing exalting, nothing exulting, just senselessness, senselessness, nothing miraculous, just a nuisance—Life, Love, Your One Love . . . your *one* love . . . (*Pause.*) . . . send her away . . . a mistake . . . too late . . . carry on as if it didn't matter. . . . It Did. . . . It *did* . . . but now it doesn't . . . for who can hear you, in no time at all you're shunted off yourself and there you go—all's forgiven, if only because . . . all's *forgotten.* . . . I used to be a librarian . . . what have I done . . . I don't know. . . . "To prove one life, and justify another . . . " . . . with scraps . . . I'm sorry . . . I'm sorry . . . I'm sorry. . . . (*He begins putting scraps back in the box, and packing up, when suddenly he sees the World's Fair recording in the box [either a shellac disc or a cassette purporting to be a recording from the record], picks it up, perplexed.*) . . . And yet . . . to say . . . or yell out . . . or carve in a wall, if but once . . . "*I was here* . . . " . . . well, there's this—last scrap, I promise. . . .

(*And we see a slide of the World's Fair, and of the time capsule exhibit.*)

At the 1939 World's Fair, in Queens, a time capsule was lowered, preserving all sorts of artifacts in a shell of titanium, to be unearthed a thousand years hence, a declamation of our little existence in the twentieth century. . . . Was our man there, being attracted to such a notion? (*Pointing to photograph*) Is he somewhere in this crowd? Hard to say. But. There was a little booth at the Fair where you could make a record of yourself . . . for fifty cents. A few were left unclaimed. This *(Holding up tape)* is a recording of one of them.

(And we hear a scratchy, and eerie, recording of an old man, perhaps slightly reminiscent of THE LIBRARIAN *[with him echoing in a whisper "and yet . . . "].)*

RECORDING

I am here . . . I am here . . . at the World's Fair. . . . Is it? . . . Is the World Fair? . . . Hardly. . . . And yet . . . I'll say this . . . to any who can hear . . . I am here . . . I am here . . . I am here . . . I am here . . . I am here. . . .

(And as the recording continues with numerous "I am here's" THE LIBRARIAN, *overlapping, sings slowly and softly, his eyes lighting up as a much-desired realization sinks in.)*

We're here because we're here because we're here because we're . . . here. . . .

(The recording fades out, and with a sort of beatific grin.)

You don't have to believe me. . . . Say I made it all up. . . . "He made it all up," I don't care anymore. . . . I'm tired. . . . Yes, I'm tired . . . but I'm not stopping my pursuit neither . . . no. . . . And why? Because I don't think Mister A Period has stopped, no, not given in, No, and never will. And if one day He Above tells our man, at last, that he may lie down . . . he'll sit. "Sit then," he'll stand. "Stand then," he'll *walk.* *(God increasingly angry/exasperated)* "Walk then," *he'll dance.* On principle. No, no repentance—no, for in the greatest act of defiance known to humankind, our man *will* find a way, this I know, mark my words, to behold this hash of a creation, to take this muck and holy mess of a life, and winnow out and revel in every bit of beauty and worth that's in it so long as he's in it, so there. And so. We Shall Proceed. Although . . . the trail trails off. The last promising sighting of him was over fifty years ago—testimony of a fellow doing a sort of buck dance outside the fences at Buchenwald. . . . "The doomed souls within were probably delirious," you'll say . . . and what did they see after all but a ragged Jew on the other side of the camp fence. . . . *But, you see, our man lives incognito.* He could be there everywhere you look, but you won't see him. . . . If in Mexico, in a sombrero he'll be. A kimono in Kyoto, a thong in New Guinea, wooden clogs in Zander aan Zee . . . And I'll be right there behind him . . . and after all these years, both of us . . . beginning to learn . . . to *dance.* . . .

(*Up on the Yiddish tune "Zetz" by Annie Lubin [or some spirited klezmer tune or Yiddish song from the 20s/30s] as he exits the stage, with the* Baedeker's *in his hand.*)

END OF PLAY

NOTE

An afterword by the playwright and Slide List from the original off-Broadway production can be found in the Broadway Play Publishing edition.

SHORT PLAYS

SHORT PLAYS

DEAF DAY

Leslie Ayvazian

Deaf Day was written for and performed by actress Kaitlyn Kenny. Leslie Ayvazian was the director. Nina Steiger was the assistant director. It was produced in the Spring Marathon of One Act Plays at the Ensemble Studio Theatre, 1999.

Deaf Day can be performed by a deaf actress or a hearing actress. The Sign Language must be authentic.

SET

The set for *Deaf Day* is very simple: A chair. Maybe a footstool. Perhaps some toys on the ground.

Deaf mother speaks to her seven-year-old deaf son, who is offstage. Spoken in English and Sign Language.

Okay.
Ready?
Come on!
Sun's up, Day's here.
Let's go!
Rise and shine.
That means: Get up and . . . be happy!
Come on.
Don't ignore me.

Look at me! Yes!

We have to practice English.
Yes. Today is a practice day.
Your teacher said.
So look at me. Look at me!

Put your hearing aids in. Yes!

(*Looks at him.*)

Now!
Good.
Okay.
We're going to the playground.
No, not at Deaf School.
In the Park.

Yes, there will be hearing children there.
I don't know if there will be any deaf kids.
You can speak to the hearing children.
Yes, you can.
Sure, you can.

Remember the new boy on our Street? Roger!
Maybe we'll see new boy Roger and his Dog!
You can talk to them. Yes!
And to other kids too.

Yes, you can.

You stand in front of them.
Look directly in their faces.
If they look away, say: (*No Sign*) "Could you please repeat
that?"
(*No Sign*) "Could you please repeat that?"
Yes, you can.
Say: (*No Sign*) "I can't hear you because I'm deaf."

Some will laugh.
Some won't laugh.
Talk to the ones who don't laugh.
Come on, honey.
Yes.
Put your shoes on.
Put your shoes on!
I'll put them on you!
Then sit down and put them on!
Sit down!
Now tie your shoes.
Good.
Okay.
Get up.
Get up!
Get up!
Look at me!
Don't turn your head away.

Come on.

Okay.

I'll wait.

(*She waits.*

She taps her foot.)

Hi.

Yes, I'll stay in the Park with you, of course.
I'll sit on the closest bench.
You can talk to me whenever you want.
People may watch you.
And some may think: "WOW! Look at this kid!
He knows two languages! How cool!"

Well, some will think, "WOW!"
Some might be stupid.
We will ignore the stupid ones.
Do we feel sorry for the stupid ones?
Nah.
We think they're stupid.
But, some people will see how wonderful you are.
And those people will want to talk to you.
So, watch their faces.
Read their lips.

If they walk away without telling you where they are
going, don't be mad.
Hearing people talk with their backs to each other.
At those times, wave to me.
We will talk.
And then, we'll come home. Yes.
And you can be quiet for as long as you want to be quiet.
No voices. Quiet.
Quiet.
Okay.

You ready?
Hearing aids, turned on!
Eyes open!
Let's go!

No, we don't have to march.
We can walk slowly!
We can walk real slowly.
And we'll look at each other.
And we'll talk.
In Sign.

We'll talk
I promise.

(*Without Sign.*)

Good.

(*Lights shift.*)

(*Lights come up.*

It is the same day: evening.)

Hey.
It's almost time for bed!
Yes it is!
And you have sleepy eyes.
Yes, yes, yes you do.
But first . . .
Look at me, honey.

(*Hits floor for his attention.*)

(*In Sign*) Look at me! Good.

Let's practice English before we go to bed.
Practice Day is nearly finished.

Watch my face.
Come on, watch.

Let's talk about the Park.

No. No Roger! No dog. No.

But the Seesaw! Yes!
That girl!
No, we don't know her name.
But you two were perfectly balanced!
You sat in the air at the same time!
That's very special.

But the slide. I know.
They pushed you down the slide.
They wanted you to go faster.
They said: "HEY! . . . HEY!"

They didn't know that you couldn't hear them.
So, they pushed.
They pushed hard. I know.

It surprised you.
And it hurt you. I know.

They pushed you because they were frustrated with you.

But I think you can understand.
Sure you can.
Think about your deaf friends at school.
When you want their attention, sometimes you grab
them. Sometimes you hit them. Sure you do.
Because you want them to look at you.
And you get frustrated. Yes you do!

So, next time, if the kids are waiting, you go fast!
Okay!
Go fast down that slide.
You kick butt!
Yes!

Then no one will push you.
And no one will laugh.

You need to be fast and quick, quick, quick.
Like a bunny.
Yes.
A fast bunny who kicks butt!
That's you!

Yes!
Right! Jackie Chan!

Okay.

(*Jumps up and does Jackie Chan stance.*)

Jackie Chan!

Auhhhhhh!

(*Does tae kwon do kick.*)

We are Jackie Chan!

(*Another move.*)

But you have sleepy eyes!

Yes.

(*Said in Korean, no Sign.*)

Cherry ut. Cun yay. (*Bows to him.*) Tae Kwon.

(*Back to Sign and English.*)

So get in bed, Jackie Chan!

And maybe, tomorrow we'll go to the Planetarium.

Or the Zoo?

Maybe the Park.
And you can get back in the saddle.

That means: When you ride a horse and fall off, you
need to get back on the horse right away. So you don't
feel scared.

Back in the saddle.
Back in the Park.
Back on the slide.
Okay?

Okay.

Now sleep, honey.
Sweet dreams.

(*She waves.*)

Sweet dreams.

(*She leaves "his room" and sits.*

She waits.

Then she gets back up and goes to his room.

She sees he is still awake, but sleepy. She waves again.

She leaves and goes back to her chair.

She waits.

Then she goes again and checks on him.

He's asleep.

She returns to her chair and sits.

She breathes a sigh of relief.

Beat.

She notices he has walked into the room.)

What's up?

Tomorrow?

Stay home?

All day?

No voices?

Quiet?

I'm thinking.

(*She gets up and sits on floor.*)

Okay.

Tomorrow.

Quiet.

I promise.

Yes.
(*In Sign*) Quiet. Quiet. I promise.
(*In Sign and English*) Good night.
(*In just Sign*) Good night.

(*She sits watching her son.*)

Lights fade.)

END

THE DEFENESTRATION
OF CITIZEN
CANDIDATE X

Adam LeFevre

The Defenestration of Citizen Candidate X was first performed at Actors & Writers in Olivebridge, New York, in May 1997. The author played the role of X.

NOTE

X periodically refers to an earpiece, through which his handlers are speaking to him, trying to keep him on track.

A podium. A microphone. All flooded in bright white unforgiving light.

Enter x. *He crosses to podium. He blows twice into the microphone.*

x

Is it transpiring?

(*He blows again.*)

Yes? Good. So.

Good evening, ladies and gentlemen. And thank you for coming with so little preconception. Kind ladies and gentle men. Gents. Tangents—ears so attentively cocked. And you of the media. Hello, you media-types. Newshounds. Culture vultures. Deconstructionists, and others unable to suppress your critical proclivities. Citizens all. The gamut. Lapwing to bottom-feeder. Ditty-mongering, finger-pointing, dis-abused paranoics. Deepwater bread-casters. Historians. Futur-ists. And I hope—please, I hear you—maybe the odd, rueful clarinetist. All of you. Lefties. Righties. All of you here, well—here we are.

One or two of you I can almost make out a face out there on the fringe, the apron, if you will, of the dark. But I sense a whole galaxy of faces, a host of eyes aswim beyond that wall of lights—that impenetrable, inevitable, remorseless wall.

On the surface, let's face it. Okay. This can't be a happy occasion for any of us. Strolling over here to the pressroom from the Larval Office with Butch Carilli, my secretary of the last—oh, Hecate!—Butch has been my right hand since we gave up our tails and climbed down from the trees. "Butch," I said as we strode, "it's times like these—desperate, unhappy times—when measure and grace, all the Apollonian pie charts and pushpins, are going to have to undergo a kind of red shift, and submit to the sticky, disgusting embrace of a distant ululation, an inner sobbing so ravenous it gnaws its own memory." And you know what he said to me? "Mr. President, I don't have a clue what you mean." So, I shot him in the forehead with the .22 pistol I have here in my breast pocket. Now there's a clarification for you. I'll pause here.

(*Pause.*)

That empty space just now was intended for your chuckle, your knowing laugh, because you understand that what I said about shooting Butch was merely an example of black humor, that skewed wit so often employed in the poetics of distress and uncertainty as a kind of safety valve—although, let me remind you Butch, wherever you are, in the old days in Egypt, the most trusted counselors would in fact be strangled and interred with their Pharaoh and be mighty glad of it. Where are you Butch? I know you're out there. No, I love Butch. Really. Butch is a gas.

Okay. I hear you. Let me get to the point. Because the Air Force helicopter idling out there on the egg-rolling lawn waiting to swallow me up and take me away, that's costing us all taxpayer dollars that might better be spent elsewhere— say, stripping, sanding, and restoring old furniture, all the old rocking chairs in America, say, that were so lovingly crafted lo those many years ago by hands tough and calloused, but tender too—skin like a reptile, but a touch like an angel. Think of all those beautiful rockers we could resurrect with that money. And we could just give them away to poor, tired, old people, who have a God-given right, not only to sit down, but be in motion too, at the same time, back and forth, back and forth. Oh America! America! You deserve moving chairs!

I have sat with myself, let me tell you. I have sat with myself long nights asking, have I misconstrued? Have I misapplied the confidence and trust you bestowed upon me in free and open election? Have I failed to recognize your true desires? Have I betrayed you by not creating public policy by which you—each of you—could articulate your individual souls? Have I kept you purposely from my innermost heart? *Contradiction. Obfuscation.* These are not pretty words. Pretty words are words like: *Monongahela; bosom; lollipop; melancholy; teleprompter.* I have asked myself: am I guilty of merely dazzling and bamboozling you like some grinning, patter-happy Las Vegas magician, while I all the while pick your pocket—stealing you blind—robbing you of everything of value, including your faith, bit by bit—even your faith in yourself?

I have sat with myself long nights and I have thought these things. And if I am guilty, if I am: what would be just and sufficient punishment? I ask you. Should I braid my tongue? Should I lick the tears from your face and spit diamonds? I never professed to be the "great communicator." It was you who asked me to speak. What can I tell you about your heart? Jesus! I mean, I'm just a farm boy from Idaho. Or Ohio. Or one of those damn O states. Butch knows. Where's Butch? We grew up together during the intermission. The Great Intermission some of you older folks may remember. Okay. Okay. Yes. They want me to stick to the program. I have one of those little things in my ear, one of those bugs. Voices of instruction. Yes, okay.

Effective midnight tonight, I am resigning this office. That's the crux of it. Some of you I will miss terribly, with a pain like a bubble in my heart. Some of you I will be glad never to see again, especially you tub-thumping pseudo-realists who wear your sanity like a crown of thorns. Begone, I say. Good riddance to bad rubbish. Yes, I hear you. Okay.

(*He touches his nose.*)

They asked me to touch my nose if I could still hear them. Yes? They want me to reemphasize that that bit about shooting Butch was just a joke. I don't have a gun. I'm afraid of guns. And let me add, on a personal note, I believe anyone who is *not* afraid of guns should be shot. Thank you.

Ladies and gentlemen, at midnight tonight I will be gone. As of midnight tonight, you are on your own. But before I go, I just want to say a word about hate. My mother . . . well, I suppose most people would say the same thing about their mothers, but my mother was a saint. She was actually a saint. She used to hang from the wall and stare down at us with big, sad eyes. We kids would take turns climbing up to feed her, jamming little bits of cheese and graham crackers in her mouth to keep her from starving, because she was our mother. She loved licorice. I remember that. You could always get her to take licorice. I can see to this day the brownish-black saliva that would dry in a crust at the corners of her mouth, making it seem as if she were perpetually smiling. Okay! I know! The point I'm making is: don't hate. Please. It's not good for you. Don't hate me. I don't hate you, even those of you who hounded me here to this dawn as if I were some kind of vampire.

So, here it is: I apologize. I apologize if I have not been what you expected, what you signed up for, what you thought you could use. I'm sorry if I disappointed you. If I hurt you, or confused you. I'm sorry if I misrepresented myself in any way.

I have sat with myself and wondered: what can I possibly offer you in just restitution for my sins, the errors of my ways. And I have come up with only one answer: clarity.

The utter clarity that will come only with absence, with my permanent and irreversible absence. So, when I leave you in a few minutes on that aeronautical dervish, that chopper, that whirlybird—you will see me no more. Hear me no more. Ever. And, after a short time, you will think of me no more, remember me only vaguely, like an old dream, or like that snowflake you caught on your tongue in the first thrilling winter of your memory.

(*He puts his hand to his ear.*)

Yes. Oh, yes. Oh, good. The voices seem to have stopped now. That means it's over. Good. I can stop. It's the end. Or the beginning—depending on your point of view. Your point of origin. Your politics, let's say. So . . .

Good evening, ladies and gentlemen. And thank you for coming with so little . . . preconception.

(*He blows on the microphone, twice*)

I hope this thing transpired. I hope this was transpiring.

(*Lights out.*)

END OF PLAY

GLASS STIRRING

Eric Lane

Glass Stirring was originally produced by Orange Thoughts Productions at Nikolais/Louis ChoreoSpace in New York City in April 1990. The director was Scott Stohler; the production designer was Gary Jennings; the stage manager was Cindy Tolan. The cast was as follows:

AGNES	Sarah Noll
JOHNNY	Jed Diamond
JEAN	Margery Shaw
DADDY	Zeke Zaccaro

CHARACTERS

AGNES: Late teens to early twenties. Fun, spirited, likes to talk.
JOHNNY: Her older brother. A pilot in World War II.
JEAN: Their mother. Forties to fifties.
DADDY: Their father. Forties to fifties.

PLACE/TIME

Small-town America. World War II.

SET

As simple as possible. Four areas: Daddy's workbench is downstage left. Jean's rocker is left center and upstage of Daddy. Johnny's area is just right of center and upstage of Jean. The dance hall is down right. A table with a tablecloth, two chairs. A Coke with a straw and Agnes's pocketbook are on the table. A mirror ball above.

NOTE

All four characters remain onstage throughout. When not speaking, Daddy polishes his fishing reel; Jean reads her bible; Agnes listens to the music, sips her Coke, fixes her makeup; Johnny listens. Movements should be kept to a minimum not to distract from the character speaking. Only Johnny actually hears what each character says.

Music plays, Frank Sinatra sings "I Guess I'll Have to Dream the Rest," accompanied by the Tommy Dorsey Orchestra. Lights up. The characters assembled as though in a family photo. DADDY *and* JEAN *seated.* JOHNNY, *in uniform, behind* DADDY. AGNES *behind* JEAN.

Lights down. The characters move into their areas. DADDY *sits on a workbench polishing a fishing reel.* JEAN *sits on a rocker, a crocheted blanket on her lap, reading her bible.* JOHNNY *stands, listens. Lights up, as* AGNES *dances with an imaginary partner at the dance hall, trying out different opening lines.*

AGNES

> Hello.
> Hi. How are you?
> Don't I know you? I guess in uniform you just looked like someone I once knew.

(*To audience.*)

> I don't think anybody's coming. Not that I'm surprised. (*Music fades.*) Sunday's always a slow one. Either the boys on leave are heading back or the ones getting it don't get off 'til morning. Preacher gave a strong sermon this morning, all about the danger of Nazis, Japanese and dance halls. Lumped us right in with Hitler and Hirohito. "Watch out for those dance halls men. They're the enemy on home soil." My Daddy made like—well, he didn't move. Just sat there staring straight at the back of Mrs. Harris's hairdo.

Like he wasn't angry or embarrassed or nothing. My Momma put her head down like she does, like if she doesn't look up no one can see her. And what am I doing anyway, it's just dancing. I know they got all these ideas of what goes on but I just dance and talk, sometimes more talk than dance even. The other night this boy and me, we're dancing. He's in uniform, we're dancing and he starts crying. Not like he wants me to see but . . . well. So I ask him what's wrong. He tells me he's a marked man. Real blank when he says it, a marked man. Every time something falls it lands on him, since a kid he tells me. Can't walk down the street without an acorn hitting him on the head or falling in some hole. "You even stepped on my feet," he tells me. "Soon as we stepped out." It's true. And I never step on no one.

"Maybe all this is happening now, so when you ship out trouble'll stay clear of you." But he didn't buy it. A marked man. That's what he called it.

(*Looks off, thinks she sees someone.*)

Oh, I thought . . .

(*To bandleader.*)

Tommy, play something, that new one. That Ida song.

(*Sings.*)

Ida from Idaho
Stiffest gal you ever want to know
Comes from all the starch in her head to toe
Ida from Idaho.

They have them play even if no one's here. Nothing worse than pulling up to a dance hall and no noise coming from inside. Except maybe going in and seeing nobody there.

I don't know why the Preacher has to make such a fuss. Seems like soon as folks start enjoying something, religion runs in to tell you it's bad. I know soon as folks start liking fish, they're gonna tell you you *don't* have to eat it on Friday.

My Daddy did seem embarrassed though. Trying so hard like he's not but . . . And Momma. Like all those people sitting on her head. I tried propping her back up but it gets hard with all those people sitting on her.

"What's wrong with dancing?" I ask my Daddy. "Folks sing in church. I don't see it all that different."

"Folks sing the name of Jesus," my Daddy tells me. Well, I never said I danced with Jesus.

The boys are scared. I can see. They pretend like they're not but I see it. In the eyes mostly. Behind. "Papers say looks like the War's coming to an end," I say. But I don't say that's what the papers saying since the War started.

My brother Johnny'd write me the papers are trying to make it look better. They don't want folks to lose hope. Don't tell Mom and Dad. "What's it like there, in Europe?" I'd write. He says it's all brown. Sky's brown. Earth's brown. Sometimes it's hard to tell the difference.

Preacher's talking Armageddon. The whole earth going up in a ball of flame. "Just read your Bible," he tells us. "The Lord knows what's coming." Collection plate was real full that day.

You think God was born God or did he have to grow up to be God? I think he was born God. Otherwise there'd be a Commandment, honor thy children.

I miss Johnny. Sometimes I see him like he's this close.

(Sings.)

Ida from Idaho
20-20 vision from all those eyes
French fried fingers and hash brown thighs
Ida from Idaho.

The other night that swing started swinging. I thought it was him but it was just the rhythm same, him and the breeze.

The other day I passed Mary Frances on the street. She's pregnant now, six months. Married a boy she hardly knew, shipping out. Seemed the thing to do. Showed me her ring and I could see she was scared. I don't know she more scared of him coming back or not.

We received Communion together, same class. She went first. Best thing about receiving Communion, we decided, was we got to wear stockings the first time. I miss stockings. But I don't mind much 'cause I know the silk's going into parachutes.

My Daddy got real mad when I told him one of the boys said there really is plenty of gasoline, Roosevelt just wants everybody to think they're giving up something so they'll feel like it's patriotic. "These are the boys you dance with," my Daddy said. I could see he was mad.

War ends, this place is through. Base'll close and with plenty of gas around, nobody's hanging around here.

(*Sings.*)

Ida from—

"A ball of light," Preacher says.

You know sometimes that's how I see my brother. Brown sky. Brown earth. And this ball of light not knowing which is which.

I planted tulips on his grave. Daddy wanted geraniums but I said the only reason people plant geraniums is they don't need any care. So I planted tulips. Bloom early then they're gone like Johnny.

Ten thirty and nobody here. It used to bother me but I don't care. Nobody shows I dance alone.

(*She dances with an imaginary partner.*)

JOHNNY

I've been looking for God. I haven't seen him and I keep looking. What I'll ask I'm not sure but I keep looking.

They planted tulips on my grave. Everyone else gets geraniums, maybe a few daisies. Tulips. (AGNES *sits*.) It was Agnes's idea. At the funeral she had to hold our Momma up. Momma was wearing those heels she does, the low square ones. Seemed like she was sinking in the ground faster than I was, so Agnes held her. My Daddy, he just looked straight ahead like he does, not showing anything, but I know he cries when nobody sees.

I miss Momma. The other day I tried that swing out back. Agnes saw but she didn't know it was me. "What's it like over there in Europe?" she'd write. I told her it was brown, all brown. Sometimes I think the reason the men are so horny is they want to taste some other color—maybe a peach or some yellow. Once I had a girl back home, she was blue with some forest green around the edge. One thing they didn't prepare us for was how brown it was gonna be. And their faces. The Germans, I mean—that they'd have them. First bombing mission I went on, after we drop them, I think of when I was a kid stepping on ant holes. All these shapes running around. One thing about the ants, they never fired back.

The Bible talks about Lot and his wife leaving the burning city. Don't look back they're told. She does and she's turned into a pillar of salt. Anytime I see somebody crying that's what I think. The salt in the tears, that's Lot's wife looking back.

Papers saying the War's gonna be over soon but I don't see how.

I used to think what I'd think about if I knew I was dying. Someplace maybe or something I'd remember, someone. But I didn't think nothing. Just color all around—blue yellow orange and me not separate from any of them.

I've been looking for God. I haven't seen him yet and I keep looking. Maybe when I find him that's what I'll ask. How he did that—Color.

JEAN

The Lord is my Shepherd; I shall not want.

I miss Johnny.

Church had a Bake Sale Sunday to raise money for a memorial they want to build for all the boys. Everybody's been saving what they can but with the rations, cakes don't taste the same—except Mrs. Harris. Her Sister send her her canning points from the City, so her pies are sweet as before the War. One thing about a Bake Sale now, it all goes.

Mrs. Thompson, she made that apple pan dowdy she does. Her boy Jimmy was there wearing Johnny's coat. I gave it to him. I didn't think I was favoring him, I just knew they were the same size. Looked real good in it, too. I asked the Preacher, he said they'd give away the rest to boys in need. I still don't know what we're gonna do with Johnny's room. I go in there and it's like I feel him, in the walls, the headboard of that bed.

Preacher's talking Armageddon. I must've heard that passage a hundred times, then one day it just makes sense.

War's going on longer than anybody expected. Sunday night we had another air raid drill. Whole house sealed tight, that old blue army blanket over the window so no light's coming out. So the Japanese won't be able to tell us from the woods.

Agnes, she's trying to get us to come down to the dance hall. Daddy, he won't go. "Momma," he tells me. "You want to go, you go alone." We went that one time—he just sat there looking out. Agnes and me, we danced. She's real

good, too. Knows how to lead and everything. All those
songs they're playing about you leaving me and dreaming
the rest. Daddy thought it was loud, but not if you're dancing. I know Johnny liked to dance. I still don't know what
we're gonna do with that room.

Preacher's giving out the clothes and the books, but I still
feel him. I even knew when he died the moment it happened. Preacher's up there reading about Lot and his wife
leaving the burning city. And just when he gets to the part
where she turns to look back—everything stops. I see Jesus
behind him on the cross looking down and it's like he's
looking right at me and then he lights up—Jesus. None of the
apostles or Mary—just Jesus. The light through the glass—
pieces of red, blue, the brown in his beard, all lit. And looking down at me. I hear an airplane over and I know the
Lord's taken my boy.

Nobody else sees. And I don't say nothing. I know if I do
they'll tell me it was just a cloud passing by or a shadow
from the plane but I know it was Johnny.

Next day the telegram came.

We buried him out in the family plot. Agnes, she planted
tulips. Goes every Sunday after church with me and Daddy
to see if they come up yet.

Sometimes I feel like that house during air raid, all
boarded up and no light showing through.

The Lord giveth; and the Lord taketh away. I know he
told Lot's wife not to look back, but maybe she just couldn't
see nothing ahead.

DADDY

I never liked dancing. I told Jean when I married her. I
didn't like it then, War hasn't changed that. "Momma," I tell

her. "You want to dance, you dance with Agnes." They play that music so loud, so maybe it'll help them forget.

Preacher's raising money for a memorial, a plaque, I thought, with the names. "One thing about a plaque," Preacher says. "It's only the Lord knows how much room we'll need for all the names."

I thought I saw Johnny the other day. But then I see it was the Thompson boy wearing that coat Momma gave him. Looked just like Johnny from behind.

They're calling this the War to end all Wars. But I remember that's what they called the last one.

Preacher says folks are asking where's God in all the destruction? And I say same place as always, folks just got to open their eyes to see.

War's no time to forget but remember.

I think of Johnny, of the two of us fishing out by that lake. First time I took him he must've been five years old. We're sitting and that light's bouncing off the water. Johnny looks at that light then looks at me. "It's the angels dancing," he tells me.

One thing about fish, I don't care what you do with it, it's still gonna taste like fish.

I think of Johnny. Two days after the funeral I remember I get up early. Momma and Agnes, they're still asleep. I'm sitting in that chair and light starts to fill the room, a beautiful yellow, the sun just rising in the east. I'd been thinking how my boy could've been somebody. And I stop and I see. I'd been thinking how he could've been somebody, and I remember—he was. "The angels dancing."

(*Lights fade.*)

THE END

IDA FROM IDAHO

Music & Lyrics
by Eric Lane

I-da from I-da-ho   Stiff-est gal   you'd

ev-er   want to   know   Comes from all the starch in her

head to   toe   I - da from I - da - ho

I - da   from I - da - ho   Twen-ty twen-ty vision from

all those eyes   French fried fin-gers   and

hash brown thighs   I - da from I - da - ho

GUARDING ERICA

Leslie Nipkow

Guarding Erica was first performed at Solo Arts Group in New York City on October 6, 1998. Leigh Silverman directed. The play was performed by Leslie Nipkow.

Lights up.

The phone rings.

It's my agent.

Not my ex-boyfriend the stalker. Not Citibank MasterCard. Not someone I don't know, asking me to subscribe to something I don't want, with money I don't have!

Thank you caller ID.

This time I smell good news.

"Hello?"

I pretend not to know who it is, because I don't want to sound like I'm paranoid or controlling or recovering from an addiction to inappropriate men. One date at a time.

I have an audition.

For *All My Children.*

I don't watch that crap. I'm a serious actress. I play plain girls who never get fucked or prostitutes who fuck for a living. Could they be confusing me with somebody else?

They need to see me in half an hour?

A television emergency.

My hair. My nails. My legs aren't shaved. I need a lipwax. I haven't done *Buns of Steel* in months.

Fuck.

I ate General Cho's Chicken last night and I'm swollen up like a poison dog.

My shoes. You're screwed if you wear cheap shoes.

I can't afford to take a cab. Not public transportation.

I CAN'T DO IT.

WAIT. I am a trained professional. I do this for a living. Sometimes.

Breathe. Feel the life force flowing up through the soles of your feet as through the roots of a tree and out the top of your head.

In with the pink Shakti Gawain Creative Visualization Living in the Light light. Out with the voice of my anorexic college dance teacher telling me I'll never work until I lose at least fifty pounds. Per leg.

"I can't be there in half an hour."

What do you mean, "Don't panic"?

I'm perfect for the part?

The role is Prison Guard #1.

Once again, I am an officer of the law.

Okay, so my first deeply sexual fantasies were of *The Man from U.N.C.L.E.* So I dreamt of the cast of *Emergency*—naked—while I made love to my pillow. When I was eleven years old. Must I continue to pay for it? Isn't it enough that I never got my Randy Mantooth Fan Club Kit? Look at me, Higher Power. I'm surrendering to the fact that Randy Mantooth stole my only dollar and never wrote back. I forgive him. Do I deserve to spend my life in uniform pants?

See, the models-turned-actresses who play cops on your highly rated network prime-time series, your *Homicide,* your

Law & Order, your *NYPD Blue,* they don't have to wear uniforms. They've been promoted. They are detectives because they're so thin but still so expert at crime solving and somehow they always find time to blow-dry their hair in the morning. They wear plainclothes. Armani plainclothes.

Twenty-five pounds of shit hangs off those cop belts. How much is it worth to me to hang twenty-five pounds of shit around my hips and put it on TV?

One thousand dollars a day?

I'll go.

It's not like it's a date.

If it were a date, I'd spend twenty minutes in the shower attempting to shave my legs.

If I get this job, I can get people to shave my legs for me. Then I won't have to look at the Edge Gel in its manly silver container and remember Steve.

Steve, who, while showering off my DNA and trace fibers from the bath mat where we just . . . before going home to his wife let fly the immortal words, "Gel works better," dooming me to forever avoid shaving my legs because I cry when I lather up.

Or maybe I just don't want to spend that much time naked and alone.

Cleansing breath.

I visualize a beautiful and talented single man with laughing brown eyes that I don't know yet.

He is smiling at me and telling me *I'm* beautiful and talented and that I'll never have to be naked and alone again.

Unless I want to be, of course. In which case, no problem. He understands that I need my space. Just page him when I have had enough and I want a hot oil massage which I do not need to reciprocate. He'll pick up some high-quality sushi on the way. Which he will eat from between my toes. Which will be perfectly pedicured. With hot paraffin wax. At the Bliss Spa.

I surround the image with a big pink bubble just like Shakti and Deepak taught me, and toss it into the air, and watch it float off into the distance getting smaller and smaller.

I thud over to the closet. Thudding is what I do when I— thudding is what I do. I thud over to my denim shirt and my big-butt pants.

I dig for my cop socks and my combat boots.

Could these be the boots that kick the ass of Erica Kane? In front of millions of people?

Until Tad visits Erica in my dayroom and slips my boots off one by one as tango music plays and stagehands smear the lens with Vaseline. A dream sequence.

Our eyes meet across the empty gray reaches of prison atmosphere. The airwaves crackle with static electricity. Satellite signals are jammed from here to the Ukraine. Veterans with steel plates in their heads begin to hum.

Tad cradles my guard face in his leading man hands, the music soars, and just as our lips are about to meet—FLASH-BACK. The world goes black-and-white. What long road has brought her to this moment? What are her thoughts?

The thoughts of Pine Valley's officer of the law.

She was once a frontrunner in the race for America's Junior Miss. She was—I—I was banking on brains and not bathing suits. But moments before the talent competition (in which I was heavily favored for my interpretive baton routine in which I embodied the spirit of Walden Pond while singing a Shaker hymn—"Tis a Gift to be Simple Tis a Gift to be Free"—Miss Junior West Virginia waved a box of Krispy

Kremes under my perfect turned up non–surgically corrected nose and—well, the hillbilly bitch had done her research. I was a power twirler. And the chocolate residue left on my fingers combined with the spike in my blood sugar turned my right baton into a heat-seeking missile.

In time, the French judge regained the use of his legs.

After the trial, I cartwheeled headfirst into a morass of drugs, alcohol, meaningless sex, and fast-food restaurant jobs. "Welcome to Bob's Big Boy, may I take your order?"

Until one August afternoon, when a motorcoach carrying the Salvation Army brass band pulled into the rest stop for some all-you-can-eat Texas Toast. And through the grease-splattered French fry and strawberry shortcake haze, the band-leader, the guy with the really big baton, recognized in my I've seen it all, I'll be your server today eyes a spark that flickered still.

He loves me, but he is married

No.

He loves me, but he is gay.

No.

He loves me, but he is a monk.

Yes.

A priest.

It's hopeless, because the Church is his bride.

He sets me on the long road back to respectability. Bye-bye Bob's Big Boy. I now guard the lawless at this cushy upstate penal institution.

I am one tough cookie. Tough, but compassionate. As Father Patrick—Father Julian—Father Steve—NO—No—just Father—was with me.

And all the while a flame burns deep within my heart space.
A pilot light of love for him.

I love children. And although years of sloppy sex and cheap
abortions have ravaged my internal organs with assorted
venereal diseases, there is a ray of hope.

I can bear Father's love child. That is my destiny.

Father Father was born to be a father, but when he watched
his mother hack his father to death with a nail file and serve
him for Thanksgiving dinner, he renounced the love of
women forever. But I can open his eyes to the perils of organized religion and an appreciation for a good square meal
not cooked by nuns. Together, we will open a center for
terminally ill children and live surrounded by joy and gratitude and Fisher-Price toys, and Erica Kane will finance the
whole thing because I allowed her to use the dayroom phone
while she was incarcerated.

I can make soap opera history. Thud by thud.

I could be the first soap star with a real body.

And then I will be so rich that I can hire a personal trainer
to pummel it into submission. If I get this job, I can afford
workout clothes without holes in the crotch so I look like
an actress should look while working out, which is what she
should be doing if she ever wants to work in this town
again. I will belong to the Reebok Sports Club. On the
Upper West Side. Near my co-op. Next door to Diane
Keaton.

If I get this job, I can fire my Serbian cleaning boy—the
Ethnic Cleanser—the one who I know went through my
bedside table and found Mr. Buzz and the dog-eared pages
of *Delta of Venus*.

I don't want to be your friend. I want you to clean my tub.
Without judgment. I mean, your country is in rubble, thank
you very much.

And if you forage for food in my refrigerator and find my last apple, for Christ's sake, don't eat it. Because at three in the morning when the chocolate chips doo-wop my name, I need that apple.

In: cleaning women who bring their own lunches. Out: Bosnia-Herzegovina.

No. I will hire a cleaning person who just shuts up and cleans.

Like I shut up and guard.

Unless they expect me to handle props. Like the time I was hired to be a guest at the wedding of Clay Alden's daughter Trisha on *Loving*. Clay Alden was played by Randolph Mantooth. Formerly Randy Mantooth of *Emergency*, and star of my early erotic dreams, where I'd seen him naked many, many—many times. And there I am—a guest at his TV daughter's wedding. My job? Pretend to eat the same hors d'oeuvre over and over, while subtly palming it for reuse in the next scene. I am good at this. So good that I am promoted and handed a glass of ginger ale to fake swill while I fake celebrate with the other fake guests near the very real Randolph Mantooth, fake father of the fake bride. Could all my teenage visualizing finally be paying off? Am I soon to feel his moderately hairy chest vibrate against my yearning flesh? I get very, very—hot, and I must have started sweating because at the sound of ACTION the champagne glass slips in agonizingly slow motion out of my nondominant left hand and shatters all over the fake marble floor. Which smears. Randy's eyes meet mine—he sees me—he knows me—he says—"She doesn't look like she lives in Corinth." And out the door I go. Before they've shot one single frame of videotape. Why was that glass the only real thing on the set?

I drop things when I'm nervous. God knows what I could do to Erica Kane.

What's left? I mean, she has been married twelve times, if you include the ones that weren't legal.

It all began with Dr. Jeff Martin, husband number one, who spends too much time at the office not worshipping Erica, who was really only in love with the idea of getting out of her mother's house and into the cold, cruel world.

Good-bye, Dr. Jeff; hello Phil Brent—who secretly loved Tara the Virgin, until Erica got pregnant—so the honorable Phil begged her to marry him, until she had a miscarriage and went berserk and he committed her to the Pine Valley nuthouse and yo-yoed back to the innocent Tara.

Bye Phil; Hello Tom Cudahy, former football player—muscular, but not meathead—whom Erica stole from prissy upstart and former street girl Brooke English. Tom gives Erica love, until he discovers she's been taking birth control pills so she doesn't ruin her modeling career.

Bye-bye Tom; hello worldly silver fox Adam Chandler (formerly Candy, adopted Cartwright brother, of _Bonanza_ fame). Adam wants to produce a TV movie of Erica's autobiography, _Raising Kane,_ and he dangles the title role in front of her like a carrot, until her screen test. She sucked, but still . . .

Erica Kane does not get the part of Erica Kane.

Hip deep in the slough of despond, Erica meets her one true chance at happiness, superspy Mike Roy, but Adam gets him shipped to Tibet and marries Erica who discovers Adam's good twin Stuart hiding in the west wing so the silver fox fakes his own death. Erica marries superspy Mike, but since he's her one true chance at happiness, she divorces him.

Or there'd be no show.

Good-bye spy; hello sexy dark politico Travis Montgomery, who impregnates Erica with his Democratic seed. She doesn't want to tell him and ruin his political campaign, but some Republican blabs—it's their nature—and they marry. But not before Erica gets shot in the stomach, endangering the baby. Bianca is born; Erica fakes her own kidnapping and then discovers that she's still married to Adam, who faked their divorce as well as his own demise, so Erica and Travis are not legally married and Bianca is a bastard.

This is daytime TV. She must be legitimized.

So Erica divorces everybody and remarries Travis to cheer up ailing Bianca (who these days is old enough to have anorexia and her own phone), but even as Erica is walking down the aisle toward Travis, she is throwing secret love looks at Jackson Montgomery, unscrupulous attorney and Travis's brother. At the inevitable divorce-slash-custody hearing, Erica suggests that she date both brothers on alternate nights, but this doesn't go over so well, so she remarries Adam until she meets the hottest of all husbands, Dimitri Marrick—Hungarian count—marries him twice, tries to kill him once, and becomes addicted to prescription drugs which she gets by fucking the physician who prescribes them for her.

Personal message to Dimitri Marrick: The woman's trouble. History will repeat itself.

So now she's Erica Kane Martin Brent Cudahy Chandler Roy Montgomery Montgomery Chandler Marrick Marrick, mother of Bianca, kidnaptress of Maria's baby (who may actually be Erica's husband Dimitri's accidental love child conceived in a random act of passion when Maria had a fight with her husband Dimitri's illegitimate brother Edmund who happens to be married to Maria in real life).

I think Erica Kane Martin Brent Cudahy Chandler Roy Montgomery Montgomery Chandler Marrick Marrick needs a strong female influence. Someone to talk to. Someone whose job it is to listen. Someone who's seen it all and is surprised by nothing. Erica Kane needs guarding. Erica Kane needs Guard #1.

This is my lucky shirt. The unlucky part is that it came from Steve. But this shirt gets me jobs.

I offset the bad karma with the DKNY tie I fought and killed for at the sample sale. I actually bought it for Steve, but he thought it was too loud.

He never seemed to mind it when I was loud.

I dream of Sunday mornings under a perfectly white goose-down duvet with *The New York Times,* a naked man that I actually like, and a bagel.

Except I'm off carbs.

Sunday in bed, napping without snoring, crossword, coffee, having sex, "Arts & Leisure," sex, nap, sex, coffee, sex, nap, great sex, movie, Chinese, mind-blowing sex, and *The X-Files.*

I've hit on Scully as my guard name.

Too derivative.

Hester. India. Clytemnestra. Scout. Mary.

MARY.

Just saying it does something to me.

MARY.

I don't personally know any Marys, except the alleged Virgin and the Magdalene.

The old evil twin dichotomy! My guard will have an evil twin!

No. A split personality. They haven't done one of those in years.

Virgin. Whore. Virgin. Whore.

No. Less is more.

My job: Be The Guard. The distillation of corrections officer. Sublimate my sexuality. Supervise the outcasts of society.

Including Erica Kane. Babynapper.

Mary's not a mush like me who can't deal with the phone
not ringing. She doesn't have a phone. She doesn't even
have cable. Not with night school bills and rent in the trailer
park.

I can relate to that.

I go through my pockets for bus fare to ABC. If I get this
job, I will never ride the subway again.

But a taxi is wrong today. To be Mary, I need to be out
there, with the common people. Look through their eyes.
Find the corrections officer within.

How does Mary stand for hours, occasionally crossing right
or left, with a mere hour for lunch and two fifteen-minute
breaks? Does she dream herself Debra Winger in the finale
of *An Officer and a Gentleman,* skinny enough to be picked
up by Richard Gere and kissed at the same time?

Is Mary dreaming of being someone else?

Does Mary climb up on her couch to check the depth of
the crease under her butt to see how much she should hate
herself today?

What do you say to a girl with a butt? "You've got such a
pretty face," they all wrote in my high school yearbook.
"And you wear such pretty pins."

Look at me now, preppie girls. Without my butt, where
would I be?

I am expected at ABC.

On the M11 uptown, I wonder how many fellow passengers will soon be watching me on the twenty-seven-inch screen. I smile and make eye contact. Three months from now they'll look at their husbands and say, "She looks familiar."

Perhaps a write-in campaign will follow. "How can we see more of Erica's guard? We think she should have her own storyline. In fact, we insist."

Secret meetings will be held at ABC.

The creators of *Homicide, Law & Order* and *Oz* will begin a bidding war for my time. My image. My common touch.

Unless I have to touch anything that resembles poultry.

I audition to play a Perdue chicken inspector (a poultry worker)—when I walk in the casting guy hands me a rubber chicken and says, "Inspect it."

I go by instinct and immediately look up its ass. Or where the ass of a rubber chicken should theoretically be. Really there's just an air hole and a product number there. And I can't think of anything else to inspect.

"Come on. Inspect it."

What am I looking for?

"We're rolling."

Nothing's coming.

I have sabotaged myself because I can't personalize rubber food. They said I was too Method.

It must be my destiny to be the Joan of Arc of correction facilities.

How can you tell when you've discovered your destiny?

I look around and I see my future.

My future not riding the bus to 66th Street and the River, because I live on the Upper West Side (near Diane Keaton), and when I am not working on the new Coen Brothers movie, I am giving my time to those who need it—the elderly, the indigent, the Democratic Party.

And I don't think too much anymore.

I can just be.

After all, the phone rings when I want it to, and I've hog-tied my fears and smudged them with sage and feng shuied myself into the life of a Zen mistress. Simple and fat free, but rich as hell.

Shit.

I'll never get this job. My feng shui is totally fahkacht.

They didn't teach the Chinese art of placement at St. Paul's School for Girls.

I've tried to counteract the negative energy by performing a simple white-witch ceremony.

I chanted, sang "Something Good" from *The Sound of Music*—the movie—both parts—did that little dance Maria does with Captain Von Trapp when they fall in love—the *Laendler*, and placed a Valentine under the couch cushions in the romance quadrant.

So my cats can commiserate over how weird their mother has gotten.

If I get this job I can hire a feline psychoanalyst to regress them to kittenhood.

If I get this job, I can move.

I lunge for the tape, and the M11 pulls over at 66th Street and 10th Avenue, directly in front of the Lincoln Center Library of the Performing Arts.

I eye the security guard in her booth behind the stolen-book detectors. We face off, guard to guard. In my bag I am carrying a copy of *Dylan Thomas in America* that I borrowed in 1996. The fines exceed the price of a ticket to Cardiff.

Am I close enough to set the book sirens off? Will I never make it to my appointment because I am being strip-searched by the New York Public Library?

Does Mary strip-search Erica Kane?

I strut toward ABC and my destiny.

My eyes meet those of my brother guard behind the desk. We're everywhere. He recognizes the guard piece of myself that I am conjuring up with a fever and buzzes me right in.

ALL MY CHILDREN—VISITOR, says the pass he gives me.

This will be worth money someday.

I take the elevator down down down to the land of casting. (Just below the seventh circle.)

Last time I was here I read for Palmer and Opal's Irish maid.

Would *you* fancy some tea? Would you *fancy* some tea? Would you fancy *some* tea? Would you fancy some *tea*?

The casting guy asked if I could start work on Monday. He'd be speaking to me by the end of the day. "Be sure to check my machine."

What was wrong with the way I said, "Would you fancy some tea?"

Should I have mimed the tray?

Six months later, I'm still waiting for the call to say I start work on Monday.

Maybe my butt was too big for the maid's costume.

But today, my ass is on my side.

Television is my friend.

I sink into the couch beneath the windswept airbrushed well-lit studio photographs of *All My Children*'s stars—not one of them with better clavicles than me.

Roots of a tree.

I channel the guard inside me.

They hand me the script. It is a tome.

Not enough time.

Focus.

I count my lines.

This is not difficult.

There are nine.

"Visiting hours are over, ma'am. Where do you think you're going. You have a visitor. Jackson Montgomery. I can't let you do that. No physical contact. You have another visitor. No physical contact. You have five minutes. No physical contact."

I am prepared.

Just think thoughts. It doesn't matter what. As long as there are thoughts being thought.

These are pages from thirteen episodes.

$13,000.

I'll think of what I'll do with the money. Those are thoughts.

That will give me the proper edge.

Watchful.

Suspicious.

But what if I'm too edgy? Too *Oz*? What if they want Auntie Em?

Oz? Em? *Oz*? Em?

WAIT.

Don't panic.

Not for the next fifteen minutes.

Don't worry if Susan Lucci will fit inside your trouser leg.

Don't make yourself small.

Look where you are. The Network!

Behind that door is the man who holds my health insurance and the respect of middle America in his hands.

I am up to guarding Erica. Daytime drama needs me.

I will leave all my doubts and unworthiness here on this chocolate brown couch.

Where Tad can look out for it for me. Thanks Tad. Heck, hang on to it. Give it to Dixie, take her down a peg. I'll be waiting.

What if Susan Lucci hears about the Guard #1 Write-In Campaign? She'll be out to get me.

I can't lose this job!

But I'll be a sight gag next to her. No makeup. Blue hat. Giant keys. And Erica with her jewels and her hair and her heels.

She's got to wear heels or they'll never get my face in the shot. Erica Kane will be talking to my breasts.

My torso will have its fifteen minutes, and then be overexposed.

But first I have to walk through that door. Not trailing debts and temp jobs. I am an actress. I can act like I don't need this job. Like I have lots of better things to do and yet am perfectly capable of doing whatever they throw at me.

"Visiting hours are over, ma'am. Where do you think you're going. You have a visitor. Jackson Montgomery. I can't let you do that. No physical contact. You have another visitor. No physical contact. You have five minutes. No physical contact."

What is it in me that fills the big-butt pants besides my butt?

Jennifer Lopez has a big butt. And she did an Oliver Stone movie. I could do an Oliver Stone movie. A biopic. A biopic of the woman who played the matron at the orphanage in Louise Brooks's *Diary of a Lost Girl*. What's-her-name. Who was once a great German femme fatale, but after terrorizing Louise Brooks in *Diary of a Lost Girl,* never saw herself out of uniform again. Her pleas fall on the deaf ears of the silent film powers that be. "I am not the guard. Guard is only one side of me. Mein sexy ich ist immer noch hier unter der Uniform. Die Vixen in mir will raus!"

Corrections officers don't win Academy Awards. "And the Oscar goes to Guard #1"? I don't think so.

That door is heavy for a reason. Cause once it closes behind me, my butt may never wear anything found in nature again.

What if Martin Scorsese watches *All My Children*?

I am standing in front of him in my best mob moll attire with bright red lips and a lipstick red Wonderbra, visualizing myself naked underneath Ray Liotta, and Marty decides— thanks to some random neuron firing stretching way back to a leisurely afternoon watching Erica Kane in his trailer— Martin Scorsese decides that I would really look better in uniform being beaten up and brutally murdered by Joe Pesci in a jailbreak.

This involves hours of rehearsal and close contact with Joe Pesci, and my first line is: "NO PHYSICAL CONTACT." My other line is "Oh," as I groan and die because I have had my head split open on the bars of my own prison door.

Joe takes my precious keys and lets all the prisoners out of jail and Robert De Niro is called in to clean things up, but I never get to meet him, because I am dead.

The credits roll, and in very tiny letters we see: Dead Guard: Leslie Nipkow.

My résumé: Dead Guard, Security Guard, Cop, Female Officer, Toll Collector, Immigration Officer, Crossing Guard, First Guard in the All-Lesbian Production of Oscar Wilde's *Salome*.

I can't go in there.

What if I become possessed and blurt out—"Don't you see? Don't you see that I can serve tea any way you ask me? I've trained for this. Just tell me what you want."

NO physical contact. No PHYSICAL contact. No physical CONTACT.

It used to be so easy. Acting is what happens while you're doing whatever it is you need to do. So what does Mary need to do?

Thud (because this is where thudding rules).

But some kind of distillation of a physical activity.

OPEN DOOR. CLOSE DOOR. OPEN DOOR. CLOSE DOOR.

There could be some kind of repetitive motion hazard involved with this.

I NEED MORE TIME.

The job is mine to lose.

Like the Olympics. A billion eyes are upon me. It's a fish-bowl. I'm the last hormonally arrested fourteen-year-old gymnast to go over the horse thing. I've got to get a 6.0.

I can't even reach down to check whether my leotard is creeping up my ass and exposing a well-muscled butt cheek.

The job is mine to lose.

It's the Wheaties box or the Betty Ford Center.

I will not stare at these pages. I Am Mary. Pine Valley corrections officer.

Erica Kane must pay for her crime. Baby stealing is not something that can be swept under the rug, even if you are in love with the District Attorney.

Again.

My life could never be a soap opera. I haven't got the hair for it. When I get ill, I look sick. When I cry, tears come out. I don't get engaged to everyone I sleep with. I rarely wear lingerie. I wear cheap shoes most of the time. I'm not proud of it. Music never plays when I look pensive. I don't own a single ball gown. Why? I wear a size twelve. Size twelves don't live in Pine Valley. It might cause a revolution.

But if there's going to be a daytime drama revolution, who better to be its Paul Revere? The butt girls are coming!

I fix the doorknob with my spirit.

And the knob turns.

Hi. I shake. Nice grip. Warm.

Shit. Did I squeeze too hard? I always squeeze too hard. I'm over-eager.

Look. I stood and I hardly noticed. I must be in the Zone.

The perfect picture people watch me go. See you soon, Tad.

I follow the casting guy through the DOOR. Blond wood. I like that. Expensive.

A candle. He burns a candle on his desk.

"I love your candle."

Fuck, that was stupid. I love your candle? I don't even know it.

"Sorry?"

Questions?

Visiting hours are over ma'am? Is there a trick to that? As far as I can see, Erica has spent too much time in the dayroom and I'm telling her to leave. Of course, I've never actually been in prison or, to the best of my knowledge, known anyone who has, so—

Oh, except that girl I knew whose Nigerian boyfriend muled heroin to get a, you know, a grub stake in this country.

Grub stake.

That's a term from my Michael Landon/*Little House on the Prairie*-watching days. They recently re-aired the episode where Mary Ingalls—the older sister—goes suddenly and irrevocably blind and gets sent away to the blind school.

"Pa, I have a headache. Things seem a little blurry. Pa! Pa! I can't see!"

"Mary, we've heard about a school."

"I've never heard about that kind of school here."

"It's in Iowa, dear."

"Make your good-bye brief, Mr. Ingalls."

"Pa!"

"But I thought we'd spend the afternoon together."

"Pa!"

"Unpack your bag."

"I can't."

"Dinner's at six. See you there."

Blind groping. Feel the mirror. Moment.

"No. I think I understand. Just stop me if I go off track."

Off track? An orangutan could do this. Less is more. Read.

He reads all the parts.

It's like Sybil fucked the Three Faces of Eve and this is their Spawn.

He has a conversation with himself as both Erica and Jackson. I am transfixed.

My line is coming up.

Visiting hours are over, ma'am. (Clearly still a formal point in our relationship.)

Visiting hours are over, ma'am.

Pa. Pa, I can't see!

Focus.

Get present. Think Mary's thoughts.

I think it's time for Miss Kane to go back to her cell. After all, it's five o'clock and the sign on the wall says visiting hours are over at five.

THUD, THUD, THUD.

Shit. Should I have stood still? Get out of your head. Remember Father Father!

"Visiting hours are over, ma'am."

Good. Less was more. He turns the page.

Now he's Opal. He's terrific.

I can almost see the Joan Rivers jewelry. Opal and Erica are plotting her escape. Does Mary notice? Do I foil the plot? Do I get knocked out? What if I have stage combat with Susan Lucci? What if I break her?

What's my next line?

Where do you think you're going?

He's not going anywhere. I can't play this. Are you sadistic? Do I pretend he's going? Do I say the line to the lamp as if it's leaving the room? Make a choice. His spirit is leaving the room. Yes. His body is still here, but his attention is wandering. I will bring him back. You bastard.

"Where do you think you're going?"

He stops. He closes the script.

Is it over? What about my other seven lines? Don't you want to see the strip search?

I can say it better. I can be blue collar.

Did I suck?

Do you want it a different way? Because I can be different. I'm a character actress.

Give me another chance.

Please.

He's smiling. You are a sadist.

We'll be speaking by the end of the day.

Resist the impulse to say:

"Is this a pattern you've addressed in therapy? Because this 'We'll be speaking by the end of the day' thing—to be frank, I've heard it before."

And I have caller ID now, so you can't say you tried, but I wasn't in. I'm electronically backed up.

Not that I'm paranoid or controlling or anything. I just don't want to miss anything.

And I'm still waiting for your call from last year. You know, the one where you hire me to be Sara the Irish maid who serves tea regularly for a thousand dollars a day to Opal and Palmer and Kelsey who isn't even on the show anymore so I guess I didn't get that part?

I've gone over every detail of my audition a million times, and I fucking well know how to serve tea, so if you're going to snatch my livelihood and my health insurance right out from under me again, DO IT LIKE A MAN!

"Give him a chance, my neurotic child."

Deepak? What are you doing here? Are you on the show?

"This is your complimentary visitation upon your millionth use of the Pink Bubble Technique. It's kind of like Frequent Flier Miles."

Thank God you're here. Could you just tell this bozo to give me the answer? He knows. He's just afraid I'm psychotic and wants to put distance between us.

"Well, are you psychotic?"

No. I'm enlightened.

"Well then, is the glass half empty or half full?"

I've read the book, Deepak, but clearly I'm missing something. I surround every little wish with a big pink bubble and does the phone ring? With all due respect, don't you read your e-mail? Because I'm a little behind in my rent. Sir.

"In Calcutta, you would be very wealthy."

Well, that's very nice, but this is Manhattan and I have cheap shoes and a slightly desperate edge, and these things don't add up to a highly successful career in television.

"If you love something, set it free—"

Fuck Jonathan Livingston Seagull. I hate poultry.

Deepak's gone. And I'm on West 66th Street, thudding toward the library again.

How did I get out?

What did I say?

Should I stop in at the Army Recruiting Center on the corner and explore being all that I can be?

Four-thirty. What time is the end of the day?

How long do I wait before I check the machine?

Should I put Susan Lucci in the pink bubble?

Is Deepak mad?

Can I possibly have done that pink bubble bullshit a million times?

I should have been doing lunges instead. But right now, my butt is my fortune.

I thud to the bus.

At least I can screw the MTA with my free transfer. This feels good. Like I am personally stealing two bucks from the Antichrist.

Take that Bloomberg. And I'm home free.

I smile.

A hairy old man in baggy khakis with a zipper that stands at half-mast smiles back. I choose that he thinks I have a nice smile, and has no idea that I can see his dick.

If I'm going to create my own reality, I am not going to include perverts today.

I tie my lucky shirt at the waist. So the pervert can see that I have one. And I feel someone's eyes on me.

I look up, and they're clear and blue and he's exactly my type. The kind of guy who'd be on *The Man from U.N.C.L.E.* if it were on today. That keen intelligence. Like the guy from *Cop Rock,* which was seriously underrated. The lean and hungry look.

Willem Dafoe, but available.

Our eyes meet across the empty gray reaches of public transportation.

I read in the "Science Times" that scientists have found particles that mirror each other for all eternity. No matter how far apart they are. Up to seven miles. But they say if it works at seven miles, it will work at seven thousand.

I am looking for my particle, and if I have to go seven thousand miles, I will, but I'd sure like to find him riding downtown on the 104.

I am temporarily blinded by the reflection of something, and I look down.

A hook.

My potential particle has a hook for a hand.

My destiny takes a sharp left turn.

Farm accident? War injury? Hand cancer?

Maybe a man with a hook could love me.

Maybe he has other attachments at home.

Here's the man who needs me. A man with a hook.

Fuck—I press the tape and we screech to a halt on my corner.

I glance back at my particle and the man with the hook isn't looking back.

FUCK YOU, HOOK MAN! I'M WHOLE!

Your loss.

Is it really the size of my butt, or am I just too sick and stunted to ever let anyone in?

Even my particle?

Even Erica Kane?

Have I been talking to myself?

I suddenly feel very Mary Tyler Moore. When she had her own show. Or *That Girl*. Minus Donald.

I slip the key in the lock after a quick stalker check. It slides right in. It always does. Home.

Wait. Is that ringing? The phone is ringing.

Is it my destiny?

Phone? Not in cradle. Where did I last wait for it to ring?

Bathroom. No. Desk? Couch cushions? Fridge? Pillow?

Silence. The familiar click, click, click of the answering machine.

I edge to the box.

The American Broadcasting Company.

My outgoing message voice. Do I sound needy? Please God, don't let me sound needy.

I NEED THIS JOB.

I send $13,000 floating off in a big pink bubble as fast as I can. Look, Higher Power! I am unattached!

"Leslie Nipkow, welcome to Pine Valley. We'd like to offer you the role of Guard #1."

Welcome to Pine Valley?

The man with the candle likes me. Likes Mary.

Visiting hours are over, ma'am. Where do you think you're going. You have a visitor. Jackson Montgomery. I can't let you do that. No physical contact. You have another visitor. No physical contact. You have five minutes. NO PHYSI-CAL CONTACT. Pa! Pa! I can't see! Blind groping. Feel the mirror. Moment.

(*Blackout.*)

THE MAN WHO
FELL IN LOVE WITH
HIS CAT

Sam Schwartz, Jr.

The Man Who Fell in Love with His Cat was originally produced as part of a trilogy of one-acts, *Ménage à Trois: Three Plays About Love and Sex,* at The Black Box Theater, Capitol Hill Arts Workshop, Washington, D.C., on May 9, 1997. The producers were Adele Robey and Linda Norton. It was directed by Robin Ervin; the lighting design was by Lynn Joslin; the costume design was by Linda Norton; the stage manager was Kathy Rehak. The cast was as follows:

HAROLD GREEN   Paul-Douglas Michnewicz

CHARACTER

HAROLD GREEN: Sixties. A retired and retiring man, conservative and unremarkable in most ways, a widower.

PLACE

In Mr. Green's mind and his living room. There should be packed boxes and crates everywhere to represent an imminent move. Harold sits at a simple table with a bottle of wine, opener, glass.

There's a tape recorder and a few books as well.

There could be a simple screen on which slides are projected. These slides represent the pictures that Harold packs with the tape. Director's discretion can decide the content of the pictures. Suggestions: Emily and Harold together in the car or dancing; the catalog gifts; Harold's "Have you seen this cat" sign.

TIME

The present.

Lights up on HAROLD *as he snaps a cassette tape into a cassette recorder. He cuts it on, blows into the microphone, and utters:*

HAROLD

Dear Anna, Weezie, and Sean. By the time you listen to this tape, I'll be dead.

(HAROLD *shuts off the tape and rewinds it.*)

HAROLD (TAPED VOICE)

Dear Anna, Weezie, and Sean. By the time you listen to this tape, I'll be dead.

(*Satisfied,* HAROLD *pushes the record button and turns the recorder on once again. He pauses it. He un-pauses it right before he begins to speak.*)

HAROLD

I guess by now you're old enough to know what happened. Your father won't let me visit. Or call. So I probably won't see you again. Or talk to you. At least in this lifetime.

I'm leaving you a recording instead of a letter because I figured if you *heard* me tell the story, there'd be more of a chance you'd understand.

(HAROLD *pauses the tape. He opens the bottle of red wine, sniffs the cork, and then leaves the bottle to breathe.*)

And so, sit back. Better pour yourself a drink.

It all started that Christmas five years ago when you gave me a cat.

I'd just presented each one of you with a replica of a 1956 Chevy convertible when a limb on the Christmas tree shook, an angel crashed to the floor, and a six-week-old Siamese made an unexpected and early entrance. Everyone laughed and yelled, "Merry Christmas."

I have to say, I was shocked. I've never been a cat person. But here was this little—thing—and she was shivering in my arms. What I wanted to do was take it outside, let it go, turn around and walk away. What I did was let it play in one of the model cars.

Once home, I figured I'd better get her a name before I decided what to do with her. So, the next day, I went into the study with my favorite book of poems.

I searched and searched, from Whittier to Lindsay, MacLeish to Millay, Auden to Browning. And finally fell asleep. I woke up to find the book on the floor by my right foot. When I picked it up, what a surprise . . .

(HAROLD *picks up a book from the table, opens it to a marked page, and reads the first six lines of Emily Dickinson's poem, "There came a wind like a bugle." When he stops at ". . . an emerald ghost," he closes the book.*)

And so I decided that her name had always been Emily Dickinson. It just took me a day and an afternoon nap to figure it out.

On January 2, I called the SPCA. A Mrs. Trent assured me that purebred Siamese were popular pets and said I could bring Emily in anytime between two and five. I asked Mrs. Trent what happened to the kittens they couldn't place. She said, after a few weeks, well, the most humane thing was to "put them down."

Emily'd been with me eight days. And, you know, you get attached. So I thought maybe I'd find a neighbor who wanted her. Then I could see her every now and again.

I checked around the neighborhood. Put up a sign. No luck.

Emily was turning out, in the meantime, to be a bit more— wild than I'd expected.

One day I dropped a Q-tip on the downstairs bathroom floor. I was still looking for it when Emily jetted down the stairs, swung her whole body around a corner, bounded over the tuxedo sofa, jumped in the air, and pounced on the Q-tip like it was prey. She threaded her way back to me and dropped it at my feet. Wanted me to toss it to her. Again. Again. And again.

Then once, still very small, she managed to climb all the way up on the bookshelf, beyond Louise's teacups, beyond the collected works of Trollope, up even, beyond the flotsam and jetsam of every ashtray ever modeled by children and grandchildren.

"Dammit, Emily," I yelled. "You're gonna hurt yourself."

And sure enough, she fell.

And with her came the old milk-glass bowl filled with plastic fruit.

Poor Emily limped for a week.

Back then, she was like a child, big-eyed with wonder, innocent and excitable. I'd forgotten how wonderful life can be when you don't really expect anything from it, except another sunrise and a bowl of water.

At these times, she was my Shirley Temple.

Or the Shirley Temple I remember. All the little girls I first had crushes on. Realizing, for the first time, that they were different from me. And that's why I liked them.

As we got older, I kept looking at the girls with their makeup, and their tight sweaters and their knowing laughs and long, thin, onyx cigarette holders, but they stopped looking back at me.

Now Emily was getting older and she was growing up to be one of those girls with makeup and tight sweaters, the ones I used to call Marlene Dietrich.

But with one important difference. She *was* looking back at me.

All of this occurred to me one day while I was trying to concentrate on the *Times* crossword puzzle. But in between catching glimpses of Emily watching me, my thoughts kept returning to Louise.

(HAROLD *pauses the tape and pours himself another glass of wine.*)

When we met—we were both twenty-one and from that first moment, we knew we'd spend the rest of our lives together.

It was soon after my dad died and left me Green Nursery that I quit graduate school and gave up dreams of being a poet and professor. Figured it never would have worked out anyway. At some point you learn to take what you're given.

Robert was born. And there we were. Louise and me. With a life neither one of us had dreamed of.

And with a marriage—like most marriages. Passionate at first, indifferent in the course of middle age and then, toward the end, passionate again, a rediscovery of each other, after Robert had gone and thoughts of mortality began to sink in. And so it went, the life of love, that way.

Bobby. Oh Bobby. When he was born, he was a joy. And we took joy in everything he did. We even tried to have more children.

And he grew up.

And he grew into a person with a personality of his own. And parts of him were strangers to us—and we never really spoke the words, but there came a time when the calls, the picnics, the rituals were like memorizing names of flowers. Clematis. Astilbe. Hosta. We did it because we had to.

Because there was still a part of us in Robert. And we always knew he was our son.

Louise, Harold. Robert, son. Caroline, daughter-in-law. Anna, Weezie, Sean, grandchildren. Family.

Emily. Emily? Now there was Emily.

She'd been with me almost two years. And one night, late, long after the rest of the world had gone to bed, there were the first stirrings of something strange. And for all its joy and delight, I also started to feel a little afraid, because I didn't quite know where my life with Emily fit into this scheme of things.

Was she a pet?

Was she family?

What were the rules?

This fear, I reasoned, is created by the unknown. To know the unknown is not to fear. Therefore, what I needed to do was buy a book about cats. The more I knew about cats, the more I'd know about Emily. And the more I knew about Emily, the less I'd scare myself.

So the next day I bought this book called *A Book About Cats*.

By page 32, I knew how to tell the difference between the rat-a-tat-tat of a hunting cat and the guttural rowls of a cat in heat. By page 104, I realized that a depressed cat will actually stop grooming herself. By page 200, I knew that light makes a cat shed, not heat. And by the end, I knew that chocolate could kill a cat.

But the fact was, the more I learned about cats, the more I

came to realize that Emily was different from that, too. She didn't look like the pictures anymore. She didn't fit the cute little profiles in the back, that chapter called: WHAT KIND OF CAT DO YOU HAVE? She liked to go swimming. When she was depressed, what she wanted was chocolate. It seemed to make her feel better.

So if she wasn't like a child, not like a pet, not even like a cat, what was she?

It was during this time that—things—began to happen around the house.

On another sleepless night while I worked on a book of puzzles, thirty-four across gave me a fit. Norse mythology. Fifteen letters. A scattering of *e*'s, *l*'s, and *n*'s. Götterdämmerung? No. Ring Cycle? No. Valhalla? No. After fifteen minutes, I gave up, went to bed.

Next morning, first thing I saw was a book had been pushed off the bookshelf. Emily sat nearby, licking her paws.

I was about to scold her when I noticed the title of the book: *The Niebelungenlied*. Of course. That was it. Emily crouched down and yawned.

"Just a coincidence," I thought to myself.

Then several other crossword puzzles were solved as mysteriously. Usually it involved books pushed off shelves, sometime even pages bent back or pocked with what I guessed were teeth marks.

Then there was the light incident. I like to pretend the hall lamp's a candle. I blow on the bulb, then switch off the light so it looks like I'm blowing it out. On this particular night, I blew on the bulb and, before I'd even touched the switch, the light went off.

Startled, I jumped. Only to step on Emily who, from what

I gathered, had pawed the plug out of the socket the very moment I'd blown on the bulb.

Oh. And the car. Every time I'd leave, Emily would have a fit. Then one day I figured out what was bothering her. It wasn't the fact I was going, it was the fact she wasn't coming with me.

Even though my book said cats hated cars, I decided to take Emily for a ride.

At first, she cowered there, under the passenger seat. But as soon as I merged into traffic, she came alive.

With her paws firm on the door handle, she poked her little head out the window. And she seemed to love it when I sped up. Before I knew it, she'd hopped down on the seat and used her nose to nudge on the radio. I half-expected her to change the station, but Bunny Berigan's "Can't Get Started" suited her just fine.

Gosh, we had fun. We went to the beach. Botanical gardens. Or we'd just ride around with no idea where we were going. Louise had been a planner, a map-reader, an itinerary-maker. But Emily—she ate maps for breakfast.

Then—one evening, I'd gone to the McGuires' for dinner—

There'd been much talk of Louise, even though I found myself talking about Emily, too, even showed them several—well, thirty or so—pictures of her—from our excursions, picnics, days at the beach—which they seemed excited about at first, but the excitement dulled noticeably as the evening wore on.

After dinner, the McGuires mentioned several single women who would "just love to meet me." "It must get lonely," they said, nodding, "in that big house, alone."

I looked at my watch. I told them I had to go.

Maybe it was the strain of the evening. Maybe it was too much to drink. But when I got home, I found myself staring at Louise's picture, the picture of her I keep on the mantel.

And I started to cry. I even thought, for a moment—

And then Emily jumped on the mantel. I scooped her up in my arms. And she did something . . . so totally unexpected. . . .

She bit me. On the nose.

I stopped crying. And kissed her.

A real kiss.

When the reality of what we'd done hit me, I blew out the hall light and closed and locked the bedroom door.

Emily usually sleeps with me. That night she cried, put her paws under the door and shook it back and forth. That night, I held the blanket to my chin and didn't move. And that night, I felt longings and desires. Things I hadn't felt in years.

What am I saying? Longing and desires? These feelings were as different as anything I'd ever felt in my life.

Excuse me for a moment.

(*He cuts off the tape. He pours himself another glass of wine.*)

So many kinds of passion in the world.

What Louise and I felt for each other was water meant to warm up but never boil over. We both knew that. And we both knew we were probably missing something. But we took what we could get. And assumed that was enough.

I remember when Louise and I used to make love. We'd leave our bodies. And watch ourselves, there, in the bed, doing something that we did out of some kind of—habit.

It made us both uncomfortable. So we'd sit in the corner,

watching ourselves, and, together like that, in the corner, we'd hold each other's hands.

When we were trying to have another child, Louise used to keep a book, a diary, of when we made love. It was just pages and pages of dates, so no one but me understood what it was.

After she died, I looked through the book expecting something, perhaps a dried flower to fall out, or a ribbon somewhere, or a note or poetry.

But it was nothing but a long list of numbers.

With Emily, however, my love was different.

Because with Emily, I got sick.

The pain in my gut grew with a vengeance. I vomited for most of the night. I hoped I was dying.

Ironically, it was Robert who nursed me back. Came over every night, he did. Made me some soup. Fed Emily.

Eventually, the fever burned itself out. And, for a while, I walked about like the living dead, a zombie, someone without feelings or desires—

I decided I needed to want things I could have. What better way to do that then to go shopping. So I found pleasure in ordering things for Emily from several catalogs.

A diamond collar and pendant.

A small, Chinese, hand-painted screen I got for her litter box. A privacy screen.

A large, blow-up bird, an odd cross between a beanbag chair and a punching bag that cats were supposed to pounce on— or something.

This is Emily. In a special bed. It's solid mahogany. And the quilt is handmade.

All these things I bought, and Emily, dearest, wanted none of them. In fact, each time something would arrive, agitated and upset, she'd ignore me.

So I threw everything away.

Well into our third year together, there was one night—it was thundering and lightning—and suddenly, the door began to shake. I looked down and saw Emily's paws underneath.

"Emily. We can't." I said.

"Harold," came the response. "Call nine-one-one. There's a fire in the basement."

Without even thinking about it, I called 911.

Fire trucks came. And sure enough. A fire had started in the basement. Said if I hadn't called when I did, we would've lost the house.

It wasn't until after the firemen left and I'd cleaned up the mess that I realized—

Emily talked.

Not like people talk to each other. But—how can I describe it?

Do you remember the summer of the Family Reunion? There we were—all having a good time when Sean—you were just two then—you could walk, but still hadn't talked—you ran up to me. All I had to do was look into your eyes to know what you were saying: "Grandpa, come quick. Anna's fallen into the lake."

This then, is how Emily would talk to me.

Or recite poetry. Or insist on a moonlight drive and a midnight swim. Or argue local politics. Or proclaim herself an animal rights activist, except for mice and rats and fish, which she felt, were brainless and deserved to be eaten.

She made it known to me that, in cat years, she was already in her late forties.

One day, we drove out to the arboretum. That's where I finally said it. Under a white oak, I blurted it out: "Emily I love you." Then Emily said: "Harold, you must know by now. I love you, too." The two of us sobbed, wondering at the impossibility of our love one minute, and then the next we were laughing uncontrollably about the whole thing.

When we got home, I took a shower. Dressed in a coat and tie. And made a very special dinner.

I issued an invitation to Emily. She accepted. And I served her at the table.

We talked of poetry and books. Of the day at the arboretum. And after a wonderful meal and some very good wine I put on my favorite record.

(*Jo Stafford's "You Belong to Me" begins to play. A slide comes up of Emily and* HAROLD *dancing.* HAROLD *gets up and begins dancing as well. Then he sings the first stanza or two.*)

I danced on my own—then, standing there, and I swear this is true, I looked down at Emily—who hesitated for a moment, and then jumped into my arms, nuzzled her head in my chest, and placed both paws on my shoulders.

"Harold," she said. "I'm afraid you're going to have to lead."

And so we danced. The two of us.

Through dozens of Jo Stafford and Rosemary Clooney songs. A living room lit only by candlelight and the iridescence of crystal. I could hear Emily's heart. Her soft breathing. I stroked her warm fur. And I saw our reflections in the mirror, me and a most lovely Siamese, looking, not foolish at all, but very right, I thought, two creatures lost in something magical and not real.

(*The music stops.*)

Back then she was thin, long, but small, and she could, for a cat, be described as willowy. She had the most beautiful mask, a perfect black oval that surrounded her eyes and mouth. Her eyes, oh her eyes—they were the most amazing blue, the blue of autumn sunsets and tropical waters, almond in shape, and there were small hairs recognizable as eyelashes that flickered above each one.

"You are so beautiful."

And that is what I said to her before we walked upstairs, paw in hand. And made love. I'm still not quite sure what it was we did. It wasn't what we think of as sex. It was just a natural physical expression of love. And it left us both stunned and delighted and silly.

I'll leave it at that.

This began one of the happiest years of my life.

I don't think the habits of our days changed much. We continued our rituals, our breakfasts, our washing up. Our drives to who-knows-where. Or we'd stay at home and Emily would sit at the window and listen to books-on-tape.

It all became very normal.

And that, of course, was our eventual downfall. The ordinariness of it all.

There were times, even, towards the end—where—when we—were with each other—I'd actually fantasize about Louise. It's then I realized that sex is really just an excuse for love. And love is just an excuse for—well—for not being alone.

It's not that Emily and I ever took each other for granted. But we began to forget that what we'd become was, perhaps, something other people'd misunderstand.

On a beautiful blue September Saturday afternoon your father came by the house.

I didn't hear the car drive up the driveway. I didn't hear the doorbell. Or his insistent knocks. I didn't hear him come in the house, call my name, or walk up the stairs.

And then it was like I dreamed I was falling only to wake up and find out I was really falling.

He found Emily and me in bed together.

And, as happens with such things, the worst part of it was seeing myself in his mirror.

Without saying a word, he snatched Emily and ran for the front door.

Emily screamed in that voice only I could hear. "Harold, help me. Please help me." She was fighting Robert, tooth and claw.

The funny thing—all I could do was look for something to put on. A robe, a sheet, a towel. To think I'd just been caught making love to my cat and my only concern was not appearing naked in front of the neighbors.

Once I'd gotten my robe, I ran down the stairs at the exact moment Robert flung her out the door.

The rest, of course, I don't remember, except as emotions. Anger, mostly. And fear.

There was shouting and even now, it comes back to me as just loud. I tried to get outside to Emily, who must have been frightened to death, but your father tackled me in the doorway.

A punch to my nose. A good one to his gut.

And then I heard a car screech to a halt. As soon as I managed to break Robert's grasp, I ran outside. The driver was yelling something about a cat running in front of him.

"Where is she?" I screamed.

"In the woods," he said. "I think I hit her."

The driver left. I stood there while your father yelled something about me being a sick man who needed help. I
ignored him and took off after Emily. I searched the neighborhood all night.

And what a sight I must have been as I wandered from one
utility pole to the next hammering up my sad little photo-
copied picture of Emily, under which was scrawled: "Have
you seen this cat?"

But no one had. I never saw Emily again. And worst of all—
I never heard her voice call to me.

(HAROLD *is silent for a moment and then recites Emily Dickinson's
poem "Some things that fly there be.")*

For weeks, I just sat in the house. I unplugged anything that
made the least bit of noise. I silenced clocks, the refrigerator, the thermostat, the pipes, timers. And I listened in the
silence for—her.

"Speak to me. Say something. Emily."

Now I've packed up the house. Sold off whatever I could.
The moving van's due here in an hour. I'm off to a retire-
ment community in Sacramento. No pets allowed. I've left
you some pictures. Several of Louise. Several of Emily.

I suppose I want to tell you what I've learned from all this,
a last acorn from a dead oak.

I guess what I've finally realized is that love's just a crazy,
insane driver.

And however much you think you can map out a destina-
tion, love always takes you where it wants to go. And then,
when it's finished with you, it drops you off and leaves you
in a place you've never been before. And only then will you
know that the stranger you've just spent a day, a week, or a
lifetime with—that stranger—was love.

My only advice is—as long as you're old and wise enough to know what you're doing—go on and get in the car.

Or you'll never really end up anywhere.

Of course, the challenge is knowing how to enjoy the ride while keeping an eye on the speed limit. Love doesn't care about limits. But you have to.

So when love drops you off in some godforsaken backwoods town, maybe you'll think about the man who fell in love with his cat. And remember me, with affection, Grandpa.

(HAROLD *cuts off the tape recorder. He downs his last glass of wine and then throws the bottle away. He removes the tape. He studies the tapes and the pictures. He places them all in one of his boxes and closes the box. He laughs.*

Lights down.)

END OF PLAY

medea redux

Neil LaBute

medea redux was originally produced as part of *bash: latterday plays,* which premiered in New York City at the Douglas Fairbanks Theatre on June 24, 1999. It was produced by Eric Krebs and Stephen Pevner. It was directed by Joe Mantello; the scenic design was by Scott Pask; the costume design was by Lynette Meyer; the lighting design was by James Vermuelen; the sound design was by Red Ramona. The cast of *medea redux* was as follows:

WOMAN   Calista Flockhart

silence. darkness.

WOMAN *sits alone in a chair at an institutional-style table. a harsh light hangs down directly overhead. a tape player, water carafe and cup, cigarettes, and an ashtray are close at hand.*

WOMAN *finishes a cigarette, stubs it out, and slowly begins to speak.*

WOMAN

. . . can i just speak? 's that okay? i mean, i'll talk about, but . . . i got 'a sort of ease into it, you know? 'cause i was never, like, this major talker or anything . . . like to keep things to myself. some people'd call it "private" or whatever, but it's more like just being sort 'a "inward." right? i'm an inward kind 'a person . . . i think it depends a lot on the way you grow up, you know, family and all, and i just ended up more inward than anything . . . anyway, i found that a lot of times, when you ask for stuff, or, like, have maybe questions to things . . . there's not always an answer out there. you can ask over and over, but you don't all the time hear something back . . . (*BEAT*) speaking 'a that, you can hear me, okay, right? can ya? I guess so . . .

(*she begins to speak, then stops, considers. finally, she begins again, very slowly.*)

. . . it's interesting, you know, how things'll work out. well, not "out," i guess, not so much that as maybe just "through." right? things get worked through . . . or work themselves through. we probably don't have all that much to do with it. we like to think we do, though, right? god, like we're in on all the big planetary decisions and shit, you know? but, uh-uh . . . you wanna know what i feel, i think we're just spinning around out here, completely out 'a whack and no way of ever getting it right again, i mean, back on track or whatever . . . just can't do it. see, we been doing things wrong for so long now that it all starts to feel okay after a while, you know, like this is how it oughta be. (*BEAT*) there's a greek word for that . . . i learned it in school. he taught it to me . . . well, i guess i more like "heard" it from him, if i'd 'a learned it i could tell you what it is, right? yeah. i know it's greek, though, i caught that much, but i don't remember what it was . . .

(*she thinks quietly for a moment.*)

no . . . 's too long ago now. had something to do with the world, the whole thing, coming off its axis or something, going off in the wrong direction from how it's all supposed to be. and it's the fault of people. or "mortals," that's what my teacher said, "mortals are to blame." see, he said it was simply the fact that—and i never could understand this, maybe i just didn't listen good enough, that was the usual problem—but he said it all stemmed from just our being mortal. right? (*BEAT*) so, then every problem we got is from being mortals . . . or humans, that's what "mortals" means . . . and just because we are what we are, these "mortals," it's, like, our fault. explain me that . . .

(*she stops for a moment and lights a cigarette.*)

you know, a lot of times i just couldn't make clear what was coming out 'a his mouth. he was really smart, though, had, like, two college degrees or something, and still wanted to work at public school. i kind 'a admired that. i was in his class, one of 'em, his first year. 's great . . . he took us, my class anyway, on a bunch 'a stuff, field trips, like museums, and up to chicago one time. that was fun. we went there, maybe twenty-five or so of us, the school bus, and i remember we were going along that one road, runs past the lake up there . . . god, that was beautiful! he looked back, my teacher did, sitting up by the driver, and saw all of us kids smashed up against our windows and staring out, every one of us with our eyes glued to that water! so, he had the driver pull off at an exit and we got, maybe, fifteen minutes or so to run around on the beach—this was november—chase each other, throw rocks, whatever, but all i did was stand there, stand down by the edge of the surf and watch the waves coming in. there in my little red windbreaker. and i dunno, i felt like an astronaut. or a kind 'a time explorer, maybe, some scout or something, sent on ahead, down to earth to see just what the fuck all the fuss's about . . . and taking it all in for the first time. you know? i still remember that. 's kind 'a like that moment in that one movie, with all the monkeys and that one guy, he does those commercials for . . . *planet of the apes*, that's the one. it's like that, remember, when he rides down the beach and realizes that he's home after all, and there's no going back, and he's screaming and everything, pounding his fist up at the sky, but he's still sort 'a caught up in it all, too, like, taken in by the awesomeness of what he's seen . . . i mean, it was better than that, i thought, maybe just because of my age at the time, it was better, but it reminded me of that a little. it did . . .

(*she stops, taking an extra-long drag on her smoke.*)

you know what's funny? he hit on me, my teacher did, on one of those trips. yeah. not on that one, this was at the maritime center a couple months later . . . scared the shit out 'a me! i didn't even know what he was doing at first—i mean, okay, i did, but i was, like, thirteen—and that's just not what you're expecting at that age. well, maybe it never is . . . he came up behind me at the observation tank, right, where they've got the sharks and everything. see, this other teacher was with us and she wanted to take the rest of the children on down the passageway—'cause they have a place where you can handle different sea things, shells and crabs and stuff, and the shark tank has this dark room connected to it so that you can stand there and see without a glare all over the windows, and some kids were sort 'a scared—but i was always interested in sharks and all that, i was. you know, you have to pick a vocation in seventh grade, they make you do that in junior high, on this "career day," right? and i chose "marine biologist." i did. out 'a all the other kinds of things they had there, i picked that one, 'cause i love the water, always have . . . so, my teacher said it'd be okay if i stayed and watched, we'd catch up later . . . (*BEAT*) well, i'm keeping my eye on this one big hammerhead, that's a species of shark—you probably knew that—and he's darting in real close to the glass, this hammerhead is . . . suddenly, i feel all this weight up against me. my teacher is pushing me forward with his body, up onto the observation windows, and i can't move. he never said anything while it was happening, i mean, to me—i could hear him whispering something about the "tragic nobility of sea creatures," some shit like that—and all i can see, i can't turn at all, the way he's got me held there, all i can see is this shark, the one i'd been watching, coming out of the murk and sweeping past me, again and again . . . and it's not till he's right on top of me, and turned each time, that i can see his eye. he turns past the glass at the last second and his eye just sort 'a rolls back all white as he passes . . . fuck, that was scary. i've never forgotten it. that feeling. his weight on me, and watching as that hammerhead just kept circling around . . . (*BEAT*) well, what the hell, it's easy to scare a kid. right?

(she plays a moment with the butt of her cigarette in the ashtray.)

anyway, he wouldn't look at me after that, my teacher, not even a glance, the whole rest of the trip. and he was always real nice before, and funny to me . . . i mean, not in a bad

way, not like inappropriately so, i don't think, but—no, i
wasn't even a "teacher's pet" or whatever—he was just sort
'a open with me. jokes, and showing me pictures in maga-
zines, like, after that career thing he would hang up under-
sea stuff in class, and bringing in pieces 'a coral to look
at . . . we were starting to be friends, i thought. at least sort
of friendly. because it's hard, i think, for a teacher in school,
like, junior high, where nobody cares, kids just wanna
do sports, and dances, hang out with their friends, you
know . . . so, if you meet a person who is actually interested, like i was, and i really was—i wasn't the smartest or
remembered the most, like i said, but—i was genuinely
interested in things. i wanted to learn, right, i felt like
i needed to comprehend a little about the universe, you
know? i did. 'cause it intrigues me. the way it works. yeah.
(*BEAT*) and i think a teacher can pick up on that. and he
just responded to it . . . so, we started to sort 'a hang out a
bit . . . just at school. the library, or looking at slides in the
resource center. lunchtimes. (*BEAT*) it was good, umm . . .
's good, that's all i mean, fuck, i was thirteen, okay, it was
nice to have somebody look at you and not say to pick up
your socks . . . something like that. let's face it, thirteen's a
pretty shitty age, right?
(*pause.*)
but he wouldn't look over at me after that . . .

(*she stops a moment.*)

he did give me a ride home, though. from school. he did do
that. i mean, nothing, not a look on the outing, sits way
away from me on the bus, but back at our building, see, he's
responsible for us, and all the parents are there, this is a friday, and my dad doesn't show. he doesn't show up. we go into
the office, call his work, nothing at home, and he doesn't
come. half hour goes by, nobody at school but us. sitting
there on the curb, waiting for my dad. finally he says, my
teacher, he can drop me if i want. he drove this late-model

peugeot—i remember 'cause i once asked him to teach me how to say it—kind of a cream color peugeot, and he said he'd run me home if i'd like that. 's what he said, "if you'd like that." (*BEAT*) in the car, like this was yesterday, i recall he had this woman singing on the tape player, real soft and painful, i remember, 'cause i had to ask who this was. i mean, this was not the bee gees and i'd never heard anything like it. so fragile-sounding, you know? he said it was "billie holiday," that was her name, and it was all he ever played. first thing he'd said to me, i mean, practically, in five hours is "billie holiday." and he smiled. it was dark out, but i could see him smiling there, we're sitting at a light, and he says, "she's all i ever listen to." and then, "you kind of remind me of her, you know? you always seem just a little bit sad. smiling, but sad. i like that . . ." (*BEAT*) the fuck did that mean? you know? because, listen, you don't say stuff like that to a thirteen-year-old, okay? you just don't, uh-uh, 'cause she'll be yours for life. i mean it. if you do, she will be . . .
(*pause.*)
not in front of my house, but down from it, a block maybe, he pulls over, there's a florist shop and it's closed, this time of the evening, and he parks in the little lot they have there . . . he kissed me. jesus, he kissed me like, i guess, you imagine how it must've been when they first invented it, like back in the days of myths and shit, when, you know, men were heroes and you could get kissed like that and you'd wait a lifetime for him to return, you would, and you could still taste him on your lips, years later. because back then kisses still meant something. that's what he kissed me like . . .

(*she takes a sip of water. she fiddles again with the edge of the water cup but doesn't drink.*)

i really don't wanna, umm, elaborate too much on, well, you know, cover all the relationship stuff a whole lot, 'cause if you've talked to him you know it already, anyway, right? maybe more than you want to . . . (*BEAT*) we started seeing each other, you know, as much as a junior high school teacher and a thirteen-year-old can see each other. that's what we began to do. we starting doing that. and i know what you're thinking, or have thought it to each other, laughing and stuff, that it's my own fault or that he was some type 'a molester, whatever, but you wouldn't really be true about that. either side of that. we, umm . . . just liked each other. and would kiss and things. not so much, but kiss and little hugs and stuff—i'd sneak into his classroom at lunch for, like, just seconds sometimes, and we'd hug—that's what we'd do.

(*pause.*)

my fourteenth birthday . . . 's in march, i'm a pisces . . . "the fish." how 'bout that? i guess it was really the weekend of, the actual day fell on a thursday, but that saturday, he, umm, picked me up at the library, the downtown branch, where i did book sorting on a volunteer basis, 'cause you get a bunch of privileges and stuff if you do it twice a month . . . but i told her, the volunteer coordinator, she was just a high school girl anyway, i told her i felt sick that day and he picked me up and we went driving. i asked where but he said, "it's a surprise," so i sat back in the ol' peugeot, the sunroof was up, 's a real nice day out, and just kind 'a drifted off to the sound of the wind rushing by. the wind and billie holiday singing sad on the back speakers . . .

(*she stops, gathering her thoughts a moment.*)

when we got to chicago, he drove straight to the lake, to this pier where he'd rented a boat for us, beautiful red speedboat, and god, it was so exciting for me! he just kept doing things like this, and there's a picnic basket and it was great, just great . . . to be out there, in the water, on this boat with him, it was just real lovely . . . (*BEAT*) he gave me a bracelet, it was all wrapped up, in wax paper, inside my sandwich! yeah, you believe that, he'd hollowed out my bread and put my present inside there, and i loved that, that was just cute . . . and i got, ahh, this beautiful, like, picture book of several greek stories, mostly of euripides, 'cause, see, he felt euripides was the most, what, "humanistic" . . . had, like, the most humanity of the greek writers. he said he was the one most at war with this . . . (*BEAT*) shit, still can't think of that word, but he was the guy who was really angry about the world being all fucked up just because we happened to be mortals . . . anyhow, it had a bunch 'a nice drawings and he said i'd like it even more as i got older . . . (*BEAT*) i still have it.

(*silence.*)

i, umm . . . found out about the baby, that i was going to have one, in late april, the 23rd, i guess, and i didn't cry. i should've, fucking kid myself, you know, but sometimes you can go along, years even, and not feel like you're growing up at all, and then there's times when you age a ton, like, in a couple 'a seconds. you know? so, i found out and went straight to his place, i mean, called first, but went there and we discussed it all. talked a long time . . . (*BEAT*) we talked, like i said, and, you know, he seemed, and this caught me, 'cause i didn't know what he'd think, but he was all excited! not yelling, or all adult and shit, and said he loved children, could think of nothing better than having a son or something. said we'd have to be careful—i mean, we both understood the situation—but i promised him i wouldn't tell anybody who the father was, no matter if my dad got real shitty about it—and he did, believe me—or school, or whatever. i said i'd keep our secret . . . we made a pledge together, there on his sofa, and i kept it. (*BEAT*) he told me that day, he said he had to go away for a couple weeks, just the end of summer, he was finishing up another of his degrees at delphi, that's a university, and then we'd, you know, make some plans. (*BEAT*) that was hard, 'cause i was scared, i'm not gonna pretend i wasn't, but getting his degree was a big thing, and could help us, too, he said . . . and so we talked for a while, and we kissed. god, you know for being this big guy, he was really gentle to me . . . and then i went home. i went to my house with our baby inside me, and watched *hogan's heroes* on tv, like i did every afternoon. i mean, what else are you gonna do, right? (*BEAT*) i just need a little water . . .

(*she pours a touch more into her cup and sips.*)

okay. umm, what else? ahh . . . when i found out he'd left his position at school—this was by a fluke, anyway, i was at the general office during the summer, which was not that far from our house, bringing them a vaccination report on my brother, and the lady there, the secretary, said, "oh, i heard about your arts and sciences teacher at gardner," my school, "we're sure sorry to lose him, aren't we?"—i didn't hear much else, really, just that she said, "well, i suppose they need good teachers in phoenix as much as they do anywhere . . ." (*BEAT*) but i didn't ask for an address or anything, i didn't, because i was standing there, in that office, suddenly standing there, fourteen years old with a baby in me and this woman yacking on about my brother needing a german measles booster, and did i know if he'd had one yet, and i was frozen in time. 's like the heavens had opened above me, at that very second, and all i could hear was the universe. this woman in front of me talking on like i was her godchild and all i could make out was the howl of the cosmos . . . and you know what? it was laughing. it was. all its attention was suddenly turned and it was laughing, laughing down at me . . .

(*she stops and slowly lights another cigarette.*)

like i said, there's a bunch 'a shit you don't need to hear twice, and i don't want your sympathy, okay, i don't, so we'll skip the hardship stuff about when i did tell my family, and being pulled out 'a school, the move to my aunt's house . . . sound familiar? i told you before, or if i didn't, i meant to . . . this story's nothing special, really, practically the only

part that's of any interest is that it happened to me . . .
you know? (*BEAT*) anyways, billie, that's my son, billie,
"william," whatever . . . was born. a beautiful boy. just quite
great, and although every mom goes off on that, he was. i
mean it. he's great, and, umm, without getting all shitty
about it, i give birth and a bunch 'a years pass. okay? i did
finally make contact with his father, sent a couple letters,
and he wrote me back right away. this was, ohh, maybe a
year, eighteen months later . . . just long enough to make
him wonder, you know? i was still only about sixteen at the
time, so i guess he was pretty scared about the whole
thing—'s what he said on paper, anyway—and asked if i
could understand. not forgive . . . understand. (*BEAT*) i,
ahh, let him know that our pact was still safe, and this
wasn't, like, some money thing. i just wanted him to have, if
he wouldn't mind so much, a sort 'a relationship with billie,
through the mail or whatever. i knew there was nothing for
us, well, you know, not after that . . . but i'd send pictures
and stuff. we ended up doing it through a postal box, and he
got to know his son that way. that's how it happened. a few
presents now and again, and he had a son, and the son's
mother loved him, and kept the secret all while the father
was away. and i know you'll think i'm just talking shit now,
but honestly, if i closed my eyes and thought about it, i
could still feel his kiss on my lips. even then . . .
(*long pause.*)
the rest you know . . . on his fourteenth birthday, billie and
me, we rented a car—we were living in utah by then, out with
some mormon relatives at that point—and we drove to ari-
zona to meet his father. we'd planned this, the two of us, by
letter, and agreed it'd be just the one time . . . he was, umm,
you know, married by this time, married and teaching in
phoenix. no chidren, though, isn't that funny? no kids 'cause
his wife had a part of her uterus, i guess, some thing, that
wouldn't work properly. but they didn't adopt and just kept
trying naturally. over and over. i thought that was the only real

sad part 'a all this—so, it'd just be this once, at a motel that he'd picked in town. one time when we'd all sit down and see each other. again. at least, the two of us, again . . .

(*she fiddles with the edge of the tape player.*)

this thing's almost run out . . .

(*she looks up but there is no answer.*)

okay. (*BEAT*) we met at the room. 's a terribly hot day, at least for december it was, 's how i remember it, anyway, and we were tired from the travel, but he was there, as promised. hardly seemed any older, which kind 'a sucked, i thought, 'cause i'd changed—i mean, look at me, right?—and it was this big moment for billie, 's all excited, and we even hugged, and it was in that second, as he leaned in to kiss my cheek, his head turned toward me and maybe it was just the light, the sun coming in the room, but i saw something there, there in his eyes . . . he loved this boy, all that shit he'd said to me years ago, it was true about kids. he loved 'em. but also . . . he was satisfied. i could see that, satisfaction on his face . . . because he'd gotten away with it all. that's what i saw, shining in his eyes, as he moved forward to kiss me. he'd beaten fate . . . and gotten away with it. (*BEAT*) after dinner, we had a bucket of store-bought chicken in the room, billie got a couple packages—one was a book of myths, imagine that—he said he wanted to see us again before we left. he had to run to school for about an hour, a science fair, i guess, but he'd be back he promised he'd be right back. the last time i saw him, there at the door, he mentioned that word, that . . . umm, well, whatever, he said it and smiled, as he stepped out onto the balcony he smiled to me and whispered, "maybe it's not our fault after all. i mean, we're just human, right?"

(*pause.*)

billie was already in the bathroom, we'd driven straight through, and i could hear the water running. he was in his bath. god, he loved the tub! since he was tiny, he loved it. so, i knew he was in there, the water filling up around him, and "lady day"—'s what he liked to call billie holiday, 's her nickname, and he called her that—playing on his tape player. "stormy weather." i, ahh, went into the room, the bathroom, and i could see him there, through a little opening in the liner he had pulled shut, eyes closed and the steam coming up. he didn't really struggle, couldn't actually, the shock of it, i suppose, when the recorder first hit the water . . . there was really only a quick kind 'a snapping sound, like the pop of a flashbulb or whatnot, and then the softer sound of him, billie, as he kicked a second or two in the water. i turned the taps off a little later . . . (*BEAT*) after, i just sat there, on the linoleum, and watched him, lying in that cloudy pool of bathwater. his eyes open and so still. i thought i could almost see, i mean, if i squinted, i could almost make out . . . *"adakia,"* that's the word. the word i was trying, you know, that's it. "the world out of balance." you can look it up if you wanna, but i'm sure that's the one . . . i knew it'd come to me, if i waited long enough.

(*she lights another smoke.*)

i was picked up in vegas, at a restaurant, you're aware of that, though, obviously . . . and brought back here. and that's it. so, now you know. i mean, what you really wanted, anyway, right? now you know . . . yes. i planned it, yes. but . . . maybe longer than you thought, huh? lots longer . . .

(*she laughs to herself.*)

and i worry about what's gonna happen, i mean, to me and all, i do—'s natural, though, right, to wonder about things— but i'll tell you. tell you what gets me through today, the next hour . . . it's him.
(*pause.*)
i can almost see 'em, you know, i can, down there in phoenix, probably wandering around on some playground

at school, a saturday, and he's just stumbling there by himself
near the monkey bars. can't be consoled, right, the truth all
spilled out now like it is, and all these tears running down,
yelling up at the sky, these torrents of tears and screaming,
the top of his lungs, calling up into the universe, "why?!
why?!!" over and over. (*BEAT*) but you know what? in my
fantasy, there's never an answer. uh-uh. there never is . . .

(*she sits and smokes now as the tape player continues to quietly hum on.*

silence. darkness.)

MOBY-DUDE

OR: THE THREE-MINUTE WHALE

David Ives

Moby-Dude Or: The Three-Minute Whale was commissioned by the Public Radio International program *Studio 360,* hosted by Kurt Andersen. It was originally broadcast in spring 2004. The Narrator was performed by Mark Price.

CHARACTER

OUR NARRATOR: A stoned-out surfer of seventeen.

SFX: sound of waves and gulls. Distant ship's bell.

OUR NARRATOR *is a stoned-out surfer of seventeen.*

OUR NARRATOR

> *Call me Ishmael,* dude. Yes, Mrs. Podgorski, I *did* read *Moby-Dick* over the summer like I was supposed to. It was bohdacious. Actually, y'know, it's "Moby-*hyphen*-Dick." The title's got a little hyphen before the "Dick." And what is the meaning of this dash before the "Dick"? *WHOAAA!* Another mystery in this awesome American masterpiece, a peerless allegorical saga of mortal courage, metaphysical ambiguity and maniacal obsession! *What,* Mrs. Podgorski? You don't believe I really *read* Herman Melville's *Moby-Dick Or The Whale*? Five hundred sixty-two pages, fourteen ounces, published 1851, totally tanked its first weekend, rereleased in the 1920s as one of the world's gnarliest works of Art? You think I copped all this like off the back of the tome or by watching the crappy 1956 film starring Gregory Peck? Mrs. P., you been chasing my tail since middle school, do *I* get all testy? Do *I* say, what is the plot in under two minutes—besides a whale and a hyphen? *Moby-Dick* in two minutes, huh? Okay, kyool. Let's rip.

(*SFX: ship's bell, close up and sharp, to signal the start and a ticking watch, underneath. Very fast.*)

Fade in the boonies of Massachusetts, eighteen-something. Young dude possibly named Ishmael, like the Bible, meets-cute with, TAA–DAA!, *Queequeg,* a South Sea cannibal with a heart of gold.

(*SFX: cutesy voice going, "Awwww."*)

Maybe they're gay.

(*SFX: tongue slurp.*)

Or maybe they represent some east-west, pagan-Christian duality action. Anyway, the two newfound bros go to Mass and hear a sermon about Jonah . . .

(*SFX: one second of church organ.*)

Biblical tie-in, then ship out on Christmas Day (*could be symbolical!*) aboard the USS *Pequod* with its mysterious wacko Captain Ahab . . .

(*SFX: madman laughter.*)

. . . who—*backstory*—is goofyfoot because the equally mysterious momboosaloid white whale Moby-like-the-singer Dick bit his leg off.

(*SFX: chomp.*)

Freudian castration action. I mean he's big and he's got sperm and his last name is "Dick," right? Moby is also a metaphor for God, Nature, Truth, obsessisical love, the world, the past, and white people. Check out Pip the Negro cabin boy who by a *fluke* . . .

(*SFX: rimshot.*)

. . . goes wacko too. Ahab says,

(*SFX: echo effect.*)

"*Bring me the head of the Great White Whale and you win this prize!*"

(*SFX: echo effect out, cash register sound.*)

The crew is stoked, by *NOT* first-mate like-the-coffee-Starbuck. Ahab wants the big one, Starbuck wants the whale juice. Idealism versus capitalism.

(*SFX: an impressed "Whoo."*)

Radical. Queequeg tells the carpenter to build him a coffin shaped like a canoe.

(*SFX: theremin.*)

Foreshadowing! Then lots of chapters everybody skips about the scientology of whales.

(*SFX: yawn.*)

Cut to . . .

(*SFX: trumpet fanfare.*)

Page 523, the Pacific Ocean. *"Surf's up!"* Ahab sights the Dick. He's totally amped. The boards hit the waves, the crew snakes the Dick for three whole days, bottom of the third Ahab is ten-toes on the-nose, he's aggro, Moby goes aerial, Ahab's in the zone, he fires his choicest harpoon, the rope does a 360 round his neck, Ahab crushes out, Moby totals the *Pequod,* everybody eats it 'cept our faithful narrator Ishmael who boogies to safety on Queequeg's coffin . . .

(*SFX: resounding echo effect, deeper voice.*)

"AND I ONLY AM ESCAPED ALONE TO TELL THEE!"

(*Resume normal voice.*)

Roll final credits. The End.

(*SFX: ship's bell to signal end of fight. End ticking watch.*)

So what do you say, Mrs. Podgorski? You want to like hang and catch a cup of Starbucks sometime . . . ?—*Tubular!*

END OF PLAY

MY CALIFORNIA

Lisa D'Amour

My California was first produced as a part of Frontera Fest '96, an annual New Performance Festival produced by Fronter@Hyde Park Theatre, Austin, Texas (Vicky Boone, Artistic Director).

CHARACTERS

MARY SEATON: Frontierswoman in the California gold region, 1851.
DOREEN MARY BAKER: San Francisco socialite, 1927.
ASHLEY SEATON ROTH: Teen runaway in Los Angeles, 1995.

PRODUCTION NOTES

My California is composed of three interlocking monologues spoken by three generations of women from the American West. The voices of the women overlap in the way that memory overlaps with the present: they are separate, yet inherently entwined. In order for the story of these women to accurately reveal itself, the monologues should overlap in the way I have written them. However, I encourage groups who perform the piece to find their own rhythm to the interlocking voices, while striving to stay as true as possible to the structure I have created.

My California was inspired by a letter from Mary Ballou to her son Seldon, published in *Let Them Speak for Themselves: Women in the American West 1849–1900* (edited and with an introduction by Christine Fisher; Hamden: Shoe String Press, 1977).

Darkness. Lights reveal a tableau. MARY SEATON *stirs three boiling pots. She wears a durable brown nineteenth-century dress and an apron.* DOREEN MARY BAKER *sits on a stool smoking a long cigarette. She wears a bathrobe and gold dancing shoes.* ASHLEY SEATON ROTH *wears tattered jeans and a T-shirt. She holds her knees tightly to her chest. Lights remain only on* MARY SEATON. *She composes a letter as she cooks.*

MARY

From the California gold region, October 30, 1851.

Dear Elizabeth:

I am far away, my dear child, and you are too young to read this testament but I will try and tell you a bit of what I'm doing here in this gold region so you might understand why I must be so far away from you for a time. Well I will try to tell you what my work is here in this muddy place. All the kitchen that I have is four posts stuck down into the ground and covered over the top with factory cloth no floor but the ground. This is a boardinghouse kitchen. I am at work in a boardinghouse.

Now I will try to tell you what my work is like in this boardinghouse. Well sometimes I am washing and ironing sometimes I am making mince pie and apple pie and squash pies. Sometimes frying mince turnovers and donuts. I make biscuits and now and then Indian Johnnycake and then again I am making minute pudding filled with raisins and

Indian bake puddings and then again I am stuffing a ham of
pork that cost forty cents a pound. Sometimes I am making
gruel for the sick now and then cooking oysters sometimes
making coffee for the French people strong enough for any
man to walk on that had faith as Peter had.

(MARY *reaches into a pouch that hangs around her waist. She reaches in,
and sprinkles some gold powder into her soup. Lights reveal* DOREEN
MARY BAKER.)

This morning I awoke and it rained torrents. Well I got up
and thought of my kitchen. I went and looked in. The mud
and water was over my shoes so I could not go into the
kitchen to do any work. I felt badly that I was destined to be
in such a place. I stood digging my toes into the very middle
of the mud floor, water wishing 'round my ankles. I wept
for a while and then I commenced to singing and made up
a song as I went along. My song was this:

To California I did come
and thought I under the bed would run
to shelter me from the piercing storm.

(DOREEN *takes a drag from her cigarette and begins speaking.*)

DOREEN

You ready, Doctor?
Analyze this.
Doreen Mary Baker
Saturday night, September something, 1927.

Dinner at Tracy's.

Fooping at
Snakey Jake's
Baby Boo's
Moon's
Maud's

Chantilly Meringues (In Jack's roost)

The rent party at sha sha's

Then
Late night screech back at Jake's

Silver Dollar cakes at Jill's

Some shut-eye at Jo Jo's
till the sun screamed its way
into the room . . .

And that was my Saturday night

Your diagnosis, Sugarshack?

(MARY *hums her song quietly as* DOREEN *speaks.*)

Momma says you're gonna read my dreams.
Straighten me out.

Well momma knows best, don't she?
Sitting round with her fancypants
talking poetry
politics
money
like she knows the difference between caviar and fish farts.

Then she runs her mouth hot to me
'bout spending my Grandma's money bone dry.

My Grandma left me money to do as I please.
And I know how to spend it:
On Pure Experience.

MARY

I've seen things here
you would never believe, my
child

                    DOREEN

                    Pure Experience is all we got
                    that's gold, Doctor.

MARY

On the ninth of September
there was a fight took place
in the saloon down the road.
I saw two men strike each
other
through the window.

One went and got a pistol
and started towards the other
man.

DOREEN

You know what that means?

It means
I'll romp stomp and bellyrub
till my prayerbones howl
and my dogs walk themselves

I never go into the saloon
but your mother's tender
heart
could not stand it so I ran
into the store and begged and
pled
with him not to kill him
for eight to ten minutes not
to take his life
for the sake of his wife and
three little children
spare his life!

Foop
fa bop
Hoop
Swoop
shim sham shimmy shop

Fa bop
sha sha
Fa bop
sha sha sha
ZOOP!
Till your eyes
pop from their eyeholes
fall through the floor
and sprout into bushes of
envy.

And then I ran back
to my boardinghouse sleeping room
and buried my face in my bed
so as not to hear the sound
of the pistol and wept bitterly.

DOREEN

It's 1927 Doctor.
The world's a changing place.
And I ain't no dinosaur girl.

MARY

That night at the supper table
he told boarders if it had not
been
for what that Lady said to
him that man
would have been a dead man
so you see that your mother
saved one human being's life.
You see that I am trying to
relieve
all the suffering and trying to
do
all the good that I can.

(MARY *sprinkles a little gold dust into her soup. Lights rise on* ASHLEY
SEATON ROTH. *She sits in front of a small tape recorder, knees pulled tightly
into her chest. A crude crayon drawing of a window hangs on the wall.*)

DOREEN

Don't try getting me to talk to Momma.
I've talked the talk to deaf ears long enough.
You know what she says?

Dancing dries up your pussywillow, young lady
Drinking sours your mothersmilk
Smoking turns ovaries to ashes.
And then young lady just where will you be?

Well.

(*She puts her hand on her abdomen.*)

If what my mother says is true
I will birth an ashen child.

That's right.
I take her out with me to
woop and wag and holler
when I stomp and hoot and wail
she is right there with me.
My little ash girl.

What?
A Daddy?
She don't have no daddy.
This is a child of pure experience.
Shhhhhhhh.

MARY

These frightening things here I know are part of something larger, some bigger greatness that you and I will have a piece of someday, my sweet Elizabeth.

(ASHLEY *presses a button on the tape recorder.*)

ASHLEY

Testing. Testing one fuck me.

There are no windows here so I drew one. Here's the scene: A window frame filled with a gray cinder-block wall. Get it? The window leads to another wall. If you don't get it, go home, get a gun and shoot yourself in the head because you're a dumb ass motherfucker who can't unpack the simplest metaphor in the universe. They tell me I'm still in California. We'll see about that.

DOREEN

Shhhhhh.
If you're quiet, you can hear her dancing.
Listen, Doctor.

(DOREEN *hums a popular song from the 1920s.*)

ASHLEY

> You guys have my file. So what do you want to know?
> I am made of gold dust and fire.
> But that's not what you want to hear.
>
> I am a runaway. A runaway from Kansas. Where I had a sin-
> gle mother, three brothers and a two-bedroom house. All
> right, here's the scene: Wake Mom up at six to serve red
> beers to truckers for breakfast. Crank the Velvet Under-
> ground to wake my brothers. Pour Cheerios for Baby Bud,
> Froot Loops for Justin, and—no lie—Count Chocula for
> the sixteen-year-old Brick.
>
> He ate Count Chocula and made us call him Brick. No
> problem. Welcome to Kansas.

MARY

I spend my days cooking
and try not to fear, my dear.

ASHLEY

Next.
Get Brick and Justin out the
door to school and put Bud
in the playpen for a while,
And start doing what I do
every day:

I know that one day you will
be with me
and we will live fat like
queens.

Smoking cigarettes and
dreaming of California.

I stand in the middle of my
mud floor
And I sing
And think of you.

DOREEN

    Shhhhhh. Shut up doctor and eyeball this, why don'tcha.

(DOREEN *begins to dance.*)

MARY	ASHLEY
To California I did come	I left when I saved enough for a bus ticket and spending money.
And thought I	California Dreams bought easy like bubble gum.
Under the bed must run.	Diamonds brushed From Babies' hair
To shelter me	Ladies spitting silver dollars Firemen filling their pockets with ashes of gold.
From the piercing storm.	California Where my days melt open new in the land of gold dust and fire.
	Whatever.
	I had a plan: Land a job writing for TV While I tried to find somebody to put my poems in a book. My English teacher was always trying to tell me they were good to send them off to colleges and journals . . . But I wanted to do it my way. . . .

ASHLEY

I would get set up and then
send for them.
Momma, Baby Bud, Justin.
Maybe even Brick. . . .

DOREEN (*Still dancing.*)

We're gonna be all right.
I got more than just my
Grandma's money.   (MARY *hums her song quietly as*
I got her ghosts.   DOREEN *speaks.*)
You with me, sugar?
I got my Grandma Lizzie,
and her momma,
My Great Grandmother
Seaton.
Now there's a lady
who WAS pure experience.
They say she saved a man
from dying once
Put herself right between
him and the gun.
Stared the gunman down till
he was
jelly in his boots.

ASHLEY

My friend Sissy says I was crazy to leave Kansas and come to
California to waste away with the nameless. She said if she
had a family as nice as mine she wouldn't stay twenty-five
minutes in California. I told her twenty-five minutes wasn't
even enough time for her to pack up all her precious leather
biker chick clothes that she lugs around the streets with her.
She says she wouldn't even pack. She'd just go. She doesn't

understand. My family wasn't all that bad. There just wasn't any space for me.

And I was gonna send for them. Really, I was . . .

Forget it. Just fuck this shit.

(ASHLEY *turns the tape recorder off. She sets to work trying to pick the lock on the door behind her.*)

DOREEN

My Great Grandma Seaton spoke in codes.
When her husband died
She left her daughter behind to come here
to California
to find her fortune.

MARY

And now I should tell you a
little more about my cooking.

Set up shop in a boardinghouse.
When she wrote letters
she spoke ingredients
spiced apples

Sometimes I am making soup

and cranberry tarts
yellow corn

and baking chicken that costs
four dollars a head.

meat
cooked slow till it fell off the
bone

I enjoy
boiling cabbage

sweet cream butter

and turnips
oven baked oysters

and cooking codfishes
sugar
for her cranberry tarts.

and boiling potatoes

DOREEN

Sounds good, don't it Doctor?

People thought:
Smart.
She makes an honest living
While trying to capture a gold-rich man
with her cooking.

Little did they know.
She had her own gold
right under her feet.

MARY

Three times a day I set my
table
which is about thirty feet in
length.
Sometimes I am
feeding my chickens
and then I am scaring
the hogs and mules out
of the kitchen

One morning her boarders
came down to her kitchen
And found nothing but a gaping hole
smack dab in the middle
of the mud floor
that was her kitchen.
She knew what was what.
She dug up her gold
sent for Grandma Lizzie
and started buying up land.

MARY

You can see by my description
that I have given you of my
kitchen
that anything can walk in
that chooses to walk in.

MARY

Sometimes I am up all night
scaring the hogs and mules
out of the house.
I will not have hogs in my
kitchen
Rooting through my kitchen
like it belonged to them.

DOREEN

By the time she died,
she had bought up enough
property
to make her a millionaire.
Left behind a lot
the size of San Francisco.

And Sundays I go to church
I am the only Lady present
among forty gentlemen.
I feel them watch me
As I pray for you, my Eliza-
beth.
As I pray for us.

In her will,
she wrote the land
was to be passed down
through the daughters
of her family.

To Grandma Lizzie

To my momma

to me

And finally

To my Ashen child.

I am here among the French
and Dutch
and Scotch
and Jews
and Italians
          and Swedes
and Chinese
          and Indians
and all manner of tongues
and nations.

MARY

And I am treated with due
respect
by them all.
As you will be,
my daughter Elizabeth.
I will make sure of that.

DOREEN

I will live out my life on that
land.

(ASHLEY, *frustrated from the lock on the door, presses "record" again.*)

ASHLEY

California is my destiny. The land of gold dust and fire.

DOREEN

So you see, I have a plan Doctor.
I will live out my life on that land.
Me and my little ash girl.

ASHLEY

I'm named for my Grandma Ashley. She lived here in California and I only visited her once but I remember every single detail of every single moment of that visit. She told me stories of her life with her mother, who was—no lie—a flapper. And I got proof.

(ASHLEY *reaches deep into her jeans, searching for something.*)

Grandma Ashley and her momma was rich on land for a time. They lived like queens till they got swindled by some businessman who turned their land into San Jose. No lie.

My Great Grandmother died penniless, but when she lived, she was way bigger than your fucking life. Believe you me.

(ASHLEY *takes a tattered old book out of her jeans.*)

DOREEN

Don't you worry doctor. We're going to be all right. You believe me, don't you?

ASHLEY

There was this Doctor fell in love with my Great Grandma Doreen. She dumped him and he spent the rest of his days writing her story. And Grandma Ashley gave the book he wrote to me. To ME. The best story is this one. This happened when Grandma Ashley was about ten. Great Grandma Doreen always kept her house open for her girl-friends, for ladies that needed space. One night they were having a huge party, dancing and smoking and shaking the walls. And then BAM! five gangsters in red zoot suits come busting in looking for Great Grandma Doreen. The head zoot suit guy points to her and says: "You. We're here for you." And Great Grandma Doreen just stands there, unmov-ing, holding Grandma Ashley in front of her. The two of them, unmoving, staring dares into the zoot suit guys. The guy says again: "Lady, we've come for you." And then— BAM! Grandma Ashley leaps down under her momma's skirts and BAM! leaps back out holding a revolver steady in her two tiny hands. Grandma Doreen says: "Could you Gen-tlemen please leave? I really don't want my daughter to see a grown man cry." And Grandma Ashley shoots a bullet straight over those gangsters' heads. All you could smell was burning hair . . .

MARY

When people ask you what I do here, Elizabeth
Be sure to tell them about my cooking.

ASHLEY

The party was back in full swing in a matter of minutes.

DOREEN

We're gonna be all right,
Sweet Doctor.

MARY

Sometimes I am cooking
rabbits
and birds that are called quails

The days of toil are over,
Sugarshack.
My Great Grandma had to   and I cook squirrels
sneak   and oats
and steal   and . . .
and hide
to get her money
But that was a long time ago.
This is 1927.
The war is over and spirits are shifting.
This is California
The United States of America.
The only place on earth a woman
can raise an ash child on her own
and live to tell about it.
We're gonna be all right.

ASHLEY

If you guys can figure out why I set that Mercedes on fire, more
power to you. All I know is I had been walking the streets in the
hot sun for weeks, peeking in the windows of Shoney's all over
town, finding that every waitress looks like my mother, and
every kid in a high chair laughs like Baby Bud.

MARY

You might think,
my dear little Elizabeth,
that when I think about the
days ahead

MARY

I see nothing
but torrents of mud and rain.
That is true, some days.

ASHLEY

When I saw that man
in his gold Mercedes
on his car phone,
his hair blowing back
from his air conditioner

But there are other days
when the clouds break away

something tore open
inside me and
I got a glimpse,
a brilliant flash . . .

And I get a flash
like brilliant sunlight

of my Grandma and her
Grandma before that
and her Grandma
before that

. . . of the children
of the children
of my children.

all standing in one
neverending line,
Staring dares into me.
And when he parked
that gold Mercedes
in an alley like a
dumb ass fool
to run into the bank . . .

And do you know what I see
my children doing?

Well. A dash of gasoline
and a couple of matches

ASHLEY

is all you need to make
Mercedes flambé.

And the paint seemed
to float from the car
into the air like a giant
cloud of gold.

I am made of gold dust and
fire.

MARY

They're cooking.
Cooking squirrels
and setting tables
thirty feet in length
in houses with floors
made not of mud
but of gold.

They drink from gold.
Their smiles
glow gold.

The very gold I
wash out from the creeks
when I'm not paining
my arms cooking.

DOREEN

I tell you I wish my Great
Grandma was here.
She wouldn't be hiring
no doctors to convince
me
I'm crazy
for keeping this baby.

Listen, this is getting facetious,
not to mention monotonous as
two nymphos fucking.

All I have to say is this:

ASHLEY

My Grandmother Ashley
died penniless but I won't.
And I'm not going to blow up
any more cars, promise.

DOREEN

If she were here, you
know what
I'd do?

I'd wrap my buzzing fin-
gers
around her hips

and foop 'em over this
way
and flop 'em like this
fob bop

zoop shoop
piggy ziggy wop
and fla fla fly her outta
that
world of toil.

From here on out I'm going
to live my life
in a state of careful vengeance.

Into a new state of mind.

I'm gonna work, scheme and gamble
my way into money the way my Grandmas
did before me.

A state of mind that sings.

ASHLEY

I close my eyes and I become Grandma Ashley

Standing at my momma's feet
Nearly buckling under the weight of that revolver
But standing. Still standing,
Ready to fire. So watch out!

ASHLEY	MARY	DOREEN
	To California	I'll romp stomp and bellyrub
I am made		till my prayerbones howl
of gold dust	I did come	and my dogs walk themselves
and fire.		foop hoop holler zoop
And one day	and thought I	till your eyes
I'm gonna swoop		pop from their holes
down into that	Under the bed	fall to the floor
Kansas Shoney's	must run	and sprout
and save my		into bushes of envy.
momma	to shelter me	
from her toil.	from the piercing	
	storm.	
		Shoop shoop
	To California	wa wazzle bam
		shag me in the middle sha
Swoop I	I did come	boom baby
Swoop I		room baby
Swoop I	and thought I	slinky dinky
Swoop		shaaaaa
Shhhhhhhh	under the bed	
	must run	
	to shelter me	
	from the piercing	
	storm.	

ASHLEY

You guys probably don't know this but Sissy made me a tape
that I smuggled in here with my favorite song taped over
and over and over. I'm out of this little nightmare therapy

crapola to my tape. This song sends me places you wouldn't believe. This one's for you, freaks.

(ASHLEY *switches out the tape.*)

MARY

One day, you will be old, my Golden Child. And you will understand my toil.

(ASHLEY *kicks the door once.*)

DOREEN

That song's for you, Doctor sweetmouth. Diagnose that . . .

(ASHLEY *kicks the door again.*)

MARY

This from your affectionate mother, Mary Seaton.

(ASHLEY *kicks the door open. Velvet Underground. LOUD.*)

END OF PLAY

TAMAM

Betty Shamieh

Betty Shamieh first performed the title role of Tamam at the Imagine: Iraq event in November 2002, which was curated by Naomi Wallace and the Artists Network of Refuse and Resist.

CHARACTER

TAMAM: A young Arab woman.

My name is Tamam.
It means enough.

I was called that because my family wanted no more
    daughters.
I am the last of seven sisters, good luck for the family.
After me, there were two brothers
and now there is only one.

Why do we rejoice when a boy is born?

Because we from Gaza understand the power of might.
The strong make the rules,
name the cities,
and decide who live in them,
or so they think.
We know what it means to be weak,
to cement a settlement of resentment,
brick by brick,
in our own ravaged hearts and shell-shocked minds,
with every corner
littered with bullets, tear gas canisters,
they say "Made in Pennsylvania" on them.

Times like these call for soldiers.
The ones we had have fallen.

A birth of a girl is different from a boy.
A girl is a gift that's too precious,
a reminder that soft things don't last long

in our world.
Parents here fool themselves,
thinking a boy child has at least almost
a fighting chance.

I want to talk about something smaller than me
that became bigger.

I want to talk about my brother.

Don't believe the stories you've heard.
I was far more religious than he.
I never had the heart to wake him to pray.
He was hoping to study medicine in Iraq
while building Israeli settlements in Gaza
so we could eat.
I let him sleep through the call.

He was caught with a rock in his hand
and a curse on his lips.
I went to the jail to visit my brother.
Most of my people looked at the Israeli guards,
with every ounce of hatred a human heart can hold,
their faces twisted not like they tasted something bitter,
like something bitter was forced down their throats.

I was smarter than that.

I knew I must navigate through the maze of might,
and did my best to be kindly, polite.
Hoping perhaps that I would
remind them of a Rachel or Sarah or Ruth
that they knew or would have liked to know.
So when they beat my brother,
that thing that started out smaller than me and got bigger,
they would lighten their touch.

I am a pretty woman.
It's not a compliment, it's not a boast.
It's a fact.

Looks are a commodity, an asset, a possession I happen to
     possess.
It's why my grandmother said no,
when my sister's brother-in-law asked for my hand.
The family that was good enough
for my plain sister wasn't good enough for me.
I'm a pretty woman.
It's not a boast.
It's a fact.

And I smiled my best smile
when the soldiers opened the gate for me.
Weighed down with baskets of food,
I brought extra,
hoping to create the illusion
that that dirty jail was one place
where there was enough and extra for all
the guards to eat twice.
Otherwise, my brother would get none,
unless there was enough and extra.

They thanked me for the food and they raped me in front
     of him,
forcing my brother's eyes open so he had to watch.
They wanted to know something
that he preferred not to tell them.
They skewered the support for their argument into my
     flesh.

I'm told that their torture specialists who study the "Arab"
     mind
realized rape would enrage our men.
Enraging a man is the first step on the stairway
that gets him to a place
where he becomes impotent,
helpless.

They not only refer to us as the cockroaches,
they examine us, experiment upon us,

as if we were that predictable, that much the same,
that easy to eradicate.
Their studies show the Arab men value the virtue of their
  womenfolk,
Their studies show something within me was supposed to
  be inviolate.

Say what you want about Arab men and women
and how we love one another,
There is one thing that's for certain.
There are real repercussions for hurting a woman in my
  society.
There are repercussions.

When the first hand was laid upon me, we both screamed.
The evolutionary function of a scream is a cry for help,
they tied down the only one who could
so I silenced myself.
That was the only way to tell my brother
I didn't want him to tell.

I flinched when I had to,
but I kept my breathing regular.
My brother tried to look every other way,
but realized I needed him,
to look me in the eyes
and understand.

They thought making us face one another
in our misery would break us.
But we were used to misery.
It's like anything else,
you can build up a tolerance for it.

Someone once told them what they wanted to know,
so they released my brother two weeks later.

That's when he built something
more intricate than the human heart,
hugged it to his chest,

and boarded a bus that was going nowhere and every-
    where.

The day he did it, he told me over breakfast—

"Oppression is like a coin maker.
You put in human beings,
press the right buttons and
watch them
get squeezed, shrunk, flattened
till they take the slim shape of a two-faced coin.
One side is a martyr, the other a traitor.
All the possibilities of a life get reduced to those paltry
    two.
The coin is tossed in the air
it spins once for circumstance,
twice for luck,
and a third time for predilection
before it lands flat.
The face that points down
towards hell
determines not only who you are,
but how you will become that way."

What he was really saying was good-bye.

Had I known, I would have said something more than—
"It's interesting
you think oppression
makes us turn into a form of money, a currency.
How odd."

Listen, I don't agree with killing innocent people
under any circumstances, ever.
The irony is
there were Palestinians who were Israeli citizens on that
    bus too.
My brother wasn't counting on that.
No one was counting on that.

I want to feel sorrow when anyone is suffering,
No matter who they are or what their people have done to
    mine,
no one's life should be snuffed out.
I am the kind of human being
who refuses to get high on the drug of hate.
In my opinion, that's the only kind of human being there is.

In other words, no one is going to reduce me to a coin.

There are absolutes,
it's wrong to kill, period.
And since the Israelis have killed five times the number of
    my people,
as we have killed theirs,
I think they are five times as wrong.
It's hard to feel sad for them sometimes,
but I swear to you that I try my best.
But it's not easy.
They complain they can't go to a pizza parlor
while they bomb us in our homes.

I should have known what my brother was bound to do,
I could have stopped him.

I said every time he went out to face their guns with our
    rocks.
"Don't go.
Let's achieve peace by peaceful means.
Let's use nonviolence.
Don't be a pawn.
What kind of fool would face a gun with a rock?
Let others risk their lives.
They can never truly win.
They could kill every Palestinian and the wind will howl
    our names and the rocks will
rise up and throw themselves."

I'd always say, "Don't go."

But I didn't say,
"You are the most precious thing in the world to me.
The fact that you exist makes the earth spin on its axis,
it's rolling for joy because you are here.
The sun shows up to see you,
and the moon chases the sun off to be in your sky
and none of them love you like I do, brother.

Not even close.

There is no goal, no political means,
worth wrenching your life from mine.
If Palestine is Utopia, Palestine is already here.
Palestine is my brother being by my side
and screaming for joy when I have my firstborn
and living long and laughing loud with me
over hot tea and warm bread,
each morning,
which is all we can afford
but, if you are by my side, is more than enough.

If you think this is a gift for me,
the box will be empty, brother.
How can it not be?
Everything will be empty, if you're not here.

Don't hurt yourself and others in my name or for my sake.
I will not forgive you if you leave me.
I will not be comforted.
I will not be."

Instead I said, "don't go," and I didn't say it loud.

They bulldozed our house
because you blew up that bus.
In all this, I didn't realize what true fear, true dread, was
till I watched our younger brother
watching them destroy our home,
witnessing each swoop and scoop,
with more anger in his eyes than I had ever seen in yours.

I was engaged to be married
to the love of my life and the richest man in Gaza.
My father went to his house
and told his father what had happened to me.
He didn't want scandal if we went ahead and married
and it was found I was not . . . as I was before.
My love left me,
because of his father's insistence.
His mother, who never liked me anyway,
took him and married him to a girl from her town.
He moved to London with her
and I haven't seen him since.

I try to convince myself
that I wouldn't want to be married to a man
who could ever betray me.
I try to convince myself I'm better off without him.

Try is the operative word.
His cowardice was a violence
that hurts and haunts me more than what the guards did to
     me.
Because I have no one to blame but my own people,
which is as hard to do as blaming yourself.

I married my sister's brother-in-law,
who was made aware that I was not . . . as I was before.

My youngest brother went to Iraq
the week before my first child was born.
He went to study engineering.
I'm worried about him.
Our friends there say he disappears for months at a time.
He never tells me where he goes or when he'll return.

I'm worried about him.

My husband and I understand each other,
which is not exactly a good thing.

My husband never lets me live it down that my family
    once rejected him,
He calls me a whore when he is angry
and stuck-up when he is not.

He gets angry often,
especially when I tell him he is worthless and not a man
when he can't find enough food.
It's the only way to make him steal it.
Like I said before, we understand one another.

I think of my first love who deserted me.
Every day, I visualize a new way I'd tell him
what a traitor he was to leave me,
in case I happen to ever see him again.
It makes me sad that,
though he wronged me in more ways than one,
he'll only have ears to listen to the first words I say.

You only get one chance to tell people they are wrong,
You get that chance because it takes people a minute or
    two
to realize you're telling them stuff they don't want to hear.
Then, they shut you out,
though they might be still standing before you,
smiling,
they make sure the door between the ear and the heart is
    locked
and they forever take away your key.

Because they know if they keep listening,
they might not change,
but it will be a little harder
to stay the same.

If I saw him today, I would tell him:
"You should have married me.
I was still a virgin, even after what the Israeli soldiers did to
    me.

I was still a virgin,
because I don't consider the men who raped me human
    and,
if you had any inkling of what a true man was
or how to be one,
neither would you."

My name is Tamam.
It means enough.

WHEN I WAS A
LITTLE GIRL AND MY
MOTHER DIDN'T WANT ME

Joyce Carol Oates

When I Was a Little Girl and My Mother Didn't Want Me was first performed at Ensemble Studio Theatre in New York City in 1997.

Lights up. An elderly WOMAN *speaks. Her voice alternates between urgency and bemusement; emotion and reflection.*

My father was killed and I never knew why.
Then, I was given away. By my mother.
I was so little . . . six months.
There were too many of us, nine of us,
    my mother gave me away.
When I was old enough to know . . . I cried a lot.

My father was killed and I never knew why.
No one would tell me.
Now there's no one I can ask.
"Why? Why?"
It happened in a fight, in a tavern, he was only
    forty-four years old.
My father I never knew. Forty-four! Now, he could be
    my son.

I wasn't always an . . . old woman. Eighty-one.
I was a girl for so long.
I was a little girl for so long.
I was six months old when my father died.
And there were too many of us to feed, and my mother . . .
    gave me away.

There were nine children. I was the baby.
I was born late, I was the baby.

My mother gave me to her sister Lena who didn't have
    children. This was in 1918.
This was in the Black Rock section of Buffalo,
    the waterfront on the Niagara River.
Germans, Poles, Hungarians . . . immigrants.
We were Hungarians. We were called "Hunkies."
I don't know why people hated us . . .

(WOMAN *pauses; decides not to explore this.*)

Uncle John and Aunt Lena were my "parents."
We moved to a farm far away in the country.
And my real mother and my brothers and sisters
    moved to a farm a few miles away.

Uncle John and Aunt Lena were good to me.
I don't know if I loved them . . . I think I loved them.
I think . . . I think they loved me.
They wanted children but couldn't have them so it was
    right, I think, that my mother gave me to them . . .
It was a, a good thing, it was a . . . (*Pause.*)
necessary thing.
I would learn one day that it happened often.
In immigrant families in those days.
In poor immigrant families.

My father was killed and I never knew why.
They said he was a bad drinker, he got drunk
    and was always in fights.
The Hungarians were the worst, they
    said—the drinking, and the fighting.
They said he was so handsome, my father.
My mother Elizabeth was so pretty.
Curly hair like mine.
They said he had a temper "like the devil."
In the tavern there was a fight, and he died.
A man took up a poker and beat my father to death.
I never knew why, I never knew who it had been.
Yet this was how my life was decided.

There is the moment of conception—you don't know.
There is the moment of birth—you don't know.
There is the moment your life is decided—you don't know.
Yet you say, "This is my life."
You say, "This is me."

(WOMAN *regards herself in wonder like a stroke victim regaining some of her awareness.*)

When I was a little girl and my mother didn't want me
I hid away to cry.
I felt so bad and I felt so ashamed.
When I was old enough I would walk to the other farm.
There was a bridge over the Tonawanda Creek a few
    miles away.
They didn't really want to see me I guess.
My name was Carolina, but they didn't call me that.
I don't remember if there was a name they called me.
They weren't very nice to me I guess.
They didn't want me, I guess I was a reminder of . . .
    something.

Elizabeth, my mother, never learned English.
She spoke Hungarian all her life.
She never learned to read. She never learned to drive
    a car.
My Aunt Lena never learned to drive, so the sisters didn't
    see much of each other.
They lived only a few miles apart, and were the only
    sisters of their family in America, but they didn't
    see much of each other.
That was how women were in the old days.

I loved my mother.
She was a short, plump woman.
Curly brown hair like mine.
People would say, "You look just like your momma!"
Then they would be surprised, I'd start to cry.
My mother scolded me in Hungarian—

"Go away, go home where you belong. You have a home.
Your home is not here."

I loved my big brothers and sisters.
There was Leslie, he was the oldest.
He took over when my father died.
There was Mary, I didn't get to know real well.
They were born in Budapest.
There was Steve, who'd been kicked and trampled
    by a horse. His brain was injured, he would never
    leave home.
There was Elsie who was my "big sister."
There was Frank who was my "big brother."
There was Johnny . . . and Edith . . .
There was George, I wasn't too close with George.
There was Joseph, I wasn't too close with.

(*Pause.*)

They are all dead now.
I loved them, but . . .
I am the only one remaining.
Sometimes I think: The soul is just a burning match!
It burns awhile and then . . .
And then that's all.

It's a long time ago now, but I remember hiding
    away to cry.
When I was a little girl and my mother didn't want me.

YAHRZEIT

Nina Shengold

Yahrzeit was first performed at Actors & Writers, Olivebridge, New York, on November 16, 1997, with the author directing. The role of Sophie was played by Sarah Chodoff.

The Lower East Side, 1940s. SOPHIE ROBBIN, *eight, kneels on the floor next to her bed, lighting a memorial candle. There is no other light source.*

Note: SOPHIE *can be played by an adult who speaks simply, without acting "young."*

SOPHIE

My father come over this boat, he was my age. Some kid with a hat on. He tole me this while he was dyin, tube shot up his arm like a soda straw, pink Presbyterian food they got drippin inside his vein. Sophie, he tole me, that name that America give us, that name ain't your name. You come closer—his breathin like traffic—I want you should know what this is that you are. An he coughs deep an rusty, then says to me, Blood, says my father. Last words.

I was four. That was half my whole life ago. Ma went an married this Cathlic guy Tommy. Three years she'd been cryin, nights cryin, days cryin, wrapped herself up in black like the mirrors. Its good to be loved, Sophie—that's how she tole me she's gonna get married that redhead guy sells us our groceries, we'll never need fruit.

Tommy had him a wife before, died. He got kids. I got sisters now. Annie an Erin. They pray by the bedside nights, call me a Jew like it's cooties, count beads. In the nighttime they whisper at me that I'm damn, can't get into their

Heaven, I'll fry in the flame pits of Hell cause I can't take Communion. I says to em, listen, you think you fit God in some biscuit an eat Him youre sick. Annie tells on me. Tommy comes gets me an washes my mouth out with soapsuds. My Ma screamin Dont Tommy Dont. I heave on the floor. He says For My Own Good.

Daddy never.

My Ma she got mad when I went with em, Annie an Erin, to Church. I lit candles, I tole her, you use to light candles. Not those, she said, those arent the same. How come? What's it mean anyway, Jewish? So how come you marry him? Ma she just looks at me lost. An I think of my father, his life drippin out through those tubes like an icicle melting, his rainbarrel chest got a hole in it somewheres. He says to me, Sophie, mein Sophele, Blood. An he shows me the blue of his wrists. Kaddish.

(*She lowers her wrist on the candle flame, snuffing it out.*)

THE END

EXCERPTS

FROM *DEF POETRY JAM*

"in the cocina"

Mayda Del Valle

Def Poetry Jam was conceived by Stan Lathan and Russell Simmons; was directed by Stan Lathan; and was written and performed by Black Ice, Staceyann Chin, Steve Colman, Mayda Del Valle, Georgia Me, Suheir Hammad, Lemon, Poetri, Beau Sia, and DJ Tendaji. *Def Poetry Jam* played at the Longacre Theatre on Broadway, where it won the 2003 Tony Award for Best Theatrical Event.

MAYDA

mami's making mambo
mami's making mambo

in the domain of the del Valle kitchen
my mother is the dictator
I refer to it as
"Carmen's culinary queendom"
She—is a cuisine conquistadora
wielding a freshly sharpened knife
like a sword above her head
here Goya doesn't stand a chance
no prepackaged shit
she is the menu mercenary
the soldier of soul food
back the fuck up!
coz mami's making mambo
she hangs the hats of iron chefs
off the windowsill like
roast duck trophies
and laughs at the sight of any edible
food item.

Mua-ha-ha-ha-ha-ha-ha-ha

no meat in the freezer
poof
Spam and corned beef in a can are

transformed into virtual filet mignon
rice cooks itself instantly at her command
and beans jump into bubbling pots shrieking
Carmen please . . . Carmen please
cook me master please
honor me with your spice
Emeril and Julia Child's mere hamburger
flippers in her presence
It was there in my mother's kitchen that
I learned more
than how to cook
It is where
I learned the essence of rhythm and power
I learned how to dance
In the midst of clanging clave pots
and wooden mortars and pestles
she would say to me
the way to a man's heart is through his stomach
and your hips
so you better learn how to cook mija
she gave me the secret recipe for ritmo

Two and a half cups of caderas, a pound of gyrating pelvis,
a pinch of pursed lips
a tablespoon of shaking shoulders
and a generous helping of soooooouuuuuuul
combine and mix
now I'm dancing the way my mother cooks.

slow, sultry, spicy, sabrosa natural instinctively
drippin' sweet sweat like fresh leche do coco
spinnin' as fast as piraguas melt in summertime
southside heat

dancing with as much kick as cuchifrito and bacardi
standing strong like a morning time bustelo
steamy as pasteles at Christmas

blendin' my hip hop and mambo like a piña colada
my mouth watering for music with sabor en caderas
soothes down my hips
dulce as Celia's Azzzucaaaar!
Con dulcura
I'm cooking with sabor
I'm bailando con sabor
coz
mami's making mambo
mami's making mambo
Mamucha, come eat, the food's ready.

FROM *JOSEPHINE UNDONE*

Daniel Gallant

Josephine Undone was first performed at the Cornelia Street Café in New York City on May 11, 2000. The play was produced and directed by the author. The case was as follows:

NARRATOR Daniel Gallant
PIANIST Michael Gallant

CHARACTERS

NARRATOR: A single narrator plays numerous roles. The narrator is twenty-five to twenty-seven years old, personable, fairly athletic, and a strong storyteller. He changes costume slightly at the beginning of each scene.

A pianist and string bass player sit onstage throughout, but never speak.

SET AND COSTUMES

The stage is sparsely set, with a warm-colored carpet; a coatrack, stage left, holding the narrator's costume pieces; a table and chair; a piano stage right; chairs and music stands stage right and down right for the pianist and bassist. The narrator can use either a body mic or a mic stand. A glass and pitcher of water sit on the table.

The narrator's costume pieces are: a gray sports jacket; a brown leather jacket; a blue bathrobe; and a long black wool coat. A sealed letter-size paper envelope sits in a pocket of each costume piece. Throughout, the narrator wears a black ribbed T-shirt, jeans and belt, and brown boots.

The season and precise location of the action are indeterminate. The most essential elements of the show are nonvisual; the narrator's tale should exert almost the same impact on those who listen with closed eyes as on those who watch.

PERFORMANCE

Josephine Undone is performed without an intermission. Including music cues, the total running time of the show is approximately eighty minutes. The following monologue begins the play. When performed, the very last line of the excerpt may be kept or omitted, as the director wishes.

MUSIC INTRO—SINUOUS TANGO

NARRATOR *walks out from the wings as music ends.*

NARRATOR

My best friend's fallen very deep in love. Because of her attention and companionship, his health is vastly better than it used to be. But he had once convinced himself that sex was poison for the soul. So firm was his opinion on the point that, in a metropolis stuffed full of scandalously beautiful people, my friend bought himself reflective sunglasses—mirror glasses—and he took them apart and he turned the mirrors inside out, so all that he could see when he wore the glasses was a detailed reflection of his own eyeballs, distorted hugely, with all the veins sticking out and the tear ducts big like donuts. He would wear these glasses every day in public, that was to be his plan, because my friend felt an attractive female was a hazardous material. He had been burned, and he was sure that if he looked into a woman's eyes again, he would combust spontaneously. These are the circles in which I travel.

So when out in public, my friend would wear his backward glasses and he'd have his little wiener dog, named Jonas, lead him around. Lead him to the subway. Lead him to have his hair cut. Just to err a little on the safe side, my good friend decided that whenever he and Jonas were about to take a walk, my friend would not only don his goggles of outrageous penitence, he would also attach a huge metal arrow to the harness on the wiener dog, an arrow which my friend assured me he had magnetically ionized to track the earth's gravitational fields. The arrow was always supposed to point pretty much *north,* but it was a tiny little dog, and the arrow was a sizable, massive arrow, so no matter which way the arrow pointed the dog was going to be off-balance. My friend figured that the tilting of the arrow, and therefore the tilting of the harness, and therefore the angle of Jonas the dog relative to the ground would help my friend keep tabs on which way he was actually going.

Now, this dog *loved,* lived and quite nearly died for honey-roasted *cashews.* And on the morning my friend first tried his experiment, a rogue cashew vendor had just set up shop a block away, in what was previously virgin, unexploited nut-selling territory. My friend woke early, saddled up his wiener dog, and walked outside. At first, poor Jonas patiently endured the weight of the huge arrow-magnet on his back. He struggled gamely and obediently. But the smell of fresh honey-roasted cashews baking in the morning sun wafted into his receptive nasal cavity and brought about a whole, fresh new itinerary in that dog's head, and inside a head that small there's only room for one itinerary at a time. The dog dashed off downhill, gravity helping it to pull my friend, whose writstwatch had unexpectedly been ionized to his end of the magnetic harness, down the hill after the dog. The dog made an executive decision to cross the street toward the source of the cashew smell, a decision he would soon regret, because the heavy metal arrow on the dog's back did not have olfactory endowments, and it continued traveling downhill. The net effect was that this huge arrow's momentum flipped the dog over in the air, twisting the loose part of the harness around Jonas the wiener dog like a kite string being wound up on its spool, and my ionized friend was pulled forward like a kite. His feet left the ground, his wallet left his pocket, and his watchband broke.

The only witness on the street at that hour, oddly, was the cashew vendor, who might well have been more sympathetic to my friend's plight had my friend's wallet not jumped out of my friend's pocket and across the street. The vendor valued his cashews far less than did my friend's dog—in fact, the vendor left his stand, dashed several yards and snagged the wallet just before it hit the ground. He leafed right through it, finding many dollar bills and several very useful cards, he made a couple speedy calculations in his head, as speedy as a street vendor and almost none among the rest of us can make, and several minutes later there were *no* witnesses on the street any longer.

Despite the arrow-shaped cross he had to bear, Jonas the dog was now at last—in spirit and in theory—a free agent. Driven forth by lustful hunger and a sudden ache for liberty, he slowly dragged himself across the street towards the cashews with his two front legs working overtime, as his back legs were mummified by the leash. My self-blinded friend fell roughly to the ground, and, numb for the moment in both legs, began to pull himself hand over hand downhill toward where his dog had gone. He soon realized that Jonas was a canine turncoat, and he screamed for Jonas to return. The dog lay straight across the street, pinned down by leash and arrow, staring up toward honey-roasted heaven with huge, dark, watery wiener eyes.

Unbeknownst to my friend, he lay screaming directly in front of a tiny theater where a performance artist was preparing for the premiere of her new show. Susan was afraid that her drastically unusual and nonlinear production would be ripped apart by critics and ignored by audiences. Over the synthesized soundtrack playing on her Technicolored stage, Susan heard screams of "JONAS! JONAS, YOU WIENER!" and, perturbed at the disturbance, marched to the theater's front door, swung it open—and saw her before her a man sprawled horizontally, a long but skinny dog perpendicular to him with its leash spread across the street and a cashew cart behind the dog. These three items were laid out at such angles, based on Susan's line of vision, that they formed the *capital letter I,* or the *Roman numeral "one."* Susan drank in the sight and said very quietly to herself:

"I am the one!"

She fell on her knees, thanked the spirits of the earth for such a sign of their confidence in her talents and her groundbreaking show, rolled my friend over to thank him too, and noticed that while *he* could not see *her* through the inside of his glasses, *she* could stare into *his* wide eyes perfectly from the outside—she could judge without being judged. The metal arrow on the dog's back pointed toward my friend, and this let Susan know that he was the one for her.

She postponed the opening of her show; she bought the cashew cart so my friend's dog would have a fragrant place to sleep, she took my friend home and she screwed him silly. The huge magnetic arrow is now hanging on their wall, collecting paper clips.

His plan . . . had failed.

But I'm not here to talk about *that* friend. He only has *one* story.

FROM *SNAPSHOT*

"HISTORY LESSON"

David Lindsay-Abaire

Snapshot contains seventeen monologues and scenes, all inspired by the same photograph. It was commissioned by Actors Theatre of Louisville and premiered at the Humana Festival of New American Plays in March 2002. It was directed by Russell Vandenbroucke; the scenic design was by Paul Owen; the costume design was by John White; the lighting design was by Tony Penna; the sound design was by Colbert Davis; the properties design was by Doc Manning; the stage manager was Sarah Hodges; the dramaturgs were Amy Wegener and Tanya Palmer. The cast of "History Lesson" was as follows:

MAGGIE   Stacy Mayer

Lights up on MAGGIE, *a park ranger. She's in the middle of giving a speech to a bunch of tourists (the audience).*

MAGGIE

And what's interesting about George Washington, and most people don't know this about him, he wasn't just the father of our country, he was also the father of the first septuplets born in the United States. Martha gave birth to seven children on October 5th, 1762. Five of the children were very badly behaved, so they were sold into white-slavery, while the two remaining, Maxwell and Hortense, drowned tragically in the Potomac while trying to retrieve their father's wooden teeth, which had fallen out of his mouth while he was beating a seagull with a canoe paddle.

(*Beat.*)

For those of you just joining the group, my name is Maggie, and today's my last day here at the Mount Rushmore National Memorial. There have been some cutbacks at the National Park Service, so I've been let go, which in my opinion is a huge loss to tourists like yourselves who are hungry for history, because I happen to be what we in the industry call "A font of knowledge."

(*Back to the speech.*)

Now if you look to the right, you'll notice the next head belongs to Thomas Jefferson, who, and this may come as a surprise to you, was actually born without skin from the neck down. In fact, he spent most of his childhood in and out of hospitals because of his susceptibility to disease, what with the exposed muscle and sinew and whatnot. But in 1772, his good friend Benjamin Franklin fashioned a crude epidermis out of sheep bladders and carpenter's glue, held together by pewter hooks that Paul Revere forged in his silver shop. Paul Revere, you may have heard, was a Smithy, which is one of my favorite words. He was also a eunuch, which was not very common in the 1700s, though there were a few. I believe Sam Adams was also a eunuch, and . . . Nathan Hale, who I've been told had a wonderful singing voice. So, that's probably something you haven't heard on any other tour today. It's interesting, isn't it?

(*Suddenly.*)

Oh, by the way, if any of you happen to have a question, feel free to raise your hand and stick it up your ass. That's just the kind of mood I'm in. I see I'm losing some of you. Well that's all right. It's more intimate this way, isn't it? And I happen to be very comfortable with intimacy, unlike a certain Victor Collins, my direct supervisor here at the National Park Service, and my former lover. He's the man responsible for my layoff, as well as my monthly herpes outbreak.

(*Back to the speech.*)

Moving on, we have the esteemed Theodore "Teddy" Roosevelt, our twenty-sixth president, and a well-documented pederast. He spent much of his presidency traipsing through Cuba and Panama in search of little boys to induct into his Rough Rider Club, whether they liked it or not. Bully, indeed. He appeared briefly in a burlesque-house comedy titled *Tally-Ho, Kathleen!* He enjoyed playing chess, and long walks on the beach.

(*Off-topic.*)

Coincidentally, so does my Ex-Lover slash Boss, Victor Collins. Any complaints about today's tour can be directed to him. His office is located just past the gift shop, behind the glass doors. He'll be the fat fuck in the stupid hat and chinos. He's hard of hearing, so I encourage you to yell whenever speaking to him, and use as much profanity as possible. He's more responsive when berated and under pressure.

(*Back to the speech.*)

Next up, we have Abraham Lincoln, our first Jewish president, and the inventor of dirt. He was, of course, our tallest president, standing ten feet, two inches tall, he spoke fluent Mandarin and walked with a peg leg. A thrice-convicted arson, Abraham Lincoln grew up in an adobe hut and had X-ray vision. He was one of our greatest presidents and his wife was mentally unhinged. Speaking of mentally unhinged, let's pretend I'm Victor and you're me.

(*As Victor.*)

"Aw gee, Maggie, it's nothing personal. I gotta fire *someone,* and heck I was gonna break up with you anyway. You're incredibly passive-aggressive, and that's not the kind of person I want to spend my life with. You were gonna be upset either way, so this is like two birds with one stone."

(*Now herself.*)

Hey anyone have a stone? Let's go throw it at Victor's head!

(*Beat.*)

I'm just kidding. Violence is never the answer, as was so wisely stated by our thirty-ninth president, Chita Rivera.

(*They're leaving.*)

Okay, well you two obviously have places to go.

(*Calling after them.*)

Have a great afternoon, and enjoy the rest of your stay here
at Mount Rushmore, the only monument in America made
entirely out of cheese.

(*Blackout.*)

FROM *STRAY CATS*

"JAGUAR JESUS"

Warren Leight

Stray Cats was produced by All Seasons Theatre Group (John McCormack, Artistic Director) in New York City, on May 14, 1998. It was directed by Kevin Confoy; the set design was by George Xenos; the costume design was by Veronica Worts; the lighting design was by Greg MacPherson; and the stage manager was Adrienne Willis. The cast of "Jaguar Jesus" was as follows:

JAGUAR JESUS   Chris Messina

NOTE

The full-length play *Stray Cats* is a series of nine monologues originally performed by nine men.

A thin, pale young kid—maybe eighteen, alone in the city, late at night, an a cappella saxophone plays in a Coltrane or "Rahsaan" Roland Kirk style. The kid speaks with a definite musical rhythm; up tempo: he and the saxophone player are essentially in a duet for the piece, trading phrases and riffs, pushing each other to the finish.

I hadn't heard chops like that in centuries.

I mean he wasn't the Bird or Coltrane or like that, but for a street saxman he was really blowing. He stood in this arcade with his change-filled case open up front of him and ripped phrases through his horn. He was stroking the night, blazing out of control and the thing was . . .

The thing was I just stumbled upon him. Judy told me to meet her in the square at ten but she was late so I heard this jazz rising and I had to check it out.

It was raining. Maybe drizzling but the word sounds too lame 'cause it was summer. I mean, in the summer it doesn't drizzle, maybe it mists. But, but here's the thing: It's a chilly summer night and you could see your breath.

Since it was chilly you could actually see the breath coming out of the gold bell of his horn.

I wished I had a camera cause here was this street player just smoking on this sax and there was real smoke coming out of it.

I crossed over and leaned on a no-parking sign and started to listen. Just as I lean on the sign he starts playing like Charlie Parker. I didn't see the connection at first, but . . . look, it's a no-*park*ing sign I lean on that starts him playing *Parker's* stuff. He was plugged into us; like a mother who can't see her kids but knows they're there.

He couldn't have *seen* me leaning either because he was concentrating completely. There was a good crowd watching and occasionally tossing lucre, ya dig that word, into his case. But he was gone: a five-alarm fire. His eyes were closed and his right foot tapped and I swear his hands and mouth never left the horn. He could do that circular breathing trick so he never had to stop playing. Clark Terry does that, where you breathe in through your nose while exhaling through the horn. Course it's harder on trumpet, what isn't?, but it's still not easy on sax.

So I lean on the sign and light up a Marlboro. I don't smoke much but when you're outside in a rainy city on a cool summer night watching a guy play his guts out for some spare "c" it seems like a natural thing to do. I only had one match so I realized I'd have to chain-smoke'm until Judy came by which shouldn't have been long since it was way after ten.

But anyway, he wouldn't have known I leaned on the sign because to him the world was a blur. He was standing in this dark arcade, burning brass oblivious. It was like when you're singing to yourself in an elevator and all of a sudden the elevator is crowded and you're still do-dahing away.

But even though he's gone he subconsciously is there. This mother and her little kids walk by and she gives the kids two coins to toss in. "Ping, ping" they go and right away this guy, who'd been blowing "dah do doop be dodo dah" blows "dah do doop be *bing bing*" 'cause he melts the coins into his riff. You know you're dreaming and the alarm goes off and all of a sudden it's not an alarm but church bells in the Easter parade? Well, same thing. He hears the coins and reforms the sound. The mother smiles 'cause she caught it.

My ma was like that too. Whenever we'd pass a street musician she'd dig into her purse for some change and hand it down to me and I'd put it in the case. We didn't have a lot but she always spared something. Had me put it in because she never took credit for what she did.

She helped people but when she needed help they weren't there.

I don't think she was crazy, at least not at first. But no one responded when she was down and when she was up. When she was up she had no outlet.

This sax guy, he has an outlet. He's got a million things to say and a million ways to say them. That horn would be nothing without him. It'd be empty.

Have you ever been in an old, pee-reeking elevator, the kind where you cross yourself before getting in? You wouldn't think it could hold a lot of people, let alone lift them up, but it doesn't. I mean does, it does. The sax is the same. It's holding this guy's energy and lifting up his sound.

My ma didn't play sax. When she was up and energized she'd try and organize a rent strike or a union fight or like that but she didn't have any education so people ignored her and thought she was wacko.

This upstairs neighbor of ours was really gone. But he had his outlet. He'd get manic and stay awake for weeks—no food, no sleep—just pure wig. He'd go into one of these fast phases and focus incredible amounts of energy.

One time he set up a publishing house for Lithuanian dissidents. Then they put him away. Six months later he was in Korea: I swear to God he set up the entire educational system of Korea. South Korea. He was a genius. When his wife divorced him we all got his modern art posters to hold.

There's a link between what those guys were painting and what the jazzmen were blowing; different melody but the same chords. I could walk through a museum and just know that Paul Klee used the same bass lines as Thelonius. Just couldn't miss it.

This sax guy was Picasso. He could do anything. One minute he'd be playing a standard ballad and the next he'd blow some hyper hip, cubist jazz. Then he'd turn into a Pollock, spraying notes everywhere.

He never stopped concentrating. If it weren't for the bottleneck at the reed you would have seen his entrails just flooding down and through his horn and into his case. There was no way he could keep playing that hard; a sax is like kryptonite after a while.

Gold kryptonite 'cause that's the kind that takes your powers away permanently.

But he was immune. Like the Bird or Trane. You see how they name guys who play sax? They name them after magic: a bird soaring on sky, a train churning on rail.

I had to find a name for this fireman because he was blowing the truth.

Finally I realized this cat was a Jaguar pouncing on reality. Fast and strong but soft and sleek.

A cop blows his whistle and someone hits his horn. All of a sudden he's playing:

Tweet

Honk

Tweet Honk

Tweet Honk yadoo Tweet Tweeeet Honk yade dedoo dyudah

The city filtered through his reed.

Then I got scared because when I was thinking about our upstairs neighbor, the manic depressive, Jag started playing fast then slow; fast then slow.

My mother wasn't manic-depressive like that guy though, I don't think. She had it tough. She was born Catholic and when she got divorced her whole family quit on her like she never existed. She used to have these flip-outs and stuff.

Once we were in a taxi coming home from visiting dad and she opened the cab door on the highway. Fifty miles an hour and she tries to roll out. But she wasn't crazy, she was too sensitive.

It's always like that. See: Creative or sensitive people can't hack it. Parker ran his body into the ground. Van Gogh mailed his ear. His own ear, my God! Tolstoy was kablooey. She didn't kill herself, I mean officially. But after the breakdown she stayed drunk all the time so people wouldn't think she was crazy.

This guy was probably crazy but he had his Korean elevator. My ma couldn't play sax.

I open another Marlboro box top 'cause Judy still hadn't shown and the guy started playing bebop. He knew I had the 'boro box top but see he takes and fakes it into 'borobob, bobop, bebop—and that's when it hits me how he's not playing his guts out but that it's a constant cycle.

If he'd just kept blowing into the horn pretty soon he'd a been sucked through it. But it was like his circular breathing thing, we were feeding off him and him off of us. A geodesic saxman.

The arcade he was in belonged to a clothing store for fat women but somehow there was a resonancy in its tiles that was yeast to his sound. It was like that. With the sax and the rain and the arcade it was like the half-lame elevator lifting people to the sky.

He had to be feeding off of us because he wasn't suffering. I mean, it was like Jesus on the cross, I don't think he suffered. I'm not sure 'cause my ma never talked religion after the divorce, but from the paintings it looks like Jesus just coped with it. He knew the truth so it was cool.

He was playing his guts out but he just kept tapping his foot. He knew there was a reason.

That's when it hit me the Jag was Jesus. I mean Jesus didn't tap his foot on the cross, it was nailed anyway, but he wasn't suffering.

And the Jaguar, he was nailed to his sax but it was okay.

His hands were nailed to it. They flew up and pounced down but they couldn't leave it. And his mouth was stuck to it too. Instead of his feet it was his mouth; same beat though. Same beat.

The reed clinched it. Christ had come back but this time his cross to bear was a saxophone. Most people wouldn't catch it 'cause that's the way people are, but it was obvious.

I stopped wishing Judas would come 'cause I knew she wouldn't. You can't rely on people, Ma. But it was okay 'cause dig it: I was chain-smoking Bebops in a cool summer rain and the Jaguar Jesus was blowing the truth.

FROM *TWILIGHT: LOS ANGELES, 1992*

"TO LOOK LIKE GIRLS FROM LITTLE"

Anna Deavere Smith

Ms. Smith dedicates this play to the memories of her father, Mr. Deaver Y. Smith Jr., and her stage manager, Mr. Richard Hollabaugh.

Twilight: Los Angeles, 1992 was originally produced by Berkeley Repertory Theatre (Sharon Ott, Artistic Director; Susan Medak, Managing Director) in Berkeley, California, on January 31, 1996. It was directed by Sharon Ott; the set design was by Christopher Barreca; the lighting design was by Pat Collins; the costume design was by Candice Donnelly; the sound design was by Stephen LeGrand; the original music was by Joshua Redman; and the stage manager was Leila Knox. It was performed by Anna Deavere Smith.

Twilight: Los Angeles, 1992 is a collection of sixty monologues, performed verbatim from the words of people who experienced the Los Angeles Riots following the Rodney King verdict. The excerpted monologue was originally performed toward the end of Act One.

ELVIRA EVERS

General Worker and Cashier, Canteen Corporation

*With a baby bottle in her hand. At her kitchen table. A black woman
from Panama in her forties. Children can be heard offstage. A Panaman-
ian accent. She had a gold front tooth.*

> So,
> it was like a carnival out there
> and I say
> to my friend Frances,
> "Frances, you see this?"
> and she said, "Girl, you should see
> that
> is getting worse."
> And I say, "Girl, let me take my butt
> up there before something happen."
> and um
> when somebody throw a bottle
> and I just,
> then I felt,
> like moist
> and it was like a tingling sensation right?
> And I dida like this (*Touching her stomach.*)
> and it was like itchin',
> and I say, "Frances, I'm *bleedin'*."
> And she walk with me to her house

And she say, "Lift up your gown, let me see."
She say, "Elvira, iss a bullet!"
I say, "What?"
I say, "I didn't heard nothin'."
She say, "Yes, but iss a bullet."
She say, "Lay down there. Let me call St. Francis and tell
    them that
you been shot
and to send a ambulance."
and she say,
"Why you,
you don't mess with none of those people
Why they have to shoot you?"
So Frances say the ambulance be here in fifteen minutes
I say, "Frances,
I cannot wait that."
I say,
"I'm goin'!"
So I told my oldest son I say,
"Amant take care your brothers
I be right back."
Well by this time he was standing there he was crying.
All of them was crying.
What I did for them not to see the blood,
I took the gown and I cover it,
and I didn't cry
that way they didn't get nervous.
And I get in the car
I was goin' drive
Frances say, "What you doin'?"
I said, "I'm drivin'."
She say, "No, you're not!"
And we take all the back street,
and she was so supportive
because she say, "You alright?
You feel cold?

You feel dizzy?
The baby move?"
she say, "You nervous?"
I say, "No, I'm not nervous, I'm just worried about the
    baby."
I say, "I don't want to lose this baby."
She say, "Elvira everything will be alright." She say, "Just
    pray."
So there was a lot of cars we had to be blowing the horn
So finally we get to St. Francis (*Hospital*.)
and Frances told the front desk office she say,
"She been shot!"
and they say, "What she doin' walkin'?"
and I say, "I feel alright."
Everybody stop doin' what they was doin'
and they took me to the room
and put the monitor to see if the baby was fine
and they find the baby heart beat
and as long as I heard the baby heart beat I calmed down.
Long as I knew whoever it is boy or girl, it's alright,
and
matter of fact my doctor, Dr. Thomas, he was there
at
the emergency room
what a coincidence, right?
I was just lookin' for that familiar face
and soon as I saw him
I say, "Well I'm alright now."
Right?
So he bring me this other doctor and then told me:
"Elvira, we don't know how deep is the bullet
we don't know where it went. We gonna operate on
you.
But since that we gonna operate we gonna take the baby
    out
and you don't have to

go through all of that."
They say, "Do you understand
what we're saying?"
I say, "Yeah!"
and they say, "Okay sign here."
And I remember them preparing me
and I don't remember anything else
Nella! (*Calling to her child.*)
No.
(*Turns to the side and admonishes the child, a girl about five
    years old.*)
She likes company.
And in the background
I remember Dr. Thomas say, "You have a six-pound-
    twelve-ounces
little girl,"
he told me how much she weigh and her length
and he
say, "Um
she born
she had the bullet in her elbow,
but when we remove,
when we clean her up,
we find out that the bullet was still between two joints
so we did operate on her and your daughter is fine
and you are fine."
(*Sound of a little child saying "Mommy."*)
Nella!
She *wants to show the baby.*
(*Listening to a question.*)
Jessica. (*Is her name.*)
Bring the baby, Nella (*The baby is brought [imaginary]. She
    laughs.*)
Yes—(*Listening to a question.*)
yes
We don't like to keep the girls without earrings, we like
    the little girls

to look like girls from little.
I pierce hers
when I get out on Monday
by Wednesday I did it.
So by Monday she was five days
she was seven days,
and I
pierced her ears.
And the red band is just like for evil eyes
we really believe in Panama . . .
In English I can't explain too well.
And her doctor he told,
he explain to me,
that the bullet
destroyed the placenta
and
went through me
and she caught in her arm.
(*Here you can hear the baby making noise, and a bell rings.*)
If she didn't caught it in her arm,
Me, and her, would be dead.
See,
So it's like
open your eyes!
Watch what is goin' on!

CONTRIBUTORS

LESLIE AYVAZIAN'S play *Nine Armenians* has been produced at many theaters including Manhattan Theatre Club and the Mark Taper Forum. It won the John Gassner Outer Critics Award, Susan Smith Blackburn Prize (second place), and Roger L. Stevens Award. One-act plays include: *Plan Day, Deaf Day, Twenty-Four Years,* and *Hi There, Mr. Machine,* all produced at EST. Her short film *Every Three Minutes,* starring Olympia Dukakis, ran on Showtime, winning a Telly Award.

GLEN BERGER'S *Great Men of Science, Nos. 21 & 22* won both the *L.A. Weekly* Award and the Ovation Award for Best Play. *The Wooden Breeks* was nominated for Best Play by the *L.A. Weekly. Underneath the Lintel* played over four hundred performances off-Broadway and won the Ovation Award for Best Play. Mr. Berger is a member of New Dramatists and lives in Manhattan, with his wife and son.

DAVID CALE'S shows include the solos *Lillian, Deep in a Dream of You, Smooch Music, The Redthroats,* and the duet show *Betwixt.* He is the author, lyricist, and cocomposer of the musical *Floyd and Clea Under the Western Sky.* He is the recipient of an OBIE and two Bessie Awards, and is a regular contributor to NPR's *The Next Big Thing.*

LISA D'AMOUR writes plays and creates collaborative, often site-specific theater. Recent projects include *Nita and Zita,* created with Katie Pearl and Kathy Randels (2003 OBIE Award); *16 Spells to Charm the Beast,* produced by Salvage Vanguard Theater (Austin); and *LIMO,* a performance installation commissioned by the Whitney Museum of Art. She is a core member of the Playwrights' Center and a member of New Dramatists.

MAYDA DEL VALLE is one of ten young poets who wrote and performed her work in Russell Simmons' *Def Poetry Jam* on Broadway. As a little girl, she saw Rita Moreno perform onstage at the Longacre Theatre. Years later, she realized her dream of performing on the same stage. A Puerto Rican woman originally from Chicago, she intends to help fill the void of positive role models for young people of color.

DANIEL GALLANT is a writer, director, producer, and actor. His plays have been staged at the 92nd Street Y, New Dramatists, Galapagos Artspace, the Actors Studio, and other venues. Daniel has produced numerous events at the 92nd Street Y and elsewhere. He holds an MA in Arts Administration from Columbia University and a BA from Swarthmore College.

JEFFREY HATCHER's original plays include *Three Viewings, Scotland Road,* and the critically acclaimed *Work Song,* written in collaboration with Eric Simonson. He has also adapted Mitch Albom's *Tuesdays with Morrie* into a play; *Swing Time* into a Broadway musical *(Never Gonna Dance)*; and his own play, *Compleat Female Stage Beauty,* into a feature film.

DANNY HOCH's *Some People* won an OBIE Award at PS 122 and the Joseph Papp Public Theater. It was filmed for HBO and nominated for a Cable Ace Award. Mr. Hoch is the recipient of a Solo Theatre Fellowship from the NEA and a Sundance Writers Fellowship. *Jails, Hospitals & Hip-Hop* premiered at Berkeley Rep, then opened in New York City at PS 122, where it was nominated for a Drama Desk Award.

DAVID IVES is probably best known for his evenings of one-act comedies: *All in the Timing* (available from Vintage Books) and *Time Flies* (available from Grove). His full-length comic fantasia *Polish Joke* was produced by Manhattan Theatre Club. Mr. Ives' young-adult novel *Monsieur Eek* is published by HarperCollins.

LISA KRON'S *2.5 Minute Ride* received an OBIE Award, L.A. Dramalogue Award, GLAAD Media Award, and Drama Desk and Outer Critics Circle nominations. Other plays include *101 Humiliating Stories* (Drama Desk nomination) and *Well*. With the Five Lesbian Brothers, Ms. Kron has cowritten and appeared in four plays: *The Secretaries, Brave Smiles . . . another lesbian tragedy, Voyage to Lesbos,* and *Brides of the Moon.*

NEIL LABUTE'S *In the Company of Men* received the New York Film Critics Circle Award for Best First Feature and the Filmmakers Trophy at Sundance. He has written and directed *Your Friends and Neighbors* and *The Shape of Things,* and directed *Nurse Betty* and *Possession*. Plays include *The Shape of Things* and *bash: latterday plays,* which he also directed for Showtime.

ERIC LANE'S plays include *Heart of the City, Times of War, Cater-Waiter,* and *Dancing on Checkers' Grave.* Honors include the Berrilla Kerr Playwriting Award, the La MaMa Playwright Development Award, and a Writers Guild Award. Mr. Lane wrote and produced two short films: *First Breath* and *Cater-Waiter,* which he also directed. He has received numerous Yaddo fellowships and the St. James Cavalier Centre for Creativity fellowship in Malta.

ADAM LEFEVRE'S plays include *Yucca Flats, The Crashing of Moses Flying-By, Windowwashers, Grant at Windsor,* and *Americansaint,* with productions in New York at Manhattan Theatre Club and Manhattan Punchline Theatre, and regionally at Actors Theatre of Louisville and Theatre Three in Dallas, Texas. His play *Waterbabies* won the 1999 Heideman Award. He makes his living as an actor.

WARREN LEIGHT'S *Side Man* won the 1999 Tony Award for Best Play. His other theater includes *Glimmer, Glimmer and Shine, No Foreigners Beyond This Point,* and *James and Annie.* He is currently co-executive producer on *Law & Order: Criminal Intent.* Mr. Leight is Vice President of the Writers Guild of America, East Council; and a member of the Dramatists Guild Council.

DAVID LINDSAY-ABAIRE'S *Kimberly Akimbo* received the L.A. Drama Critics Award and was hailed by *The New York Times* as "The Comedy of the Year." His plays include *Wonder of the World* and *Fuddy Meers,* which has received over a hundred productions around the country and has been translated into several languages. Mr. Lindsay-Abaire is a proud member of New Dramatists, the Dramatists Guild, the WGA, and the Tony Award Nominating Committee.

AASIF MANDVI is an actor and writer currently living in New York City. *Sakina's Restaurant,* his first play, was the recipient of two 1999 OBIE Awards. Mr. Mandvi's acting credits include roles in such films as *The Mystic Masseur, Analyze This, The Siege, Eddie, Spider-Man 2, Undermind, American Chai, ABCD,* and *Peroxide Passion.* He regularly appears on numerous television shows as well as stage productions on and off Broadway.

MARTIN MORAN appeared on/off-Broadway in such plays as *Cabaret, Titanic, Bells Are Ringing,* and *Floyd Collins,* among numerous others. He performed his own work at HERE,

Dixon Place, and many other venues. For *The Tricky Part* he won
an OBIE Award. Beacon Press will release *The Tricky Part,* developed from his memoir, in the spring of 2005. In 2001 Moran
received a NYFA Fellowship Award in Creative Nonfiction.

LESLIE NIPKOW is a member of the Women's Project Playwrights
Lab, where she is currently developing her new play, *Beauty,
1953.* Her screenplay, *Sara Charlotte,* was a 2004 Sundance and
Chesterfield finalist. *Guarding Erica* has been performed at
HERE, PSNBC, and Solo Arts, and featured on SoapNet.
Leslie is an Emmy and Writers Guild Award nominee.

JOYCE CAROL OATES' plays have been performed at the Humana
Festival, McCarter Theatre, Contemporary American Theater Festival, Circle Rep, and American Place Theatre,
among others. Her newest collection is *New Plays* (Ontario
Review Press). Honors include the 1970 National Book
Award and the 2003 Commonwealth Award for Distinguished Service in Literature. She is the Roger S. Berlind
Distinguished Professor in the Humanities at Princeton University.

JOSÉ RIVERA's plays have been seen across the country and translated into six languages. They include *The House of Ramon
Iglesia, Each Day Dies with Sleep, Cloud Tectonics, Giants Have Us
in Their Books,* and *References to Salvador Dali Make Me Hot.*
Honors include two OBIE Awards, as well as grants from the
NEA, the Rockefeller Foundation, and a Fulbright Arts Fellowship.

SAM SCHWARTZ, JR., (1957–2002) was a playwright, scriptwriter,
and screenwriter in Washington, D.C. He was playwright-in-
residence at Capitol Hill Arts Workshop and had productions
in Washington, New York, Boston, and Los Angeles, among

others. *The Man Who Fell in Love with His Cat* is part of a trilogy of one-acts, *Ménage á Trois: Three Plays About Love and Sex.*

BETTY SHAMIEH is a Palestinian-American playwright. Her play *Roar* was presented at the New Group in 2004. She performed in her play *Chocolate in Heat* off-off-Broadway. A recipient of the New Dramatists Van Lier Fellowship, Shamieh is a graduate of Harvard College and the Yale School of Drama and currently the screenwriting professor at Marymount Manhattan College.

NINA SHENGOLD won the Writers Guild Award for *Labor of Love* and the ABC Playwright Award for *Homesteaders.* Her short plays, including *Finger Food, Lives of the Great Waitresses, No Shoulder, Emotional Baggage, Lush Life,* and others, have been performed off-Broadway and throughout the country.

ANNA DEAVERE SMITH'S work as a solo performer include *Fires in the Mirror,* about Crown Heights; *Twilight: Los Angeles, 1992,* about the response to the Rodney King verdict; and *House Arrest,* an examination of the American Presidency. Ms. Smith has acted in TV and films. She has performed her own plays at numerous theaters, including Berkeley Rep, the Joseph Papp Public Theater, on Broadway, as well as for PBS.

ABOUT THE EDITORS

ERIC LANE and NINA SHENGOLD are editors of eleven contemporary play collections. Their other titles for Vintage Books include *Under 30: Plays for a New Generation, Plays for Actresses, Leading Women: Plays for Actresses II, Take Ten: New Ten-Minute Plays,* and *Take Ten II: More Ten-Minute Plays.* For Viking Penguin, they edited *The Actor's Book of Contemporary Stage Monologues, The Actor's Book of Scenes from New Plays, Moving Parts: Monologues from Contemporary Plays, The Actor's Book of Gay and Lesbian Plays* (Lambda Literary Award nominee), and *Telling Tales: New One-Act Plays.*

NINA SHENGOLD received the ABC Playwright Award and the *L.A. Weekly* Award for *Homesteaders,* published by Samuel French. Her *Romeo/Juliet,* a five-actor adaptation of Shakespeare's play, is published by Broadway Play Publishing; *War at Home,* written with Nicole Quinn and the students of Rondout Valley High School, is published by Playscripts, Inc. Her ten-minute plays have been performed at the Actors Theatre of Louisville and dozens of other theatres. Ms. Shengold won the Writers Guild Award and a GLAAD Award nomination for her teleplay *Labor of Love,* starring Marcia Gay Harden; other screenplays include *Blind Spot,* with Joanne Woodward and Laura Linney, *Unwed Father, Double Platinum,* and a film adaptation of Jane Smiley's *Good Will.* She is artistic director of upstate New York theatre company Actors & Writers. Her first novel, *Clearcut,* is forthcoming from Anchor Books in 2005.

ERIC LANE is an award-winning playwright and filmmaker. Plays include *Heart of the City, Times of War, Cater-Waiter,* and *Dancing on Checkers' Grave,* which starred Jennifer Aniston. Mr. Lane has written and produced two short films: *First Breath* stars Victor Williams, Kelly Karbacz, and Melissa Leo, and is directed by Jimmy Georgiades. *Cater-Waiter,* which Mr. Lane also directed, stars David Drake, Tim Deak, Lisa Kron, and John Kelly. For his work on TV's *Ryan's Hope,* he received a Writers Guild Award. Honors include the Berrilla Kerr Playwriting Award, La MaMa Playwright Development Award, numerous Yaddo fellowships, and a St. James Cavalier Centre for Creativity fellowship in Malta. Mr. Lane is an honors graduate of Brown University, and is artistic director of Orange Thoughts, a not-for-profit theater and film company in New York City.

INDEX

Information pertains to characters in the play.
*Indicates a solo show, originally performed by the author.

PERMISSIONS
ACKNOWLEDGMENTS

and vital dramatic work, and protect them against theft and abuse of their work. All performances must be approved and licensed, whether or not admission is charged. Copyright infringers can be subject to heavy statutory damages. To purchase authorized acting editions of this play, and to obtain stock and amateur performance rights, you must contact: Playscripts, Inc., Web site: http://www.playscripts.com, e-mail: info@ playscripts.com, Tel. 1-866-NEW-PLAY (639-7529).

Aasif Mandvi: *Sakina's Restaurant* by Aasif Mandvi, copyright © 1998 by Aasif Mandvi. Reprinted by permission of the author.

For all performance rights, contact: Ron Gwiazda, Rosenstone/Wender, 38 East 29th Street, New York, NY 10016. Tel. 212-725-9445.

Martin Moran: *The Tricky Part* by Martin Moran, copyright © 2004 by Martin Moran. Reprinted by permission of the author.

For all inquiries, contact: Lisa Loosemoore, Viking Entertainment. Tel. 212-620-5100.

Leslie Nipkow: *Guarding Erica* by Leslie Nipkow, copyright © 1998 by Leslie Nipkow. Reprinted by permission of the author.

For all inquiries, contact: Ricki Olshan, Don Buchwald & Associates, 10 East 44th Street, New York, NY 10017. Tel. 212-867-1200.

Joyce Carol Oates: *When I Was a Little Girl and My Mother Didn't Want Me* by Joyce Carol Oates, copyright © 1997 by Ontario Review, Inc. Reprinted by permission of Rosenstone/Wender on behalf of Joyce Carol Oates.

Permission for stock and amateur performance rights in this play must be obtained from Samuel French, Inc., 45 West 25th Street, New York, NY 10010.

For all other rights, contact: Phyllis Wender, Rosenstone/Wender, 38 East 29th Street, New York, NY 10016.

José Rivera: *Sonnets for an Old Century* by José Rivera, copyright © 2003 by José Rivera. Reprinted by permission of the author.

For all inquiries, contact: The Joyce Ketay Agency, 630 Ninth Avenue, Suite 706, New York, NY 10036. Tel. 212-354-6825.

Sam Schwartz, Jr.: *The Man Who Fell in Love with His Cat* by Sam Schwartz, Jr., copyright © 2003 by the Estate of Sam Schwartz, Jr. Reprinted by permission of Betsy Kulamer.

For all inquires, contact: Betsy Kulamer, 201 Massachusetts Avenue, NE, Apt. 315, Washington, DC 20002. E-mail: Bkulamer@aol.com.

Betty Shamieh: *Tamam* by Betty Shamieh, copyright © 2001 by Betty Shamieh. Reprinted by permisison of the author.

For all performance rights, contact: Rosenstone/Wender, 38 East 29th Street, New York, NY 10016. Tel. 212-725-9445.

Nina Shengold: *Yahrzeit* by Nina Shengold, copyright © 2004 by Nina Shengold. Reprinted by permission of the author.

For all performance rights, contact: Phyllis Wender, Rosenstone/Wender, 38 East 29th Street, New York, NY 10016. Tel. 212-725-9445.

Anna Deavere Smith: "Elvira Evers—To Look Like Girls from Little" from *Twilight: Los Angeles, 1992* by Anna Deavere Smith, copyright © 1994 by Anna Deavere Smith. Reprinted by permission of Doubleday, a division of Random House, Inc.

Anthologies edited by Eric Lane and Nina Shengold

TAKE TEN
New Ten-Minute Plays

In this splendid collection, thirty-two of our finest playwrights hone their skills on a form that has been called the haiku of the American stage. The plays range from monologues to an eight character farce and contain parts across the entire spectrum of age, race, and gender. Eminently producible, ideally suited for the classroom and audition, *Take Ten* is a marvelous resource for teachers and students of drama, as well as a stimulating read for lovers of the theatre.

Drama/0-679-77282-0

TAKE TEN II
More Ten-Minute Plays

In this splendid follow-up to *Take Ten*, Eric Lane and Nina Shengold have put together a veritable bonfire of talent. *Take Ten II* provides a fast-track tour of the current theatrical land-scape, from the slapstick ingenuity of David Ives's *Arabian Nights* to the searing tension of Diana Son's 9/11 drama *The Moon Please*. This outstanding anthology includes thirty-five short plays by major American playwrights as well as exciting new voices.

Drama/1-4000-3217-2

PLAYS FOR ACTRESSES

Gather any group of actresses, from students to stars, and some-one will inevitably ask, "Where are all the great roles for women?" They are right here, in this magnificently diverse col-lection of plays with female casts. Their characters include up-rooted Japanese war brides, outrageously liberated Shakespearean heroines, and nuns who double as Catholic schoolgirls. Whether you're looking for a script to produce, a scene for acting class, or a new audition speech, this book will provide you with a wealth of juicy female roles.

Drama/0-679-77281-2

LEADING WOMEN
Plays for Actresses II

Eric Lane and Nina Shengold once again have gathered an abundance of strong female roles in an anthology of works by highly acclaimed authors and cutting-edge newer writers. The characters who populate these full-length plays, ten-minute plays, and monologues include a vivid cross-section of female experience: girl gang members, Southern debutantes, pilots, teachers, and rebel teenagers. Each play in *Leading Women* is a boon for talented actresses everywhere.

Drama/0-375-72666-7

UNDER THIRTY
Plays for a New Generation

For the vast generation of actors in their teens and twenties, *Under Thirty* is an unparalleled source of varied and challenging roles. There are snappy romantic duets, large-cast ensembles, and everything in between, populated by richly dimensional, mold-breaking characters: misfit cheerleaders, nurturing drifters, rich petty thieves—even a rogue SAT tutor. The contributing playwrights include award-winning dramatists such as Sam Shepard, Donald Margulies, Warren Leight, and Kenneth Lonergan, hilarious humorists such as David Ives and Douglas Carter Beane, and an array of fresh voices.

Drama/1-4000-7616-1

VINTAGE BOOKS
Available at your local bookstore, or call toll-free to order:
1-800-793-2665 (credit cards only).